The Future of
Organised Labour

Craig Phelan (Ed.)

The Future of Organised Labour

Global Perspectives

PETER LANG

Oxford · Bern · Berlin · Bruxelles · Frankfurt am Main · New York · Wien

Bibliographic information published by Die Deutsche Bibliothek
Die Deutsche Bibliothek lists this publication in the Deutsche Nationalbibliografie;
detailed bibliographic data is available on the Internet at ‹http://dnb.ddb.de›.

British Library and Library of Congress Cataloguing-in-Publication Data:
A catalogue record for this book is available from The British Library, Great Britain,
and from The Library of Congress, USA

Cover design: Thomas Jaberg, Peter Lang AG

ISBN 3-03910-508-6
US-ISBN 0-8204-7514-9

© Peter Lang AG, International Academic Publishers, Bern 2006
Hochfeldstrasse 32, Postfach 746, CH-3000 Bern 9, Switzerland
info@peterlang.com, www.peterlang.com, www.peterlang.net

Printed in Germany

Contents

DAN GALLIN

Foreword

There is today general agreement among trade unionists, concerned political activists, scholars and independent observers that the labour movement is in crisis, and the crisis usually referred to is the crisis of the unions, manifested in several ways: serious loss of membership in most countries of the world, especially in their industrial heartland in Western Europe and North America; inability to organise the growing mass of unorganised workers; lack of power to resist repression, whether soft (as in the United States) or hard (as in Colombia or China); lack of capacity to resist the neoliberal agenda (as in most of Europe, North America, Australia and Japan).

This crisis is generally attributed to the economic, social and, ultimately, political effects of globalisation, unfolding in the 1980s and 1990s: the dramatic worldwide shift in social power relations in favour of transnational capital, to the detriment of labour and of the national State in its role of administrator of a social compromise between labour and capital. This is explained by the new and unprecedented mobility of capital, whilst labour remains confined within the boundaries of the national State. At the same time, massive and permanent unemployment, also in industrialised countries, has caused the unions to lose control of the labour market even where they were traditionally strong and has substantially weakened their bargaining power.

These are true insights, but they are partial truths and partial insights. The crisis of the trade union movement today is in fact the outcome of the larger crisis of the broader labour movement, which began much earlier, much before the onset of globalisation. The trade union movement would not be in its present predicament, fighting defensive battles in isolation, if it had not lost, by stages and over time, its anchorage in society at large.

History advances in long cycles. To understand what has happened, we need to do a flash back, about seventy years ago or more. Fascism in Europe, whatever else it may have been, was a gigantic union-busting exercise. Its consequences, and the consequences of World War II, are too often forgotten. A whole generation of labour activists, the best people, disappeared in concentration camps, in the war, or did not come back from exile. At least two generations perished in Spain and in Portugal, where fascism had lasted longer.

At the end of the war, the labour movement re-emerged, superficially strong, because it was part of the Allied cause, and had won the war, whereas capital was on the defensive, having largely collaborated with fascism in the Axis countries and in occupied Europe. In reality, the labour movement had been greatly weakened, with a decimated leadership and its capacity to act as an independent social force severely undermined. All democratic governments in postwar Europe were initially supportive of the labour agenda and consequently the trade unions developed an over-reliance on the State. No longer was there any aspiration to represent an alternative society, and the social tissue of labour institutions, which had provided the material and ideological underpinnings of the movement, was allowed to erode amidst the complacency generated by newfound peace and prosperity.

In the USSR and in the countries of Eastern and Central Europe under its domination, all traces of an independent labour movement were erased. Nearly all the cadres and activists of the socialist, syndicalist, or dissident communist movements who had survived the war perished in the labour camps and prisons of the system. A new class of bureaucrats took total control of society: in that system, 'trade unions' were in fact State agencies of labour administration. In China, the same system still exists, but independent trade unionism, although heavily repressed, is a reality.

In the former colonial countries of Africa and Asia, the labour movement, allied to the national liberation movements, had played a key role in the liberation struggle. Soon, however, in many of these countries it faced the choice of submitting to the new one-party States or being repressed (India and South Africa after 1990 are the major exceptions).

In Latin America an old movement, most of it with anarchist and syndicalist roots, faced violent repression since the early 20th century, with thousands massacred by the military in Chile, in Argentina, and in Ecuador. Later in the century, it again had to face military dictatorships and suffered heavy losses from which it is only now recovering, with difficulty.

The early US labour movement faced repression of almost the same level of intensity. Some authors attribute the later dominance of conservative syndicalism and of political conformism, the characteristic feature of the politics of the AFL and later of the AFL–CIO (American Federation of Labor–Congress of Industrial Organizations), despite the radical upsurge of the CIO in the 1930s, to the ingrained memory of repression. One author has said that the central need of American labour was 'refocusing on the excessive and repressive powers of US economic elites, the perilous distortions they cause in the American economy and in the whole fabric of society, and the class war they have conducted against labor for well over a century'.[1]

The global labour movement we have today is the survivor of these struggles against enormous odds. It has survived, it is resurgent in many places, but it has suffered great losses, not least in its sense of purpose. In most countries, it is on the defensive: too often unions have retreated into what they assume to be their 'core business', leaving a vacuum in society that has been filled by other social movements. Because of contrasting experiences in different parts of the world, the labour movement is ideologically and politically fragmented, but most of the time absence of politics is even more of a problem than political division. Underlying its loss of power and authority is a crisis of identity and orientation. The need of the hour is a serious challenge to global transnational capital and to the world order it has fashioned, but such a challenge cannot be mounted unless

---

1   Sexton, P.C. (1991) *The War on Labor and the Left: Understanding America's Unique Conservatism*, Boulder, Colo: Westview Press.

the movement recovers a common identity based on an alternative vision of society.

Historically, this alternative has been socialism, but socialism is also undergoing a crisis, and that is a crisis of the meaning of socialism. Yet the labour movement is engaged in a global struggle, whether all parts of it are aware of it or not, and whether they are ready for it or not. In that struggle, it cannot do without a political dimension and a common vision. Clearly, we need to re-define socialism so it again becomes recognisable as the politics which are naturally ours, those of the historical labour movement – recognisable and acceptable even by those who have rejected, for good reason, the damaged goods sold under that label.

Those who are developing the concept of global social movement unionism, or of the global justice movement, are seeking to rebuild a labour movement with a shared identity and shared values – not the lowest common denominator, that is what we have today and this movement, as it is, can only lose. Beyond the lowest common denominator, we need an alternative explanation of the world, alternative goals for society and a program on how to get there that all can subscribe to. A new international labour movement, armed with a sense of a broader social mission, can become the core of a global alliance including all other social movements that share the same agenda. Such a movement can change the world. It can again be the liberation movement of humanity it set out to be one hundred and fifty years ago.

The contributors to this volume on *The Future of Organised Labour: Global Perspectives* have studied different aspects of the crisis of the labour movement we have outlined here, both in a national and a global context. Many of their contributions point to what needs to be done to overcome this crisis. We hope that this book will help bring about the global labour movement the workers of the world need and deserve.

August 2005

Craig Phelan

The Future of Organised Labour

Introduction

Organised labour has been the vanguard of participatory democracy and social justice in the developed world for more than 150 years, and it has been the dominant voice for a more equitable distribution of wealth. On the shopfloor, in working-class communities, in corporate boardrooms, in local and national legislatures, and in the international arena, organised labour has been at the forefront of struggles to improve the quality of life for the majority of people. The movement has always had two apparently contradictory approaches, 'sword of justice and vested interest' (Alan Flanders, quoted in Hyman 2004: 19), but it has employed both with remarkably beneficial effect for working people, and it has been a mainstay of life in the modern world.

But now organised labour has reached a critical juncture, and the question of whether it will continue to play its vanguard role is in doubt. The sense of crisis that emerged in the 1980s now permeates the movement in virtually all advanced economies. In the past quarter century, the power of organised labour has been significantly undercut by intensified global competition, radical corporate restructuring, increased capital mobility, the inexorable shift of employment from the industrial to the service sector, the breakdown of long-established industrial relations systems, and a hostile political climate. Plummeting memberships, the rapid decline of collective bargaining coverage, and loss of influence on the shopfloor and in the political arena have dissipated the confidence that earmarked organised labour in the decades following World War II and have given rise to forebodings about the movement's future.

In developing and transitional economies, organised labour has historically played a less prominent, although by no means an insignificant role. By the 1970s, as developing and transitional states started to emerge as preferential sites for Fordist manufacturing, organised labour in Latin America, Asia, and Africa assumed increasing prominence as the defender of workers' rights and a vital element in democratisation processes. Its strategic position was often enhanced with waves of industrialisation since labour peace was vital to the health of both the economy and the state. Yet as in the advanced economies, labour movements in developing and transitional economies began to experience crises of their own in the 1980s. The movement's distress in the developing world has related but different causes, since state labour policies have been heavily influenced by the imperatives of the World Bank and International Monetary Fund (IMF). But the sense of crisis for trade unionism in developing and transitional states is just as profound, and the solutions put forward are equally innovative.

Organised labour has long evidenced a tendency to progress through dramatic bursts rather than incremental growth, and many sympathetic observers scramble to identify strategies that might revitalise, rekindle or reawaken the movement. They look for signs in the economy, in the body politic, and especially in the creative trade union responses to the harsh new environment, for some indication that labour is about to embark on its 'next upsurge' (Clawson 2003). Other often equally sympathetic observers are convinced that the heyday of organised labour has passed forever, that it is unlikely the movement will ever again play a privileged role in the crusade for human betterment. 'Labor militants will undoubtedly be a part of new, transformative social dynamics', lamented Manuel Castells (1997: 360). 'I am less sure that labor unions will.'

This book is a collective study of the current state and future prospects of organised labour worldwide. It offers analysis of the causes and extent of the movement's current malaise from a variety of vantage points. It provides eight national and regional studies – China, Britain, France, the US, Eastern Europe, Brazil, Ghana and Cameroon – that detail problems faced and the inventive strategies trade unions have adopted in response. It also provides fresh scholarly perspectives on a host of global labour issues: the extent and impact of global corporate restructuring; the ongoing fight to achieve core labour standards; the enduring importance of gender and diversity; the fortunes of the international labour movement; the relationship between trade unions and NGOs; the intellectual response to organised labour's present predicament; and the role of labour in the global social justice movement.

I should also make clear what this book is not. It makes no pretence of comprehensive coverage. There are many aspects of the movement that might have and perhaps should have been covered. And there are many national and regional movements that could have been included, most obviously those in Germany, India, South Korea, Mexico and South Africa. This book represents the first of what I hope will be two volumes; even then, given the vastness of the topic, comprehensive coverage cannot be expected. This book has no illusions of disciplinary coherence. Contemporary labour studies is a fractious field, one represented by a variety of disciplinary approaches, many of which are represented in the chapters herein. And this book does not provide a coherent plan of action designed to rekindle organised labour. Many of the chapters make abundantly clear what strategies the authors deem most likely to achieve success in their respective areas, but readers looking for simple global solutions to complex problems will be disappointed.

If lack of comprehensiveness, disciplinary uniformity and clearly formulated strategies for renewal can be seen as the principal faults of this volume, they might equally be regarded as its dominant virtues. Rather than trying to touch on all subjects superficially in a single volume, the book provides readers with representative coverage of labour movements around the globe, national and regional movements from every continent, and the latest scholarly word on many of the most prominent issues of concern to all who are interested in organised labour's fate. The book reveals the expansiveness of labour studies as a discipline, and hopefully it can kick start the process by which historians, economists, industrial relations scholars, political scientists, sociologists and activists can enter into a fruitful dialogue about methodology and findings. The book also affords some indication of the wide variety of tactics for survival and renewal employed by organised labour around the world, revealing as well that strategies are often path dependent and culture bound; strategies that offer promise in one organising environment may be inappropriate in another.

The remainder of this introductory chapter will contextualise and summarise the principal findings of each of the contributions. Before doing so, it provides a necessarily truncated history of how organised labour in both the developed and developing world has reached its present crisis, an assessment of the depth of the problems facing the movement in various states and regions, and an overview of the many ways in which labour movements around the world have sought to overcome the grave difficulties that beset them.

The Rise and Fall of the Postwar Accords

In advanced capitalist economies (the Organisation for Economic Co-operation and Development or OECD countries), the three decades following World War II are often described as the 'golden age' of capitalism, and it was then that the strength and influence of organised labour reached its apex. In most OECD countries, despite their significant differences, a postwar accord between capital and labour took root as economies moved toward a production regime with numerous common characteristics. With the breakdown of this coherent production regime in the 1980s and 1990s, the postwar settlement that was the basis of organised labour's power was undermined, thus precipitating the movement's current crisis.

Despite a myriad of national peculiarities, labour relations in OECD countries during the golden age shared certain fundamentals. Fordist mass production prevailed, characterised by economies of scale, standardised parts, and Taylorist workplace organisation that divided work into numerous discrete units that could be carried out by low skilled workers. Labour relations systems also shared the desire to remove wages from competition to the extent possible, which was achieved through a variety of mechanisms: state-directed incomes policies in France, centralised wage negotiations in northern Europe, and central wage 'signposts' in the US and Britain. Labour relations systems during the golden age were also marked by a clear although often implicit division of authority between management and organised labour: the prerogatives of the former included questions of investment and the organisation of production, while the latter primarily concerned itself with wages, hours and working conditions. The principal role of the state in these labour relations systems was to stabilise the macro-economic environment, achieved through Keynesian polices.

Given the enormous political, economic and social diversity among advanced capitalist economies, the similarities of the industrial relations systems that emerged following 1945 were quite striking. In many European countries – Germany, Austria, the Low Countries, and Sweden, for example – the labour-capital accord was sanctified by national social pacts. Japan witnessed high levels of labour militancy following the war, but by the mid–1950s it too had adopted a comparable system. In France and Italy, where the labour movement was dominated by Communists, and where the state assumed a more interventionist role in the economy, the same pattern emerged. Even in Britain and the US, where collective bargaining traditionally had been more decentralised, an analogous postwar accord was adopted, although the supporting institutional framework was not as deeply embedded. By the late 1960s, all OECD countries 'shared an institutional set-up for governing the economy which was, in all its superficial variations, remarkably similar' (Hancké 2003: 8).

For organised labour, the postwar accords meant power and influence beyond the dreams of prewar trade unionists. By 1950 trade unions had established themselves as key players in the capitalist democracies of Europe, North America and Japan. Union density rates began a long period of growth, and in every advanced industrial economy unions organised between one-third and two-thirds of all workers. Organised labour wielded considerable clout in national politics and became a bulwark in the pursuit of economic growth and social improvement (Western 1997). It is true that many workers outside the mass production sector were excluded from the high wage and secure job contracts that were part and parcel of the postwar agreements, but organised labour was in a position to wield its sword of justice and benefit society as a whole through promotion of social welfare legislation. It is also true that organised labour had in effect accepted a subordinate role in industrial policy since it had tacitly agreed not to impinge on managerial prerogatives, but such was the trade-off for its influence in matters of social and political policy.

These stable, generally pro-labour, and convergent industrial relations systems suffered dramatically from the economic shocks of the 1970s. At first it was by no means obvious that the entire edifice would be destabilised. But as economic woes precipitated by the oil crisis showed no signs of abating at the end of that decade, and as advanced capitalist economies failed to resume their former growth rates, it became clear that the Fordist system and the labour-capital accords based on it faced a fatal structural crisis. In the 1980s leading firms in all advanced economies displayed a strong desire to restructure in order to compete in the new economic environment, but the nature of their reorganisation was often dependent on the institutional power of unions in their respective industries and national settings.

Where organised labour was powerful, and where employers were equally well organised, as was the case in Germany, reorganisation in the 1980s proceeded along highly cooperative lines. In other countries where labour-dominated governments were in power, employers' freedom to manoeuvre was restricted and the restructuring of labour relations followed a similar route. But in situations where powerful organised labour faced weakly organised employers, as was the case in both France and Britain, employers sought partnership with the state to impose their restructuring plans and thereby exclude labour from decision-making processes. The result was the replacement of the postwar accords not with a new, unified industrial relations scheme in OECD countries, but with new patterns of labour-capital relations that yielded radically different outcomes for union movements by the end of the tumultuous 1990s.

While industrial relations systems continued to exhibit 'persistent diversity' (Crouch 1993), it is helpful to discern two general patterns of capitalist labour relations that became evident even before the recession of the early 1990s. The patterns by and large reflected the strength of the institutional structure of the postwar accords (Ebbinghaus and Visser 1999). Strong institutional structures shielded union movements from market forces that intensified competition among workers (Western 1997). In countries such as Germany, Austria, Belgium, the Netherlands, the Scandinavian states, Italy and Japan, where the institutional framework for incorporating trade unions was deeply embedded, firms tended to make use of existing arrangements when restructuring, building upon and modifying the postwar accords rather than abandoning them. Management continued to depend on worker input and co-determination of training schemes as they sought to establish a system in which production techniques could be permanently upgraded and labour peace maintained. The result was to reaffirm organised labour's importance. Thus the emerging industrial relations systems in these countries was characterised by strong labour movements, stable and centrally co-ordinated wage bargaining, relatively harmonious workplace labour relations, and a viable framework for worker input in company decision-making. Countries that followed this path are now often referred to as co-ordinated market economies (CMEs) (Hall and Soskice 2001; Thelen 2001).

Other countries, most notably the UK, US, Australia, New Zealand and Israel, pursued an entirely different path. Part of the reason for this is that firms in these countries were more likely to be dependent on short-term financing, and the need for quarterly profits precluded the long-term co-operative solutions promised by the CME approach. But a deeper reason was the lack of well-defined institutional arrangements for workforce retraining, centrally co-ordinated bargaining, and worker involvement in corporate decision-making. In effect, these countries could not simply upgrade their labour relations systems; employers therefore could join hands with sympathetic states to undermine the power of organised labour and radically reorganise labour relations. In Britain in the 1980s the Thatcher government's defeat of both the printers' and miners' unions symbolised the new political resolve to assist corporate restructuring. In the US this was matched by Reagan's decision to fire striking air traffic controllers and hire non-union replacements. Australia followed a similar pattern despite the fact that the country had a Labour government between 1983 and 1996. Industrial relations in these countries came to be characterised by deregulated labour markets, decentralised wage bargaining, enhanced managerial prerogatives, and as a result, weak national union movements. This group of countries is often lumped together under the rubric of liberal market economies (LMEs) (Hall and Soskice 2001; Thelen 2001; Howell 2003).

Both of these emerging industrial relations patterns were modified during the 1990s and early 2000s as a result of intensified global competition and a painful recession. In the LMEs deregulation of labour relations and the weakening of trade unionism and collective bargaining continued apace. In Britain continued state hostility and employer aversion to collective bargaining saw union density, which had risen from 43 to 55 percent between 1965 and 1979, drop steadily to 29 percent in 2001 (Heery, Kelly and Waddington 2003: 79). With the election of Tony Blair and a Labour government in 1997, a mildly more propitious atmosphere has seen union density rebound to 31 percent in 2004,[1] but the Labour government continues to fashion Britain as a low wage, deregulated economy so as to attract foreign capital, and it is often a handmaiden to employer efforts to decentralise collective bargaining, de-recognise trade unions, and introduce flexible, individualised labour contracts (Howell 2005; Coates 2005). The US in the 1990s witnessed a spectacular rise in non-union employment in automobiles, telecommunications and the industrial sector as a whole, while in the hostile climate trade unions made little headway in organising the burgeoning service sector. Trade union density in the US peaked at 34 percent in 1954 (Kaufman 2004: 45–7); between 1980 and 2004 density fell from 20 percent to a paltry 13 percent, with three-fourths of union members in the public service sector, meaning that the manufacturing sector in the US has become virtually union free (Fantasia and Voss 2004; Bennett and Kaufman 2002). Australian labour also experienced rapidly declining fortunes. From a centralised and union-friendly corporatist system in the 1970s, by the end of the 1990s Australian industrial relations became decentralised and virtually excluded union participation. As a result, union density rates in Australia fell precipitously from 46 percent in 1980 to 25 percent in 2004 (Wooden 2000; Griffin, Small and Svenson 2003; Strachan and Burgess 2004).

---

1   Unless otherwise stated, union density rates in this chapter are taken from Golden, Lange and Wallerstein 2002, and OECD 2005.

Trade unions in the CMEs came under increasing pressure in the 1990s as well, but their response was and remains quite different, with more sanguine results for organised labour. In Germany an employer push for greater flexibility in the centrally co-ordinated system of wage determination and for the deregulation of labour laws, coupled with the profound challenge of unification, placed enormous strain on its much vaunted labour relations system. There has also been a weakening of the works councils in Germany, representing an increase in managerial prerogative and the undermining of institutional arrangements for worker input. Changes in the German system were largely the result of negotiations between organised labour and capital through the auspices of an 'enabling state' (Schmidt 2002), and therefore organised labour has retained much of its strength, but union density has dropped nonetheless from 34 percent in 1980 to 25 percent in 2004 (Behrens, Fichter and Frege 2003; Thelen and van Wijnbergen 2003). In Sweden too there has been a shift from a highly centralised system of bargaining to an industry-based one that allows for plant-level differentials, weakening the power of trade unions to some extent. But in part due to high levels of public employment and the institutionalised role for trade unions in distributing welfare benefits, union density levels in Sweden actually climbed from 78 percent in 1980 to 81 percent in 2004 (Swenson and Pontusson 2000; Piazza 2002). Japan also followed this pattern, although there has been a significant drop in Japanese unionisation rates (from 30 percent in 1980 to 22 percent in 2004) stemming from the labour movement's inability to organise newer sectors of the economy (Gordon 2001; Weathers 2003).

The relative resilience of organised labour in the CMEs does not imply that such movements are problem free. Along with their counterparts in the LMEs, they now operate in a new and far more difficult economic and political environment, labour's 'brave new world' (Martin and Ross 1999). Capital is more mobile today, and freer to pursue spatial and technological 'fixes' to any challenges to profitability (Silver 2003). De-industrialisation and the shift from Fordist to post-Fordist, flexible production have undercut the traditional core occupational and industrial constituencies of trade unions: the male, blue-collar mass-production worker. Organised labour must learn to organise many groups of workers who were often deemed 'unorganisable' in the not-so-distant past: those who work part-time under flexible, individual contracts; the ever-growing number of female workers; those employed in the service sector. And organised labour must accomplish this transformation in what might well remain for some time a hostile political climate. Revitalising organised labour in OECD countries is not simply a question of renewed commitment; it requires bold experimentation.

Labour's Predicament in the Global South

Historical focus on the 'golden age' of capitalism in OECD countries (1950–1980) has overshadowed an equally impressive and simultaneous 'golden age' of development in the world's poorer nations. While there had long been significant levels of industrialisation in some areas of what has become known as the global South, most notably Latin America and India, prior to 1950 colonialism had established a division of labour by which the raw materials of the colonies were exploited to sustain industrialisation in the imperial North. Yet by the 1970s a 'new international division of labour' had developed with the rapid expansion of the world market for industrial production sites and cheap labour. Often transplanting mass production techniques to sites in the developing world (peripheral Fordism) in order to escape the heavy labour costs of OECD countries, international firms led the way for the rapid industrialisation of significant areas of the global South (Munck 2002: 106–9; Singh 1994).

Trade unionism had long-established roots in many pockets of the global South that enabled it to exercise influence during the golden age of development. In sub-Saharan Africa, the movement never represented more than a small minority of the working population, but trade unions tended to be concentrated in urban centres and occupied strategically important sectors of the economy. They thus were in a position to wield far more economic and political weight than their numbers implied. African trade unions were often deeply involved in the struggle against colonial rule, showed remarkable resilience under authoritarian post-colonial regimes, and as key civil organisations have been at the forefront of resistance to oppression and exploitation (Akwetey 1994; Kester and Sidibé 1997). In Latin America, trade unionism expanded rapidly under state-directed, import-substitution industrialisation. Often the target of vicious repression by dictatorial regimes, organised labour in Latin America was highly politicised, fighting for improved conditions in state-owned and directed factories, and leading movements to establish democratic rights and welfare systems at the national level (Sanchez Bajo 2002; Fernandez Jilberto and Riethof 2002; Seidman 1994). In the transitional economies of the Asia-Pacific region, a complex trade union history has a common thread: the imprint of state authoritarianism. Some regimes sanctioned official trade unions and incorporated them into decision-making processes. Others excluded worker organisations of all stripes. In all cases, autonomous labour organisations were often the victims of harsh repression (Frenkel 1993). Thus independent trade unionism in the Asia-Pacific region has traditionally been sporadic and often ineffectual. Nor did profound industrialisation give rise to powerful union movements that exercised significant influence in the political or economic arenas, although South Korea may be seen as an exception to this rule (Hutchison and Brown 2001; Kuruvilla et al. 2002; Ranald 2002; Deyo 1997).

When the global South became seen as an attractive site for mass production in the 1970s, labour organisation was transformed. Wherever capital moved in the search for a 'spatial fix' in the highly competitive global environment, labour unrest and often explosive trade union growth followed. Beverly Silver (2003: chapter 2) has described the process in the automobile industry. In 1937 a militant minority shut down Fisher Body plants in Flint, Michigan and thereby crippled the largest industrial corporation in the US. General Motors was forced to jettison its fiercely anti-union stance and embrace collective bargaining, a process that was extended to all major US car manufacturers. By the 1950s and 1960s, US automakers were investing heavily in Western Europe, using much the same production techniques. In the late 1960s Western European autoworkers exploded in a wave of strikes that bore a striking similarity to those in the US in the 1930s and 1940s. This pattern of organising and unrest was then replicated with increasing speed as auto manufacturing shifted to Brazil (where autoworkers were at the forefront of a strike wave from 1978 to 1986), to South Africa (again with autoworkers in the vanguard of the wave of strikes between 1979 and 1986), and to South Korea, where autoworker unrest erupted in 1987 and ushered in a period of intense state repression and automaker technological innovation designed to make production impervious to such disruptions.

Erecting viable trade unions in developing and transitional economies is not simply a matter of replicating earlier developments in OECD countries however. Organised labour in the developing South faces a unique set of problems. Industrial production is often confined to certain pockets in developing countries, and the presence of an enormous labour surplus in the country as a whole places a powerful strain on wage levels and the labour market. Instead of an expansive welfare state to act as a buffer against unemployment and the vicissitudes of the business cycle, developing and transitional economies possess large informal sectors that can inhibit the effectiveness of industrial action by providing a ready reservoir of replacement labour. Since the marginalised and unprotected informal sector often operates beyond the legal pale, the passage of beneficial labour legislation is a problematic undertaking (Fernandez Jilberto and Riethof 2002).

The burden of debt, and the structural adjustment policies of the World Bank and IMF, has had enduring implications for many labour movements in the global South by shaping the economic and political environment in which they operate. The Latin American debt crisis of 1982 represented a stark demarcation between an era of state-led development based on import substitution and one of neoliberal policies. In the wake of the 'lost decade' of the 1980s, Latin American and other developing states increasingly opened their economies to foreign competition, slashed social welfare budgets, privatised many state-owned companies, and legislated labour market flexibility. Resulting labour unrest in reaction to those policies is often regarded by elites as a threat to economic stability and foreign direct investment, and thus it often provokes renewed efforts to liberalise labour relations. In many ways, structural adjustment programmes, public sector retrenchment, and high debt burdens 'constrain the possibilities for organised labour to struggle for better wages and working conditions' (Fernandez Jilberto and Riethof 2002: 16; Bensusán and Cook 2003).

In much but not all of sub-Saharan Africa, for example, the evidence is clear that structural adjustment programmes had a deleterious impact on organised labour. Public sector layoffs and new private sector labour laws have led to heavy membership losses and depleted trade union treasuries. Despite often heroic efforts to combat structural adjustment, trade union resistance has generally proved ineffectual. Mounting job insecurity and a falling off of real wages has forced many trade unionists into the informal labour market, thus leading some commentators to lament the virtual elimination of the wage-earning class as a distinct entity (Konings 2002: 313).

As one might expect, union density rates and collective bargaining systems vary dramatically among states in the global South. Yet in accord with OECD nations, density rates have fallen for virtually every state which has adopted neoliberal reforms and labour market liberalisation. In Kenya, for example, union density fell precipitously from 41.9 percent in 1985 to 16.9 percent in 1995; in Argentina density dropped from 48.7 percent in 1986 to 25.4 percent in 1995; in Singapore density plummeted from 26.8 percent in 1980 to 15.6 percent in 1995. Union density rates in liberalising India rose marginally between 1980 and 1993 (from 18.2 to 18.9 percent), although many observers believe decline will commence once liberalising reforms are fully implemented (Verma and Kochan 2004: 3; Banerjee 2005).

Labour liberalisation has not signalled wholesale retrenchment for all labour movements in the global South. Taiwan's union density rate jumped from 26.2 percent in 1980 to 50 percent in 1995 after a state social insurance benefit was made available to union members only, once again underscoring the importance of the institutional framework for the health of organised labour (Kuruvilla et al. 2002). And in South Africa, after years of repression, the labour movement has exploded with the fall of apartheid. In 1985 union density stood at 18 percent. By 1997 that figure reached 36 percent, although by 2003 it had slipped to 32 percent (Braude 2004). Yet these cases are exceptions to the general pattern of decline and crisis that has gripped organised labour in developing and newly industrialising countries. In many parts of the developing world, trade unionists continue to face dismissal and discrimination, even imprisonment, while obstacles to organising and collective bargaining mount in the increasingly competitive global marketplace (ICFTU 2005).

The Future of Organised Labour

It is a bitter irony that trade union decline is occurring precisely when the labour movement is needed most. Not only are unions losing their influence in areas of traditional concern (wages, hours and working conditions), and not only is organised labour, historically one of the most important civil actors, losing its capacity to promote the broader aims of political democracy and social rights; the decline of organised labour has also meant the weakening of what should be the key counterbalance to the forces of neoliberal globalisation. Poverty rates are increasing within many OECD countries (especially the US and Britain) and between OECD countries and the global South (most notably sub-Saharan Africa). Such trends will no doubt continue as long as the driving force behind redistributive justice is too weak to influence events.

Yet the continued demise of organised labour is not a foregone conclusion. Although some observers have been quick to suggest that trade unions, as products of industrialisation, have become super-fluous in the 'post-industrial' world, evidence suggests otherwise. Organised labour has not been a passive victim of recent economic and political shifts. As it has throughout its history, labour has demonstrated a capacity to adapt, to make its voice heard, to re-assert its power. The scale and scope of experimentation taking place in the labour movement today is testimony not just to the depth of the crisis but also to the possibility of resurgence in the years ahead.

Not surprisingly, the question of union revitalisation has become the principal focus of contemporary labour studies. The large and ever-growing body of literature on the subject is marked by a wide variety of perspectives. One approach is to assess revitalisation schemes worldwide by their impact on relations with the social actors of greatest concern: existing and potential members, employers, and the state (Cornfield and McCammon 2003). Another is to differentiate between top-down strategies of union elites and bottom-up initiatives from the rank and file (Hurd, Milkman and Turner 2003). Arguably the most fruitful framework is to categorise the range of possible initiatives available to unions and determine to what extent and with what effect they have been adopted by labour movements in various locales. Frege and Kelly (2004) articulate this approach in the context of Western Europe and the US, and it is one that holds enormous potential for understanding the complexity of revitalisation efforts worldwide.

Frege and Kelly posit six overlapping and mutually dependent strategies by which trade unions can advance their interests: organising, labour-management partnership, political action, reform of union structures, coalition building, and international solidarity. They make clear that revitalisation is not a simple question of identifying a strategy or combination of strategies that is universally applicable. What works in one national setting may be inappropriate for another (for an illustrative case study, see Carter et al. 2003). Since employer and state policies, industrial relations institutions, and union identities vary from country to country, each national setting offers unique constraints and opportunities for union advance. Moreover, labour movements are to a large degree path dependent, meaning that labour institutions, while certainly capable of reform, progress along lines shaped by their institutional legacies and structures.

In countries such as Spain and Italy, for example, where organised labour benefits from the existence of social pacts created from political opportunities that arose in the 1990s, unions depend on such resources as the ability to mobilise workers politically and to win votes in works council elections, but organising the unorganised has played a secondary role. In the US, however, where bargaining coverage is closely tied to membership density, organising has become the dominant revitalisation strategy. Given the relentlessness of union decline in the US, this emphasis is hardly surprising. Farber and Western (2002) demonstrate that only a ten-fold increase in organising success will return union density rates to their pre-1980 levels. Yet since nearly half of all new workers organised by the American Federation of Labor-Congress of Industrial Organizations in 2000 were recruited by just three unions (the Service International Employees Union, the United Food and Commercial Workers, and the International Brotherhood of Electrical Workers), the innovative organising efforts of these and other dynamic unions has convinced some that 'American unions have repositioned themselves for a potential organising renaissance' (Hurd, Milkman and Turner 2003: 99).

It is the revitalisation strategy that originated in the global South, however, that has drawn the most attention and inspired the most sanguine speculations about the future of organised labour: social movement unionism. 'If in the Golden Era it seemed that the workers of the North were the undisputed pioneers of organisational methods and ideological innovation', argues Ronaldo Munck (2002: 122), 'in the era of globalisation the lead has in many ways passed to the workers of the South'. Born in the days when labour joined hands with other progressive forces to throw off the yoke of colonialism, or when labour and other groups fought side by side to contest authoritarianism, social movement unionism connotes coalition-building, often at the local level, with community groups, students, political activists, environmentalists, human rights campaigners, and others around such issues as living wages, sustainable development, civil liberties, fair trade, labour standards and organising rights. Social movement unionism also implies an expansion of the trade union vision beyond workplace issues, a readiness to again raise its sword of justice on behalf of the dispossessed majority rather than protecting the vested interests of its own membership (Waterman 1998). Social movement unionism has been particularly pronounced in South Africa, where the labour movement was part of the grand coalition that overthrew apartheid (von Holdt 2003; Adler and Webster 1995), and in Brazil, where it was an essential element in the movement that democratised politics and brought Luiz Inácio Lula da Silva to power in 2002 (Riethof 2004; Seidman 1994).

Much of the recent literature on social movement unionism focuses on its applicability to the US (Turner and Hurd 2001).

Although the US labour movement did play a role in the civil rights movement, it largely absented itself from the social movements of the 1960s. As Dan Clawson reveals in chapter 9, however, social movement unionism might provide the means for labour's 'next upsurge'.[2] After detailing the extent and reasons for union decline in the US, Clawson argues that the best hope for revitalisation is through the exercise of community power in combination with allies in the new social movements. Such an approach would lead to less reliance on hostile state institutions, in particular the National Labor Relations Board, to guarantee industrial fair play, and to greater corporate awareness that anti-union behaviour will generate public condemnation that will impact profit margins. He summarises the types of initiatives already underway that point in the direction of social movement unionism in the US: anti-sweatshop activity, worker centres, living wage campaigns, Justice for Janitors, multi-union coalitions, graduate student unions, cross-border alliances, and anti-war organising.

On a global scale, non-governmental organisations (NGOs) represent potentially powerful coalition partners for trade unions in building social movement unionism. Both NGOs and trade unions are part of the institutional fabric of all democratic societies. In some national settings and for some groups of workers, especially those in the informal economy of the global South, the distinction between an NGO and trade union can be ambiguous (Ratnam and Verma 2004). In chapter 6, Peter Waterman[3] explores the possibilities for true coalition-building between these two sets of global, socio-political actors. After exploring the differences and commonalities between them, Waterman passionately asserts that global union revival is not possible without the two groups acting in concert, and he challenges both to recognise the necessity of moving beyond older paradigms and

---

2   For an extensive scholarly discussion of Clawson's arguments, see (2004) '*Labor History* Symposium: Dan Clawson, *The Next Upsurge: Labor and the New Social Movements*', *Labor History* 45(3): 333–82.

3   See also Waterman's essay on social movement unionism and scholarly responses in (2005) '*Labor History* Symposium: Labor and the New Social Movements', *Labor History* 46(2): 195–243.

embracing alternatives percolating in the Global Justice and Solidarity Movement. In chapter 5, Ronaldo Munck looks at social movement unionism from an intellectual perspective. Through an examination of Karl Polanyi's ideas, which have gained increasing popularity among labour movement sympathisers in recent years, Munck asks whether labour is presently equipped ideologically to be at the forefront of a broad social movement capable of countering global market forces, and he speculates on what a new, radical yet viable global strategy for labour might look like. Rob Lambert, in chapter 7, finds amidst the pain and hardship of plant closings in Australia's white goods industry, small signs of hope that global social movement unionism is being born. His involvement with workers resisting the closings provide him with some optimism that there exists an historic opportunity for intellectuals, union officials, shop floor militants, and social activists to join hands in creating a powerful oppositional force.

Along with organising and coalition-building, political action is central to revitalisation. Forms of trade union political action vary from state to state, depending on a variety of factors, including the type of regime and the extent to which labour institutions are embedded in frameworks for policy-making. In chapter 10, Anita Chan examines the role of the official Chinese trade union federation, the All-China Federation of Trade Unions, from its origins in the Maoist period through the economic reforms and political liberalisation of the 1980s when it sought greater autonomy from the Chinese Communist Party. She highlights the trend toward greater responsiveness to the plight of workers on the part of the Federation today, although she places equal emphasis on the constraints placed on it by the authoritarian regime. Piet Konings, in chapter 13, cautions against easy generalisations about trade union responses to neoliberal policies in African states. Through a comparison of trade unionism in Ghana and Cameroon, he demonstrates that the nature of the state and the organisational capacity of unions, among other factors, account for why trade unionism can continue to prosper under neoliberalism in some states while it declines in others. And in chapter 12, Andréia Galvão details the reactions of the two major trade union federations in Brazil to neoliberal reforms that swept that country from the 1990s. Despite clear ideological differences between the two federations, the pressure of neoliberal reform has led to a convergence in strategy and a narrowing of vision, even after the election of Lula in 2002.

A fourth and increasingly important' labour revitalisation strategy is international solidarity. In recent years there have been tentative signs of greater activism and more radical demands from the international union movement, represented by the International Confederation of Free Trade Unions (ICFTU) and the International Trade Secretariats, in its efforts to slow the spread of neoliberal economic policies (O'Brien 2000; Harrod and O'Brien 2002). In chapter 3, Mark Anner analyses the campaign of to establish global core labour standards through the World Trade Organisation, the IMF and the World Bank.[4] Paying careful attention to the internal dynamics and diverse composition of the ICFTU, in particular the differing power resources and viewpoints of unions from the developed North and global South, Anner reveals the inherent difficulties of achieving reform at the international level.

Any effective revitalisation strategy for organised labour must come to grips with the issue of workforce heterogeneity. Modern workforces are increasingly diverse in terms of race, ethnicity, and age, but the majority of unions have been slow to make the necessary adjustments to recruit and service the needs of a heterogeneous pool of potential members (Ledwith and Colgan 2002). Above all, the movement must reckon with its long-standing failure to organise women. Although women now comprise fully half the global workforce, they are grossly underrepresented in trade union leadership positions. In chapter 4, Sue Ledwith surveys some of the creative efforts by women to develop more inclusive forms of organising within, across, and outside the traditional boundaries of established labour movements. She argues that traditional trade unionism has a great deal to learn from groups it has long marginalised.

As many of the chapters reveal, revitalisation is increasingly conceptualised as more than simply a question of devising new strategies and tactics, but also a matter of re-visiting the more fundamental

---

4   For a wide-ranging discussion of this subject, see (2004) '*Labor History Symposium: Kimberly Ann Elliott and Richard B. Freeman, Can Labor Standards Improve under Globalization?*', *Labor History* 45(4): 497–535.

question of union identity. Renewal may well demand that union movements everywhere must redefine fundamentally their sense of purpose and identity, re-examine and broaden their goals, re-think their role in society, politics and the marketplace (Hyman 2001). David Ost, in chapter 11, illustrates how organised labour in Eastern Europe, after half a century of communism and fifteen years of post-communism, is still struggling with bitter legacies as it begins to shape a new identity and viable, independent movements. He finds that the most debilitating legacies are not those of communism but of postcommunism, with its often wildly optimistic free market sensibilities. In chapter 8, Steve Jefferys weaves together the recent histories of trade unionism in both Britain and France. Digging even deeper than union identity, Jefferys suggests the different legacies and trajectories of trade unionism in these two countries can be traced to basic differences in world view, the Lockean tradition in Britain and the legacy of Rousseau in France, and in particular the different meanings of liberty.

Although the principal emphasis of contemporary labour studies is now revitalisation, many scholars are still wrestling with the exact nature of the problems faced by organised labour. Globalisation is invariably cited as one of chief causes of union decline, yet the term itself and its impact are still very much contested. Bill Dunn, in chapter 2, offers an illuminating and provocative discussion of global restructuring.[5] He warns that exaggerating the incapacity of the state in the face of globalisation, and the rush to embrace new transnational strategies to combat labour decline may possibly lead the movement to lose focus on national political solutions, which, Dunn argues, remain as important as they ever were.

What is the future of organised labour? Amidst the often brutal economic and political realities that have undercut the powerful labour movements of the postwar world, and in the flickering hopeful signs from around the world that a different and even more vibrant movement is being born, can we discern what will be the role for organised labour in the years to come?

---

5   See the extensive debate on Bill Dunn's arguments in *'Labor History Symposium: Bill Dunn, Global Restructuring and the Power of Labour'*, *Labor History* 47(1).

Certainly not. Events in Britain from 1888 to 1892, the US in the mid 1930s, Western Europe in the late 1960s, Brazil in the early 1980s, South Korea in the late 1980s, and South Africa in the early 1990s – all momentous upheavals in industrial relations that represented dramatic advances for organised labour – caught observers, sympathetic and hostile alike, by surprise. Many of the contributors to this volume have graciously consented to offer possible future scenarios for the movement in their respective chapters, but they would be the first to admit that the predictive powers of analysts have not improved over the years. One thing is certain. The future of organised labour is incubating today. It is being written in corporate boardrooms, legislatures and judiciaries, and powerful international agencies. It is also being written by factory workers in China, machinists in Brazil, impassioned organisers in Eastern Europe, living wage coalitions in the US, informal sector workers in Cameroon, and concerned citizens around the world. It is hoped that this volume will in some small way contribute as well.

References

Adler, G. and Webster, E. (1995) 'The Labor Movement, Radical Reform, and Transition to Democracy in South Africa', *Politics and Society* 23(1): 75–106.

Akwetey, E.O. (1994) *Trade Unions and Democratization: A Comparative Study of Zambia and Ghana*, Stockholm: University of Stockholm.

Banerjee, D. (2005) *Globalisation, Industrial Restructuring and Labour Reforms: Where India Meets the Global*, Thousand Oaks, CA: Sage.

Behrens, M., Fichter, M. and Frege, C.M. (2003) 'Unions in Germany: Regaining the Initiative?', *European Journal of Industrial Relations* 9(1): 25–42.

Bennett, J. and Kaufman, B. (eds) (2002) *The Future of Private Sector Unionism in the United States*, Armonk, NY: M.E. Sharpe.

Bensusán, G. and Cook, M.L. (2003) 'Political Transition and Labor Revitalization in Mexico', in D.B. Cornfield and H.J. McCammon (eds)

Labor Revitalization: Global Perspectives and New Initiatives, Oxford: Elsevier.

Braude, W. (2004) *South Africa Country Analysis*, Johannesburg: National Labour and Ecocomic Development Institute.

Carter, B., Fairbrother, P., Sherman, R. and Voss, K. (2003) 'Made in the USA, Imported into Britain: The Organizing Model and the Limits of Transferability' in D.B. Cornfield and H.J. McCammon (eds) *Labor Revitalization: Global Perspectives and New Initiatives*, Oxford: Elsevier.

Castells, M. (1997) *The Information Age: Economy, Society and Culture, Vol. II: The Power of Identity*, Oxford: Basil Blackwell.

Clawson, D. (2003) *The Next Upsurge: Labor and the New Social Movements*, Ithaca, NY: ILR Press.

Coates, D. (2005) *Prolonged Labour: The Slow Birth of New Labour Britain*, Basingstoke: Palgrave Macmillan.

Cornfield, D.B. and McCammon, H.J. (2003) 'Revitalizing Labor: Global Perspectives and a Research Agenda', in D.B. Cornfield and H.J. McCammon (eds) *Labor Revitalization: Global Perspectives and New Initiatives*, Oxford: Elsevier.

Crouch, C. (1993) *Industrial Relations and European State Traditions*, Oxford: Clarendon Press.

Deyo, F.C. (1997) 'Labour and Industrial Restructuring in South-East Asia', in G. Rodan, K. Hewison and R. Robison (eds) *The Political Economy of South-East Asia: An Introduction*, Melbourne: Oxford University Press.

Ebbinghaus, B. and Visser, J. (1999) 'When Institutions Matter: Union Growth and Decline in Western Europe, 1950–1995', *European Sociological Review* 15(2): 135–58.

Fantasia, R. and Voss, K. (2004) *Hard Work: Remaking the American Labor Movement*, Berkeley: University of California Press.

Farber, H.S. and Western, B. (2001) 'Accounting for the Decline of Unions in the Private Sector, 1973–88', *Journal of Labor Research* 22: 459–486.

— and — (2002) 'Ronald Reagan and the Politics of Declining Union Organization', *British Journal of Industrial Relations* 40(3): 385–402.

Fernandez Jilberto, A.E. and Riethof, M. (2002) 'Labour Relations in the Era of Globalization and Neo-Liberal Reforms', in A.E. Fernandez Jilberto and M. Riethof (eds) *Labour Relations in Development*, New York: Routledge.

Frege, C.M. and Kelly, J. (2004) 'Union Strategies in Comparative Context', in C.M. Frege and J. Kelly (eds) *Varieties of Unionism: Strategies for Union Revitalization in a Globalizing Economy*, Oxford: Oxford University Press.

Frenkel, S. (1993) 'Variation in Trade Union Patterns: A Synthesis', in S. Frenkel (ed) *Organized Labour in the Asia-Pacific Region: A Comparative Study of Trade Unionism in Nine Countries*, Ithaca, NY: ILR Press.

Golden, M., Lange, P. and Wallerstein, M. (2002) 'Union Centralization among Advanced Industrial Societies: An Empirical Study', Dataset available at http://www.shelley.polisci.ucla.edu/data. Version dated 28 July 2004.

Gordon, A. (2001) *The Wages of Affluence: Labor and Management in Postwar Japan*, Cambridge, MA: Harvard University Press.

Griffin, G., Small, R. and Svenson, S. (2003) 'Trade Union Innovation, Adaptation and Renewal in Australia: Still Searching for the Holy Membership Grail', in P. Fairbrother and C.A.B. Yates (eds) *Trade Unions in Renewal: A Comparative Study*, London: Coninuum.

Hall, P.A. and Soskice, D. (2001) 'An Introduction to Varieties of Capitalism', in P.A. Hall and D. Soskice (eds) *Varieties of Capitalism: The Institutional Foundations of Comparative Advantage*, New York: Oxford University Press.

Hancké, B. (2003) 'Bifurcated Convergence: Labour Relations in OECD Countries 1980–2000', European Institute Working Paper, London School of Economics, April.

Harrod, J. and O'Brien, R. (eds) (2002) *Global Unions?: Theories and Strategies of Organized Labor in the Global Political Economy*, London: Routledge.

Heery, E., Kelly, J. and Waddington, J. (2003) 'Union Revitalization in Britain', *European Journal of Industrial Relations* 9(1): 79–97.

Howell, C. (2003) 'Varieties of Capitalism: And Then There Was One?', *Comparative Politics* 36(1): 103–24.

— (2005) *Trade Unions and the State: The Construction of Industrial Relations in Britain, 1890–2000*, Princeton: Princeton University Press.

Hutchison, J. and Brown, A. (eds) (2001) *Organising Labour in Globalising Asia*, London: Routledge.

Hurd, R., Milkman, R. and Turner, L. (2003) 'Reviving the American Labour Movement: Institutions and Mobilization', *European Journal of Industrial Relations* 9(1): 99–117.

Hyman, R. (2001) *Understanding European Trade Unionism: Between Market, Class and Society*, London: Sage.

— (2004) 'An Emerging Agenda for Trade Unions?', in R. Munck (ed.) *Labour and Globalisation: Results and Prospects*, Liverpool: Liverpool University Press.

ICFTU (2005) 'ICFTU Annual Survey: Grim Global Catalogue of Anti-Union Repression', Brussels: International Confederation of Free Trade Unions. http://www.icftu.org/displaydocument.asp?Index=991222870.

Kaufman, B.E. (2004) 'Prospects for Union Growth in the United States in the Early 21st Century', in A. Verma and T.A. Kochan (eds) *Unions in the 21st Century: An International Perspective*, Basingstoke: Palgrave Macmillan.

Kester, G. and Sidibé, O.O. (eds) (1997) *Trade Unions and Sustainable Democracy in Africa*, Aldershot: Ashgate.

Konings, P. (2002) 'Structural Adjustment and Trade Unions in Africa', in A.E. Fernandez Jilberto and M. Riethof (eds) *Labour Relations in Development*, New York: Routledge.

Kuruvilla, S., Das, S., Kwon, H., and Kwon S. (2002) 'Trade Union Growth and Decline in Asia', *British Journal of Industrial Relations* 40(3): 431–63.

Ledwith, S. and Colgan, F. (2002) 'Tackling Gender, Diversity and Trade Union Democracy' in F. Colgan and S. Ledwith (eds) *Gender, Diversity and Trade Unions: International Perspectives*, London: Routledge.

Martin, A. and Ross, G. (eds) (1999) *The Brave New World of European Labor: European Trade Unions at the Millennium*, Oxford: Berghahn Books.

Munck, R. (2002) *Globalisation and Labour: The New 'Great Transformation'*, London: Zed Books.

O'Brien, R. (2000) 'Workers and the World Order: The Tentative Transformation of the International Union Movement', *Review of International Studies* 26: 533–55.

OECD (2005) *OECD Employment Outlook 2005*, Paris: OECD.

Piazza, J.A. (2002) *Going Global: Unions and Globalization in the United States, Sweden, and Germany*, Lanham, MD: Lexington Books.

Ranald, P. (2002) 'Analysing, Organising, Resisting: Crisis in East Asia, South Korea and the Philippines', *Journal of Industrial Relations* 41(2): 295–325.

Ratnam, C.S.V. and Verma, A. (2004) 'Non-Governmental Organisations and Trade Unions: The Case of India', in A. Verma and T.A. Kochan (eds) *Unions in the 21st Century: An International Perspective*, Basingstoke: Palgrave Macmillan.

Riethof, M. (2004) 'Changing Strategies of the Brazilian Labor Movement: From Opposition to Participation', *Latin American Perspectives* 31(6): 31–47.

Sanchez Bajo, C. (2002) 'Institutionalizing Labour throughout Argentina's "Second Great Transformation"', in A.E. Fernandez Jilberto and M. Riethof (eds) *Labour Relations in Development*, New York: Routledge.

Schmidt, V. (2002) *The Futures of European Capitalism*, New York: Oxford University Press.

Seidman, G. (1994) *Manufacturing Militance: Workers' Movements in Brazil and South Africa*, Berkeley: University of California Press.

Silver, B. (2003) *Forces of Labor: Workers' Movements and Globalization since 1870*, New York: Cambridge University Press.

Singh, A. (1994) 'Global Economic Change, Skills and International Competitiveness', *International Labour Review* 133(2): 135–48.

Strachan, G. and Burgess, J. 'Trade Union Survival and Women Workers in Australia', in A. Verma and T.A. Kochan (eds) *Unions in the 21st Century: An International Perspective*, Basingstoke: Palgrave Macmillan.

Swenson, P. and Pontusson, J. (2000) 'The Swedish Employer Offensive against Centralized Bargaining', in T. Iversen, J. Pontusson and D. Soskice (eds) *Unions, Employers and Central Banks: Macroeconomic Coordination and Institutional Change in Market Economies*, Cambridge: Cambridge University Press.

Thelen, K. (2001) 'Varieties of Labor Politics in the Developed Democracies', in P.A. Hall and D. Soskice (eds) *Varieties of Capitalism: The Institutional Foundations of Comparative Advantage*, New York: Oxford University Press.

— and van Wijnbergen, C. (2003), 'The Paradox of Globalization: Labor Relations in Germany and Beyond', *Comparative Political Studies* 36(8): 859–80.

Turner, L. and Hurd, R.W. (2001) 'Building Social Movement Unionism: The Transformation of the American Labor Movement', in L. Turner, H.C. Katz, and R.W. Hurd (eds) *Renkindling the Movement: Labor's Quest for Relevance in the 21st Century*, Ithaca, NY: ILR Press.

Verma, A. and Kochan, T.A. (2004) 'Unions in the 21st Century: Prospects for Renewal', in A. Verma and T.A. Kochan (eds) *Unions in the 21st Century: An International Perspective*, Basingstoke: Palgrave Macmillan.

Von Holdt, K. (2003) *Transition from Below: Forging Trade Unionism and Workplace Change in South Africa*, Pietermaritzburg: University of Natal Press.

Waterman, P. (1998) *Globalization, Social Movements and the New Internationalisms*, London: Mansell.

Weathers, C. (2003) 'The Decentralisation of Japan's Wage Setting System in Comparative Perspective', *Industrial Relations Journal* 34(2): 119–34.

Western, B. (1997) *Between Class and Market: Postwar Unionization in the Capitalist Democracies*, Princeton: Princeton University Press.

Wooden, M. (2000) *The Transformation of Australian Industrial Relations*, Sydney: Federation Press.

BILL DUNN

Globalisation, Labour and the State

Introduction

In this chapter, I seek to examine the relations between contemporary
capitalism, labour and the state. I particularly want to question an
influential line of argument which suggests that something called
'globalisation' weakens the state, which in turn disempowers labour.
A corollary to such a proposition is that strategies for labour revival
must be reconceived; they cannot be oriented towards the state (from
which power has disappeared) and must be 'upscaled' to confront
capital at the global level. I argue this sets labour an unnecessarily
daunting task; one that implies workers should abandon what remain
crucial arenas of struggle. Understanding capitalism as a global
system still requires labour supporters to examine the specific ways in
which social relations are mediated and contested at the national and
local levels and how different forms and arenas of action are related.

The first half of the paper considers the implications for workers
of debates between globalisation theories and sceptical critiques. The
latter emphasise continuities and enduring state strengths and therefore, at least by implication, the importance of national action for
workers. However, I then diverge from such discussions, suggesting
that an overtly pro-labour perspective highlights the limitations of
many of these debates and the shared assumptions of the apparently
antagonistic stances. Labour supporters should indeed be wary of af-
firming neoliberal perspectives that national political action has
become irrelevant. However, labour's situation cannot adequately be
conceived in national terms and notions of sovereignty and statist
alternatives to capitalism (of either a Stalinist or social democratic
hue) were never entirely adequate. I suggest that elements of a Marxist

understanding of political economy, notions of 'combined and uneven development' and 'relative autonomy' can help to elucidate the limitations of economistic and state centred approaches and the interdependence of struggles on different scales and of different (political and economic) forms.

The New Orthodoxy of Labour Disempowerment

The literature on globalisation is huge. At least for some writers, theories of globalisation or the 'new economy' replace discourses which conceived the world primarily in terms of class relations or class struggle. Labour is seldom the explicit object of contemporary, mainstream theorising. The exclusion is often somewhat perfunctory. However, we can extract from the orthodoxy a powerful explanation of the contemporary quietude of workers' organisation; a claim that globalisation has weakened the state and that this debilitation in turn weakens labour.

Despite numerous different emphases and qualifications, the case for globalisation is well rehearsed. An economic and technological revolution moulds the world into a newly shared social space (Held et al. 1999). Territorial boundaries and distances become ever less relevant as capital becomes more mobile (Scholte 2000). It is carried by more efficient transport and communication media but perhaps most fundamentally capitalism changes its nature, becoming weightless as knowledge replaces material production as the key source of wealth (Castells 2000). Efforts to deny change, according to this perspective, rely on setting up a 'straw man', a caricature of globalisation as a completed end state, which is not yet achieved. There is no denying the radicality of transformative processes and particularly their impact on nation states.

Multilateral firms now span the globe, most of the largest more 'foreign' than 'national' in terms of their assets, sales and employment (Glasius et al. 2002). The very notion of company nationality becomes questionable and the idea that firms and nations share common interests becomes antiquated. Businesses can, as one managing director memorably put it, 'go hopping and skipping and jumping to everywhere we can find a competitive labor market' (cited in Reich 1991: 121). They can sell their wares far from production. States continue to seek investment, but the costs, the concessions needed to succeed, become ever greater (Thomas 1997). The possibilities of even big rich states effectively containing capital diminish.

Perhaps in the realm of material production the relevance of distances and borders must be reckoned declining rather than already vanished. Some goods remain harder to move than others, some capital relations less susceptible to immediate relocation. But in the increasingly important knowledge economy, it is suggested, capital is already weightless. The vital work of symbolic manipulation can take place anywhere and transfer its products instantly and frictionlessly, at the click of a button. Epitomised by finance, here we really experience the 'end of geography' (O'Brien 1992) as vast amounts of (virtual) money whiz around the world. New financial instruments and trading places proliferate. In foreign exchange, daily turnovers now exceed the annual GDP of all but the largest countries. Global finance thus renders even rich states powerless; witness the attempts to defend the pound and the lira against speculative attack in 1992 and the even greater vulnerability and more severe social consequences on poorer countries of the next round of crises later in the decade.

Thus, as they become integrated into a single market economy, all states are weakened, regardless of their size or professed political orientation (Strange 1996). This creates a new paradigm, in which the global political economy operates in fundamentally different ways to the previous era dominated by distinct national economies. Globalisation reduces states to mere 'transmission belts' from global capital to their local economies, their behaviour ever more uniform and predictable as socio-economic space becomes increasingly homogeneous. This may still be a process rather than an achieved end state but as Strange (1999) suggests there is a clear 'litmus test' giving a decisive answer: there is convergence.

This new globalised world is disastrous for labour. Capitalism, left to its own devices, is an iniquitous exploitative system. But more or less democratic states had partially tamed it. Long struggles established democratic rights and even specifically pro-worker policies, for example limiting the length of the working day, guaranteeing a degree of social security or minimum wages. National labour movements were able to win country-wide deals with the state or with employers' federations limiting labour market competition. All this apparently disappears as states' power declines and the 'democratic defence' withers.

Labour, as Hyman (1998) argues, is subject to a two pronged attack. Firstly, states can no longer afford expansionary macro-economic policies or generous welfare states. Finance capital flees to places with sounder money. Within states, the tax burden shifts onto the less mobile, from more to less nimble sectors of capital and from capital to labour (Frieden 1991). Thus capital moves 'taking jobs and incomes with it, and leaving adjustment and welfare costs in its wake' (Rowley and Benson 2000: 7).

Secondly, national systems of industrial relations are under-mined. Capital can play off workers in different parts of the world against each other, moving to wherever hours are longest and pay lowest. There is, in short a 'race to the base' as what one critic has described as the 'manic logic of global capital' (Greider 1997) sweeps all before it. The mere threat of movement is often enough to win concessions.

Some writers attempt to distinguish here between the skilled and unskilled. Capital, according to the classic Heckscher-Ohlin factor-proportions models of orthodox economics will indeed relocate from areas of relative labour scarcity to those where it is abundant; from the unskilled but protected workers in the 'North' to the millions of willing unprotected 'hands' in the 'South'. The skilled workers of the North, by contrast, may remain relatively abundant and highly valued, able to command high wages while also benefiting from cheap imports made available by the new international division of labour (Wood 1994, 1998; Reich 1991). Thus we can explain not only labour's travails but also an increasing polarisation. Even the winners, however, according to such a scenario, do so as individuals rather than collectively. It is not their own organisation but comparative advan-tage upon which success depends. Some writers question even such narrow, sectional gains, suggesting that highly skilled labour is equally susceptible to task migration (Wolman and Colamosca 1997; May 2000). In any case, the prospects for solidarity between workers, always fragile even amongst relatively homogeneous domestic workforces, become ever more remote. Thus:

> [G]roups of workers in different countries compete with each other for employment, offering employers the lowest price at a given level of labour productivity. The power of trade unions to influence this bargain without the support of the state is limited in a national context; in the international it hardly exists for most occupations (Harris 1987: 198).

Workers, men and women of different skills and nationality but also of diverse races, religions and languages are set into ever more direct competition with each other. Typically presented as passive victims, global restructuring thus has 'shattering consequences' for workers' economic well being (Piven, cited in Castree 2000: 275). According to Castells 'the labor movement seems to be historically superseded' (1997: 360) and in extremis the very notion of class becomes redundant. Even more cautious scholars often describe at least some degree of disempowerment; noting falling union densities, levels of industrial action and diminishing political influence (Strange 1998; Gray 1998; Ross 2000).

Descriptions or theories of globalisation are sometimes explicitly neoliberal and anti-labour. However, the basic claims appear to have convinced many erstwhile Marxists and other labour supporters as explanations of organised labour's decline. Some scholars qualify the characterisation of capitalist transformation and its impact. It remains possible to identify workers and to suggest they can act on their own behalf. However, they often confirm the profundity of the disjuncture, concluding that if they are to resist, workers need something quite different from what has gone before.

Strategies for Addressing Globalisation

Globalisation, even according to many labour supporters, sweeps away local resistance. Workers therefore cannot and should not attempt to oppose it. To be against globalisation makes no more sense than being against the wind; what are needed are strategies for living with it and perhaps harnessing it. Orientations and organisation, which seek power in a national arena from which it has vanished, are surely redundant. Both Marxism and conventional social democratic politics are precluded (Giddens 1995; 1998). However, it may be possible to identify more positive aspects of contemporary change and to articulate strategies that can deal with globalisation. Some writers seek new social agents beyond class and realms of struggle within a putative global civil society. However, others maintain that labour can continue to play a role if it changes direction, to compete at the same scale as global capital (Tilly 1995; Radice 1999; Mazur 2000). Although I will be critical of this perspective, there is something consistent and important in such an understanding of globalisation. Poulantzas (1978) discussed the need for concepts of strategy. 'Globalisation' may then be a useful concept for labour not because it tells us that resistance is futile (however severe labour's problems might be) but because (or in as far as) it tells us of the need for a strategic reorientation, an 'upscaling' of action.

Predictably, this need to upscale is interpreted in different ways. For some authors the global level provides an arena for redeeming the democratic deficit left by state retreat. If transnational capital is producing a transnational state (Robinson, 2002), or even more diffuse institutions of 'global governance' it is here that pro-worker policies need to be established. Imperfect as institutions such as the UN, IMF, World Bank and WTO may be as presently constituted, they can be pressured to include labour friendly policies, whether universal standards or more modest and minimal basic rights. Longstanding institutions like the International Labour Organization might also be rejuvenated to play a vital role in establishing an international labour standards regime (Hughes 2002). Established labour institutions like the International Confederation of Free Trade Unions can also adapt to their changed environment and become vehicles for a more thorough-going labour internationalism and source of influence on the international institutions. Albeit at a more limited, regional level, some writers highlight the development and potential of intra-European and North American initiatives (Strange 2002).

Other scholars identify the limitations of particular institutions, while some see problems with this general approach (Mahnkopf and Altvater 1995; Bacon 2000; Panitch 2001). Although prepared to court labour organisations and other NGOs, provided they are sufficiently 'responsible', the global institutions are tied to liberalising agendas and powerful interests apparently inimical to those of workers. Global capitalism remains an unchallengeable given. Meanwhile, within labour's own international institutions longstanding problems of bureaucracy and distance between leadership and membership, already experienced at national level, appear likely to be accentuated with the increase in size and scope.

Therefore some authors instead advocate a 'bottom-up', 'grass-roots' or 'rank-and-file' internationalism, or social movement unionism (Moody 1997; Waterman and Munck 1999). The emphasis usually remains global but now on confronting capital directly rather than relying on institutional intermediation. Perhaps most optimistically of all, anarchist approaches return from the margins, able to celebrate the demise of the state and the new importance of multiple loci of autonomous resistance (Hardt and Negri 2000).

Despite their considerable differences, all these approaches share a rejection of the national level as no longer able to offer adequate resistance to global capital and, therefore, as an appropriate arena for labour strategies. The possibilities of various forms of international or global labour action are surely worth developing. Their absence plausibly represents a crucial flaw in labour's armoury. An emphasis on internationalism, or anti-nationalism, may be particularly welcome in an era witnessing the resurgence of parochial nationalist and racist politics. More problematic is the dismissal of the other parts of that armoury. The anti-labour implications of much of the mainstream theorising about globalisation seem clear, albeit sometimes as a matter of regret rather than celebration. There is a powerful argument that the world just is becoming more liberal. There is no alternative. Of course, any potential misuse by pro-capital interests does not allow us simply to dismiss the claims of social transformation. However, it might incline labour supporters to be sceptical, in the sense of suspending judgement, to look at the evidence particularly critically, before accepting what have often been avowedly anti-labour discourses.

Globalisation 'Sceptics' and the Enduring Pertinence of 'the National'

Against mainstream characterisation of globalisation, a substantial 'sceptical' literature questions the extent and significance of contemporary restructuring and emphasises historical precedent, often drawing on evidence from the pre-World War I *belle époque* but also highlighting continuities with the post-World War II Keynesian era. This critique maintains that although the world may have become more internationalised in certain respects, this does not constitute globalisation. Increases in trade (which must in any case be contextualised through comparisons with earlier high trade/GDP ratios) take place between established nation states. If tariffs are lowered (itself a political decision) trade regulation remains. And if transport costs fall (and it is not clear they always do [Dunn 2004]), predisposing capital to move from one location to another, this constitutes not de-territorialisartion but the changing balance between alternative territorial considerations, those of place and distance (Rosenberg 2000).

There have been huge investments into some formerly poorer countries, for example into Mexico and Singapore, and most recently China, but rather than 'racing to the base', most capital remained concentrated within the rich country Triad of North America, Western Europe and East Asia, with the poorest, lowest waged locations, most obviously in sub-Saharan Africa, conspicuously ignored. Mobility seems to vary considerably with capital in relatively few sectors able to flit across the world as the caricature would have it. Most firms remain strongly 'national' in the location of key assets and activities (Doremus et al. 1998) with expansion often into neighbouring countries or close to key market locations within the developed world. For all the hyperbole, much of the economy remains resolutely 'weighty' in the sense of involving physically massive commodities (Huws 1999). Moreover, even the most immaterial sectors remain tied to place through numerous cultural, social and political links. So 'global finance', for example, is particularly highly concentrated within a few major cities. Even as total foreign exchange turnover escalated, trading became more concentrated in the US and UK (essentially in New York and London) (Henwood 1998).

While the technologies leapt forward, they did not sever knowledge and finance from the material world and while 'more fluid and mobile than other forms [...] the state tends to play an exaggerated role in mobilizing and controlling finance capital' (Winters 1994: 421–2). Powerful governments proved competent to monitor funds, when they perceived the need, for example of suspected terrorists or in and out of sanctioned countries. Similarly, the money speculated against the pound and lira, the Thai baht or Indonesian rupiah was largely borrowed from rather old-fashioned on-shore commercial banks, a practice conspicuously permitted by leading states (Gowan 1999). Even smaller, weaker ones, Malaysia and Chile for example, appeared capable of achieving at least some success in controlling capital flows. So while capital moved it was far from obvious that it swept away nation states.

Rather than heralding irrevocable moves towards marketisation, in many cases, state spending increased as a share of national GDP, without having the apparently disastrous consequences for growth predicted by neoliberal versions of globalisation (Moody 1997; Vernon 1998; Garrett 2000). In short, states appeared to retain many of their former powers and resources. They continued to engage in 'complex hedge plays' (Greider 1997) and bargains both with firms and other states, their practices influenced by numerous obstinately national social practices as well as external economic forces. Instead of convergence, we find Strange's own litmus test confirms, '[t]he gap between rich countries and very poor ones is widening, and so is the gap between the rich and poor in the poor countries and the rich and poor in the rich countries' (1999: 351–2). The evidence thus questions notions of globalisation and claims of state retreat (Hirst and Thompson 1996; Weiss, 1998).

Moreover, an 'institutionalist' theoretical current suggests we should 'bring the state back in' at a more fundamental level. Capitalism from the start, as Polanyi (1957) insists, was based on state initiative and support and it continues to require this institutions basis. To the extent the state now withdraws, it heralds not a bright new dawn but unsustainable turbulence and unmanaged conflict (Gray 1996; Kapstein 1999).

Consequently, if states appear to be becoming less democratic, more pro-business and anti-labour, this should not be interpreted as a consequence of inexorable processes of globalisation and state decline. Some states themselves engineered change. In many instances, they positively encouraged and developed capital movements. For example, the leap in FDI flows was stimulated by privatisations of state-owned companies (Tussie and Woods 2000) with Herod identifying a 'corporate surplus' in the concessions ceded 'above and beyond what is strictly necessary to attract new investment' (1991: 391). Meanwhile political offensives and moves towards liberalised labour relations (Boyer 1998; Leisink 1999) often preceded the 'globalising' economic shifts. States are not reduced to mere transmission belts from the world to the local economy. Therefore, if their conditions and organisation declined, workers would need to redress the changes within national political economies, to contest power and wealth within what remains the crucial arena of struggle.

The Enduring Efficacy of National Labour Action

Thus the sceptical critique, if usually indirectly and implicitly, affirms the importance of the national level for labour activities. In practice, most struggles still begin locally and are often oriented towards the state, for example opposing attacks on welfare, pensions or industrial relations regimes (Wood 2002). Recent strikes in several continental

European countries, while defensive rather than assertive in their nature and achieving only limited success, show at least an enduring resilience of national labour movements. Stackhouse reports that Mexican workers' wages fell despite the predictions of free trade theory, adding that it is therefore little surprise if 'they blame their own government's attacks on trade unions rather than the World Trade Organization or even the free-trade agreement' (cited in Tabb 2000: 35).

Conversely, Gindin asks:

> what kind of internationalism can we expect among the United States, Mexico, and Canada if the American labor movement can't yet organize its own South; if the Mexican labor movement doesn't yet have a common union across workplaces within a single company like GM; if the Canadian labor movement hasn't yet been able to achieve major organizing breakthroughs in its own key private service sectors? (Cited in Panitch 2001: 17).

If nothing else, the enduring differences between states would appear to confirm that internal processes and class struggle continue to shape their development.

As I will outline more fully below, I am sympathetic to important elements of this argument. There appear to be many respects in which it remains both possible and necessary for workers to fight at the national level. It also seems important to put contemporary changes into historical context, to relativise claims of restructuring and to study the unevenness and often contradictory nature of change. The world has not become, nor is yet close to becoming, a homogeneous, deterritorialised space. However, in other respects, particularly in so far as some authors appear to be trying to reassert the state as the fundamental issue of social theory, this perspective can also be misleading and disabling for labour.

Contesting Sovereignty

MacLean (1999) offers a powerful critique of the apparently hetero-dox or sceptical accounts as epitomised by Hirst and Thompson's (1996) influential work. Firstly, their defence of the 'national' or 'inter-national' depends on a mass of empirical evidence, itself often nationally derived. The conclusions, suggests MacLean, are therefore anticipated by the methodology. Secondly, and perhaps more impor-tantly, he suggests (following Bourdieu) that orthodoxy and hetero-doxy share many assumptions setting the terrain of argument in such a way that a 'doxa' or universe of the undisputed goes unchallenged. Crucially, for all the efforts to relativise and historicise change, the idea that the nation state was, at least formerly, the central problematic of social theory largely goes unchallenged in both globalist and sceptical accounts. As far as labour is concerned, we can similarly note how various forms of 'statism' were common currency amongst much of the left, whether in the form of Stalinism or social democracy. Other radical currents were marginalised and state control and planning appeared to be the epitome of socialism.

Assumptions of state sovereignty are perhaps particularly exag-gerated within disciplines like international relations employing trans-historical conceptions of inter-state competition essentially running unchanged from antiquity through the 17th-century Treaty of West-phalia to the present day. However, this is no mere peculiarity of American political realism. Within the sociological tradition too, Weberian presumptions of nation states as sole legitimate authorities within given territories run deep. Giddens understands 'a capitalist society [a]s a "society" only because it is a nation state' (1990: 57).

This seems to be the real 'straw man'. So conceiving the past, it becomes a relatively simple task to demonstrate a new paradigm and a post-sovereign world. Any number of powers encroach national sovereignty. All sorts of social relations exist beyond state authority. The litany of International Financial Institutions, regional authorities, private finance, multinational firms and so on, is familiar.

However, notions of absolute sovereignty were always at best a 'convenient exaggeration' (Strange and Tooze 1981). States' actions have always been constrained by forces from within and without; not simply by the structures of interstate competition but by rival claims, religions authorities and by economic forces. The debates between liberals and mercantilists, already raging in the 18th century were concerned with how policy could best steer the ship of state in the potentially troubled waters of the international economy. If the mercantilist strategies were not the ignorant or narrowly self-serving follies suggested by their critics, nor were they wholly or unproblematically successful. What states could 'do' about their situation was already limited.

Any such limits became clearer in the 20th century. Globalised finance and restrictive national policies, speculative capital movements and hot money flows that overwhelmed the resources of central banks were a recurring characteristic of the 1920s and 1930s. Keynes was responding to a dominance of financial markets similar to that occurring today (Sassen 1996). Again, however, the achievements of Keynesianism and the extent to which nation states could ever control capital are contested (Burnham 1997). 'Keynesian countercyclical demand management policies were only pursued in Germany during 1926, and on a broader scale, during the 1970s. Such policies generally proved to be unsuccessful and short lived' (Notermans 1997: 206). For Callinicos '[t]he tale of reformist governments defeated by economic constraints imposed notably through the flight of capital on the financial markets is almost as old as social democracy itself' (2001: 27). The effectiveness of earlier national reform processes even in the richest countries and the notion that we have entered a new period are therefore doubtful (Callaghan 2002). Social democracy was, of course, always much weaker in the poorer majority of the world.

This suggests that we should be cautious about arguments of 'democratic defence'. We do not need to adopt anarchist or more careless Marxist formulations to appreciate that national states are neither necessarily democratic nor pro-labour. This should not be read as a blanket rejection of the efficacy of national reformism. To repeat, domestic struggles have moulded policies in many ways. Popular mobilisation and the workers' movement have made a difference. For example, their role in establishing the post-1945 settlements in various countries is well documented. At the same time, however, it is necessary to emphasise the limited nature of such achievements. Labour's democratic gains, real enough in many places, were limited in their extent and depth and often contradictory.

At best big labour became a 'junior partner' within postwar national economies. Even more benign forms of 'corporatism' gave labour some voice on the presumption that capital accumulation would not be fundamentally challenged. Moreover, a reliance on top level deals may have served capital well, undermining lower tiers of worker organisation, leaving it particularly vulnerable when state support was withdrawn in the 1980s and 1990s (Fairbrother and Yates 2003).

In the US, social democracy never developed as in Europe but there are parallels in the deals struck between big business and labour. As *Fortune* said at the time of the 1950 'Treaty of Detroit', 'GM Paid a Billion for Peace. It Got a Bargain'. Such deals may have facilitated long term productivity gains – and a declining wage share if not income – but also undermined the union strengths which had won them in the first place. Rank-and-file militancy was diffused while full-time union workers became more concerned with narrowly focused pay bargaining (Rupert 1994). In the US, perhaps even more than elsewhere, labour also became committed to a pro-government project, supporting domestic capital against its competitors. This also plausibly undermined independent labour organisation facilitating the decline of unions, which even in strict numerical terms, began not with recent 'globalisation' but in the late 1940s.

For all their contradictions, any gains were important for workers. But so too are many contemporary conditions, of welfare and democratic rights and legal protection for union activity. These might be under attack but there seems to remain much to fight for at the national level. Increasing internationalisation may have changed states' roles and labour's tasks; the contemporary state may have been undermined in various ways. Nevertheless, it seems expedient to be cautious. If the state is not yet powerless, neither was it ever absolutely powerful.

Re-Conceptualising Political Economy and Labour's Tasks

If states were never absolutely sovereign they were nevertheless – and I believe continue to be – hugely important social institutions. In this section I want to argue that concepts of Marxist political economy, of 'combined and uneven development' and of state 'relative autonomy', can help to articulate more positively labour strategies and overcome the dualist juxtaposition implicit in competing notions of globalisation or national development and the separation of economic and political. I am aware that this will rankle with some labour supporters who insist we should abandon outdated vocabularies and instead address contemporary problems through a more appropriate 21st-century language (Waterman 1997). To use the terminology of 'Marxism' and 'socialism' is indeed to court misunderstanding. However, with apologies for any unimaginative phraseology, I think the greater danger lies in insisting on novelty and thereby dismissing theoretical and historical lessons upon which labour can draw. There is a long tradition which, however imperfectly, has conceived the global and the national and the economic and political as interdependent not as exclusionary alternatives. It may yet help us examine the manner of these interrelations and the consequences for labour strategy in the current conjuncture.

The concept of combined and uneven development seems to be a useful starting point. Initially used by Trotsky (1962) to understand social relations and the prospects of revolution in Russia in the early 20th century, I want briefly to highlight two aspects of combination and unevenness which seem to remain essential in attempting to articulate contemporary development and the tasks of labour. Firstly, there is a geographical sense. Development is 'combined' in that capitalism operates as a world system. The development of each part has to be understood in relation to the whole. This is not then a recent achievement, although its salience might have become greater in recent years. This development is 'uneven', not simply because it is an anarchic and unplanned system but also because even strictly economic imperatives continue to upset any momentarily established equilibrium (Storper and Walker 1989). There is a continual tension, in Marxist language, between the extraction of relative and absolute surplus value, with the geographical correlates of imperatives to intensify investments and productivity at existing concentrations of labour or of moving to new locations and new, cheaper sources of exploitation.

The point for labour strategy is that although we live in a global world economy, and perhaps one in which globalisation has increased in recent years in the sense of shifting geographies of production, workers may need to act at different geographical scales. Change continues to disrupt all 'fixed, fast-frozen relations', including established labour practices but the universal does not obliterate particularities. Empirically, it would appear that in some instances, the effective reach and power of localised groups of workers increases. As examples from the auto-industry have shown, a single factory may be crucial to extended production chains (Herod 2000). Even in a global economy, there remain countervailing tendencies, increased concentrations of labour and just-in-time production systems that may be particularly vulnerable to disruption. Again the auto-industry provides powerful evidence (Thelen and Kume 1999) but even in the supposedly most globalised sectors like finance, concentrations of workers, whether in particular global cities, or even more specifically, for example in individual call-centres, appear to have increased rather than decreased. Other groups of workers, for example those involved in transport and communications, with a power to disrupt the movements of capital have been admitted as a potential exception to claims of labour disempowerment (Strange 1996). Conversely, other workers in particular locales may have become weaker, more vulnerable and more dependent upon solidarity across distance. The point is that the sweeping generalisation fails to capture labour's situation or potential.

In terms of their effects, too, labour's actions can be understood as combined and uneven. Struggles can and often do move beyond the particular places and the specific issues around which they are provoked. The possibilities of achieving links and solidarity between workers may change but in certain contemporary situations be enhanced, for example by the availability of new media. Labour faces many problems and new challenges. The point is that there is no *a priori* appropriate scale of action. 'Upscaling' local action may always be desirable but specific localised power may still be effective. Even studies of recent labour disputes with a significant international dimension suggest that not only global but also national and (especially) local scales of struggle were crucial (Castree, 2000). Budd even suggests that still 'domestic struggles are the key to the development of a thoroughgoing internationalism, rather than vice versa' (1998: 194).

This anticipates a second sense of combined and uneven development in that it has to be understood both politically and economically. In Trotsky's Russia the state mobilised resources, especially with regard to the military and armaments manufacture, which helped to create concentrations of labour out of proportion to its absolute weight in the population and thus gave it a political importance, which could not be read off from Russia's overall level of development. Therefore, relations within any particular country are not shaped simply by evolutionary domestic economic development, nor by international economic processes but also by international and internal political relations. Moreover, the conclusion that it was possible in certain circumstances for workers to take power even in an economically backward country challenged any simplistic evolutionist or reductionist reading of social change and the relationship between politics and economy. It says what others have articulated in terms of the relative autonomy of the state.

As mentioned above, an institutionalist tradition of social science emphasises that states remain important and retain a significant autonomy. Such accounts criticise what they perceive as the parallel economic determinisms of contemporary neoliberalism and 'orthodox' Marxism (Skocpol 1985; Gray 1996). In these, they suggest, the state is reduced to mere superstructural adjunct of dominant economic interests. This is a common charge against Marxism and perhaps one with some foundation. *Capital* did not extend to include any anticipated systematic treatment of the state while in the *Manifesto* we do read the famous characterisation as nothing 'but a committee for managing the common affairs of the whole bourgeoisie' (Marx and Engels 1975: 35). Many followers have added any number of awkward and contradictory formulations. However, as Cammack (1990) suggests, such a critique relies on either denying or appropriating more nuanced Marxist interpretations. These offer important elements of explanation of the relative separation of politics and economics and hence a guide for understanding labour's tasks.

In feudalism and other pre-capitalist class societies, economic relations were directly political. The separation of 'politics' and 'economics' is a particular achievement of capitalism. It creates aspects of independence never previously possible. Commodification of production relations allows the power inherent in these unequal economic conditions to co-exist with equal political rights (and for politics and economics to be conceived as separate realms). Of course, the separation of politics and economics is incomplete. In some respects it is more apparent than real, is one of the illusions that 'scientific socialism' seeks to dispel. In particular, the capitalist economy and nation state continue to condition each others' existence. Nevertheless, the uniquely capitalist nature of the state for Marx involved precisely its relative autonomy from the economy. This is not therefore a reluctant concession to critiques of Marxist determinism.

This has a number of implications. Firstly, because there is not an immediate correspondence between economic and political relations, the state form has to be understood in its historical specificity. Again contra anarchist or more careless Marxist formulations, certain activities can be seen as based on needs for organisation and social authority found in virtually all societies, its legitimacy is not wholly arbitrary, however much any general social needs are institutionalised for specific class purposes (Draper 1977). Labour cannot support or oppose all state institutions, the hospital, prison or meteorological office, for example, with equanimity. It also highlights the vacuity of claims of state retreat that focus only on certain activities, ignoring others which show no sign of diminution.

Secondly, the autonomy of the state can be double edged. On the one hand, it means it can be flexible and adaptable; not directly serving particular capitalists whose competing interests would prevent any effective general representation. On the other hand, it means that as states develop they can be shaped by particular social struggles; states which have evolved out of feudalism bear traces of that birth, others of revolutionary struggles. Reformist successes for example in winning postwar welfare states may be more or less successfully institutionalised and endure even as the struggles that achieved them subside. This can also be contradictory for labour. It was already clear to Marx in the 19th century, for example in the struggles over the length of the working day, that reform processes within capitalism were taking place. It seems reasonable to add that the degree of reform achieved by political action exceeded anything he envisaged. However, the shift to the 'political' in at least some instances may have reflected 'economic' weakness or failures of industrial action. This may also have strengthened a social democratic ideology in perceptions that capitalism can only be fought 'politically', through the state and that economic struggles are in some intrinsic sense secondary, less important or likely to succeed. Moreover, more or less successful practices, accommodation to norms of parliamentary democracy may also have had unforeseen but significantly moderating effects on the labour movement providing a materialist rather than simply ideological explanation for the transformation and successive 'betrayals' of the ambitions of more radically transformative projects (Prezorski 1985).

Thirdly, however, autonomy is only 'relative'. The state within capitalism is necessarily a distinctly capitalist state. It may have a degree of autonomy, serving the interests of those who staff it or of particular social groups who win representation through it but it cannot for any prolonged period escape the logic of capital accumulation, cannot represent any specific interests freely or independently but under conditions of pressure and constraint. States need funds to sustain the growth strategies and to sustain the political support of leading groups in society.

The separation of politics and economics is therefore conditional and the reconstitution of the economic 'base' might still lead to pressures or even political dislocations. So generalisations about the autonomy or interdependence of politics and economy can only be the starting point for more concrete investigations. Indeed, because the capitalist state is a relatively recent historical invention, has come into being, this perspective allows us to suggest it might therefore also decline. Nevertheless, it does challenge claims that capital mobility now necessarily requires a reconception of political forms. Labour should, in principle, neither ignore, nor limit itself to, struggles within and against the nation state.

Such an emphasis on the relative autonomy of the state, the (partial) separation of the economic and political seems vital for understanding contemporary processes of restructuring. Politics and economics are in a real sense separated or autonomous under capitalism in a way not conceivable in previous societies. This separation means that whereas economic mobility would directly challenge political forms in previous societies this need not be the case in capitalism (Rosenberg 2005). Indeed, not only the possibility, but also the fact, of capital mobility has been an intrinsic part of capitalism since its inception (Holloway 1995).

Thus there appears to be a utility in identifying not only change but also continuities with the past, considering which aspects of strategy, including those which built nationally based resistance and won national reforms, may still be of use. At the same time it remains possible and necessary to evaluate particular strengths and weaknesses. This contrasts with liberal economics and accounts of globalisation which assert a homogenisation and attempt to exorcise politics from the study of the economy. Conversely, it also differs from 'sceptics' who may continue to insist that nation states remain the key actors and see statecraft as the appropriate object of study. The separation of politics and economics has not been confined to the academy but runs deep within the labour movement. Social democratic and Stalinist 'statism' has long been opposed by a 'workerist' economism. These old debates appear to be played out again. A politicist tendency of some on the left continues to conceive labour's struggles either in terms of national reform or in a rather undifferentiated celebration of resistance as an act of political will (Holloway 2002). Meanwhile, for example, an insistence that Social Movement Unionism can now provide an adequate response to state decline rediscovers many of the principles of an earlier anarcho-syndicalism. Evidence of a more open, militant and participatory unionism on which the latter draws seems attractive. But neither can labour afford to ignore the struggles within or initiated by the state. It is precisely state attacks that have provoked some of the biggest response from organised labour.

Of course 'relative autonomy' remains controversial and imprecise. It nevertheless seems to offer a sounder basis than alternatives, which conceive the economy and politics as wholly separate spheres or imply the outright dependence of one on the other. The point is not simply that old Marxist texts repay revisiting. It is more that labour supporters need to study concretely the complex interdependence of contemporary political economy. Labour's situation cannot simply be read-off from processes of economic restructuring and state decline. Rather, workers' conditions and their potential for changing them need to be understood in terms of more complex and articulated processes of material, institutional and ideological change (Cox 1986).

Conclusion

Neither theories of globalisation nor state-centred sceptical critiques offer adequate characterisations of contemporary political economy or guide for labour perspectives. Increased integration has not overridden national or local distinctiveness and does not mean that labour can only act effectively at the global level. It is misleading to talk of state retreat, but less because state sovereignty remains intact and inviolable than because it was always partial and conditional. What states 'do' may have changed but many struggles within and against specific nation states continue to matter. If these are ultimately insufficient this is nothing fundamentally novel. A more thoroughgoing internationalism may now be required but is more likely to develop from specific, real, all be they partial, strengths than an insistence on the futility of national struggles. Different scales and different forms of action, both economic and political, remain necessary and labour strategies need to articulate their interaction.

References

Bacon, D. (2000) 'World Labor Needs Independence and Solidarity', *Monthly Review* 52(3).

Boyer, R. (1998) 'The Changing Status of Industrial Relations in a More Interdependent World. An Interpretation and Agenda for Further Research', in T. Wilthagen (ed.) *Advancing Theory in Labour Law and Industrial Relations in a Global Context*, Amsterdam: North-Holland.

Budd, A. (1998) 'Workers in a Lean World: Unions in the International Economy – Reviewed', *Historical Materialism* 3.

Burnham, P. (1997) 'Globalisation: States, Markets and Class Relations', *Historical Materialism* 1(1): 150–60.

Callaghan, J (2002) 'Social Democracy and Globalisation: The Limits of Social Democracy in Historical Perspective', *British Journal of Politics and International Relations* 4(3): 429–51.

Callinicos, A. (2001) *Against the Third Way: An Anti-Capitalist Critique*, Cambridge: Polity.

Camack, P. (1990) 'Statism, New Institutionalism, and Marxism', *Socialist Register 1990: The Retreat of the Intellectuals*, London: Merlin.

Castells, M. (1997) *The Information Age: Economy, Society and Culture, Volume 2: The Power of Identity*, Oxford: Blackwell.

—— (2000) *The Information Age: Economy, Society and Culture, Volume 1: The Rise of the Network Society*, Oxford: Blackwell.

Castree, N. (2000) 'Geographic Scale and Grass-Roots Internationalism: The Liverpool Dock Dispute, 1995–1998', *Economic Geography* 76(3): 272–92.

Cox, R.W. (1986) 'Social Forces, States and World Orders: Beyond International Relations Theory' in R.O. Keohane (ed.) *Neorealism and its Critics*, New York: Columbia University.

Doremus, P.N., Keller, W.W., Pauly, L.W. and Reich, S. (1998) *The Myth of the Global Corporation*, Princeton: Princeton University Press.

Draper, H. (1977) *Karl Marx's Theory of Revolution, 1: State and Bureaucracy*, New York: Monthly Review Press.

Dunn, B. (2004) 'Capital Mobility and the Embeddedness of Labour', *Global Society* 18(2): 127–43.

Fairbrother, P. and Yates, C.A.B. (2003) 'Unions in Crisis, Unions in Renewal?', in P. Fairbrother, P. and C.A.B. Yates (eds) *Trade Unions in Renewal: A Comparative Study*, London: Continuum.

Frieden, J.A. (1991) 'Invested Interests: The Politics of National Economic Policies in a World of Global Finance', *International Organization* 45(4): 425–51.

Garrett, G. (2000) 'Shrinking States? Globalization and National Autonomy', in N. Woods (ed.) *The Political Economy of Globalization*, Basingstoke: MacMillan.

Giddens, A. (1990) *The Consequences of Modernity*, Cambridge: Polity.

— (1995) *A Contemporary Critique of Historical Materialism*, Basingstoke: MacMillan.

— (1998) *The Third Way*, London: Polity.

Glasius, M., Kaldor, M. and Anheir, H. (2002) *Global Civil Society 2002*, Oxford: Oxford University Press.

Gowan, P. (1999) *The Global Gamble: Washington's Faustian Bid for World Domination*, London: Verso.

Gray, J. (1998) *False Dawn: The Delusions of Global Capitalism*, London: Granta.

Greider, W. (1997) *One World, Ready or Not: The Manic Logic of Global Capitalism*, Harmondsworth: Penguin.

Hardt, M. and Negri, A. (2000) *Empire*, Cambridge, MA: Harvard University Press.

Harris, N. (1987) *The End of the Third World: Newly Industrializing Countries and the Decline of an Ideology*, Harmondsworth: Penguin.

Held, D., McGrew, A., Goldblatt, D. and Perraton, J. (1999) *Global Transformations: Politics, Economics and Culture*, Cambridge: Polity.

Henwood, D. (1998) *Wall Street: How it Works and for Whom*, updated edition, Verso, London.

Herod, A. (1991) 'Local Political Practice in Response to a Manufacturing Plant Closure: How Geography Complicates Class Analysis', *Antipode* 23(4): 385–402.

— (2000) 'Implications of Just-in-Time Production for Union Strategy: Lessons from the 1998 General Motors-United Auto Workers Dispute', *Annals of the Association of American Geographers* 90(3): 521–47.

Hirst, P. and Thompson, G. (1996) *Globalization in Question*, Cambridge: Polity.

Holloway, J. (1995) 'Capital Moves', *Capital and Class* 57: 136–44.

— (2002) *Change the World without Taking Power*, London: Pluto.

Hughes, S. (2002) 'Coming in from the Cold: Labour, the ILO and the International Labour Standards Regime', in R. Wilkinson and S. Hughes (eds) *Global Governance*, London: Routledge.

Hyman, R. (1998) 'Industrial Relations in Europe: Crisis or Reconstruction', in T. Wilthagen (ed.) *Advancing Theory in Labour Law and Industrial Relations in a Global Context*, Amsterdam: North-Holland.

Kapstein, E.B. (1999) *Sharing the Wealth: Workers and the World Economy*, New York: W.W. Norton.

Leisink, P. (1999) 'Introduction', in P. Leisink (ed.) *Globalization and Labour Relations*, Edward Elgar, Cheltenham

MacLean, J. (2000) 'Philosophical Roots of Globalization and Philosophical Routes to Globalization', in R.D. Germain (ed.) *Globalization and its Critics*, Basingstoke: Macmillan.

Mahnkopf, B. and Altvater, E. (1995) 'Transmission Belts or Transnational Competition? Trade Unions and Collective Bargaining in the Context of European Integration', *European Journal of Industrial Relations* 1(1): 101–17.

Marx, K. and Engels, F. (1975) *Manifesto of the Communist Party*, Beijing: Foreign Languages Press.

May, C. (2000) 'Information Society, Task Mobility and the End of Work', *Futures* 32(4): 399–416.

Mazur, J. (2000) 'Labor's New Internationalism', *Foreign Affairs* 79(1): 79–93.

Moody, K. (1997) *Workers in a Lean World*, London: Verso.

Notermans, T. (1997) 'Social Democracy and External Constraints', in K.R. Cox (ed.) *Spaces of Globalization: Reasserting the Power of the Local*, New York: Guilford Press.

O'Brien, R. (1992) *Global Financial Integration: The End of Geography*, London: Pinter.

Panitch, L. (2001) 'Class and Inequality: Strategy for Labour in the Era of Globalization', paper presented to the International Studies Association, Chicago, 23 February.

Polanyi, K. (1957) *The Great Transformation*, Boston: Beacon Press.

Poulantzas, N. (1978) *Classes in Contemporary Capitalism*, London: Verso.

Prezorski, A. (1985) *Capitalism and Social Democracy*, Cambridge: Cambridge University Press.

Radice, H. (1999) 'Taking Globalization Seriously', in L. Panitch and C. Leys (eds) *Global Capitalism versus Democracy, Socialist Register 1999*, London: Merlin.

— (2004) 'Nation-states in Global Capitalism: A Critique of International Political Economy', unpublished manuscript.

Reich, R.B. (1991) *The Work of Nations*, London: Simon and Schuster.

Robinson, W.I. (2002) 'Capitalist Globalization and the Transnationalization of the State', in M. Rupert and H. Smith (eds) *Historical Materialism and Globalization*, London: Routledge.

Rosenberg, J. (2000) *The Follies of Globalisation Theory*, London: Verso.

— (2005) 'Globalization Theory – A Post-Mortem', *International Politics* 42(1): 2–74

Ross, G. (2000) 'Labor Versus Globalization', *Annals of the American Academy of Political Science* 570: 78–91.

Rowley, C. and Benson, J. (2000) 'Global Labor? Issues and Themes', *Asia Pacific Business Review* 6(3–4): 1–14.

Sassen, S. (1996) *Losing Control? Sovereignty in an Age of Globalization*, New York: Columbia University Press.

Scholte, J.A. (2000) *Globalization: A Critical Introduction*, Basingstoke: Macmillan.

Skocpol, T. (1985) 'Bringing the State Back In: Strategies of Analysis in Current Research', in P.B. Evans, D. Rueschemeyer and T. Skocpol (eds) *Bringing the State Back In*, Cambridge: Cambrdige University Press.

Storper, M. and Walker, R. (1989) *The Capitalist Imperative: Territory, Technology, and Industrial Growth*, New York: Basil Blackwell.

Strange, G. (2002) 'Globalisation, Regionalism and Labour Interests in the International Political Economy', *New Political Economy* 7(3): 343–65.

Strange, S. (1996) *The Retreat of the State: Diffusion of Power in the World Economy*, Cambridge: Cambridge University Press.

— (1998) 'Globalony?', *Review of International Political Economy*, 5(4): 704–20.

— (1999) 'The Wesfailure System', *Review of International Studies*, 25(3): 345–54.

— and Tooze, R. (1981) 'States and Markets in Depression: Managing Surplus Industrial Capacity in the 1970s' in S. Strange, S. and R. Tooze (eds) *The International Politics of Surplus Capacity: Competition for Market Shares in the World Recession*, London: George Allen and Unwin.

Tabb, W.K. (2000) 'Turtles, Teamsters, and Capital's Designs', *Monthly Review* 52(3): 1–12.

Thelen, K. and Kume, I. (1999) 'The Effects of Globalization on Labor Revisited: Lessons from Germany and Japan', *Politics and Society* 27(4): 476–504.

Thomas, K.P. (1997) *Capital beyond Borders: States and Firms in the Auto Industry, 1960–94*, Basingstoke: Macmillan.

Tilly, C. (1995) 'Globalization Threatens Labor's Rights', *International Labor and Working-Class History* 47(1): 1–23.

Trotsky, L. (1962) *The Permanent Revolution and Results and Prospects*, London: New Park.

Tussie, D. and Woods, N. (2000) 'Trade, Regionalism and the Threat to Multilateralism', in N. Woods (ed.) *The Political Economy of Globalization*, Basingstoke: Macmillan.

Vernon, R. (1998) *In the Hurricanes' Eye: The Troubled Prospects for Multinational Enterprises*, Cambridge, MA: Harvard University Press.

Waterman, P. (1997) 'Conceiving an "International Social-Movement Unionism" Requires a 21st, not a 19th Century, Vocabulary', at <www.labournet.org.uk/oct97/waterman/html>

— and Munck, R. eds (1999) *Labour Worldwide in the Era of Globalisation: Alternative Models in the New World Order*, New York: St Martins Press.

Weiss, L. (1998) *The Myth of the Powerless State*, Cambridge: Polity.

Winters, J.A. (1994) 'Power and the Control of Capital', *World Politics* 46: 419–52.

Wolman, W. and Colamosca, A. (1997) *The Judas Economy. The Triumph of Capital and the Betrayal of Work*, Reading, MA: Addison-Wesley.

Wood, A. (1994) *North-South Trade, Employment and Inequality: Changing Fortunes in a Skill-Driven World*, Oxford: Clarendon.

— (1998) 'Globalisation and the Rise in Labour Market Inequalities', *The Economic Journal* 108(450): 1463–82.

Wood, E.M. (2002) 'Global Capital, National States', in M. Rupert and H. Smith (eds) *Historical Materialism and Globalization*, London: Routledge.

MARK ANNER

The Paradox of Labour Transnationalism: Trade Union Campaigns for Labour Standards in International Institutions[1]

Introduction

In response to declining union membership,[2] there is a growing perception that labour will have to develop strategies that complement local organising and national activism with international campaigns (Gordon and Turner 2000). One option is for labour to pressurize global governance institutions to provide mechanisms that ensure compliance with core labour standards (van Roozendaal 2002; Wilkinson and Hughes 2000).[3] The leadership of the International Confederation of

---

1   A version of this chapter was presented at the Workshop of the Transnational Contention at Cornell University. Segments of the paper were published as 'The International Trade Union Campaign for Core Labor Standards in the WTO', *WorkingUSA* 5(1): 43–63. The author thanks Roy Adams, Teri Caraway, Peter Katzenstein, Sidney Tarrow, and Danielle Van Jaarsveld for their comments on earlier versions of this chapter.

2   According to a study by the International Labour Organisation, 'Workers' organisations are experiencing serious difficulties almost everywhere and are losing members'. Of the countries studied by the ILO, 'about half have seen a considerable drop in their membership' (ILO 1997: 6). The decline in unionisation rates in some countries is much less than in others; unionisation rates remain above 50 percent of the work force in many European countries. See OECD 2005, <http://www1.oecd.org/scripts/cde/queryScreen.asp?DSET =CDELFS_C6T01I&SETNAME=Trade+union+density&DBASE=LFS_INDI CATORS&EMAIL=&DBNAME=Labour+Market+Statistics+%2D+INDICAT ORS>, (accessed 27 July 2005).

3   The goal is not to supplement national strategies with global strategies. National struggles remain a vital part of union activism because, while market-oriented

Free Trade Unions (ICFTU), the world's largest international trade
union organisation, has been particularly interested in adding a labour
standards clause to the mechanisms of the World Trade Organisation
(WTO). Yet not all ICFTU union affiliates were equally enthusiastic
about the idea. While WTO-inspired market-oriented reforms may
hurt organised labour in both developed and developing countries,
labour is hurt in different ways and to different degrees. As a result,
while some organisations supported the ICFTU's focus on labour
standards for formal sector workers, other wanted to broaden the
scope of the campaign to included development-related issues. Different perceptions of the problem also influenced the debates. Some
unionists saw the WTO as an institution dominated by powerful states
and did not trust that a labour-rights dispute settlement mechanism
would be applied fairly to less developed countries. Yet, most member
organisations of the ICFTU eventually decided to sign on to the WTO
campaign.

   To understand why the ICFTU and its member organisations
supported the demand for a labour standards clause in the WTO it is
necessary to explore how interests are aggregated and international
labour solidarity is constructed through international organisations
made up of organisations with different cultures, histories, and ideational influences. Goal formation is the result of processes that involve
the negotiation of interests and the construction of solidarity through
debate, dialogue and persuasion based on normative understandings.
This negotiation takes place through an organisational matrix of
national trade union centres with significant power imbalances. The
concept of solidarity suggests interdependence and common efforts
among groups in different structural conditions based on overlapping
interests and principles. While it may be said that southern unionists
are more adversely affected by globalisation than northern unionists,[4]

---

reforms and the deregulation of labour relations regimes may weaken states'
capacity to protect labour vis-à-vis the exigencies of capital, they have not
eliminated state capacity. Moreover, the emerging institutions of global governance are woefully inadequate substitutes.

4   For example, some of the harshest labour conditions resulting from inter-
     nationalised production regimes exist in Export Processing Zones, which are

northern unionists also experience the adverse affects of globalisation through membership loss, privatisation, declining social welfare, and increased job instability.[5]

Thus, northern unionists also have an interest in influencing the rules governing international financial institutions. Yet, northern trade unionists may have a vision of what is to be done that differs from that of the south. And, they also tend to have greater resources and greater access to international institutions. This gives them the ability to pursue their agenda and to assist southern unionists as they pursue their related demands. Yet it also gives them the ability to set global campaign agendas. That is, northern unions are better positioned to decide what to prioritise, how to frame issues, and what tactics to use.

Hence, the same factors that make northern alliances appealing for southern actors also create conditions through which southern actors can lose control over the strategic direction of campaigns. This may result in agendas that do not reflect the core concerns of everyone they portend to represent. This is what I have termed *the paradox of labour transnationalism*.[6] The ICFTU campaign for core labour standards in the WTO in many ways illustrates this paradox. On the one hand, most southern unionists supported the WTO campaign out of the recognition that national and sub-national activism was increasingly insufficient to protect workers against the adverse effects of market-oriented reforms and the growing power of capital. Yet, on the other hand, these same southern unionists expressed concern that the international campaign was more likely to reflect the priorities of the more powerful northern trade unions – i.e., labour standards for

---

much more prevalent in developing countries. In general, economic internationalisation has increased the income gap between north and south.

5   In this chapter, I will use the term 'northern unionists' to refer to unionists in the advanced capitalist countries. 'Southern unionists' refers to unionists in developing countries. Certainly there are important differences within both the north and the south, which I will indicate when appropriate.

6   By labour transnationalism, I mean coordinated actions by workers' organisations in at least two countries that target international actors, such as multinational corporations, international institutions, or foreign states. (Tarrow 2005: especially 25). I use the term transnational as opposed to international to emphasise my focus on cross-border relations among non-state actors (See Keohane and Nye 1971: especially xii).

formal-sector employees – at the expense of development-related demands sought by the south.

This paradox is not fixed in stone. The failure to achieve a labour standards clause in the WTO Seattle Ministerial made the ICFTU leadership more open to new ideas and thus provided an opportunity for southern unionists to modify the ICFTU's strategy. At the same time, southern unionists benefited from certain forms of representation and the power of legitimacy that they brought to the campaign. That is, much like social movement dynamics, resource-weak actors within international organisations may take advantage of emerging opportunities and frame issues in terms of social norms to influence organisational agendas. The ICFTU campaign slowly broadened its demands to include development related issues. The ICFTU also appeared more willing to pursue social movement alliances, albeit selectively. This shift in strategy indicates that southern unionists had more power to influence campaigns than material balance-of-power analysis would otherwise indicate.

As the ICFTU is now more aggressively targeting other international institutions, most notably the International Monetary Fund and the World Bank, the paradox of labour transnationalism has not fully dissipated. The challenge here, as in the WTO campaign, is for the labour movement to establish procedures and normative understandings that mitigate the differences and power imbalances among national trade union centres. The goal is not to supplant a northern agenda with a southern agenda, but rather to construct a truly *transnational* trade union agenda.

Labour Transnationalism, Interests and Solidarity

It is impossible to explore the issue of labour transnationalism without addressing questions of economic interests and social solidarity. Scholars have debated since the 19th century the theoretical roots of class solidarity and conflict. Karl Marx argued that capitalism was a global system that homogenised the conditions of working-class and created the potential for international proletariat unity (Marx 1977 [1887]). In contrast, Wolfgang Stolper and Paul Samuelson argued that national factor endowments differentiated the interests of workers internationally; workers in national-states where labour was abundant would be more likely to favour free trade than workers in national-states where labour was scarce (Stolper and Samuelson 1941). The debate continues to this day. While some scholars argue that economic 'globalisation' has created downward pressure on working conditions everywhere and thus a strong incentive for transnational labour alliances (Gordon and Turner 2000), others argue that globalisation has increased the heterogeneity of the international working class, augmenting conflicts of interests and making sustained cross-border collaboration unlikely (Eder 2002).

That these arguments point towards opposing outcomes suggests that economic interests are theoretically indeterminate in establishing whether labour will pursue transnationalism. The existing empirical evidence is also inconclusive; we know that there are many examples of both cross-border solidarity and economic nationalism. Thus, a strictly interest-based account only takes us so far. As Göran Therborn argues, '"[i]nterests" by themselves do not *explain* anything. "Interest" is a *normative* concept indicating the most rational course of action in a predefined game, that is, in a situation in which gain and loss have already been defined. The problem to be explained, however, is how members of different classes come to define the world and their situation and possibilities in a particular way' (Therborn 1980: 10). For a fuller explanation, we must complement economic explanations with institutional and ideational factors.

Richard Hyman explains that trade unions can create an 'imagined solidarity' of workers.[7] Hyman writes, 'Solidarity implies the perception of commonalities of interest and purpose which extend, but do not abolish, consciousness of distinct and particularistic circumstances' (Hyman 1999: 96). For Hyman, solidarity must be reinvented in order to reflect current employment conditions in which

---

7   Hyman is, of course, building on the concept of nationalism/'imagined communities' developed by Benedict Anderson (Anderson 1991).

workers are more differentiated at the same time that they are more interdependent. That is, trade unionists are in need of new ideas that help to unify and mobilise an international labour movement at the same time they do not negate differences.

The challenge is to frame issues in ways that resonate with dominant cultural understandings (Snow et al. 1986). Klotz and Lynch note, 'Emerging ideas need to be "packaged" or "sold" in reference to prevailing norms, not solely in terms of their instrumental advantages' (Klotz and Lynch). Yet it is also true that in the process of packaging their ideas, movements define themselves and their opponents. They establish what they stand for, what they oppose, and whom they oppose. The ICFTU portrayed the globalising world economy as part of a fierce competition among multinational corporations in a 'race to the bottom' to find which states would offer the lowest wages, the least protective labour legislation, and the weakest health and occupational standards. To stop the race to the bottom, unionists needed to join together to pressurize global governance institutions to enforce universal labour standards (ICFTU 1999a).

How does the labour movement arrive at a particular frame? How is Hyman's 'imagined solidarity' constructed? Robert O'Brien (2000) argues that the ICFTU's frame is the result of three exogenous factors: the end of Cold War, economic globalisation, and exposure to other social movements. Yet, factors internal to movements also matter. First, change takes place through organisational structure. As Sidney Tarrow suggests, in studying transnational campaigns it is important to make the distinction between networks and international organisations. International organisations have a much easier time centralising strategic decision-making and then requesting membership compliance (Tarrow 2001). This can be both strength and weakness. It is strength because it ensures coherence and focus to the campaign. It can be weakness because the ability of less powerful members of the organisation to question or modify strategies is curtailed. Moreover, the sense of membership allegiance created by international organisations may be very strong. As one labour leader admitted in reference to the WTO campaign, it is not always clear when members in developing countries support campaigns out of conviction or out of loyalty.[8]

An alternative organisational structure is the network, for which labour scholars like Peter Waterman have expressed an understandable fondness (Waterman 1998; 2001). In contrast to the vertical structures of international organisations, networks are 'characterized by voluntary, reciprocal, and horizontal patterns of communication and exchange' (Keck and Sikkink 1998: 8). As a result, the dilemma of conviction versus loyalty is less pronounced in transnational networks than international organisations. Moreover, unencumbered by the hierarchical decision-making structures of international organisations, networks can respond much more quickly to issues as they arise. That is, networks have the potential to be more egalitarian and lighter on their feet.

But networks have limitations, such as a lack of ability to hold network leaders accountable to a membership base. And networks may not eliminate power imbalances. As Jordan and Tuijl argue, 'If [relationships are] not handled with care, they may reflect as much inequality as they are trying to undo' (Jordan and van Tuijl 2000: 2061). Uvin also emphasises the dramatic inequality among non-governmental organisations that make up many transnational networks. He explains, 'A disproportionate number [of the richest NGOs] are located on the same 50 square miles of the world's surface as are most of the other powerful institutions'. He adds, 'A small proportion of [global civil society] control the purse strings for the vast majority of the others' (Uvin 2000: 16).

What this discussion suggests is that the construction of movement goals and the implementation of movement campaigns take place in institutional contexts – be they international organisations or transnational networks – that may lessen but not eliminate power imbalances. As a result, movement activists need to take extra care to ensure that the voices of all those affected by a campaign are heard. This may be done through the actions of an enlightened leadership. It also may be the result of internal 'social movement' dynamics. Sidney Tarrow argues that social movements, when confronting more power-

---

8   Author's interview, Brussels, 20 June 2000.

ful forces, exploit opportunities, mobilise resources, and frame issues in ways that resonate favourably with dominant social values (Tarrow 1998). I will suggest that less powerful actors might use social movement strategies in order to pursue their agenda within international organisations. In the ICFTU campaign, southern unionists exploited the opportunity presented by the failure of the WTO Ministerial in Seattle and framed their demands in terms of norms that resonated within the organisation. They also looked for internal alliances with like-minded northern unionists. Sometimes the construction of 'imagined solidarities' involves a healthy degree of *internal* activism.

International Organisations: Labour and the ICFTU

Since the 19th century, trade unionists have sought to develop transnational ties through international organisations. Early trade union organisations tended to focus on specific economic sectors and were mostly limited to Europe and North America. The 20th century saw attempts at international trade union unity, but world war and the political divisions created by the Cold War eventually left the movement divided into three organisations: the communist World Federation of Trade Unions (WFTU), the social Christian World Confederation of Labour (WCL), and the social democratic International Confederation of Free Trade Unions (ICFTU).[9] The ICFTU claims 233 national affiliates with 145 million members in 154 countries, and is considered the largest of the three.

The ICFTU represents a formal, highly-structured, international membership organisation.[10] The congress is the maximum authority

---

9   At its December 2004 Congress, the ICFTU committed itself to the creation of a new international trade union confederation by joining forces with the World Confederation of Labour (ICFTU 2004c).

10   Being an international organisation does not prevent participation in networks. At its 18th World Congress, the ICFTU has stated its commitment to building

and it meets once every four years. Delegates to the congress, who have the right to vote on important matters, are chosen based on the number of members of their national organisation, with a minimum of one delegate and a maximum of twenty. There are fifty-three members of the Executive Board, of whom forty-three are nominated by geographic regions. The ICFTU's constitution stipulates that Europeans should have the largest number of representatives on the Executive Board, with seventeen. North America (the United States and Canada) has five representatives. This gives Europe, the US and Canada 53.49 percent of these seats. Asia is given eight seats, while Africa and Latin America are given six each (ICFTU 2004a). The ICFTU has struggled with its European bias. Gumbrell-McCormick (2000: 347) explains:

> The European affiliates had always been by far the largest section of the ICFTU membership; [...] [excluding the AFL–CIO] they provided almost 60% of total membership, and a significantly higher proportion of the confederation's finances. [...] It was essential that the development of ICFTU policies and structures satisfied the requirements and objectives of the Europeans [...] but it was a delicate task to achieve this without unduly offending affiliates in other parts of the world.

All ICFTU general secretaries have been European. At the 2004 Congress of the ICFTU, the president from Zambia was replaced by a woman union leader from Australia. This was an important step forward for the representation of women in the international trade union movement. Yet it also meant a drop in the participation of unionists from developing countries in the organisational hierarchy of the ICFTU. Presently, the general secretary is British, the president is Australian, and the ICFTU's steering committee chairperson is German.

The ICFTU requires affiliated organisations to pay annual dues. However, the rate of dues varies according to levels of development.

---

social movement alliances. For example, the ICFTU participates regularly in the World Social Forum. These social movement alliances are still somewhat tentative and very selective. With Peter Evans, I have referred to this combination of international organisations and networks as a 'basic rights complex' (Anner and Evans 2004).

Trade union centres in least developed countries may pay less than two percent of the rate paid by trade union centres in developed countries. As a result, dues paid by European countries, the US and Canada amount to over eighty percent of the ICFTU's dues income. This allows unions in less developed countries to maintain their membership, but it also enhances the sense of entitlement of the wealthier members to influence key decisions. This economic imbalance is further heightened by patterns of intra-union assistance. Every year, northern-based trade union centres provide approximately US$ 70 million in official support to trade union projects in less developed countries. The support is sorely needed by unionists in developing countries. But it also can create a sense of economic dependency that comes with political consequences. Unionists that depend on funding from the north may be hesitant to aggressively question the political decisions of their economic supporters.

There are no easy solutions to these dilemmas. They confront any organisation that attempts to build international solidarity among a large group of economically and culturally disparate members. Identifying the potential sources of power imbalance can minimise their adverse affects. At the same time, financial resources are not the only source of power. The participation of unionists from developing countries provides legitimacy to transnational campaigns that, when recognised and used effectively, can give southern actors an ability to influence campaigns. The goal is not to replace a northern bias with a southern bias. Rather, it is to ensure equal participation of northern and southern unionists' in the conceptualisation as well as the implementation of campaigns in order to achieve movements that are international in substance as well as form.

International Institutions:
The WTO as a Threat and an Opportunity

Charles Tilly notes that national labour movements grew and became strong with the development of national states that were able to ensure respect for labour rights.[11] He adds that globalisation lessened the capacity of national states to enforce labour rights resulting in the need for labour to develop new strategies on the international scale (Tilly 1995). This has led labour to target the institutions of global governance, most notably the World Trade Organisation (WTO), to complement national labour relations regimes with enforcement of international labour standards (O'Brien et al. 2000; van Roozendaal 2002).

The WTO, unlike its predecessor, the General Agreement on Trade and Tariffs (GATT), is potentially open to all trade-related issues.[12] Governments that systematically permit labour rights violations in export sectors to lower costs and increase competitiveness could be regarded by the WTO as engaging in an unfair trade practice (Wachtel 1998). Second, unlike the International Labour Organisation (ILO) – the international institution designed to deal with labour issues – the WTO has a dispute settlement system that has the power to sanction violators (O'Brien et al. 2000). Moreover, the formation of the WTO gave the process of multilateral trade negotiations a more structured and effective institutional framework. Since it is no longer necessary for member states to unanimously accept committee findings, it is more likely that the enforcement mechanism will move forward. This gives the WTO greater power to ensure compliance with its rules. The ICFTU hoped that the power of

---

11   In truth, this is more the case of rich, developed countries. In developing countries, the state was often a source of labor repression that worked in alliance with capital.

12   Prior to 1995, trade negotiations focused mainly on tariff reduction. With the 1995 Uruguay Round of the General Agreement on Trade and Tariffs (GATT) that established the WTO, the scope of trade negotiations expanded to include the service sector, intellectual property rights, rules on investment, and potentially many more issues.

the WTO enforcement mechanism could provide a means to enforce internationally-recognised labour standards.

Yet there are risks involved in this strategy. The WTO is not – unlike the ILO – a tripartite organisation. As a result, trade unions do not directly participate in the decision-making process nor can they present complaints to the WTO. That role is reserved for governments (Greenfield 2001). And the WTO enshrines power imbalances that favour developed countries, which may use a labour rights clause to the detriment of developing countries (Ewing 2001). Strong states could employ their power and influence to use the WTO rules against competitors based on that country's violation of labour standards. The ICFTU responded to this risk by arguing that the burden of determining whether labour rights had been violated should be in the hands of the ILO. Another risk is that the WTO could accept a workers' rights clause but the process of going through the ILO and WTO procedures would be so burdensome that very little would change in practice. The result would be to legitimise the WTO's system of market-oriented reforms without ensuring respect for labour rights (Gumbrell-McCormick 2000). In the end, the leadership of the ICFTU felt that there was no alternative than to pursue the WTO campaign. If labour did not have the correlation of forces to bring down the WTO and to create something that was better, the only strategy left for labour was to try to make the existing international institutions as least harmful to labour as possible.

Campaigning for Labour Standards in the WTO

The first opportunity for the ICFTU to pursue its demand for a labour standards clause came at the WTO's first Ministerial Meeting in 1996 in Singapore. Prior to the Singapore Ministerial, there was very little discussion among ICFTU affiliates, particularly affiliates in developing countries, regarding the core labour standards campaign.[13] The campaign was largely developed by the ICFTU's office in Brussels, which informed its affiliates of its position on labour standards at a meeting soon before the Singapore Ministerial began.[14] At Singapore, heads of state did not accept the ICFTU proposal for a labour standards clause, but the ICFTU did manage to ensure reference to core labour standards in the final declaration.

ICFTU affiliates such as the Norwegian Confederation of Trade Unions (LO-Norway) pressured the ICFTU headquarters to increase the participation of member organisations in the core labour standards campaign, particularly southern unionists.[15] In response, the ICFTU established the Task Force on Trade, Investment and Labour Standards (TILS). TILS consisted of representatives of member organisations and was designed to share information and to develop activities. The work of TILS was facilitated when the LO-Norway decided to fund many of its activities. Most of LO-Norway's funds were dedicated to ensuring the more active involvement in the campaign of unionists from developing countries. The Norwegian government and Norwegian unionists wanted to encourage the participation of unions in developing countries to ensure that core labour standards would not be used for protectionist purposes. According to a representative of LO-Norway, Norwegians are particularly aware of the need to find mechanisms to ensure the participation of less powerful members in international organisations since 'Norway is such a small country and, as a result, has struggled with this issue itself'.[16]

Prior to the second Ministerial meeting of the WTO in Geneva in May 1999, TILS organised a three-day conference for its members. One of the main goals of the pre-Ministerial conference was to prepare

---

13   Interview with Leonard Larsen, Oslo, Norway, June 2000. The exception is Latin America, where the Inter-American Regional Organisation of Workers (ORIT) began an active campaign with its affiliates prior to Singapore (interview with Barbara Shailor, Washington, 10 October 2000).
14   Interview with Jon Ivar Nålsund, Head of the International Department, the Norwegian Confederation of Trade Unions (LO-Norway), Oslo, Norway, 21 June 2000.
15   The author has worked as a global advisor to LO-Norway.
16   Interview with Leonard Larsen, Oslo, Norway, June 2000.

unionists to lobby their governments on the issue of core labour standards. This strategy had little impact at the time in part because the Geneva Ministerial was more about marking the GATT's 50th anniversary and less about discussing substantive issues. Given the ceremonial nature of the Geneva Ministerial, the ICFTU increasingly focused its attention on the Third Ministerial, scheduled to begin in late November 1999 in Seattle. For the ICFTU labour standards campaign, Seattle became somewhat of a showdown.

Most of the campaign budget prior to Seattle went to regional, sub-regional and national seminars. According to the ICFTU, the intention of these meetings was to 'galvanise support for the workers' rights clause in the mechanisms of the WTO' in preparation for the third WTO Ministerial meeting.[17] After each event, participants were encouraged to write letters to heads of state, trade ministers, and finance officials, using a model letter provided by the ICFTU. Affiliates were also encouraged to request that their governments allow them to be part of the official national delegation to the Seattle Ministerial.

These tactics combined to form a four-part strategy developed during a TILS seminar held in Geneva in December 1998. The ICFTU first developed the overall arguments and rationale of the campaign and, through regional and sub-regional activities, informed national union affiliates about the goals. National affiliates were called upon to aggressively lobby their governments. Governments would then, it was hoped, support the trade-labour rights linkage at the Seattle Ministerial and force the WTO to accept labour standards as part of its framework. Finally, the WTO would use its new labour rules to force member states to comply with core labour standards.

While many observers of the WTO-labour campaign focused on the events in Seattle that targeted the WTO, few mention the amount of work the ICFTU and member organisations did to lobby national states prior to Seattle. Yet this comprised a greater share of the ICFTU's efforts. This suggests that, in order to fully appreciate the

---

17   ICFTU/AFRO (1999) 'Report and Plan of Action on the West and Central African Sub-regional Meetings on International Labour Studies Standards and Globalisation', memo.

significance of large, transnational protest events, it is necessary to also study the many smaller events that take place in the months leading up to the large events. Moreover, it highlights that international institutions like the WTO exist due to the participation of national states and that even in transnational campaigns, unionists mostly dedicate their attention to pressurizing their national states. The ICFTU was particularly interested in achieving the support of state representatives from strong or otherwise symbolically important states or coalitions of states. These included the European Union, the United States, and South Africa. As Sidney Tarrow observes, strong states can provide international institutions with the authority, if not the normative frame, to ensure action when consensus is lacking (Tarrow 2001: 7).

The limitation of the strategy was that it relied too much on one model of activism – lobbying through letter writing – and was too focused on a narrow set of demands, core labour standards. While focus is important, it limited the ability of the movement to pursue broader demands that might have responded to the development needs affecting workers while also creating the foundation for broader alliances, particularly with governments in developing countries. The campaign never managed to assuage the fears of developing countries that a labour standards clause would not be used for protectionist purposes. Even the South African government, which in general supported the link between labour rights and trade, did not believe that the dispute settle mechanism of the WTO was the best place for a labour standards clause.[18]

The result of the Seattle Ministerial meeting of the WTO is well known. Trade ministers failed to agree upon the launching of a new round of multilateral trade negotiations. While street protesters undoubtedly put considerable pressure on state representatives, most observers concur that the Ministerial also collapsed due to irresolvable disputes among member countries. The labour rights issue was certainly one issue of contention, but disputes on more conventional issues – such as agriculture, dumping, textile and apparel restrictions,

---

18   Author's interview with Alec Erwin, Minister of Trade and Industry, Government of South Africa, Pretoria, South Africa, 5 July 2000.

and investment – also prevented countries from reaching a consensus on the negotiating agenda (Elliott 2000).

Complicating matters further was US President Bill Clinton's comment that sanctions should be applied to countries that violated core labour standards.[19] The comment provoked an immediate backlash among developing countries that had long argued that the objective of the core labour standards campaign was to apply sanctions. These countries pressured to dilute the core labour standards proposal so much that it reflected very little of the original ICFTU proposal. The suspension of the Ministerial Meeting meant that the proposal was not voted upon. But the mood was such that core labour standards did not received the same attention in the subsequent Ministerial Meetings in Doha and Cancun. Thus, the campaign did not achieve its immediate goal.[20] Governments of developing countries unanimously rejected the ICFTU proposal for a labour rights clause in the mechanisms of the WTO. No doubt, some of these governments were conservative and undemocratic, and had no interest in supporting labour rights abroad or at home. But this could not be said about the governments of other developing countries, like the South African government.

Southern Unionists and the Paradox of Labour Transnationalism

One of the ironies of the WTO campaign was that while the ICFTU leadership argued that developing countries had the most to gain from the labour standards proposal (O'Brien 2000: 544), the strongest opposition to the proposal came from governments in developing countries. Moreover, southern unionists expressed concerns about the campaign. Ebrahim Patel, Deputy General Secretary of the Congress

---

19   Michael Paulson (1999) 'Clinton Says He Will Support Trade Sanctions for Worker Abuse', *Seattle Post-Intelligencer*, 1 December, p. A1.

20   Yet the campaign did raise awareness on how labour rights violations are linked to trade-related economic competition.

of South African Trade Unions (COSATU) argues that the campaign needed to be more influenced by southern actors. He says: 'We haven't succeeded in making the social clause a demand of the South. It is still a demand of the North supported by some unions in the South'.[21] Patel notes that the international labour movement could have done a better job of convincing the media and critics that the campaign was not about northern protectionism. But to do this, northern unionists would have to show that they are prepared to pressure their governments to allow for greater market access for products from poor countries.

Patel suggests that a more global union campaign would take on not only different demands but also different tactics. He notes that the degree and the nature of trade union influence on governments in developing countries is not the same as trade union influence on governments in developed countries. There is a different logic and institutional relationship. Moreover, there is important variation among developing countries. While South African unions have a great deal of influence, other unions in developing countries have very little influence over their governments. For Patel, lobbying works best in liberal democracies while other forms of protest activities are potentially more productive in political contexts where democratic rights are curtailed. Patel highlights the paradox of labour transnationalism by noting that there is a need for southern unionists to make use of international levers to pressure for respect of labour rights, yet southern unionists face the risk of northern allies using their control over the levers in ways that are not always the most beneficial for southern workers.

Like COSATU, the Sole Labour Centre of Brazil (CUT) supports the ICFTU campaign in general, but also expresses a need for the campaign to better reflect the needs of workers in the south. Concretely, the CUT also argues that the campaign for labour rights must be integrally linked to the theme of sustainable development. For Kjeld Jakobsen, International Secretary of the CUT, the issue is employment opportunities. He observes, 'What good is it for me to

---

21   Interview with author, Cape Town, South Africa, 5 July 2000.

have the right to negotiate collectively if I don't have a job?'[22] Jakobsen notes that in order to achieve success in the future, the ICFTU and its affiliates need to clarify goals and mechanisms, and need more and better alliances with organisations fighting the adverse effects of economic globalisation on poor and working people.[23]

Sanjeeva Reddy of the Indian Trade Union Congress (INTUC), who was one of the more outspoken southern union critics of the WTO campaign, explains: 'We agree with the importance of core labour standards. We have reservations about linkage with the WTO. All trade union centres in India have reservation.' He continues, 'We are afraid of linkage. We are afraid that India will have to implement core labour standards whilst no one else will'.[24] Like other southern unionists, the Indians were concerned about not being able to control the international enforcement mechanisms for core labour standards. The Indians preferred that ensuring respect for core labour standards through international institutions be limited to the ILO, which does not have sanctioning power and where labour has an institutional presence through the ILO's tripartite mechanisms.

Other unionists from developing countries expressed concerns about the conceptualisation of the campaign. For example, in the conclusions from a conference organised in Ghana participants noted, 'Discussions should address a whole range of development aspects including developing countries' needs concerning [...] [market] access, environment, investment, poverty, unemployment, social protection and gender. Other issues that were most likely to attract the attention of government officials were agricultural policies, tariffs, anti-protectionism, debt crisis, etc'.[25] In Tunis, unionists called for the creation of permanent specialised committees in the WTO that would deal with issues such as the debt problem, poverty alleviation, technology transfers, and the rights of workers to freely emigrate, in addition to international labour standards (ICFTU 1999b).

---

22   Interview with author, São Paulo, Brazil, 10 July 2000.
23   Ibid.
24   Interview with author, Geneva, 26 June 2000.
25   Ibid.

ICFTU Campaigns since Seattle

In the wake of the Seattle Ministerial, the ICFTU began to make some important changes in the campaign. In an April 2001 declaration on the upcoming WTO Qatar Ministerial, it noted the need to focus on development priorities such as debt relief, market access, and availability of AIDS/HIV drugs.[26] Other ICFTU statements referred to the growing interest on the part of its members to 'strengthen [the ICFTU's] alliances with NGOs, including consumers' NGOs, wherever possible, including co-operating to organise demonstrations as had been done successfully in Seattle in November 1999'.[27] In early August 2001, the ICFTU announced its first ever Global Unions' Day of Action for November 9, 2001. The day of action coincided with the first day of the WTO Qatar Conference. In a message to its members, the ICFTU explained what the day may include:

> As well as meetings and information in work-places, affiliates could consider a range of actions including demonstrations; work stoppages; public information and mobilisation efforts; media-oriented actions; and petitions, based on our common demands. Given the different circumstances in each country and the specific concerns of unions in particular sectors, such a day of action will need to include many forms of action.[28]

---

26 ICFTU. 2001, April. ICFTU Statement On The Agenda For the 4th Ministerial Conference of the World Trade Organisation in Qatar, 9–13 November 2001 (2nd Draft).

27 ICFTU, TILS Task Force, unpublished memo, Brussels, Belgium, 27 June 2001. Many unionists in developing countries are less wary about developing alliances with other civil society organisations. Given the distorted and partial patterns of industrialisation in developing countries, traditional industrial unions never acquired the degree of power and representation enjoyed by similar unionists in developed countries. Workers in developing countries often relied on alliances with other sectors of society to promote their demands. This is particularly true of some left-oriented unions. More conservative union organisations have attempted to compensate for their lack of power at the plant level through corporatist arrangements at times with right-wing governments.

28 ICFTU, open letter, 27 July 2001.

The message marks two important changes. First, the ICFTU's call for direct action and protest activity is a change from its prior focus on lobbying top-level government officials. Second, the ICFTU encouraged members to develop their own strategies of action depending on what would work best in each country thus showing greater flexibility in strategy implementation.

Why did these changes take place? The power imbalance among northern and southern unionists had not been altered. Nor did the ICFTU modify its decision-making mechanisms to ensure the more structured participation of southern unionists.[29] After the failure of Seattle, the ICFTU leadership was forced to re-evaluate its strategy. This gave members who were critical of the campaign an opportunity to suggest a modification of goals and alternative tactics. The ICFTU leadership was also vulnerable to normative critics regarding how it should run its campaigns. Most notably, participants and external observers argued that if the campaign was to benefit workers in the south, then those workers should have an important say in the campaign's strategy. Such arguments, framed in this way, were hard for the ICFTU leadership to dispute.

The result of these factors appears to be a modest but important shift in campaign goals and tactics. Yet, while the ICFTU remains committed to a revised WTO campaign for core labour standards,[30] it may have missed its critical juncture at the Seattle Ministerial meeting in 1999. Since that time, it has been extremely difficult even to get the WTO Ministerials to include the labour standards issue on the agenda. And so the ICFTU turned its attention elsewhere in pursuit of international institutions that could use their power and influence to ensure respect for core labour standards.

---

29   The ICFTU has done a better job in ensuring the participation of women in its leadership structures.

30   At its 18th World Congress in 2004, delegates agreed that the ICFTU 'will continue to work for the defence and promotion of core labour standards at the WTO, including working towards the establishment of permanent structured co-operation between the ILO and the WTO'. (ICFTU 2004b)

Targeting the IMF and World Bank

In the wake of Seattle, the ICFTU's continued desire to incorporate labour rights clauses in the institutions of global governance led it to target the International Monetary Fund and the World Bank with renewed vigour. The ICFTU had long been interested in influencing these financial institutions. In 1996, the ICFTU invited the Director of the IMF, Michel Camdessus, to speak at its World Congress. Yet the relationship was far from amicable. While the IMF looked for ICFTU support to successfully implement its plans, most ICFTU members felt that IMF neoliberal policies were the root cause of many of their problems. This was especially the case of unionists from developing countries that faced the brunt of structural adjustment programmes. At the Congress, unionists from Latin America expressed strong disagreement with the IMF's suggestion that workers were responsible for their own poverty because of lack of training (O'Brien 2000: 545).

By the early 2000s, the IMF and the World Bank sought to improve their image with many civil society organisations. There are at least three reasons why they shifted their policies. First, their image was tarnished by a series of spectacular failures, the most dramatic of which was the Asian financial crisis. The subsequent crises in Russia and Brazil, and the economic collapse in Argentina led to the further discrediting of World Bank and IMF policies. Second, they were tarnished by the exposés of high-ranking staff members who provided detailed insider accounts of the failed policies and 'one-size-fits-all' approach of these institutions.[31] Finally, their images were damaged by large and powerful protest events in Quebec, Genoa, Washington, and cities throughout the global south where unionists, students, environmental groups, women's organisations, indigenous people's associations, and others demanded that international financial institutions become more accountable to people's needs. The size, breadth, and determination of the global social justice movement made these institutions realise that they had to establish better mechanisms of communication with civil society organisations. Among other changes,

---

31   See, for example, the critique offered by Joseph Stiglitz (Stiglitz 2002).

they agreed to systematic meetings with the international union movement.

In October 2002, the first high-level meeting between the IMF and World Bank, and the international union movement occurred, with the agreement that these meetings would be repeated every two years in Washington. In October 2004, the meetings with the IMF and the World Bank took place with 81 union representatives from 40 countries. Unionists from the south were well represented due to the ICFTU's renewed appreciation of their role as well as travel support provided by the Norwegian Confederation of Trade Unions. The meetings offered the opportunity for the union movement to evaluate with these international financial institutions (IFIs) progress made since the last meeting. Unionists concluded that while some advances were made in terms of processes of consultation, much more needs to be done in terms of implementation and monitoring. The World Bank had done more than the IMF in terms of incorporating promotion of core labour standards into its activities. For example, the International Finance Corporation (IFC), the Bank's private sector lending arm, agreed to incorporate reference to core labour standards as part of its lending criteria. Yet the IFC has yet to establish an effective monitoring and compliance mechanism.

The IMF acknowledges the positive role that unions can play in society. Yet it also maintains that labour market flexibility via reductions in severance pay and social security benefits is an important tool for employment generation (IMF 2005). In October 2003, the IMF established a guide to facilitate regular meetings between its staff and Civil Society Organisations (CSOs).[32] The guide, however, emphasises that the IMF negotiates with governments not with CSOs. Moreover, the guide explains that civil society organisations should not be privy to certain information considered sensitive on matters involved in negotiations between the IMF and national governments, despite that fact that these sensitive matters might be the issues that are most important for labour. Another purpose of the exchanges with

---

32   See IMF, 2003, *Guide for Staff Relations with Civil Society Organisations*, http://www.imf.org/external/np/cso/eng/2003/101003.htm (accessed 12 February 2005).

civil society, according to the guide, is for the IMF to determine the 'political viability' of its policies, that is, 'to gauge forces for and against IMF-supported policies'. This suggests that IMF staff members are to determine the relative strength of business groups and labour groups and pursue policy accordingly. Given that market reforms have tended to strengthen business associations at the expense of organised labour, it follows that the IMF will have a greater incentive to listen more closely to the opinions of the business sector.

While the leadership of the ICFTU sees exchanges with international financial institutions as an opening of which they can take advantage, southern unionists are less likely to believe that the changes in the IFIs are sincere. The Argentine unionists expressed their outrage at the consequences of the IMF policies in Argentina. A Colombian unionist noted how, as unionists continue to be assassinated, IFIs and the Colombian government have pushed for labour market flexibility at a time when workers need more, not less, protection. A unionist from Cameroon referred to the new policies of the IFIs to converse with unionists on a regular basis as a public relations ploy where Third World unionists are used to polish the image of these international institutions. Hence, the paradox of labour transnationalism re-appears, albeit in a different form. While southern unionists need international campaigns to modify IFIs' conduct in their region, the power imbalance between the southern unionists and the international institutions is so great, that southern unionists express scepticism that the incorporation of labour rights clauses into the frameworks of the IFIs will modify working conditions in their countries in any significant way.

Conclusions

Economic internationalisation has altered the terrain in which labour endeavours to pursue its demands. It is increasingly difficult for workers to improve their living and working conditions solely through local organising drives and efforts that target the national state. This does not make local and national efforts unimportant. As Bill Dunn (this volume) makes clear, national states remain an important site of labour contention. Even in transnational campaigns, states remain a crucial target. WTO decisions are, after all, made by upper-level governmental representatives. The most important component to the ICFTU strategy was for member organisations to pressurise their governments to accept the labour standards proposal prior to the Ministerial Meetings. Yet, as capital, goods, and production regimes increasingly span borders, labour has found the need to combine domestic strategies with transnational activism. This is particularly the case for workers in developing countries that never enjoyed a strong welfare state, where the state could be the source of severe forms of anti-union repression, and where international financial institutions and the US government are perceived to have more power than national legislatures.[33]

Prime targets for the labour movement included the WTO, IMF, and World Bank. The problem for the movement was in deciding how to target these institutions. Certainly, organisations like the ICFTU have internal decision-making procedures, including international congresses where delegates have the opportunity to vote on certain issues. Yet, decision making is seldom that straightforward, most especially in organisations made up of affiliates with differing economic capabilities, access to structures of power, and ideational influences. This results in the paradox of labour transnationalism. Weak actors in southern countries need alliances with strong actors in northern countries to achieve their goals, but it can become all too easy for northern actors to use their power to take the lead in designing campaign strategies, which may result in a displacement or modification of the original goals of the southern actors.

---

33   In a recent study by the United Nations Development Programme on Latin America, when asked to list who yields the most power in Latin America, interviewees listed the US government (22.9 percent), international financial institutions (16.6 percent), and national legislature (12.8 percent). The most common response was the business/financial sector, which was mentioned in 79.7 percent of responses (UNDP 2004).

Yet, southern actors have found ways to make their voices heard. They can take advantage of opportunities created by failed campaigns and use the legitimacy that they bring to movements to suggest modified goals and alternative tactics. In some cases, this may only result in minor modifications, but it does indicate that southern unionists can exert influence. This is especially true when they are able to overcome differences and communication problems within the south and speak with one voice. Since Seattle, the ICFTU has broadened its demands to include more development-related issues, has changed its tactics to include a variety of forms of protest activity, and has expanded its range of activities to target international financial institutions besides the WTO. Some of these changes are relatively minimal and incremental. But they do suggest that, while the paradox of labour transnationalism is never completely overcome, it can be mitigated.

References

Anderson, B. (1991) *Imagined Communities: Reflections on the Origin and Spread of Nationalism* (revised and extended edition), London and New York: Verso.

Anner, M. and Evans, P. (2004) 'Building Bridges across a Double Divide: Alliances between US and Latin American Labour and NGOs', *Development in Practice* 14(1 & 2): 34–47.

Eder, M. (2002) 'The Constraints on Labour Internationalism: Contradictions and Prospects', in J. Harrod and R. O'Brien (eds) *Global Unions? Theory and Strategies of Organized Labour in the Global Political Economy*, New York: Routledge.

Elliott, K.A. (2000) 'Getting Beyond No...! Promoting Worker Rights *and* Trade', in J.J. Schott (ed.) *The WTO After Seattle*, Washington, D.C.: Institute for International Economics.

Ewing, K. (2001) 'Trade Union Rights in the Twenty-First Century', *WorkingUSA: The Journal of Labor and Society* 5(1): 19–42.

Gordon, M.E., and Turner, L. (2000) 'Going Global', in M.E. Gordon and L. Turner (eds) *Transnational Cooperation Among Labor Unions*, Ithaca, NY: ILR Press.

Greenfield, G. (2001) 'Core Labor Standards in the WTO: Reducing Labor to a Global Commodity', *WorkingUSA* 5(1): 9–18.

Gumbrell-McCormick, R. (2000) 'Facing New Challenges: The International Confederation of Free Trade Unions (1972–1990s)', in A. Carew, M. Dreyfus, G. van Goerthem, R. Gumbrell-McCormick and M. van der Linden (eds) *The International Confederation of Free Trade Unions*, New York: Peter Lang.

Hyman, R. (1999) 'Imagined Solidarities: Can Trade Unions Resist Globalization?', in Peter Leisink (ed.) *Globalization and Labour Relations*, Cheltenham, UK: Edward Elgar.

ICFTU (1999a) *Building Workers' Human Rights into the Global Trading System*, Belgium: International Confederation of Free Trade Unions.

— (1999b) 'Final Declaration: Sub-Regional Seminar for the Maghreb Countries, Tunis, July 13–15.'

— (2004a) *Constitutions as Amended by the Eighteenth World Congress, Miyazaki, December 2004*, International Confederation of Free Trade Unions [Date accessed: 15 February 2005]. Available from www.-icftu.org/www/pdf/Const-E.pdf.

— (2004b) *Final Resolution (18GA/E/6.12), Trade Union Rights*, International Confederation of Free Trade Unions, available from http://congress.icftu.org/www/pdf/18GA/Final/18GA-12EN.pdf.

— (2004c) *Final Resolution, 18/GA/E/61, Globalising Solidarity: Building a Global Union Movement for the Future* [Date accessed: 15 February 2005]. Available from http://congress.icftu.org/www/pdf/18GA/Final/-18GA-01EN.pdf.

ILO (International Labour Organisation) (1997) *World Labour Report: Industrial Relations, Democracy and Social Stability 1997–1998*, Geneva: International Labour Organization.

IMF (International Monetary Fund) (2005) *Stabilization and Reform in Latin America: A Macroeconomic Perspective on the Experience Since the Early 1990s*, Washington, DC: IMF.

Jordan, L., and van Tuijl, P. (2000) 'Political Responsibility in Transnational NGO Advocacy', *World Development* 28(12): 2051–2065.

Keck, M.E., and Sikkink, K. (1998) *Activists Beyond Borders: Advocacy Networks in International Politics*, Ithaca, NY: Cornell University Press.

Keohane, R.O., and Nye, J.S. (1971) *Transnational Relations and World Politics*, Cambridge, Mass.: Harvard University Press.

Klotz, A., and Lynch, C. (forthcoming) *Constructing Global Politics: Strategies for Research*, unpublished manuscript..

Marx, K. (1977 [1887]) *Capital: A Critique of Political Economy*, New York: Vintage Books.

O'Brien, R. (2000) 'Workers and World Order: The Tentative Transformation of the International Union Movement', *Review of International Studies* 26(4): 533–55.

—, Goetz, A.M., Scholte, J.A. and Williams, M. (2000) *Contesting Global Governance: Multilateral Economic Institutions and Global Social Movements*, New York: Cambridge University Press.

Snow, D., Rochford, E.B. Jr., Worden, S. and and Benford, R.D. (1986) 'Frame Alignment Processes, Micromobilization, and Movement Participation', *American Sociological Review* 51(4): 464–81.

Stiglitz, J.E. (2002) *Globalization and its Discontents*, New York: W.W. Norton.

Stolper, W. and Samuelson, P. (1941) 'Protection and Real Wages', *Review of Economic Studies* 9(1): 58–73.

Tarrow, S. (2001) 'Transnational Contention and International Institutions', *Annual Review of Political Science* 4: 1–20.

— (2005) *The New Transnational Activism*, New York: Cambridge University Press.

— (1998) *Power in Movement: Social Movements and Contentious Politics* (2nd edition), New York: Cambridge University Press.

Therborn, G. (1980) *The Ideology of Power and the Power of Ideology*, London: NLB.

Tilly, C. (1995) 'Globalization Threatens Labour Rights', *International Labor and Working-Class History* 47(1): 1–23.

UNDP (2004) *Democracy in Latin America: towards a Citizen's Democracy*, United Nations Development Programme, available from http://democracia.undp.org/Informe/Default.asp?Menu=15&Idioma=2.

Uvin, P. (2000) 'From Local Organization to Global Governance: The Role of NGOs in International Relation', in K. Stiles (ed.) *Global Institutions and Local Empowerment: Competing Theoretical Perspectives*, London: MacMillan.

van Roozendaal, G. (2002) *Trade Unions and Global Governance: The Debate on a Social Clause*, New York: Continuum.

Wachtel, H. (1998) 'Labor's Stake in the WTO', *The American Prospect* March–April.

Waterman, P. (1998) *Globalization, Social Movements, and the New Internationalisms: Employment and Work Relations in Context*, Washington, DC: Mansell.

— (2001) 'Trade Union Internationalism in the Age of Seattle', *Antipode* 33(3): 312–36.

Wilkinson, R. and Hughes, S. (2000) 'Labor Standards and Global Governance: Examining the Dimensions of Institutional Engagement', *Global Governance* 6: 259–277.

SUE LEDWITH

The Future as Female?
Gender, Diversity and Global Labour Solidarity

Introduction

This chapter is about women's relationships with trade unions and
labour movements. It is about how women work collectively within
and across gender exclusion zones, how they carry their project inside
into labour organisations' mainstream and how they work transversally across all of these and also together with a range of allied
organisations, campaigns and NGOs. The context is trade unionism in
crisis in the face of globalisation and its devastating impact on organised labour worldwide. Questions of trade union survival and revival
are increasingly centred on organising the unorganised: women,
young workers, part time workers, minorities, migrants, the disabled.

Three important and unfolding strategies both of unions and of
excluded groups are discussed: organising, mainstreaming, and
affirmative action approaches, including separate structures. In
particular, women's autonomous organising is examined for its
efficacy as a creative and strategic form of organising. It is compared
with and countered by the more institutionalised strategy of mainstreaming, and the question of balancing the two is addressed. Ways
in which diverse groups develop diverse strategies, especially at grassroots, in and across communities, as open systems, mobilising, linking
with and forming alliances and coalitions with new social movements,
together with mainstreaming, are explored, drawing on micro case
examples and illustrated in more detail through a joint transnational
union gender project between western and eastern European trade
unions.

Above all the chapter attempts to identify ways in which there are always women actively organising, in communities, in labour movements, across networks and alliances, working for change, as part of the larger transformative 'women's project'.

Labour Market Changes

The speed of globalisation and its doubling of the global labour force (Freeman 2005), trade liberalisation and its accompanying mantra of deregulation and flexibility, frequently accomplished through the violation of human, worker and trade union rights, has changed the landscape of work and workforces both within and across countries and continents. Changing patterns of gender relations have been at the centre of the restructuring of employment and social systems (Rubery et al. 2003). Women now make up around 50 percent of the workforce world wide, and as Juliet Mitchell (1986: 36) observed early on in the process of globalisation, within a period of critical change in capitalism they are the frontline: 'women are used within the economy as a temporary advance guard...'

In addition, patriarchal gender regimes (Walby 1990) shape women's affective and familial responsibilities, circumscribe their roles, and mark the locations, sites and timeframes of women's workforce participation. They designate women's particular aptitudes and skills as being those based in the domestic sphere and which come 'naturally' to women, eliminating the need for costly training initiatives by employers. Thus women predominate in caring, servicing occupations and industries, in the public sectors of education, of health and social care, in the private services such as catering and hospitality, homeworking, sewing in clothing and knitwear factories, and women's 'nimble fingers' and alleged passivity offered opportunities for work in electronics and other fine assembly work. Within feminised labour market segmentation, black and ethnic minority women make up those lower in the pay and skills hierarchy (EOC 2005), with, in the UK, Bangladeshi and Pakistani women at the bottom. A common reason for this is that the majority of Bangladeshi and Pakistani women are outside the labour market, conforming to cultural traditions of looking after the home and family. These patterns are replicated worldwide, with women's pay systematically lower than men's. Yet increasingly, as globalisation shifts the contours of work and with it family subsistence, it is women's earnings which are critical for family survival.

As globalisation has spread its tentacles, formal sectors have been shrinking, compelling people to move into the informal economy as the only way to make a living. This is where new employment 'opportunities' often are, especially in developing and transitional countries and where women mainly work. The ILO's 2002 report, 'Decent Work and the Informal Economy', makes it clear that contrary to earlier thinking, this is no longer a temporary or residual state of affairs. The authors comment that there are important and complex forces at work that are 'expanding the size and changing many of the characteristics of the informal economy' and that 'these forces are seldom gender-neutral' (ILO 2002: 27). Among such forces they identify that women are much more likely than men to leave and re-enter the labour force over their life cycle, but because they do not have access to education and skills training, they often end up in informal jobs.

As the 'advance guard', women have been moving into labour markets faster than men in most parts of the world in recent decades and now make up the largest share of informal employment and whose share of which is probably underestimated. As the ILO points out (2002: 12), women are more likely than men to be in informal activities that are under-counted, such as home work, paid domestic work in private households, production for own consumption and in small units where their contribution is invisible. Not only do a higher percentage of women than men work in the informal economy, but women are concentrated in the lower-income sectors, working in survival activities or as casual wage workers or homeworkers (ILO 2002: 31). In many countries women make up the bulk of agricultural workers, who are often excluded from employment surveys. The very term informal means there is little or no framework of rights and protection. Activities are often outside or on the margins of the law, it is difficult and dangerous to organise collectively, there is greater likelihood of exposure to serious occupational health and safety hazards, and HIV/AIDS has special implications. It is here, the ILO emphasises, that informal social protections, extended family, and local communities are being stretched beyond breaking point as adult breadwinners are struck down in their prime, leaving children and the elderly to cope: 'never was it more clear why social solidarity and risk-pooling must be organized on the widest possible basis' (ILO 2002: 70).

Globalisation is mainly at the expense of women, often through labyrinthine networks of unregulated contracting and subcontracting. In export garment manufacturing informal work ranges from women working in Bangladeshi factories under conditions of almost total non-compliance with protective legislation, to sweatshops exploiting local and sometimes migrant labour in Los Angeles, Bulgaria or Indonesia, to homeworkers in the Philippines who embroider baby clothes for smart New Yorkers as 'disguised wage workers' in multi-layered systems of subcontracting (ILO 2002: 36). Garment making being 'women's work' it is a feminised sector – over 80 percent female, the ILO estimates.

In the transition countries of central and eastern Europe to market economies, and especially in the CIS, the informal sector has expanded rapidly, building on small existing, often illegal, activities such as foreign currency exchange and drugs traffic, and fed by the closure of state-owned enterprises, privatisation, and collapse of social insurance systems (ILO 2002: 19, 20). Women in southern European countries are most likely to work in the informal sector, or the underground economy as the ILO report refers to it (ILO 2002: 24).

At the end of the 20th century the huge expansion of western supermarkets and our growing obsession with 'fresh' food has impacted especially on women in Latin America and Africa with the production of non-traditional agricultural products, especially fresh vegetables and flowers. Women often work on large-scale 'factory farms' for very low wages and poor working conditions (ILO 2002: 37). The extensive use of pesticides in such flower factories as shown in Colombia has a damaging effect on their health, including birth defects. The 'rights gap' is especially serious for those in the informal economy, principally women (ILO 2002: 69).

Union Crisis and Revitalisation Strategies

Labour movements themselves have been among the least flexible organisations and on their own are no longer able to withstand pressure 'if not open attack' from employers, governments or both (Turner 2004). Within the past few decades the model has become prey to globalisation and restructuring, and labour movements worldwide are in crisis as memberships among the traditional workforces plunge (Verma et al. 2002: table 1). Their success in the old order was based on selectivity and exclusivity, which was ensured through a complex web of rules and procedures and which shaped a particular kind of representative democracy within the narrow confines of primary labour markets of highly trained, skilled, paid and organised male workers. Not for nothing were these known as closed unions, and while later unions opened up to accommodate a wider range of workers, on the whole, their rules and structures were similarly protective. Whatever the fine differences, labour movements across the world were, and often still are, seen as inflexible, arcane strongholds of maleness and masculinity, and increasingly among younger workers, irrelevant. A survey by the ICFTU Women's Committee in 2000 found that 72 percent of non-unionised women said the most important reason they did not join unions was because they did not understand how unions could help them. (ILO 2002: 81).

Not surprisingly, those members remaining become less and less representative of the workforce; they are 'male, pale and stale'. The new workforces are young, culturally and ethnically diverse, over-whelmingly female, and unorganised. They are employed mainly either in secondary and flexible labour markets, in developing countries and transitional economies, in informal sectors in extremely precarious work, or in Export Processing Zones (EPZs) which are frequently ring fenced, excluding workers from their country's protective laws and trade union organisation. Among the former, few see themselves reflected in union memberships and union business and even more rarely in leadership positions. Among the latter, collectively organising is a high risk activity. Yet the need for protection and organisation of workers is strong.

These difficulties and trade unions' own tardiness in adapting to the hegemony of globalisation, its new world order and widening 'rights gap', sees labour movements in crisis, or even 'perdition' as one UK academic comments (Metcalf 2005).

A recent example of such decline, fall and maybe resurrection, is the 2005 schism in the American union movement. Since 1980 union density has fallen to 12 percent (Labour Research 2005), with more former members outside than in unions alongside the unorganised working poor. Impatient with what they saw as stasis in the AFL-CIO, six of the largest US unions formed the Change to Win Coalition, representing 40 percent of federation members. Their leader, Anna Burger, is described as 'part of a new generation of leaders who cut their teeth in the civil rights and antiwar movements' (Edsall 2005). In the summer of 2005 they split. A trigger point was the high profile Justice for Janitors campaign,[1] where the Service Employees International Union (SEIU), has combined with community groups and opinion leaders in organising such 'tough-to-mobilize groups as home health care and child care workers, building service workers and private security workers, all heavily female and minority' (Edsall 2005). The coalition aims to become the voice for the nation's lowest-paid workers, many living on the margins of society. Although the coalition has developed innovative organising techniques, the question remains as to whether even this group, with all the individual coalition union leaders men, with one a minority, is capable of reaching the unorganised (Edsall 2005).

---

1   'Justice for Janitors' is a campaign of union organising and contract negotiations for cleaning workers. It relies on aggressive outreach to immigrant workers, particularly Latino workers and their communities, along with high-visibility direct action and protests against large corporations that subcontract cleaners (Jeff Booth, Member of Harvard Clerical and Technical Workers Union, AFSCME Local 3650, at www.socialistalternative.org/justice29/9.html).

As in the US, increasingly, remedies for union revitalisation focus on organising and mobilising the unorganised, the working poor; women, and also young workers, part time workers, minorities and those with low human capital (education and skill), among whom women are of course significant. The paradox of labour movements is that their traditional strength has been vested in an exclusive core membership of highly-skilled, blue-collar male workers which habitually has not spoken to or for women, and who now stand to be the 'saviours' of organised labour. Whether the opportunities opened up by the crisis offers the chance for real revival, are questions increasingly being asked both within labour movements and among engaged academics and researchers (Colgan and Ledwith 2002c; Frege and Kelly 2004; Taylor and Mathers 2004). Is there sufficient purchase here for the development of counter-hegemonic mobilisation among labour movements, a willingness to engage more widely and openly, to make concert and coalition with allies such as NGOs and new social movements? And if so, what can traditional homosocial trade unionism learn from women's trade unionism and that of other marginalised groups and from contemporary social movement action?

Some of this work is informed by gender research and writing which discuss and debate these issues both in the industrial relations mainstream and in women's studies, and some of which is drawn on in this chapter. Research and analysis of strategies of previously excluded and marginalised groups have produced new insights, especially into the social processes of traditional trade unionism's patriarchal, racialised and homophobic oligarchic tendencies and forms of struggle against these.

These are now explored in relation to three main union equality strategies: forms of organising, mainstreaming and affirmative action, especially separate structures,[2] and autonomous organising. These will be discussed following an exploration of the social construction of exclusion which informs modes and practices of revival adopted by unions, and of strategies developed by the marginalised themselves.

---

2   I am addressing these three here as they are key in relation to organising the unorganised and concomitant trade unionism transformation. Other writers have discussed different strategies; see Frege and Kelly 2004; Heery et al. 2003.

The discussion draws on a model developed elsewhere of overlapping regimes of closure and power within labour organisations (Ledwith and Colgan 2002). These involve practices of and responses to exclusion and demarcation, to modes of inclusion, consequences of usurpation, strategies of transformation and coalition, and throughout, intersecting relationships with difference and diversity of class, gender, race and ethnicity, sexuality, and disability.

Gendered Traditions

Exclusion

Women's exclusion from trade union movements stems from pre-existing gender labour market segregation and segmentation. Exclusionary strategies by traditional trade unionism have involved resistance and closure to outsiders such as women, part timers (often women), and minority or subordinate ethnic and racial groups in order to secure and maintain cultural and class homogeneity and access to rewards and resources. Dominant discourses such as the family wage, and the concept of the male breadwinner, reinforce gendered power relations of exclusion at work and in unions, which in some countries include marriage bars.

The early model of protection and exclusivity of the pre-entry closed shop which emerged from the mediaeval guild and apprenticeship system provided powerful class solidarity, not only in relation to capital, but also to gender and race/ethnicity. In Britain for example this was exemplified through attitudes and practices of the print unions where women, the semiskilled and, during wartime, youth labour substituting for craftsmen going to fight, were branded as 'dilutees', and collusion by employers ensured women did not 'penetrate' the shopfloor (Cockburn 1983; Ledwith 1991). It was precisely through such practices of exclusivity and sectionalism that unions were able to regulate the supply of labour, calibrating pay levels to the top of the manual pay league for generations. Intra-class sectionalism has been the 'hallmark of trade union action' (Hyman 2001: 31), a tradition which also provided the exemplar for gender exclusion among the later semiskilled unions.[3] In the 20th century such practices were extended to block potential dilution by immigrant labour. Exclusion may also be achieved through collusion between capital and organised male labour against 'dilution' by women, unskilled and outsider racial and ethnic groups. The image of privileged masculinist unionism is frequently reinforced through mainstream capitalist media especially in the post-industrial economies, leading many women workers to eschew this model as not speaking to them.

The state and employers, especially in emerging economies, may also practice exclusion both of trade unions altogether and of groups from particular spheres. For example, EPZs in many countries are given 'freedom' from trade union organising, and women are restricted from working in certain occupations such as seafaring and mining. In apartheid South Africa restrictions on black workers impacted especially on black women. The two largest categories of employed black women were domestic and agricultural workers, neither of which was protected in law (Kabak and Ravenhill 2004).

In developing countries exclusion of women from formal employment sectors through discriminatory practices involving caste and religion, such as in India (Hensman 2002), is of increasing importance. This usually entails exclusion from legal employment rights and formal trade union organisation, as well as being invisible within their unions, where women rarely hold leadership positions.

In the developed world trade union practices of total exclusion have largely broken down as the closed-shop and other similar systems have given way under pressure of technological, economic, political and social change. However in spite of embracing women, workers from ethnic groups, disabled members, lesbians and gay men into membership, these are still excluded proportionally from leader-

---

3   Notable exceptions were the cotton workers of Lancashire and the northwest
     (Boston 1987; Drake 1920).

ship positions. Surveys by international trade union confederations continue to show serious under-representation of women in trade union decision-making, especially in positions of responsibility and leadership, and in collective bargaining (ETUC 1999; ICFTU/ILO 1999; AFL-CIO 2004; TUC 2005).

In the UK research about union membership recruitment and retention has found that women were more likely than men not to have been asked to join unions, and to cite shortcomings in union organisation as a reason for leaving the union (Waddington and Kerr 1999). TUC surveys of black members (2000a) of lesbian and gay members (2000b) and of the unorganised, especially young workers (2000c) have found that while all were vital to the revitalising of unions, many did not see unions as helpful or relevant to them. An international survey of gender equality in trade unions found that often unions had not targeted 'atypical' workers to organise. Instead they kept them at arms length, helping set up their own organisations and then establishing alliances with them (ILO/ICFTU 1999). There are important distinctions here; if informal workers are not members of the union, then it cannot speak for them and cannot represent them. It can only be an advocate for them (ILO 2002: 84).

Women running for union leadership positions also find that gender is a key issue. In Australia the last two presidents of the ACTU (Australian Council of Trade Unions) have been women, with the most recent, Sharan Burrow also taking on the top job at the ICFTU. Yet, as discussed by Kathie Muir (1997: 186) women's professional status, qualifications and abilities can easily be undermined by representations of her gender as a weakness. In the UK in the 1980s and until the 1991 merger to form the GPMU (Graphical, Paper and Media Union), the leader of SOGAT '82, the largest print union, was a woman, Brenda Dean. When her union merged with the smaller, formerly closed and masculinised craft-based NGA (National Graphical Association), an academic journal reviewer speculated that allowing SOGAT's journal to run pages dedicated to women members – a third of the membership – and their issues, perhaps had been a factor in her failure to win the leadership election for the new union (Metcalf 1996).

Sexual Politics

As observed above, sexual politics are firmly embedded in union movements. Connell (1995) demonstrates how hegemonic masculinity becomes a dominant form of exclusion and control, pursued through a range of mechanisms of gender power, including sexual harassment and domestic violence. Cobble and Michal (2002) identify how the labour movement in the US helped men achieve 'manhood' through traditional sexual practices built on deeply embedded gender norms at work. Sexual harassment plays a key role in policing the boundaries of traditional homosocial patriarchal trade unionism. In study after study sexual harassment is shown to be a central and contentious issue in trade union gender relations, going as it does to the heart of union sexual politics (Franzway 2002). Union mainstreams also tend to ignore or deflect dealing with harassment in relation to race, sexuality and disability, being intent on maintaining distance from and containment on issues which challenge gender and race cultural norms and hierarchies (Ledwith and Colgan 2002).

Disability

An analogous analysis can be applied to disability (Humphrey 1999, 2002). Notwithstanding the move away from the medical and welfare models of disability which situate the disabled as victim and outsider, towards social and rights models of disability activism and self-help, able-bodiedness and able-mindedness remain the hegemonies of the body and mind in many societies, especially through the post-industrial and postmodern discourses commodifying and constructing the perfect body.

Ethnicity and Race

Racial and ethnic hegemonies also contribute to hierarchies and diversities of inclusion and exclusion. In the 21st century, issues of diversity and difference of race and ethnicity, of cultural, religious and ideological belief, and national identities have become a touchstone of dissent, debate, exclusion and conflict. Closely bound up with issues of immigration and the roles and position of immigrants in competitive labour markets, attitudes of unions and their members are ambivalent, characterised by dilemmas over their position. Penninx and Roosblad (2000) discuss these attitudes as: do unions resist and exclude or assimilate them as part of the working class, and in each case under what conditions and in what forms?

Examples of exclusion are also given by Virdee (2000) of how in the postwar years large numbers of Caribbean workers were encouraged to move to work in Britain's new welfare state, and Asians moved to the manufacturing sector. White trade unionists resisted the employment of black workers, or insisted on quota systems, colluding with employers in restrictive practices of racist exclusion in key sectors of employment sustaining and reinforcing institutionalised racism (McPherson 1999). The result has been placing black and minority ethnic workers at the bottom of the British class structure (Virdee 2000: 210), where they remain. A study of black and ethnic minority women in four UK unions also found that they suffered a complex set of disadvantages, and experiences of racism and sexism pervaded their working lives (Healy et al. 2004). They also responded positively to systems and structures which the four unions had put in place to recruit and involve such women. Significantly, a large number of the women in the survey were also actively involved in their own communities, illustrating ways in which women work across organisational boundaries.

Inclusion: Union Strategies

By the end of the 20th century, unions were accepting that women, black and minority ethnic (BME) members, disabled members, lesbian and gay members should no longer remain unorganised. Driven by loss of memberships and of economic and political influence, together with increasingly confident and well organised groups of the formerly marginalised, organised labour had begun to move forward agendas and strategies of inclusion.

These can be seen to have three main trajectories, which after an earlier period of backlash and standoff, and when none was maximising effectiveness on its own, have moved to work more closely together; mainstreaming, organising, and affirmative action.

Mainstreaming

Gender mainstreaming (GM) as an international phenomenon originated in development policies and was adopted by the UN at the 1995 Beijing conference on women and its subsequent platform for action. GM is about inclusion and integration of those from oppressed groups into mainstream structures and processes. It is described by the European Trade Union Confederation (ETUC 1999) as, rather than the adoption of a catalogue of measures, aiming to 'infuse a preoccupation with equal opportunities into all trade union decision-making processes, so that the gender question is incorporated wherever decisions are made. In this way it becomes a permanent subject for discussion and negotiation within trade union organisation', especially in training and collective bargaining. GM is the preferred practice of labour movements since it is compatible with the trade union ethos and discourse of unity and collective solidarity. European trade unionism and European Union equality policies have been especially forceful in advocating mainstreaming and in developing measures and practices to develop it. In a recent survey, the ETUC found that most of the national union confederations had 'attempted to gender mainstream trade union policies', yet the methods were limited mainly to collecting gendered statistics, training, publications and research. The main problems identified with gender mainstreaming were the lack of awareness, training and inadequate statistics. Among the eleven affiliated industry federations interviewed, there was little or no emphasis placed on GM. These disappointing findings strengthen the case for combining mainstreaming with affirmative action measures such as special structures, rather than a single strategy. The ETUC (2004: 100), observing that close to 100 percent of union confederations in Europe had women's structures, believes that 'in a male-dominated environment, these women's structures *ensure* (emphasis in the original) that the points of view and interests of women are taken into account and are not neglected'. Quite how the ETUC expects such a guarantee to be upheld is not discussed, even though the special structures were identified as being mainly only advisory, and few had a budget.

This sort of GM seems to be located largely at the level of public rhetoric and institutional bureaucratic action. While clearly this is important in legitimising and making visible the significance of the gender question, on its own it is not sufficient. As Dahlerup (1988) has made clear, it is the critical act, informed by a gender consciousness which is significant in moving to political action. Walby (2003) also discusses this tension between GM as either 'expertise' or 'democratisation', concluding they are complementary rather than in opposition, and that where there is a low level of political activism the existence of an effective bureaucracy is key. However, there is also a need for strong mobilising networks both within and outside the bureaucracy, and if the appropriate 'frames' are available, such mobilising could make a positive difference.

Organising

Organising is a strategy in its own right, but it also belongs within the labourist attachment to mainstreaming as a solidaristic model. New approaches to organising and recruitment are being developed by trade union movements around the world. Particularly strong examples are unions in Anglophone countries, which, through their close international links, have developed sophisticated strategies of organising, recruitment and retention, drawing on one another's experiences to do so. So union-building organising work in the US (Bronfenbrenner 1997) has informed developments such as Australia's Organising Works campaign and its later 1999 project *unions@work*, which also built on the UK TUC's own model, the Organising Academy. The key here has been organising 'like with like', using mainly women and young workers to recruit those like them. The main motivation for these new unionism projects is membership crisis, 'a trade unionism for the new insecure world of work' (TUC 1997). While evidence indicates a 'relatively conservative orientation' among unions targeting workers in proximate job territories and traditional blue collar constituencies, there is also an increasing tendency to target women, ethnic minorities and 'atypical' workers, thus extending organising to these 'previously neglected' groups (Heery et al. 2003). Internal resistance to such measures has sometimes been strong and ranges from apathy to active opposition to both new methods and new, 'non-traditional' organisers – with younger and female organisers reporting harassment (Heery et al. 2003). These represent new and, for many traditionalists, unwelcome and threatening changes.

While primarily about mainstreaming, such strategic developments have also draw on characteristics and techniques of autonomous organising, which in turn owe much to the 'new social movements' of the 1970s and more contemporary developments, especially the use of electronic communications. Unions see this as an opportunity to import new 'blood' and the methods of new social movements into unions, albeit somewhat warily (Heery et al. 2003). In particular, organisational characteristics of the women's movement and feminism have been adopted by the UK TUC Women's Conferences, where in recent years informal non-resolution-based discussions have been included. In these, the usual formal procedural rules are dropped for sessions which are run in smaller-group workshop formats with the intention of being inclusive and testimony-based. In 2004 the informal session was about Women's Rights Worldwide and focused on the Play Fair at the Olympics campaign (discussed below) (TUC Women's Committee 2005).

Affirmative Action: Women's Structures and Self-Organisation

Women have been the primary movers in shifting labour movements towards addressing gender and other democratic deficits. Feminists raised labour's consciousness about discrimination, difference and diversity, developed the idea of self organising into caucuses, and once women started making gains, the doorway was open for others (Hunt 1999).

Special Structures

Special structures for target groups have emerged as a key strategy for addressing democratic deficits in unions. Most common are committees and conferences. These are situated inside the union, are most likely to have advisory status only, and there is no guarantee of acceptance of their often limited number of resolutions by the mainstream conference. Least favoured are reserved seats on elected mainstream decision-making bodies. Within union circles, these are frequently seen as being undemocratic, unrepresentative and incompatible with customary (for which read gender-blind) union electoral traditions.

Special, separate structures or autonomous or self-organisation may be either or both outside the union entirely, or in an outsider-insider relationship to the mainstream through women's committees, conferences, women's education and so on. These are all forms of affirmative action which in the lexicon of equal opportunities (EO) can be described as radical initiatives whereby existing structures, attitudes and cultures are challenged in pursuit of change. Radical EO seeks to intervene directly in organisational practices in order to achieve a fair distribution of rewards among groups as measured by ethical and moral criteria. It focuses on fairness in outcomes calling for positive discrimination and consciousness raising in order to 'release a struggle for power and influence' (Jewson and Mason 1986).

Structures for women and other diversity groups have not been won without such struggles, which, as identified here, are at the centre of complex power relations of gender, race/ethnicity, sexuality and disability. Nevertheless a 1998 survey of ICFTU affiliates found that 70 percent of national centres and 58 percent of trade unions now do have measures to increase the participation of women in leadership positions, with reserved seats for women being the preferred strategy.

In the UK, in its 2004 survey, the South Eastern TUC Women's Rights Committee (2004) found that few unions now have no equality committees, networks or groups. Nevertheless, only 55 percent of those surveyed had women's structures, and only three had dedicated national women's officers.

The significance of women's and diversity structures organisation cannot be overemphasised. They may involve relatively small numbers, but the effects are far reaching. Women's participation in women's groups encourages women's representation in the mainstream and vice versa, and as women's activism gains visibility it provides models for broader networks of women unionists (Elliot 1984; Parker 2003: 221). Similarly our research with UNISON women found that black women were more likely to join the union because it had a special structure – a self organised group – for black members and this spoke to them (Colgan and Ledwith 2000a).

UNISON is probably the best known UK union to have adopted radical structures. In 1993 when UNISON was formed from three former public service unions, equality was at the heart of the new union's constitution. UNISON saw itself as setting 'new standards for trade unionism' and as taking a lead in public sector unionism across Europe (Mann et al. 1997). In fact that lead was watched with intense interest by unions worldwide. The UNISON constitution tackled the balance between autonomous organising and mainstreaming gender equality through legitimising and recognising the rights of self organisation of women, black members, lesbian and gay members and disabled members. Semi-autonomous Self Organised Groups (SOGs) were established for each, with a dedicated national officer, committee and conference for each, and a commitment to resources (Mann et al. 1997). The leadership sought to maintain control through a rulebook statement that the SOGs were to 'work within the established policies, rules and constitutional provisions of the union' (UNISON rules 1997; Colgan and Ledwith 2000a). As well as tensions arising from the clash with another rule exhorting SOGs to establish their own priorities, problems arise when the main development of new ways of doing union policy is left to the members with the lowest degree of power (Hansen 2004; McBride 2001). A SOG which strategically managed this balance was the lesbian and gay group which used self organisation to bypass union bureaucracy and overcome some of the blockages created by homophobia (Colgan 1999). Self organisation as a means of encouraging representation of and participation among diverse constituencies can only work where unions are prepared to ensure adequate links and resources (Colgan and Ledwith 2002b: 160). Working collaboratively across SOGs on key agendas, is also important for strategies of participative democracy in the union – what Humphrey (2002) refers to as rainbow politics.

Usurpation

Separate or self organisation presents ideological and practical difficulties to traditional trade unionism, which see such practices as divisive, as detracting from espoused main aims and methods, as setting up alternative centres of power, and of entrism. Critical tensions, resistance and backlash arise when traditional power holders see their position and status threatened, usurped by the new democratic order.

An important part of the gender and diversity equality project in trade unions entails changing the balance of power between groups in order to achieve equity and proportionality. Where women make up the majority of the membership but have not been present in leadership and decision-making positions this necessarily will mean replacing men with women, white or dominant racial and ethnic members with those from marginalised groups. In the US women union leaders surveyed by the AFL-CIO (2004) identified 'push back' from male leaders who seemed to think they would be forced to 'give up something', as one of the most common barriers to women entering leadership positions. Even though union rules and constitutions may be changed formally to 'let in' such members, in practice these may be fiercely resisted by those who risk being shut out, by deploying exclusionary, discriminatory and intimidatory tactics such as harassment and bullying. As Malehoko Tshaoedi (2002: 17) has observed about South African unions, the closer women's challenges go to the centre of male power the more vigorous the resistance. Franzway (2002) comments, if relations of male domination shape women's subordination, then successful challenges to that domination are likely to be strenuously resisted – as are challenges to homophobic, racialised and dis-ablist regimes and discourses. As a result there is also a continuous process of resistance and backlash to confront (Parker 2003; Healy and Kirton 2000). For example, the recent report to the AFL-CIO (2004) in America on overcoming barriers to women in unions found a lack of affirmative action structures, with few resources in those that did exist. Indeed they were so marginalised that they became 'holding pens' for women members and women's issues while allowing the union's leadership to consider they had completed their duty. Although, as the report stated, such structures energise women, foster leadership skills, and are a source of education and networking, without adequate staffing and funding it is difficult for them to be effective. In the UK union UNISON, such resistance took a number of forms; systems of self organisation were described as 'political correctness', as a 'drain on (the union's) resources' and 'opening the union up to ridicule'. Although the SOGs were also charged under the rule book with 'establishing their own priorities' (Mann et al. 1997), formal resolutions requesting firm constitutional links to the mainstream, better resources for self-organised groups, a voice in regional budget setting and a range of similar demands were not achieved without long and substantial prevarication (Colgan and Ledwith 2000b). Power relations and practices of resistance such as harassment, of exclusion from caucusing around critical elections, leaders denying diversity and minority members information or access to education programmes and conferences, persist widely across labour movements (Ledwith and Colgan 2002).

At Ruskin College, in the UK, I work with many trade union activists from overseas, mainly southern and sub-Saharan Africa. When we discuss gender issues in their unions and societies, they frequently tell of patriarchal attitudes and backlash, of oligarchic and factional tendencies, as well as of increasing examples of union women's initiatives. In Zimbabwe one union leadership's attempt to encourage the election of women into leadership positions resulted in an unofficial male caucus rejecting this route and producing their own preferred (male) leader. In Ghana there are women's regional and national structures, including a women's desk at the TUC, although it remains unoccupied at the time of writing.

Autonomous Organising

A principal expression of struggle by excluded, outsider groups is autonomous or self organisation, whereby oppressed and marginal groups develop outside of the mainstream as both an alternative community and/or a constituency where change strategies, possibly as a counter-hegemonic, are built and then carried across the margins into the union and towards a more transformational agenda.

The development of women's autonomous organising in unions arose during the 1970s when second wave feminism and the women's liberation movement(s) connected with an upsurge in new social movement and political activism. Excluded from 'old' labour unionism, women set up their own groups.[4] In Canada for example, Hunt (1999) records the presence of informal lesbian groups at union women's conferences in that period. In the USA white-collar and professional women broke away from 'men's' unions and formed their own in a bid to challenge the gendered norms of their work as clerks and flight attendants where there was pressure to 'appear forever young, slim and sexually alluring' (Cobble and Michal 2002). South African women, fighting against racism and sexism both within apartheid and within their own ethnic communities, organised themselves in a wide range of interest groups both inside and across race, class and union divides (Ravenhill and Kabak 2004).

---

4   There is a long tradition of women's autonomous union organising. Among the best known from the early days of 19th-century industrialisation were the Women's Trade Union League, and the National Federation of Women Workers set up in the UK by Mary Macarthur and colleagues (Boston 1987; Drake 1920).

These examples illustrate two strands in women's autonomous organising; women's space for empowerment and politicisation in its own right, and as a springboard to carry the gender agenda from the margins into the mainstream of the union. For women and diversity group constituents organising autonomously, there is a difficult balance to be struck. As Briskin (1993, 1999) has argued, separate organising depends on maintaining a balance between autonomy and integration. The dangers are two-fold. Too little integration and the separate organising is marginalised; too much and the radical edge can be blunted. Achieving a successful balance, a 'both-and' position, generates powerful representation for the particular interest group, together with the legitimacy awarded through formal rules and structures. This can be described as Cockburn (1989) has theorised, a long, transformative agenda which goes to the heart of trade unionism aiming to melt the 'masculine monoculture', changing the organisation on the grounds that 'the on-going chances of all groups are to be equalised and sustained, democratised and opened' (Cockburn 1989).

The social and political processes involved have been discussed in detail elsewhere (Colgan and Ledwith 2000a, 2002a). These entail strategies of social creativity, social change and collective action. Social creativity involves individual empowerment through development of skills, self-confidence, and possibly political consciousness. If and when these combine collectively into group consciousness, they may lead on to mobilising strategies of social change and collective action. Three factors are important in moving groups towards collective action: group members need to perceive themselves as having a shared identity and concerns; they need to perceive the opposing group or constituency (in the case of trade union exclusion and demarcation this would include the union oligarchy, hierarchy and mainstream) as not legitimate or as unstable; and there needs to be leadership by vanguard equality activists, women with a strong political and feminist consciousness. Foley (2003) illustrates aspects of such 'micromobilization', in her study of a Canadian union women's committee's project to increase union responsiveness to the concerns of its female members.

Among women's groups, emotion and personal testimony have been important in both personal empowerment and feminist consciousness-raising. Strongly associated with the women's movement, these also map onto wider social movement framing theory in which emotion, especially anger, has become recognised as integral to the framing process. Framing involves an intellectual account of injustice which legitimises the moral indignation and righteous anger directed towards the source of injustice and oppression, through which develop rationales and strategies for action (Hercus 1999; Hunt et al. 1994; Taylor 1999).

Other researchers have also identified the efficacy of such a model in relation to consciousness development and activism through women's trade union education (Greene and Kirton 2002) and women's groups within trade unions (Parker 2003). Freire's model of 'conscientizacao' as a pedagogical dialogue in which the oppressed come to critically reflect on and act on their oppressive situation is also relevant. His term refers to the dialectic of critical reflection and action as a method of self liberation achieved through the cooperative involvement of all participants, including in collaborative educational projects, attempts by academics to move knowledge out from the academy and share it with 'those who do manual (sic) work' (Freire 1985).

Women Do Things Differently

Significant in the equality field is the debate around sameness and difference, and while I do not intend to raise this generally, that women and men experience both sameness and difference is no longer contested. In the discussion here, it is relevant that in some spheres of trade unionism women share political and solidaristic ideologies and action with their brothers. But since their material lives are also different, they also 'do' labour politics differently. In Sierra Leone for example, the teachers' union women's committee organises community activities: an annual sports event for women, a carnival, and other celebratory and inclusive actions as well as education and organising programmes. As in many countries, Ugandan union women run education programmes for women which, in addition to addressing trade union issues, include practical familial care aspects such as pregnancy and women's health. AIDS/HIV are commonly included in union programmes across the continent; in South Africa women activists strive to work on the practicalities of living with the condition. The region's union movements are also supported in joint projects by European unions, especially those from the Netherlands, Scandinavia and Germany, and increasingly, as in the UK examples below, more widely through alliances and joint working with international development departments and NGOs (Ledwith 1998–2005).

Importantly, unlike traditional male, industry and mainstream politics routes into trade unionism, women in service and white collar work especially, are more likely to have learned their politics and activism through women's organising, feminist student politics, anti-Vietnam rallies, anti-racist campaigning, community, and environmental groupings. Often these experiences have led such women to remain active in grassroots unionism, although research has also found that it is in local, 'malestream' branches and workplace union organisation where women often encounter the fiercest resistance (Colgan and Ledwith 2002a: 172).

Women's relationship with militancy is another example. Researchers have found that women's propensity for striking and other forms of industrial action are related not to their gender but rather to structural and cultural factors which they share with their brothers (Purcell 1981). On the other hand, the discourse of militancy is essentially a masculinised one, and as Briskin (2005) has pointed out, women's militancy has often been interpreted and re-configured to fit into, rather than challenge the dominant gender order. More recently however women's militant action, especially in the feminised public and services sectors, has been transformed for the women involved and in the public imagination (Briskin 2005). Women's work in public and service sectors is often directed to the welfare of others rather than directly to the employer's purse, making it difficult and maybe inappropriate to take traditional forms of industrial action. Not only this, but women's connectedness with family and local community inform different forms of militancy, such as in the Canadian Eaton's dispute where striking women 'questioned the industrial style picketing tactics they were expected to use. They learned to run successful picket lines in their own right and develop creative ways to sell their cause to the public' (McDermott 1993). Women's involvement in militant action is also important in personal empowerment and politicisation. For some women involved in the Eaton's dispute; 'the strike changed my personality. I went from being mouse to mouth' (McDermott 1993: 40).

A different, but related form of women's militancy can be seen in community-union action, where female support for industrial action taken by their male partners, family members, friends and colleagues, is both welcomed and resisted. In her discussion of the activities and politicisation of UK miners wives support groups and networks, to the Women on the Waterfront in the Liverpool docks and those in Australia, and many others, Sandra Jones (2002) identifies this as a gender model of community industrial relations exchange. Such activity has also long been recognised as a site for women's empowerment and politicisation, often leading to challenges and changes in domestic gender power relations.

Such strategies and formations transmute in different ways in different sectors and in different countries. In the developing world, in informal sectors, the connections between community, work and organising are especially significant. In development circles of gender planning there is a view that for disadvantaged groups, the identification of strategic interests can only really emerge 'from below' (Kabeer 1994). These include cases like the women working for 'small' changes in third world communities (Hamdi 2004), and then linking with unions, for example around action on HIV/AIDS, especially through educational projects. The ILO (2002) provides many examples, such as in Zimbabwe an IUF project which focuses on training women as educators and counsellors on HIV/AIDS to reach as wide a community as possible, and Education International's materials for teachers to help and encourage them to lead open discussion on HIV/AIDs in the classroom.

These community unionism approaches are also especially appropriate to women's organising, through women's connectedness to family and community. Briskin (2005) writes of its importance in the US where union density is low, state and employer antagonism is high, and there has been a long history of creative initiatives such as civil rights organisations becoming de facto bargaining agents to ensure job access and equity for black communities, and mainstream unions representing workers in fast food companies where union organisation was outlawed. In these ways, 'poor workers' unions' whose membership is largely people of colour and women, and which include low wage workers and no-wage workers (unpaid domestic workers, the unemployed and in the US, workfare workers), are rebuilding labour 'from below' (Tait 2005). Similar community campaigning work in Australia involved women trade union activists working with community, church, arts and other groups, and holding night vigils with garment workers (Ledwith 2000). In UNISON, regional women's self organised groups have developed 'fun days' in local communities as a grassroots strategy both for organising women into membership and drawing them into activism (Mann et al. 1997). In the summer of 2005 in the UK those at the centre of the Gate Gourmet dispute were mainly female Asian contract workers employed by the firm supplying British Airways meals. Their indissoluble connections with family and community meant sympathetic industrial action rapidly spread through the 'world's favourite airline', mirroring in a post-industrial, modern society, the characteristics of women in similar situations in the poorer, developing world. Strategies too illustrated much of that outreach. As well as strong support from their trade union, community backing was especially vital, and the dispute gained a high media profile with debates being located variously in discourses of globalisation and unstable labour markets, trade union rights, and the 'passive' Asian woman turned militant (Gupta 2005).

Transformation through Alliance: Transversal Politics

Women are not a homogenous group, whether locally at grassroots, in the workplace, in their union, or internationally. Gender always intersects with other diversities. Women too are divided by class, sexuality, ethnicity and race, disability, age, and so on. The ongoing debates about whether or not there is still a women's movement exemplify this diversity and difference. However, since all women share a position of gender subordination in their own particular sphere, there will also always be areas of commonality where their interests meet at a particular point of time, in struggle. In discussing how to deal with this, Nira Yuval-Davis (1998) argues for the idea of 'transversal politics' whereby feminist politics should incorporate the notion of 'women's positionings' into their agendas. Thus women (and men) from different constituencies may remain rooted in their own membership and identity, but simultaneously be prepared to shift into a position of exchange with those from different groups and group interests in pursuit of a common agenda. Transversal politics can be seen as a new form of democracy which can develop new political projects that cross and transcend old barriers (Walby 2003).

The concept of transversal politics was developed as a feminist politics in Italy at meetings of feminists from Israel, and Palestine, and from the different components of former Yugoslavia (Yuval-Davis 2004) to seek ways of building peace. They were following a tradition of autonomous left politics in Bologna under the name 'transversalism', the constant flow of communication both horizontally and vertically in the construction of a radical political group as a collective subject. Building on these traditions, Yuval-Davis (2004) distinguishes between transversal politics being used descriptively, referring to political activities and organising which take place in a variety of locations, and normatively, as a model of political activism.

Cynthia Cockburn (1998) has also written about these transversal feminist politics in places and projects 'where peace was done' between and among women of different religious and ethnic backgrounds or national belonging, in the Palestinian/Israeli conflict, in Northern Ireland, and in Bosnia/Hercegovina. 'Doing' it hinges on 'facing up to difference and constantly renegotiating the terms of solidarity. Cockburn describes such an alliance as 'a creative structuring of a relational space between collectivities marked by problematic differences'. As alliances these groups were committed to cooperative action which required of them a shared belief that apparently deadlocked situations can transform or be transformed over time; what, Cockburn has termed elsewhere, 'a long agenda' (1989, 1991).

Coalition and Alliances

Women's community unionism like the broader women's movement, also illustrates the strength of working across the range of interests and groupings, as appropriate, developing open systems, links, alliances and coalitions. I borrow here from a social movement model of three concentric rings, an outer ring of sympathisers, a middle ring of activists able to commit resources and legitimacy, and an inner core of leaders; a modern version of Gramsci's intellectuals engaged in developing a counter-hegemony,[5] or in this context, feminist animating spirits (Delmar 1987) and 'movement intellectuals' (Nash 2002) acting as the 'leaders, organisers, publicists, lobbyists of the much broader and diverse women's movement' (Colgan and Ledwith 1996). Among these must also be counted the female and feminist researchers and activists engaging with and working with trade union women in gender and labour movements in a range of ways – joint research projects, round tables and international e-networking takes place through such fora in for example Australia, Canada, the US, Denmark, the UK, to name just a few.

---

5   An alternative hegemony developed through alliances needs to have developed a 'cohesive world view of its own' (Williams 1977: 27) in readiness to seize the moment of crisis and disintegration in the old order. In the discussions here, the concept of a feminist or women's counter-hegemony is being used both as a potential process against traditional masculine trade unionism in crisis, and also as a much wider, universal women's project of transformation. Gramsci discussed two main ways to subvert the dominant hegemony; war of manoeuvre, or revolution, and war of position – a long struggle across the institutions of civil society (Strinati 1995). It is this 'longest revolution' (Mitchell 1971) which feminists and others interested in a counter-hegemony of gender and diversity continue to work towards.

Practical, emotional and ideological strategies of coalition and alliances enable movement beyond the narrow interests of sectoral and sectional organised labour towards a framework of rights (Sen 2001) and are especially important for women and members of racial, ethnic and sexual minorities where such groups are weak. One example is SEWA (Self-Employed Women's Association) which, already functioning as a union in the informal sector in India, started many of its coops because its women members either needed work or had lost their jobs when they tried to organise and fight for improvements (Hensman 2002).

The 1995 Platform for Action of the Fourth World Conference on Women at Beijing was a rallying point for international women's networking and transversal working. It was also a highly visible event and continues to be a symbolic rallying point for women worldwide. In developing countries, in the informal economy especially, those who attempt to organise may face intimidation, threats, violence and murder. Other excluded groups are often agricultural, domestic and migrant workers, and in the formal sectors, women working in EPZs, for example in Malaysia (Todd and Bhopal 2002). Working transversally becomes increasingly significant.

Ukrainian Women Trade Unionists – and a World-wide Campaign

I now move to illustrate the efficacy of key gender issues discussed here through two case studies. First the relationship between women's autonomous organising, and gender mainstreaming in Ukrainian public sector trade unions as a means of women's empowerment and change from traditional unionism towards the 'inclusionary gender project' union is discussed. This is followed by a discussion of alliance making and transversal politics as it relates to the Ukrainian case and a wider example of global coalition building in the 2004 campaign Play Fair at the Olympics.

A critical feature of the Ukraine project was that it was women-led at all levels, and for a central period, involved women-only working and aimed to challenge and change women's gender sub-ordination in their unions and in the wider society (Ellis 2002). These goals can also be seen as part of the wider undertaking of achieving citizenship parity, justice and recognition for women (Fraser 2003; Young 1990), especially in a country and culture undergoing rapid change such as Ukraine.

Following the collapse of the Soviet Union, a desperate situation ensued for women. In newly independent Ukraine, women formed 80 percent of those losing work and over two-thirds of the registered unemployed. The non-payment and arrears of wages (Simon 2000) and with it the loss of social welfare and women's rights guarantees all hit women particularly hard. There was increasing sex and age discrimination against women at work and in society, and a shift in women's status from the Soviet icon of superwoman who can do it all – although this lingers – to a re-emergence of the myth of ideal Ukrainian woman as 'hearth mother' (Rubchak 2001: 149, 158; Pavlychko 1997: 231). In addition, violence at work and in the home, and sexual exploitation and trafficking of women and girls was increasingly an issue. These new discursive formations, the demands of the greedy institutions of home and work, together with the economic situation and fear of job loss, militated against campaigning for equality.

In this context, as part of the western trade union response to their sisters in eastern Europe, and following a resolution at a conference in Budapest in 1999, the Public Services International (PSI) women's committee set up a collaborative CEE (Central and Eastern European) twinning project. In this western European trade unions worked with eastern European unions to promote action on gender equality (particularly work–life balance and sexual harassment), to increase women's representation and develop their campaigning skills, with the political aim of giving issues affecting women workers higher visibility. On both sides the unions involved volunteered to take part in the project. In the UK case these were UNISON, Prospect and PCS. There were seven Ukrainian public service union partners, covering workers in health, gas, customs, science academy, culture, municipal, local and state employment (Ellis 2002).

The project combined overall joint decision making between the Ukrainian union leaders and a UK steering group of women planning and overseeing delivery. At various stages women educators from Ruskin and from UNISON joined the steering group and also took lead roles in facilitating the workshops. A research element involved a series of short questionnaire surveys of the Ukrainian unionists in order to identify priorities and concerns, together with some personal background data. The project ran from 2001–02 and was organised in three stages. First was securing commitment of the trade union leadership in each country and raising money (in the UK); awareness-raising and campaign planning with the Ukrainians via a week-long seminar at Ruskin in Oxford which included high profile visits to UK unions and NGOs. Stage two was in Kyiv and involved training and empowering the Ukrainian trade union women to develop campaigns, and the third stage was rolling out the two main campaigns, on sexual harassment and on work-life balance.

Keeping a balance between mainstreaming and women-only working was an important part of the project. As elsewhere, Ukraine trade unions are patriarchal. From our survey of the Ukrainian participants we found an absence of union structures or committees responsible for gender equality, and a corresponding under-representation of women in leadership positions. Mainstream senior officers were almost entirely male, with masculinised discourse driving gendered hierarchies, union agendas and gender relations. This was replicated at the Ruskin seminar where the agenda was set by the male leaderships. Two of the men hoped to be candidates in the imminent national parliamentary election. It was important therefore to maintain and strengthen the alliance between the men and women union leaders if gender equity was to be taken forward into the mainstream of both the unions and the wider civil and political society. The issue of balancing work and family life was agreed by the union leaderships as a clear campaign priority, and was already being pursued, especially through joint work with NGOs and parliamentarians.

Sexual harassment (SH) was a more contentious issue, going to the heart of gender politics. Given the strength of the dominant male discourse which belittles sexual harassment and treats it as a joke, it was perhaps not surprising that it had not been raised by the Ukrainians as an issue to address in the project. Even the women, including their confidential, individual questionnaire responses, had not identified SH as a problem. Mindful of its centrality in constructing gender power relations, and its place on the PSI gender agenda and our own UK unions, we had included it as part of the Ukraine programme (Ledwith et al. 2003).

At the first workshop of Ukrainian trade union leaders at Ruskin, the matter of SH had been tricky. The women had been reticent to raise or discuss it in the presence of their male colleagues, with whom they colluded in joking about it, although there was some uneasy laughter. Clearly the discourse trivialising sexual harassment in mainstream masculinised trade unionism was an important factor here in controlling both the agenda of sexual politics and women themselves as sexual objects. As Cockburn (1991) has argued, men's social power gives them sexual authority which conveys the message to women that 'you're only a woman'. MacKinnon (1979), Walby (1990) and others have also theorised SH as a male control strategy to keep women in their place. However outside the mixed-gender 'classroom' environment, several women did show an interest in the issue, and also in domestic violence, and women-only sessions on these topics were organised for them.

At the Kyiv workshop, the controlling masculine discourse around SH and was partly reflected in the very small number of (younger) women who were willing to be involved in the SH campaign group. Nevertheless, the women-only space enabled this group to work closely together to develop a tightly argued and costed proposal. These skills, combined with their increased confidence and the support from their coalition UK partners (including funding) enabled them to actively reclaim and re-formulate sexual harassment as something unacceptable to women and not to be tolerated by them. It was no longer 'just a joke' (Collinson and Collinson 1996). By making it publicly visible among their union colleagues, the women were able to challenge prevailing ideas and stereotypes of SH, and legitimise its seriousness as both a women's and an official union discourse. Even so, the new discourse remained precarious. The woman mainly driving the SH campaign emailed four months later, reporting that among the workshop participants she could not find anyone who wished to help run the campaign. She herself developed a number of initiatives with significant allies outside the union, such as the national Olympic committee on women's problems and later, another two members of the campaign group did take action. In a follow-up survey of the workshop participants one year later, the women reported that despite difficulties they had rolled out a number of sexual harassment initiatives, working transversally across a number of interest groups: students and student union leaders and activists, the university library; discussions with and the distribution of leaflets and booklets; publishing information in a magazine on women's health and liaising on a book for young people. Outreach work included collaboration with the international women's NGO against trafficking, La Strada, networking with a number of leaders in Kyiv and together with a women's organisation, launching a telephone help line in another town.

The other main strand of this gender project was the concern with participative, active learning: a women's conscientizicao, and the development of gender awareness, skills and strategy development within an autonomous women-only space which could then be carried into the mainstream as well as maintaining women's coalition politics. Personal comments by the women during the workshop were reinforced in the evaluation questionnaires at the end, and still held when surveyed again the following year. In reply to the question about why they had signed up for workshop, in addition to identifying their role as a union leader, several added that they 'wanted to hear something new on gender issues and to teach my women' (members and work colleagues). A senior trade union leader who had been involved in gender work for some time explained her involvement as: 'Because nowhere, in the government, the Supreme Council, the state administration, are women represented (0.1 percent of the number of men).' Another described the weight to be carried by the small vanguard of feminists in 'the lack of understanding of women themselves of their own problems; their inability to make their problems known and put them forward for public discussion, especially at government level', although a different woman reported how she helped devise a project which was included in a government scheme and put forward for discussion in the Ukrainian Supreme Council.

Evidence of personal empowerment from the project ranged from making new friends, networking, learning new skills and new ways of working, as well as raised consciousness: 'I've become wiser and more liberated and I'm teaching this to my trade union colleagues.' Cross-union and country working was another important plus: 'It was wonderful to meet professionals from the international trade union movement. Their experience and approach was untraditional and rather new for us. I got a great deal out of it that was new and interesting.' And for another woman it 'strengthened my conviction that choosing the path of women's struggle was correct'. Others wrote about how the experience had impacted on their sense of self and on relations within their family. For one woman: 'most of all it has influenced me. I have reviewed my attitude to myself' and in her family there was a 'revolution taking place. Many questions have been raised.'

The efficacy of self organising at the levels and sites discussed in this project is clear. The provision of space for women's social creativity and for collectively rallying for transformational change was effective, especially in the case of sexual harassment which was raised as a serious matter in the union. The project managed to maintain a balance between autonomy and integration into the mainstream at the level of the home, the workplace, and the union and also working in alliances with NGOs on women's trafficking issues, and the wider politics in order to work towards citizenship parity, justice and recognition. This was a project about moving gender and women's equality out of the margins into the mainstream. At the limited level discussed in this chapter, it appears to have helped make a start.

And More Widely

Globalisation itself also offers the means for its own confrontation, especially via satellite and electronic communication, and the world-wide web. New social movements particularly mobilise this way, and increasingly labour movements are doing the same.

Global campaigns are especially important for workers where unions are proscribed and the dangers for those establishing collective workers' organisations outside official structures include forms of repression, imprisonment and maybe death. Play Fair at the Olympics (2004) was a high profile global campaign using strategies of coalition with alliances between the UK TUC, Oxfam, and the Labour Behind the Label pressure group, backed by the ICFTU and the International Textile, Garment and Leather Workers' Federation. It demanded that sportswear companies change their purchasing practices, persuade their suppliers to respect international labour standards, including freedom to join and participate in trade unions, pay a living wage and ensure workers do not experience harassment, inhumane working hours and enforced overtime and unsafe and unhealthy work practices (Labour Research 2004). The majority of the workers in the industry, and in the garment factories, are women. In their 2004 report based on research interviews with 186 workers in six countries, the alliance partners in the campaign write how these reveal a pattern of 'abysmally low wages, workers being forced to work excessively long hours, exploitative terms of employment, bullying, sexual harassment and physical and verbal abuse' with involvement in trade union activity virtually outlawed (Oxfam 2004). Many pregnant women suffer miscarriages because of the long working hours. Although women workers do try to improve their situation, often at great personal risk, they face huge obstacles when they try to join or form trade unions. At two Indonesian factories producing predominantly for the company Nike, women said that traditional attitudes towards women's roles made it difficult for them to become active union members. The authors identify three commonly interrelated reasons for both the high level of women employed in such workplaces and the constraints on their unionism: traditional patriarchal values, economic discrimination, and gender-based skills. They quote a 21 year old woman as saying 'We women follow orders more than men do because we are already used to following orders from our fathers, brothers and husbands. So the manager just becomes another man to follow orders from' (Oxfam 2004: 40). The campaign identified such issues as crossing from the developing countries where globalisation hones in on cheap labour driving down pay in the interests of global competition, to those where such companies are owned, such as Japan, Italy, Germany, the UK. And it also identified situations where 'glimmers of hope' had been achieved through making alliances (Oxfam 2004: 48). The Australian Council of Trade Unions (ACTU), whose president became the first woman leader of the ICFTU, adopted together with the Labour Council of New South Wales, a code requiring the payment of fair wages, limits on working hours and respect for the collective rights which was subsequently adopted by the Australian Olympics organising committee, which also signed an agreement with the Textile Clothing and Footwear Union of Australia. Following lobbying and visits by Australian and Fijian unions, two factories in Fiji producing shirts for the Sydney Olympics became unionised. They point out that, where there have been successful resolutions of workers' rights violations, they have tended to result from companies working together and in collaboration with unions and NGOs.

As mentioned earlier, in the UK, the campaign was launched at the 2004 TUC Women's Conference with the aim of raising awareness about international development, and to discuss the role that unions can play in doing this more widely, and campaigning on international labour standards for women workers. Here was another example of women working across formal and informal alliances and coalitions. Women from global unions, Oxfam, Labour Behind the Label, and other development NGOs acted as facilitators in the group sessions at the women's conference. This led to campaigns by a number of unions to promote the rights of women workers in global supply chains. Another Play Fair at the Olympics initiative was a roundtable at Ruskin College of women academics and union organisers to encourage further research in the field and an exchange of expertise between gender specialists on workplace equality and development practitioners (TUC Women's Committee 2004).

Conclusions

As the assault of globalisation on labour has strengthened resistance to feminism among working class men (Epstein 2001), so it has galvanised women and other marginalised groups to work both separately and transversally on strategies of inclusion, alliance, and coalition. Verity Burmann has argued that corporate globalization has threatened or transformed established social movements and sparked powerful new forms of social protest (2003). As discussed here, women's global labour campaigning such as the Play Fair at the Olympics project has made alliances with the new anticapitalist and anti-corporate activism. Within labour movements, western and eastern European women unionists have partnered one another, also making alliances and coalitions with educators, researchers, NGOs and parliamentarians. These are just some of the revitalisation strategies identified by contemporary commentators as overlapping and combining political action, reform of union structures, coalition building and international solidarity. John Kelly (2003) points out that workers do not need to move around the world in order to confront multinational corporations: it is international worker organisation mobilising in different ways from the old that is critical; mobilising through the internet, building coalitions around religious and community groups – and women's groups should be included. The future of labour mobilisation is one where the field of solidarity is 'greatly broadened' (Turner 2004), from politics to local coalitions to international collaboration – something that women have long been doing from a position of liminality – a creative and resourceful place which speaks to labour movements in crisis.

Once again, as was hoped in the 1960s and 1970s, the new social struggles of the 21st century are now combining with working-class organisations and have the potential to lead to significant social transformation. As Mitchell observed two decades ago, and Cobble and Michal comment in the new millennium (2002: 234), 'women are at the forefront of economic change and they are at the forefront of devising new forms of unionism that will appeal to a new generation of workers'.

This chapter has discussed some of these forms which are of central importance not only to women, minorities, the oppressed, but more widely as part of the project of labour movement survival, revival and mobilisation. New forms of unionism involve women doing things differently – women in their families and communities, joining with other groups on single issues and on longer campaigns and projects, in regional and national alliances, and on international stages. It also involves new feminist and political consciousnesses as well as women's empowerment and skills development if women are to keep going against, and somehow transcend the gender politics that is part of their everyday life.

References

AFL-CIO (2004) *Overcoming Barriers to Women in Organizing and Leadership*, Washington: AFL-CIO.

Boston, S. (1987) *Women Workers and Trade Unions*, London: Lawrence and Wishart.

Bronfenbrenner, K. (1997) 'The Role of Union Strategies in NLRB Certification Elections', *Industrial and Labor Relations Review* 50(2): 195–212.

Briskin, L. (1993) 'Union Women and Separate Organizing', in L. Briskin and P. McDermott (eds) *Women Challenging Unions: Feminism, Democracy and Militancy*, Toronto: University of Toronto Press.

— (1999) 'Autonomy, Diversity and Integration: Union Women's Separate Organizing in the Context of Restructuring and Globalization', *Women's Studies International Forum* 22(5): 543–54.

— (2005) 'Feminization, Gendering and Worker Militancies', paper presented at 'Labouring Feminism and Feminist Working Class History in North America and Beyond' Conference, University of Toronto, 29 September–2 October.

Burmann. V. (2003) *Power, Profit and Protest: Australian Social Movements and Globalisation*, London: Allen and Unwin.

Cobble, S. and Michal, M. (2002) 'On the Edge of Equality? Working Women and the US Labour Movement', in F. Colgan and S. Ledwith (eds) *Gender, Diversity and Trade Unions: International Perspectives*, London: Routledge.

Cockburn, C. (1983) *Brothers*, London: Pluto Press.

— (1989) 'Equal Opportunities: The Short and Long Agenda', *Industrial Relations Journal* 20(4): 213–25.

— (1991) *In the Way of Women: Men's Resistance to Sex Equality in Organisations*, London: Macmillan.

— (1998) *The Space Between Us*, London: Zed Books.

Colgan, F. (1999) 'Recognising the Lesbian and Gay Constituency in UK Trade Unions: Moving Forward in UNISON?', *Industrial Relations Journal* 30(5): 444–63.

— and Ledwith, S. (1996) 'Sisters Organising: Women and Their Trade Unions', in S. Ledwith and F. Colgan (eds) *Women in Organisations: Challenging Gender Politics*, Basingstoke: Macmillan.

— and — (2000a) 'Diversity, Identities and Strategies of Women Trade Union Activists', *Gender, Work and Organization* 7(4): 242–57.

— and — (2000b) *Women in UNISON: Report to the Union*, London: UNISON.

— and — (2002a) 'Gender and Diversity: Reshaping Union Democracy', *Employee Relations* 24(2): 167–89.

— and — (2002b) 'Gender, Diversity and Mobilisation in UK Trade Unions', in F. Colgan and S. Ledwith (eds) *Gender, Diversity and Trade Unions: International Perspectives*, London: Routledge.

— and — (eds) (2002c) *Gender, Diversity and Trade Unions: International Perspectives*, London: Routledge.

Collinson, M. and Collinson, D. (1996) '"It's Only Dick": The Sexual Harassment of Women Managers in Insurance Sales', *Work, Employment & Society* 10(1): 29–56.

Connell, R. (1995) *Masculinities*, Cambridge: Polity Press.

Dahlerup, D. (1988) 'From a Small to a Large Minority: Women in Scandinavian Politics', *Scandinavian Political Studies* 11(4): 275–98.

Delmar, R. (1987) 'What is Feminism?', in J. Mitchell and A. Oakley (eds) *What Is Feminism?*, Oxford, Basil Blackwell.

Drake, B. (1920/1984) *Women in Trade Unions*, London: Virago.

Edsall, T.B. (2005) 'Anna Burger to Head Breakaway Labor Group Coalition: Hopes to Reverse Setbacks and Organize More Women and Minorities', *Washington Post*, 27 September.

Elliot, R. (1984) 'How Far Have We Come? Women's Organisation in the Unions in the United Kingdom', *Feminist Review* 16(1): 64–73.

Ellis, V. (2002) 'Report and Evaluation of Ukraine Gender Project', paper presented at PSI *CEE Gender Equality Project Steering Committee*, Bucharest, November.

Epstein B. (2001) 'Response to Acker and Eisenstein', *Monthly Review* 53(5).

Equal Opportunities Commission (2005) 'Ethnic Minority Men and Women', in *Women and Men in Britain Series*, Manchester: EOC.

European Trade Union Confederation (1999) *The Second Sex of European Trade Unionism*, Brussels: ETUC.

— (2004) *Women in Trade Unions: Making the* Difference, Brussels: ETUC.

Foley, J.R. (2003) 'Mobilization and Change in a Trade Union Setting: Environment, Structures and Action', *Work, Employment and Society* 17(2): 247–68.

Franzway, S. (2002) 'Sexual Politics in (Australian) Labour Movements', in F. Colgan and S. Ledwith (eds) *Gender, Diversity and Trade Unions: International Perspectives*, London: Routledge.

Fraser, N. (2003) 'Social Justice in the Age of Identity Politics', in N. Fraser and A. Honneth *Redistribution or Recognition? A Political-Philosophical Exchange*, London: Verso

Freeman, R. (2005) 'China, India and the Doubling of the Global Labor Force: Who Pays the Price of Globalization?', *The Globalist* August 30.

Frege, C. and Kelly, J. (eds) (2004) *Varieties of Unionism: Strategies for Union Revitalization in a Globalizing Economy*, Oxford: Oxford University Press.

Freire, P. (1985) *The Politics of Education: Culture, Power and Liberation*, London: Macmillan.

Greene, A-M. and Kirton, G. (2002) 'Advancing Gender Equality: The Role of Women-Only Trade Union Education', *Gender, Work and Organization* 9(1): 39–59.

Gupta, R. (2005) 'Heroines of the Picket', *Guardian*, August 27.

Hamdi, N. (2004) *Small Change*, London: Earthscan.

Hansen, L.L. (2004) 'Gender Equality, Policy Problems and Possible Solutions: Gender, Power and Change in LO and UNISON', Roskilde: Unpublished PhD thesis (English summary).

Healy, G. and Kirton, G. (2000) 'Women, Power and Trade Union Government in the UK', *British Journal of Industrial Relations* 38(3): 343–60.

Healy, G., Bradley, H. and Mukherjee, N. (2004) 'Individualism and Collectivism Revisited: A Study of Black and Minority Ethnic Women', *Industrial Relations Journal* 35(5): 451–66.

Heery, E., Kelly, J. and Waddington, J. (2003) 'Union Revitalisation in Britain', *European Journal of Industrial Relations* 9(1): 79–97.

Hensman, R. (2002) 'Trade Unions and Women's Autonomy: Organisational Strategies of Women Workers in India', in F. Colgan and S. Ledwith (eds) *Gender, Diversity and Trade Unions: International Perspectives*, London: Routledge.

Hercus, C. (1999) 'Identity, Emotion and Feminist Collective Action', *Gender and Society* 13(1): 34–55.

Humphrey, J.C. (1999) 'Disabled People and the Politics of Difference', *Disability and Society* 14(2): 173–88.

— (2002) *Towards a Politics of the Rainbow: Self-Organization in the Trade Union Movement*, Aldershot: Ashgate.

Hunt, G. (ed.) (1999) *Laboring for Rights: Unions and Sexual Diversity across Nations*, Philadelphia: Temple University Press.

Hunt, S.A., Benford, R.D. and Snow, D.A. (1994) 'Identity Fields: Framing Processes and the Social Construction of Movement Identities', in H. Johnston, E. Larana and J.R. Gusfield (eds) *New Social Movements: From Ideology to Identity*, Philadelphia: Temple University Press.

Hyman, R. (2001) *Understanding European Trade Unionism: Between Market, Class and Society*, London: Sage.

ILO/ICFTU (1999) 'The Role of Trade Unions in Promoting Gender Equality and Protecting Vulnerable Women Workers', First Report of the ILO-ICFTU Survey.

ILO (2002) *Decent Work and the Informal Economy*, Geneva: ILO.

Jewson, N. and Mason, D. (1986) 'The Theory and Practice of Equal Opportunity Policies: Liberal and Radical Approaches', *Sociological Review* 34(2): 307–29.

Jones, S. (2002) 'A Woman's Place is on the Picket Line: Towards a Theory of Community Industrial Relations', *Employee Relations* 24(2): 167–89.

Kabak, B. and Ravenhill, D. (2004) *Ahead of their Time: History of the Women's Legal Status Committee*, Johannesburg: DS Print Media.

Kabeer, N. (1999) 'Resources, Agency, Achievements: Reflections on the Measurement of Women's Empowerment', *Development and Change* 30: 435–64.

Kelly, J. (2003) *Union Revival: Organising Around the World: TUC New Unionism*, London: TUC.

Labour Research Department (2004) 'The Firms Who Go for Gold', London: *Labour Research*, July.

— (2005) 'American Union Federation Faces Challenge from Largest Affiliates', London: *Labour Research*, July.

Ledwith, S. (1991) 'Sweet Talk, Soft Deals? Gender and Workplace Industrial Relations', Working Papers in Economics, Business and Management 35, London: Business School, Polytechnic of North London.

— (2000) 'New Unionism, New Women? Women's Careers in Australian Trade Unions: Case Studies in an Australian State', paper presented at British Universities Industrial Relations Association Annual Conference, University of Warwick, 7–9 July.

— (1998–2005) *Informal Conversations with Overseas Trade Union Scholars*, Ruskin College, Oxford.

— and Colgan, F. (2002) 'Tackling Gender, Diversity and Trade Union Democracy: A Worldwide Project?', in F. Colgan and S. Ledwith (eds) *Gender, Diversity and Trade Unions: International Perspectives*, London: Routledge.

— , Ellis, V., and Radford, I. (2003) 'Feminist Praxis in a Trade Union Gender Project', paper presented to Gender and Industrial Relations Special Seminar: From Margins to Centre? Researching Gender in Industrial Relations, International Industrial Relations Conference, Berlin.

MacKinnon, C. (1979) *Sexual Harassment of Working Women. A Case of Sex Discrimination* (with T.I. Emerson), New Haven: Yale University Press.

Mann, M., Ledwith, S., and Colgan, F. (1997) 'Women's Self-Organising and Union Democracy in the UK: Proportionality and Fair Representation in UNISON', in B. Pocock (ed.) *Strife: Sex and Politics in Labour Unions*, St. Leonards: Allen and Unwin.

McBride, A. (2001) *Gender Democracy in Trade Unions*, Aldershot: Ashgate.

McDermott, P. (1993) 'The Eaton's Strike: We Wouldn't Have Missed It for the World!', in L. Briskin and P. McDermott (eds) *Women Challenging Unions: Feminism, Democracy and Militancy*, Toronto: University of Toronto Press.

Macpherson, Sir W. (1999) *The Stephen Lawrence Inquiry: Report of an Inquiry into the Matters Arising from the Death of Stephen Lawrence*, London: HMSO.

Metcalf, D. (1996) 'Review of *SOGAT: A History of the Society of Graphical and Allied Trades*, by John Gennard and Peter Bain', *British Journal of Industrial Relations* 34(2): 315–16.

— (2005) 'British Unions: Resurgence or Perdition? An Economic Approach', in S. Fernie and D. Metcalf (eds) *Trade Unions: Resurgence or Decline?*, London: Routledge.

Mitchell, J. (1971) *Women's Estate*, Harmondworth: Penguin

— (1986) 'Reflections on Twenty Years of Feminism', in J. Mitchell and A. Oakley (eds) *What is Feminism?*, Oxford: Basil Blackwell.

Muir, K. (1997) 'Difference or Deficiency: Gender, Representation and Meaning in Unions', in B. Pocock (ed.) *Strife: Sex and Politics in Labour Unions*, St Leonards. Allen and Unwin.

Nash, K. (2002) 'A Movement Moves: Is There a Women's Movement in England Today?', *European Journal of Women's Studies* 9(3): 311–28.

Oxfam GB (2004) *Play Fair at the Olympics*, Oxford: Oxfam.

Parker, J. (2003) *Women's Groups and Equality in British Trade Unions*, Lampeter: Edwin Mellen.

Pavlychko, S. (1997) 'Progress on Hold: The Conservative Faces of Women in Ukraine', in M. Buckley (ed.) *Post-Soviet Women from the Baltic to Central Asia*, Cambridge: Cambridge University Press.

Purcell, K. (1981) 'Militancy and Acquiescence among Women Workers', in S. Burman (ed) *Fit Work for Women*, London: Croom Helm.

Ravenhill, D. and Kabak, B. (2004) *Ahead of Their Time: History of the Women's Lobby*, Johannesburg: DS Print Media.

Roosblad, J. (2000) 'Trade Union Policies Regarding Immigration and Immigrant Workers in the Netherlands 1960–1995', in J. Wets (ed.) *Cultural Diversity in Trade Unions: A Challenge to Class Identity?*, Aldershot: Ashgate.

Rubery, J., Humphries, J., Fagan, C., Grimshaw, D. and Smith, M. (2003) 'Equal Opportunities as a Productive Factor', in B. Burchell, S. Deakin, J. Michie and J. Rubery (eds) *Systems of Production: Markets, Organisations and Performance*, London: Routledge.

Rubchak, M.J. (2001) 'In Search of a Model: Evolution of a Feminist Consciousness in Ukraine and Russia', *European Journal of Women's Studies*. 8(2): 149–60.

Sen, A. (2001) 'Work and Rights', in M. Fetherlolf Loutfi (ed.) *Women, Gender and Work*, Geneva: International Labour Office.

SERTUC Women's Rights Committee (2004) *Waving Not Drowning*, London: Southern and Eastern Region TUC.

Strinati, D. (1995) *An Introduction to Theories of Popular Culture*, London: Routledge.

Tait, V. (2005) *Poor Workers' Unions: Rebuilding Labor from Below*, Boston: South End Press.

Taylor, G. and Mathers, A. (2004) 'The European Trade Union Confederation at the Crossroads of Change? Traversing the Variable Geometry of European Trade Unionism', *European Journal of Industrial Relations* 10(3): 267–85.

Taylor, V. (1999) 'Gender and Social Movements: Gender Processes in Women's Self-Help Movements', *Gender and Society* 13(1): 8–34.

Todd, P. and Bhopal, M. (2002) 'Trade Unions, Segmentation and Diversity: The Organising Dilemmas in Malaysia', in F. Colgan and S. Ledwith (eds) *Gender, Diversity and Trade Unions: International Perspectives*, London: Routledge.

Tshoaedi, M. (2002) 'Women in the Labour Movement: Perceptions of Gender Democracy in South African Trade Unions', in F. Colgan and S. Ledwith (eds) *Gender, Diversity and Trade Unions: International Perspectives*, London: Routledge.

TUC (1997) *Partners for Progress: Next Steps for the New Unionism*, London: TUC.

— (2000a) *Resisting Racism at Work*, London: TUC.

— (2000b) *Annual Report*, London: TUC.

— (2000c) *Reaching the Missing Millions*, London: TUC.

— (2004) *World Trade Union LGBT Rights Network Launched*, www.tuc.org.uk/equality/tuc-9143.

— (2005) *TUC Equality Audit*, London: TUC.

TUC Women's Committee (2005) *Report of the TUC Women's Committee 2004–5*, London: TUC.

Turner, L. (2004) 'Why Revitalize? Labour's Urgent Mission in a Contested Global Economy', in C. Frege and J. Kelly (eds) *Varieties of Unionism: Strategies for Union Revitalization in a Globalizing Economy*, Oxford: Oxford University Press.

UNISON Rules (1997) London: UNISON

Verma, A., Kochan, T.A. and Wood, S. (2002) 'Union Decline and Prospects for Revival: Editor's Introduction', *British Journal of Industrial Relations* 40(3): 373–84.

Virdee S. (2000) 'Organised Labour and the Black Worker in England: A Critical Analysis of Postwar Trends' in J. Wets (ed) *Cultural Diversity in Trade Unions: A Challenge to Class Identity?*, Aldershot: Ashgate.

Waddington, J. and Kerr, A. (1999) 'Trying to Stem the Flow: Union Membership Turnover in the Public Sector', *Industrial Relations Journal* 30(3): 184–96.

Walby, S. (1990) *Theorising Patriarchy*, Oxford: Blackwell.

— (2003–4) 'Gender Mainstreaming: Productive Tensions in Theory and Practice', Contribution to ESRC Gender Mainstreaming Seminars, Department of Sociology, Lancaster University, at www.comp.lancs.-ac.uk/sociology/papers/pdf.

Williams, R. (1977) *Marxism and Literature*, Oxford: Oxford University Press.

Young, I.M. (1990) *Justice and the Politics of Difference,* Princeton: Princeton University Press.

Yuval-Davis, N. (1998) 'Beyond Differences: Women, Empowerment and Coalition', in N. Charles and H. Hintjens *Gender, Ethnicity and Political Ideologies*, London: Routledge.

— (2004) 'Human/Women's Rights and Feminist Transversal Politics', in M. Marx Ferree and A. Tripp (eds) *Transnational Feminisms: Women's Global Activism and Human Rights*, Minneapolis: Minnesota University Press.

Ronaldo Munck

Globalisation, Labour and the 'Polanyi Problem'[1]

Introduction

The labour and 'new' social movements are an integral element for a progressive solution of the so-called '*Polanyi problem*', that is to say, how the current tendency towards the creation of a global free-market economy can be reconciled with a degree of stability and cohesion in society. Taking a 'Polanyian' perspective allows us to develop a much-needed historical perspective on the dual transformations of globalisation and labour, too often viewed in a 'presentist' manner. This contribution develops in three 'moments', to use a Gramscian term. It first outlines what the '*Polanyi problem*' consists of and some of the implications that arise in developing a Gramscian/Polanyian strategy of counter-hegemony for the labour and the new social movements today. The question to be answered is whether labour is capable of acting as part of the broad social counter-movement to the world-scale self-regulating market that globalisation is creating. A second moment, called *Perspectives*, outlines some of the main theoretical perspectives deployed in the study of labour and globalisation with a view to moving beyond narrow disciplinary constraints. The question is whether a new global labour studies is emerging even if a new paradigm has not yet emerged. Finally, we move to *Politics* where some of the key strategies and practices of labour and the new social movements are critically examined. The contours of a new 'global strategy for labour' are explored in broad outline. Inevitably, in such a broad synthesis there is considerable loss of texture and specificity

1   This article previously appeared in (2004) *Labor History* 45(3): 251–69. For this journal's website, see http://www.tandf.co.uk/journals. The author would like to thank Taylor & Francis for granting permission to reproduce the article.

and more research is called for. In terms of the opposing classificatory strategies of the 'lumpers' versus the 'splitters', first adumbrated by Darwin, I am probably a 'lumper'[2] in that I take a position in the round and do not dwell on nuances. However, I believe it is sometimes necessary to stand back from the concrete to develop a more abstract reasoning before going on to advance a new synthesis that is both grounded and rigorous.

The Polanyi Problem

Towards the end of the Second World War Karl Polanyi wrote of how a self-regulating market 'could not exist for any length of time without annihilating the human and natural substance of society' (Polanyi 2001: 3). This 'stark utopia', according to Polanyi, would destroy humanity and transform the world into a wilderness, an opinion mirrored by today's eco-socialists of course. The current strategy and ideology of globalisation as transformative revolution seem to echo and confirm Polanyi's account of the 19th century industrial revolution, the last 'attempt to set up one big self-regulating market' (Polanyi 2001: 70). This capitalist project was not achieved and the social history of the 19th century was transformed by what Polanyi calls a 'double movement': while the market spread and all around it was commodified, society at the same time protected itself through 'a network of measures and policies [that] was integrated into powerful institutions designed to check the action of the market relative to labor, land and money' (Polanyi 2001: 79). This deep-seated counter-movement resisted the pernicious effects of the self-regulating market and sought to 're-embed' its economic structures within society.

Perhaps one of the most influential and 'topical' of Polanyi's concepts is, indeed, that of 'embeddedness'. Before the emergence of

---

2   'Lumpers are comfortable with large categories that display considerable within-group heterogeneity. Splitters want to create a new, homogeneous category for every small variation' (Scott Acton 2001:15).

an unregulated market system towards the end of the 18th century, markets (that is to say exchange relations) were governed by certain 'moral' principles (such as reciprocity) that could be seen as 'embedded' in the social and political order of the day. In the course of the 19th century (as in the late 20th century), there was a strong bid to 'disembed' market regulations so as to remove them from social, political or moral regulation. There have been since several cycles of embedding, dis-embedding and re-embedding of market relations. Most famously, the long postwar boom has been characterised as a period of 'embedded liberalism' (Ruggie 1982) in which a transnational liberal order was combined with state intervention at the domestic level. This was known as a 'compromise state' and took various forms. The question then today, from a Polanyian perspective, is whether, after a twenty-year period during which capital has moved to free itself from any restrictions set by society or local communities, we might be heading back towards a phase of re-embedding and the development of a 'compromise state' as seems to be implicit in the 'globalisation and governance' debates (see for example Prakash and Hart 2000).

If economic liberalism was the organising principle of society when Polanyi was writing, neoliberalism holds that dominant role today. As Polanyi once wrote: 'The true implications of economic liberalism can now be taken in at a glance. Nothing less than a self-regulating market on a world scale could ensure the functioning of this stupendous mechanism' (Polanyi 2001: 145). During the 1970s and 1980s there was a concerted bid by the transnational capitalist class to create a 'disembedded liberalism' that led to the triumph of 'globalisation' as discourse and practice in the 1990s. This was Polanyi's 'double movement' in reverse as it were, with the market successfully defending its prerogatives against what it saw as the encroachments of society and politics. As with the first 'great transformation', this move towards a de-regulated market system was achieved through strong state intervention. Capital mobility was encouraged, free trade was sanctified, labour was made more 'flexible' and macro-economic management became fully market compliant. This was no smooth, gradual and organic evolution of the market according to natural principles. On the contrary, as Polanyi put it for his day and equally relevant today: 'the market has been the outcome of a conscious and often violent intervention on the part of a government which imposed the market organisation on society for non-economic ends' (Polanyi 2001: 258). Following this lead, we can now develop a more realist account of the rise of globalisation, and its attendant marketisation and commodification, fully cognisant of the conscious political intervention it sprang from.

This is not the place for a proper evaluation of Polanyi's contribution to a critical social science of transformation (but see Polanyi-Levitt 1990 and Mendell and Salé 1990 for a broad overview). However, in terms of the study of social movements in the era of globalisation we need to consider his incipient theorising of a concept of counter-hegemony in a way that complements rather than contradicts Gramsci (for which see Burawoy 2002). For Polanyi, 'The countermove against economic liberalism and *laissez-faire* possessed all the unmistakable characteristics of a spontaneous reaction' (Polanyi 2001: 156). The attempt now, as in the case of the 19th century dealt with by Polanyi, to set up 'one big self-regulating market' (Polanyi 2001: 70), was bound to create resistance in those social sectors 'most immediately affected by the deleterious action of the market' (Polanyi 2001: 138). While economic liberalism forged ahead to create a self-regulated market, untrammelled by any social constraints or even political prudence, the principles of social protection come into play to protect people and the environment. Markets could spread across the globe and the circulation of commodities could accelerate to an unprecedented degree, but the capital, currency and commodity markets would need to be organised and ultimately regulated. If this was the case when Polanyi wrote, it is doubly so today as a successor strategy to the Washington Consensus is debated in the corridors of power to prevent the global system being destabilised further by a utopian project to create a global self-regulating market.

While Polanyi's problematic can serve as an inspiration to today's student of labour and globalisation it is by no means beyond critique. There is in Polanyi's work a distinct lack of mediations to explain how the 'double movement' might operate. Who precisely would 'spontaneously' move against the unregulated, disembedded market system and why? Polanyi's rejection of the mechanical Marxism of his day is understandable, but this means that power is somewhat underspecified in the Polanyi problematic. There is even a whiff of functionalism, and what Mangabeira Unger (1987) calls 'necessitarianism' in the way the 'double movement' is concept-ualised as arising spontaneously in reaction to the depredations of the free market. We can still argue, I believe, that a contemporary version of the notion of a counter-movement by society in response to the effects of the unregulated market system is an inspired perspective to focus on globalisation, its discontents and the counter-movements it generates. One would also have to 'globalise' Polanyi who was inevi-tably still working within the parameters of the nation-state that he saw as self-sufficient analytically and in terms of the arena in which the 'double movement' would play itself out.

In applying Polanyi's perspective to a broad sweep review of economic ideas and institutional change in the 20th century, Mark Blyth has argued persuasively that 'the double movement, in common with other interest-based explanations of institutional change, sees change as a problem of comparative statics' (Blyth 2002: 7). Thus the shift from disembedded to embedded liberalism in the mid-20th century is imputed to the punctual exogenous variable of the 1929 capitalist crisis and the economic/political instability of the 1930s. The new order is then used to explain the past, which simply does not work as an historical account. If we take a complexity perspective we will be more aware that 'causes' and 'effects' do not always correspond so neatly. Rather, 'an appropriate analysis of the "global age" necessitates the examination of various notions that are not reducible to, or explained through, single processes such as network or empire or markets or disorganization' (Urry 2003: 15). We also need to understand better the discursive construction of reality if we are to develop a more persuasive account of the rise of free market global liberalism. A crisis, for example, only becomes one when it is narrated as such, and economic ideas can actually become powerful in their own right. One need only think of the ideological operation by which neoliberal globalisation became hegemonic in the 1990s to realise the importance of this point. Likewise, counter-movements cannot be seen as spontaneous, practically automatic responses; they are rather

constructed, and then they impact back on the definition and resolution of the crisis itself.

It would also be necessary to specify rather more than Polanyi
does how the mechanism of social protection in regards to the
expansion of the self-regulating market actually operates. In a broad
review of the *Limits to Globalization,* Rieger and Leibfried draw
attention to Polanyi's contribution but argue that the different
modalities and timing of moves towards social protectionism contra-
dict Polanyi's over-general interpretation (Rieger and Leibfried 2003:
61–2). While their open-ended comparative analysis of the role of
social policy as a framing condition for the development of a market
economy is to be welcomed we do not necessarily need to accept their
Max Weber inspired rejection of what they see as the Polanyi
argument, namely that 'a market economy *per se* leads to socially
intolerable outcomes' (Rieger and Liebfried 2003: 65). A more
persuasive critique might be that of van der Pijl when dealing with
international class formation, namely that 'Polanyi's "social protection" is only one modality of a more fundamental process of
socialisation – other modalities being, e.g. corporate planning,
education or international integration' (van der Pijl 1998: 15). From
this perspective we can conceive of the different modalities of
socialisation in the era of neoliberal globalisation, taking up forms
of nonmarket coordination and other ways through which social
embeddedness takes place.

A Polanyi-inspired analysis of globalisation and labour today
would take up, for example, what Beverley Silver recently referred
to as 'Polanyi-type labor unrest [by which] we mean the backlash
resistances to the spread of a global self-regulating market, particularly by working classes being unmade by global economic transformations [...]' (Silver 2003: 20). While capitalism 'makes' the
working class as Marx demonstrated so persuasively, in its neoliberal
variant it can also 'unmake' or de-proletarianise vast swathes of the
global working class. At a less dramatic level, it can certainly undo the
'compromise state' that delivered to the working classes of the West a
degree of social stability in its long postwar boom. While some of the
older working classes are being 'deconstructed' and are resisting this
process as Polanyi's perspective would predict, new working classes

are constantly being (re)created in the West but most particularly in the East and South, which are now organising and resisting in classical (i.e. *Das Kapital*) Marxian style. This dual process is crucial to our understanding of labour and the social movements in the era of globalisation. We should also add that, as E.P. Thompson (1971) argued so passionately, the working class 'makes' itself and is thus not likely to be absent from its unmaking or re-making under neoliberal globalisation.

What is often forgotten in IPE (International Political Economy) readings of Polanyi is that he was also an anthropologist and an early pioneer of the sociology of (under)development (see his work in Dalton 1971). His research on trade, markets and money in pre-capitalist societies helped Polanyi develop a credible alternative logic to that of the unregulated market, which he refused to see as the culmination of human history. Today, as global social movements challenge unfettered market rule and commodification in multiple ways, this alternative societal logic is again being developed in practice. For Amory Starr, the counter-globalisation (or as she prefers to call it, the anti-corporate) movement 'including anti-fascist punk youth, wearily determined homeless activists, wealthy historical preservationists, organisers and housing advocates in low-income communities, and third world landless workers' (Starr 2000: 64) is today challenging the logic of commodification and development across the globe in essentially 'Polanyian' terms. The logic of profit and enclosures is being contested by an alternative social logic of non-market goods and values, and open spaces, a situation that Polanyi, as a forerunner of post-development theories (such as Escobar 1995) would probably understand quite well. It is this broad counter-movement in the spirit of an(other) development that allows us to find the common terrain where labour and the 'new' social movements may come together in a bold social transformation to match the great transformation being wrought by globalisation. Much of the current debate on globalisation and counter-globalisation can be read as dealing with the 'Polanyi problem' as we have defined it here. As a lens for analysing counter-hegemonic social movements the Polanyi perspective is arguably broader and potentially more radical than traditional (sociological) resource mobilisation or identity politics approaches. There is now a growing interest in theorising the contemporary politics of transformation through a Polanyian lens (see for example Udayagiri and Walton 2002) even if a new paradigm has not yet emerged. The social and political transformations being wrought by the globalisation processes reflect Polanyi's dark vision of the socially destructive effects of the self-regulating market. But equally his perspective allows us to understand why the architects of globalisation must also necessarily engage with the problematic of governance. 'Scaled up', as it were, to engage with global governance, Polanyi's perspective can provide a fruitful an overall framework for understanding the making and continuous re-making of actually existing globalisation.

Where Polanyi is, perhaps, most relevant today, however, is as a theorist of counter-hegemony to counter or complement Gramsci-inspired analysis of the way in which neoliberal globalisation builds and maintains hegemony. He rejects the notion that labour is a commodity or that trade unions and labour legislation should not interfere 'with the laws of supply and demand in respect of human labor, and removing it from the orbit of the market' (Polanyi 2001: 186). The social counter-movement to the ever-expanding market and commodification process is precisely designed to remove labour from the sway of market forces and to decommodify labour. The global counter-movement today includes a plethora of movements (or movement of movements) from the NGOs to anti-capitalist activists, from small farmers to big developing nations (such as the Group of 22 that led to the collapse of the Cancun WTO negotiations). Polanyi directs us away from class essentialism and towards an understanding that counter-hegemony will be a broad social and political spectrum seeking to represent the general interest of humanity. The task set by Polanyi is that 'of creating more abundant freedom for all […] This is the meaning of freedom in a complex society […]' (Polanyi 2001: 268).

Perspectives

Despite the relatively long-standing and recently renewed interest in Polanyi from an International Relations and IPE perspective, his influence over international labour studies has really been quite slight. This may well be related to the disciplinary boundaries still respected by those who work within Western modernist parameters as Polanyi was anything but bounded. Apart from my own *Globalisation and Labour: The New 'Great Transformation'* (Munck 2002) and Beverly Silver's *Forces of Labour: Workers' Movements and Globalisation Since 1870* (Silver 2003) from a world-systems perspective, there were only general allusions to Polanyi in Robert Cox (Cox 1971, 1977) of course, and a tantalisingly brief mention by Peter Evans (Evans 2000). However, international labour is back in focus since Seattle 1999 at least, and a number of substantial texts have appeared in the last few years. Four edited collections stand out: the *Socialist Register* for 2001 entitled *Working Classes: Global Realities* (Panitch and Leys 2000), a collection by political scientists, *The Politics of Labour in a Global Age* (Candland and Sil 2001), an ILO (International Labour Organisation) sponsored collection, *Organised Labour in the 21st Century* (José 2002), and IPE conference proceedings, *Global Unions? Theory and Strategies of Organised Labour in the Global Political Economy* (Harrod and O'Brien 2002) that does mention Polanyi, but only in the background and via Cox's use of him.

This set of texts brings to bear an impressive set of case studies and a number of relevant theoretical perspectives are also advanced. They must be welcomed as building blocks in the creation of an adequate understanding of labour as a social movement in the era of globalisation but they suffer, to my mind, from certain limitations. With the exception of *Global Unions?*, these texts more or less take for granted the nation-state as the natural and self-sufficient lens and arena for the study of labour. From the *Socialist Register* through to the ILO the emphasis is almost exclusively on national case studies. Yet not only has neoliberal globalisation undermined the national order of things for a quarter of a century at least, but the theoretical critique of methodological nationalism is now well established (see

Workshop on Methodological Nationalism, 2002). Equally outdated (in my view) is the continued emphasis on Western Enlightenment disciplinary paradigms: political science for Candland and Sil (2001), and the rather implausible marriage of 'the two IRs' (international relations and industrial relations) proposed by Harrod and O'Brien (2002). These perspectives, whatever their merits as tools of analysis, will not really assist labour in becoming part of the new counter-globalisation movement that is rapidly moving beyond traditional conceptions of how politics is both analysed and conducted. For some time now, disciplinary boundaries have been breaking down, even between the 'natural' and the 'social' sciences (on which see Waller-stein 1996), both of which are domains characterised by complexity, a necessary antidote to over-unified conceptions of globalisation.

Industrial relations are, of course, a product of a particular period (the 'compromise state') and pertained to a particular region of the global (the 'advanced' or 'developed' countries). It is understandable, although questionable, that a book emerging from an ILO research department (José 2002) will be set within the parameters of industrial relations and collective bargaining. Less understandable, is that other texts proposing a more radical intellectual agenda (such as Candland and Sil 2001) should also share the ILO discursive space of human relations, social partnerships and labour relations, all set within the confines of the nation-state, albeit one buffeted by the winds of globalisation. Certainly workers and trade unions operate, to some extent and in some regions, within the confines of industrial relations regimes. However, to assume tripartite (state-business-unions) or bipartite (business-unions) industrial relations as they existed in the past is hardly the most adequate paradigm to examine the changing fortunes of labour in the complex and changing era of globalisation we now live in. Not least of the problems of this perspective is that the ILO and its philosophy have been largely marginalised in a world order dominated by the free market philosophy of the WTO. So it is a bit like fighting with yesterday's weapons on today's terrain.

At the other end of the spectrum of labour studies are those who believe Karl Marx is still the single and simple beacon to guide us forward. Also here there is a certain mismatch between the changing terrain of struggle and the weapons chosen. For this approach the forward march of labour proceeds under its traditional banners and all that is needed is more energy and commitment. Thus we have the 'Monthly Review school' (for example Wood 1997) and the Socialist Workers' Party (for example Harman 2002) simply repeating the nostrums of working class primacy and rejecting any engagement with what they dub 'globaloney'. Vanguard politics are taken for granted, and socialism is assumed to be in its pristine state, pre-1989, pre-1956, pre-1917 too, probably. Interestingly, while the *Monthly Review* still firmly prioritises the nation-state as the terrain of choice for labour struggle, the SWP, in its own narrow fashion, is more 'international-ist', although still clearly within a vanguardist perspective. Seeking to transcend the limitations of these approaches but still within the same rather 'theological' domain, is the work of Peter Waterman (Water-man 1998) that seeks to develop a 'new' labour internationalism more appropriate to the era of globalisation and the global justice movement. None of these approaches is polluted by anything as open-ended and complex as the Polanyi perspective, however. Nor does an abstract internationalism really connect with the lives and needs of (most) workers on the ground. What is also a problem is a general neglect of the spatial dimension springing from a traditional Marxist emphasis on the social.

There is, of course, much grounded and theoretically astute work being carried out on labour and internationalism that is neither theological nor institutional, the two overarching problems we have identified so far. Beverly Silver (2003) takes the comparative histori-cal approach deployed productively in the past by the likes of Charles Tilly, Eric Wolf, Barrington Moore and F.H. Cardoso. There are also studies coming out of the critical industrial relations school (notably Hyman 2001, 2002, 2003) and from the political sociology school (Tarrow, 2002) that demonstrate a real and imaginative engagement with the new realities of labour in the era of globalisation. Then, of course, there are the more recent post-structuralist perspectives (see, for example, Kayatekin and Rucio 1998 and Gibson-Graham 1996) that provide the labour scholar/activist with a whole host of new perspectives. The break with class essentialism and the adoption of a broader, more 'culturalist' and gendered approach to labour is certain-ly overdue. As is an understanding of globalisation not as monolith but as a complex, contingent and hybrid set of shifting social relations. The world is changing rapidly and our theoretical lenses need to be adjusted accordingly to take account of the fluid and complex setting of labour and social movement activities.

From my own, non-geographer's perspective, what is most essential to integrate into a contemporary labour analysis is a spatial dimension. Recent debates in human geography (Marston 2000) allow us to break with previous conceptions of global/local, urban/rural, home/work as ontologically given, and direct us instead to the social construction of scale. Labour and labour practices can now be conceived of as multiscalar (with the imaginatively termed 'scale jumping' now possible) with those scales being socially constructed and embedded. Already being pushed out into the area of labour studies (notably Herod 1998 and 2002) this perspective is still being debated and developed. This approach is not without its problems, notably a tendency (perhaps inevitable) to reify the scales of human activity and to hierarchise them to some extent. Also, we sometimes (as in Herod's analysis of the East Coast longshoring industry) note a certain neglect of the historical dimension and of traditional 'socio-logical' concerns with 'race', ethnicity and gender in spite of ritual incantations of the 'holy trinity' of race, gender and class to which 'space' is now added. However, we must certainly accept that global-isation can no longer be seen to have simple causal effects on other 'levels' such as the national, the regional and the local. A focus on the interpenetration of the 'scales' of human activity is a breakthrough for conceptualising labour today. As we displace the place-space ontological distinction so we open up labour analysis and strategising in ways that recognise the complexity and fluidity of the world we now live in.

What I would like to propose to move the debate forward now is a simple spatial/social matrix as a heuristic model that would combine the 'Polanyi problem' problematic with the recent debates on the politics of scale.

Figure 1: Socio-Spatial Matrix

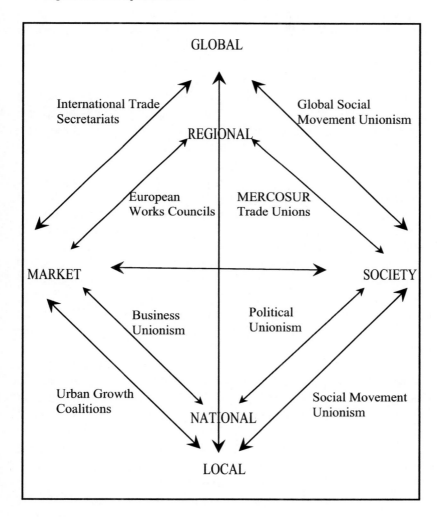

The various points of the diamond should be conceived of as poles of attraction setting up force fields affecting the activity of labour in complex and interrelated ways. Workers and labour movements operate within the parameters of the market but they are also embedded within social relations. So we can see, for example, how a business unionism is closer to the logic of the market than, say, a social movement unionism, which is more attuned to the needs of society or even a political unionism that still operates within the parameters of the nation-state. Then, without posing a hierarchy, labour actions can also be seen to have a spatial dimension, ranging from the local community level to the global transnational space that has its 'official' and more 'unofficial' sub-spaces. The International Trade Secretariats operate more in a market-dominated force field than the newer social movement unionism oriented organisations for example. Then, the regional scale of union activity can show a more market-oriented repertoire of action and approach (European Works Councils) or a more 'social' orientation as with the MERCOSUR union alliance between the Brazilian, Argentinean, Paraguayan and Uruguayan labour movements. At the local or city level, unions may participate in the 'urban growth coalitions' that many cities engaged in the race towards 'competitiveness' have developed or they may adopt a more social movement orientation towards the broader community and its complex issues. I would argue in conclusion that neither axis of social formation and political action is self-sufficient; it is rather their combined and uneven effects that shape the making of the contemporary workers' movement.

A theoretical/political task that still needs to be carried out is to relate globalisation and labour as a problematic to the counter-globalisation movement as a whole. There is a growing literature on the latter, much of it (understandably) celebratory and proclamatory. It tends to leave organised labour out of the story, relegated to the ranks of the 'old' social movements, certainly not an effective player in the era of globalisation as did Castells (1997) in his influential broad-brush analysis of the global capitalist order today. However, in practice trade unions have begun to engage, unevenly and sporadically with the World Social Forum and other more punctual initiatives of the counter-globalisation movement (see for example International Metalworkers' Federation 2003). The tensions and even contradictions in this movement are only now beginning to show and the next few years may clarify this emerging problematic. In the meantime, labour will seek to be included, albeit not always comfortably. In terms of analysis I tend to agree with Boaventura de Sousa Santos when he argues that: 'The problem with the new social movements is that in order to do them justice a new social theory and new analytical concepts are called for' (de Sousa Santos 2003: 2). Having said that, a Polanyi-inspired focus on the counter-movement generated by the self-regulating global market project can serve to sensitise us to the ways in which labour and the new (or maybe not so new) social movements emerge to contest the dominant order. From a transformationalist perspective it would be wrong, I believe, to write labour out of this ongoing story, however 'old' labour may appear in comparison to the new actors engaged against the commodification of society. Or, as Hardt and Negri put it rather more eloquently: 'Just when the proletariat seems to be disappearing from the world stage, the proletariat is becoming the universal figure of labor' (Hardt and Negri 2000: 256)

The most influential and wide-ranging alternative treatment of labour and the new social movements in the era of globalisation is undoubtedly that provided by Manuel Castells in the second volume of his *magnum opus* on *The Information Age* (Castells 1997, 2001). In a sweeping review of contemporary social movements from the Zapatistas to the American Militia and from the women's movement to Aum Shinrikyo, Castells finds no room for the labour movement. In fact, he makes the rather apocalyptic statement that: 'the labour movement seems to be historically superseded' (Castells 1997: 360). Castells thus seems to join those who see the labour movement as part of the 'old' capitalism, marooned in yesterday's politics.[3] In contrast to the 'new' social movements, labour for Castells is unable anymore to articulate a project identity 'by itself and for itself' (Castells 1997: 360), a failing which prevents trade unions from being a transformative force in the new (post-capitalist?) Information Age we supposedly live in.

---

3   However, in a journalistic piece (Castells 1996) he calls for a reinvention of the trade unions in an implicitly more positive expectation.

Politics

As neoliberal globalisation forges ahead in its project to ensure the worldwide dominance of market forces, so a global labour force is taking shape. In terms of Hardt and Negri's terminology: 'When the new disciplinary regime constructs the tendency toward a global market of labor power, it constructs also the possibility of its antithesis' (Hardt and Negri 2000: 253). While deprived of a viable socialist alternative, transnational workers' organisations did at least go into the post-Cold War period unencumbered by the politics of that era. From the ICFTU (International Confederation of Free Trade Unions), through the ITSs (International Trade Secretariats, now renamed Global Union Federations), to the international departments of the big national federations, these organisations went through a process of social and political transformation. Thus we have the veteran AFL–CIO (American Federation of Labor–Congress of Industrial Organisations) leader, Lane Kirkland declaring in the early 1990s that: 'You can't be a trade unionist unless you are an internationalist' (cited in French et al. 1994: 1). This belated return to traditional trade union values, including international solidarity, was by no means a simple radical turn. However, taken as a broad trend it can be seen as part of a developing Polanyi-type 'counter-movement' against the encroachment of the unregulated market into all areas of society.

At its 1996 World Congress the ICFTU discussed a document entitled 'Globalisation, the greatest challenge for unions in the 21st Century'. They recognised that the position of workers worldwide had changed fundamentally as a result of the complex social, economic, political and cultural processes we know through the shorthand term of 'globalisation'. Since then the ICFTU can be said to be in transition between the old statist-corporatist model and the new, more campaigning networked role it needs to play to effectively defend workers' interests (see van der Linden 2003 for this argument). A recent interview[4] with a leading member of one of the more active

---

4   This interview was conducted by Mark O'Brien (University of Liverpool) as part of his PhD research on the new labour internationalism.

ITSs reveals the changes of context and attitude that have taken place since unions began 'going global':

> The main change for us is that we are dealing much more with global institutions than we were a decade ago. That's in terms of the World Bank because of the policy decisions made there with regard to restructuring, structural adjustment programmes, their support for the neoliberal agenda, privatisation.

But it is not simply a question of will to become a counter-movement but also of resources. As the same ITS leader put it:

> [O]n the one hand you've got the whole globalisation debate and the reality that workers are facing in terms of how they're affected [...] but then, on the other hand you've got unions with a declining membership, with less resources and greater demands on the needs at a national level and therefore the amount of time and energy and money they can put into working internationally and perhaps almost taking solidarity for granted, is perhaps less not more than it was a decade ago.

The will to 'globalise' is thus tempered by national level resources implications and the simple fact that without strong national level unions there can hardly be a strong transnational trade union presence.

The regional scale of labour activity is still distinctly under-researched and problematised even though regionalism and regionalisation are seen to be crucial moments of globalisation's drive to transform the world of work. A long-standing example of regional trade unionism is that of the ETUC (European Trade Union Confederation) and the EWCs (European Works Councils), which began to operate in the mid 1990s. There is much debate on the nature of the EWCs (see for example Wills 2001 and 2003; Sadler 2000) and many trade unionists are quite sceptical of their potential, but they remain an ambitious aspect of the European Union's social charter, which could yet lead to a degree of transnational industrial relations. Firstly, if we accept that the different 'models' of capitalism mean something to workers, and then we can follow Will Hutton (2002) in tactically supporting the European model over the UK–US one. Secondly, any vehicle for the horizontal exchange of ideas and the development of even low-key joint action must be welcome elements building counter-hegemony. More explicitly, radical regional trade union organisations such as SIGTUR (Southern Initiative on Globalisation and Trade Union Rights) have also developed a regional voice (see Lambert 2002 for a positive view on this development) but the 'radical' option is, arguably, no less prone to divisions and demoralisation than the more 'conservative' or bureaucratic European model. Over and above the very particular cases we do note the importance of moving towards a better understanding of the regional movement in the making of labour in the era of globalisation and in refusing the binary opposition of global-local or global-national that bedevils much recent and more traditional labour studies.

It is in the Americas that some of the most dramatic tensions between globalisation, regionalism, nationalism and trade unions have been played out. In North America there was a fierce debate within the US, Canadian and Mexican unions over what the formation of NAFTA (North American Free Trade Association) in 1994 would mean (for these debates see French, Cowie and Littleham 1994). Nationalist and protectionist responses gradually gave way, albeit hesitantly and unevenly, to development of a common labour response to this significant step in North/South capitalist rationalisation. Establishing a community of interests amongst workers across North America was not easy and has not done away with national and sectional interests of course. In South America, trade unions in Brazil, Argentina, Uruguay and Paraguay have developed an intense regional transnationalism within MERCOSUR (Common Market of the Southern Cone), which has had a significant impact in promoting a more *desarollista* (developmentalist) agenda in response to the neoliberal agenda (see Munck 2002 on these debates). Workers solidarity in this type of context can take transnational forms but also be thoroughly imbued with nationalism. Is this type of action incompatible with 'global solidarity' or does it rather illustrate the tension between internationalism and the new global solidarity movements?

The 'death of the nation state' must surely rank as one of the weakest of the globalisation or globaliser discourses (one with its left wing as well as establishment manifestations). Certainly the state and nation have been reconfigured by the global free market initiative. However, the national terrain has not been superseded; workers still live in particular places and make demands on national governments. So, fire fighters in Britain, autoworkers in Brazil and street traders in Bangladesh are involved in 'national' struggles. However, the global level may well serve to unify these struggles insofar as the 'real enemy' in all three cases is probably the neoliberal, privatising, competitivity drives of the global neoliberal agenda. The politics of scale may have changed but internationalism is no magic answer to neoliberal globalisation. Sam Gindin is surely correct to argue, on the basis of considerable experience, that: 'Strategic international co-ordination is dependent on the strength of national movements' (Gindin 1998: 202). Many of these movements have recovered from the neoliberal offensive of the 1980s and are starting to reorganise, restructure and resist.

There are several reasons why it is wrong to 'downgrade' the national terrain from a transformative labour perspective. First of all, it tends to over-emphasise the distance between the global new social movements and the 'old' trade union movements. It is analytically incorrect and politically divisive. Second, workers in Brazil, South Africa or the Philippines will not only work at the national level but they may be nationalist as well. Neoliberal globalisation – as Polanyi showed so eloquently for a previous wave – dissolves social bonds and society resists. This resistance will often take a nationalist form that does not merit the sniffy cosmopolitan sneer it sometimes receives. Third, there is a strong argument to be made that if globalisation was created by a number of leading capitalist states, then these should be the targets for the global labour movement and not some nebulous 'globalisation'. A strategic view of the global labour movement may, indeed, wish to prioritise certain pivotal points of capital's global architecture, at a given point in time.

It is the 'local' level that is most often promoted by counter-globalisation movement intellectuals as a priority. The local is sometimes prioritised as a particularly virtuous domain where an ethic of care and solidarity might prevail. The benefits of 'community' are contrasted with the detrimental and impersonal effects of 'globalisation'. I think it is correct to point out that a transnational corporation might be particularly vulnerable at one of its local 'nodes' to vigorous labour and community action. Yet this is not always the case and often the 'militant particularism' (Harvey 1996: 19) of the local struggle will either fail or take on distinctly right-wing characteristics. The whole debate about the 'glocal' – as the new local-global hybrid – steers us away from contrasting the local domain with others. The local is hardly separate from the global, which is made and unmade in particular places. The community resources that can be accessed and mobilised at local level can also, of course, result in sub-regional, national, regional and transnational networks, alliances and struggles.

During the long Liverpool dock strike/lockout of 1995–98 many of these debates were played out in practice, offering a salutary lesson to any one-sided analysis and strategy. While the dockers had considerable support amongst the local 'community' (including some trade unions) they were essentially blocked from obtaining national solidarity due to trade union legislation and a general mood that things had 'moved on' from such actions (set-piece confrontations as the miners had previously engaged in). The Liverpool dockers were, however, able to generate considerable international support particularly in Western Europe and North America, generated to some extent by Internet networks. Now, what is interesting is how diametrically opposed views of this conflict have been articulated quite persuasively (for an overview see Castree 2000). It could equally plausibly be seen as the last kick of a particularist *macho* model of trade unionism or a harbinger of a new electronic or communication solidarity model. It was argued that the international solidarity efforts were basically a diversion from generating more effective local/national solidarity, but also that this transnational work, if more grassroots-oriented and dynamic, could have delivered victory. Perhaps refusal of binary oppositions and an embrace of complexity is the only sensible response to these conundrums.

A 'global strategy for labour' (Faux 2000) need not be global any more than the local arena can be privileged in building a counter-movement to neoliberal globalisation. The local and the global cannot exist without one another; the national scale of human activity still counts for a lot and the regional movement is incorrectly under-estimated. The brisk review of recent literature I have carried out above points, I would argue, towards the need for a strong interdisciplinary focus and an engagement with the new complexity approach gaining ground in the critical social sciences. The heuristic diamond-shaped model establishing some of the main parameters of labour activity may have some usefulness in this task. The main issue, however, is not to develop sophisticated academic models but to focus on the complexity of the new paradigms we need to understand the various processes in the world around us, and the interpenetration of the various 'scales' of human activity. As Ash Amin rightly argues in contesting any naturalistic conception of scale globalisation is best conceived as: 'an energised network space marked by the intensification of mixture and connectivity as more and more thins become interdependent (in associative links and exclusions)' (Amin 2002: 395). This is probably a sound starting point for an analysis of labour in the era of globalisation that is radical but grounded, conscious of what is new but fully cognisant of history and structure.

In terms of an overall conclusion on a labour politics of transformation for the 21st century, I would like to refer to A.V. José's bold introduction to the ILO volume *Organised Labour in the 21st Century* (José 2002). While firmly reformist in orientation and limited by the UN 'family' view of global governance, a strong Polanyian theme also emerges. José argues that: 'Throughout the twentieth century, trade unions have functioned in an environment marked by dynamic changes in the world of work [...] During the period they built organisational strength and capacity to mobilise their constituents [...] At the same time unions influenced social policy and assisted the development of institutions to regulate markets' (José 2002: 17). Trade unions have transcended narrow special interest politics to take on the Polanyian task of regulating or controlling the free market. José calls on unions to 'resume their traditional role as guardians of social cohesion' (José 2002: 13). Certainly this may be read in an integrationist manner as will the discourse of social inclusion but the ILO is also now promoting the radical strategy of 'global social movement unionism' (Bezuidenhout 2002), something unthinkable even a decade ago.

The point is not that the ICFTU or the ILO or the AFL–CIO have suddenly become radicalised by globalisation but that the 'Polanyi problem' requires a degree of global governance that in turn requires some participation by labour and hence creates some opportunities. It is significant that Joseph Stiglitz, ex chief economist of the World Bank and Chair of Clinton's Council of Economic Advisors provides an enthusiastic Foreword to the recent new edition of Polanyi's classic (Stiglitz 2002). Stiglitz challenges the myth of the self-regulating economy, in classic *laissez-faire* garb or its current Washington Consensus, and calls for greater regulation. Regulation may restrict some freedoms – such as the freedom to move capital in and out of a country – but it may enhance those of others: 'for the poor face a greater sense of insecurity than everyone else [...] there is less freedom, less freedom from hunger, less freedom from fear' (Stiglitz 2002: xvi–xvii). Taking up the tasks of development and poverty alleviation will be part of the global labour movement's strategy as it rises to the challenge of a counter-hegemonic response to the Polanyi problem faced by globalisation from above.

References

Amin, A. (2002) 'Spatialities of Globalisation', *Environment and Planning A* 34: 385–99.

Bezuidenhout, A. (2002) 'Towards Global Social Movement Unionism? Trade Union Responses to Globalisation in South Africa', in A.V. José (ed.) *Organised Labour in the 21st Century*, Geneva: International Institute for Labour Studies.

Blyth, M. (2002) *Great Transformations. Economic Ideas and Institutional Change in the Twentieth Century*, Cambridge: Cambridge University Press.

Buraway, M. (2003) 'For a Sociological Marxism: The Complementary Convergence of Antonio Gramsci and Karl Polanyi', *Politics and Society* 31(2): 193–261.

Candland, C. and S.R. (eds) (2001) *The Politics of Labour in a Global Age: Continuity and Change in Late-Industrialising and Post-Socialist Economies*, Oxford: Oxford University Press.

Castells, M. (1996) 'Empleo, trabajo y sindicatos en la nueva economía global', *La Factoria*, 1.
— (1997) *The Information Age, Volume II: The Power of Identity*, Oxford: Blackwell.
— (2002) *The Information Age, Volume II: The Power of Identity (New Edition)*, Oxford: Blackwell.
Castree, N. (2000) 'Geographic Scale and Grassroots Internationalism: The Liverpool Dock Dispute, 1995–98', *Economic Geography* 76(3): 272–92.
Cox, R.W. (1971) 'Labour and Transnational Relations', *International Organisation* 25(3).
— (1977) 'Labour and Hegemony', *International Organisation* 31(3).
Dalton, G. (ed.) (1971) *Primitive, Archaic and Modern Economics: Essays of Karl Polanyi*, Boston: Beacon Press.
Escobar, A. (1995) *Encountering Development: The Making and Unmaking of the Third World*, Princeton: Princeton University Press.
Evans, P. (2000) 'Fighting Marginalisation with Transnational Networks: Counter-Hegemonic Globalisation', *Contemporary Sociology* 29(1): 230–41.
Faux, J. (2002) *A Global Strategy for Labour*, available from http://www.globalpolicynetwork.org/faux2002wsf.html.
French, J., Cowie, J. and Littleham, S. (1994) *Labour and NAFTA: A Briefing Book*, Durham, NC: Duke University Press.
Gibson-Graham, J.K. (1996) *The End of Capitalism (As We Knew It): A Feminist Critique of Political Economy*, Oxford: Blackwell.
Gindin, S. (1998) 'Notes on Labour at the End of the Century', in E.M. Wood (ed.) *Rising From the Ashes? Labour in the Age of 'Global' Capitalism*, New York: Monthly Review Press.
Hardt, M. and Negri, A. (2000) *Empire*, Cambridge, MA: Harvard University Press.
Harman, C. (2002) 'The Workers of the World', *International Socialism* 96: 3–46.
Harrod, J. and O'Brien, R. (eds) (2002) *Global Unions? Theory and Strategies of Organised Labour in the Global Political Economy*, London and New York: Routledge.
Harvey, D. (1996) *Justice, Nature and the Geography of Difference*, Oxford: Blackwell.
Herod, A. (1998) *Organising the Landscape: Geographical Perspectives on Labour Unionism*, Minneapolis: University of Minnesota Press.

— (2001) *Labour Geographies: Workers and the Landscapes of Capitalism*, Guildford: Guildford Publications.

Hutton, W. (2002) *The World We're In*, London: Abacus.

Hyman, R. (2001) *Understanding European Trade Unionism: Between Market, Class and Society*, London: Sage.

— (2002) *The International Labour Movement on the Threshold of Two Centuries: Agitation, Organisation, Bureaucracy, Diplomacy*, available at http://www.arbarkiv.nu/pdf_wrd/Hyman_int.pdf.

— (2003) 'An Emerging Agenda for Trade Unions?', in R. Munck (ed) *Labour and Globalisation: Results and Prospects*, Liverpool: Liverpool University Press.

International Metalworkers' Federation (2003) *Trade Unions and Social Movements: New Alliances Against New Forms of Capitalism*, available at http://imfmetal.org/main/index.html.

José, A.V. (2002) 'Organised Labour in the 21st Century: Some Lessons for Developing Countries', in A.V. José (ed.) *Organised Labour in the 21st Century*, Geneva: International Institute for Labour Studies.

— (ed.) (2002) *Organised Labour in the 21st Century*. Geneva: International Institute for Labour Studies.

Kayatekin, S. and Rucio, D. (1998) 'Global Fragments: Subjectivity and Class Politics in Discourses of Globalisation', *Economy and Society* 27(1): 74–96.

Lambert, R. (2002) 'Labour Movement Renewal in the Era of Globalisation: Union Responses in the South', in J. Harrod and R. O'Brien (eds) *Global Unions? Theory and Strategies of Organised Labour in the Global Political Economy*, London: Routledge.

Marston, S. (2000) 'The Social Construction of Scale', *Progress in Human Geography* 24(2): 219–42.

Mendell, M. and Salé, D. (eds) (1990) *The Legacy of Karl Polanyi: Market, State and Society at the End of the Twentieth Century*, London: Macmillan.

Munck, R. (2002a) *Globalisation and Labour: The New 'Great Transformation'*, London: Zed Books.

— (2002b) 'Labour, Globalisation and the Regional Dimension. The Case of MERCOSUR', *Labour, Capital and Society* 34(1).

Panitch, L. and Leys, C. (eds) (2000) *Socialist Register 2001: Working Classes, Global Realities*, London: Merlin Press and New York: Monthly Review Press.

Polanyi, K. (2001) *The Great Transformation. The Political and Economic Origins of Our Time* (Foreword by J. Stiglitz, Introduction by F. Block), Boston: Beacon Press.

Polanyi-Levitt, K. (ed.) (1990) *The Life and Work of Karl Polanyi*, Montreal: Black Rose Books.

Prakash, A. and Hart, J. (eds) (2000) *Globalisation and Governance*, London: Routledge.

Rieger, E. and Leibfried, S. (2003) *Limit to Globalization*, Cambridge: Polity Press.

Ruggie, J. (1982) 'International Regimes, Transactions and Change: Embedded Liberalism in the Post-War Economic Order', *International Organisation* 36(Spring): 379–415.

Sadler, D. (2000) 'Organising European Labour: Governance, Production, Trade Unions and the Question of Scale', *Transactions of the Institute of British Geographers* 25: 135–152.

Scott Acton, G. (2002) *Classification of Psychopathology: Goals and Methods in an Empirical Approach*, available at http://www.galton.-psych.nwu.edu/acton/goals.html.

Silver, B. (2003) *Forces of Labour. Workers' Movements and Globalisation Since 1870*, Cambridge: Cambridge University Press.

Sousa Santos, B. (2003) *The World Social Forum: Towards a Counter-Hegemonic Globalisation*, at http://www.ces.fe.ua.pt/bss/fsm.php=A9.

Starr, A. (2000) *Naming the Enemy: Anti-Corporate Movements Confront Globalisation*, London: Zed Books.

Stiglitz, J. (2001) 'Foreword', in K. Polanyi, *The Great Transformation. The Political and Economic Origins of Our Time*, Boston: Beacon Press.

Tarrow, S. (2002) 'The New Transnational Contention: Organisation, Coalitions, Mechanisms', (mimeo).

Thompson, E.P. (1971) *The Making of the English Working Class*, Harmondsworth: Penguin.

Thrift, N. (1999) 'The Place of Complexity', *Theory, Culture and Society*, 16(3): 31–69.

Unger, R M. (1987) *False Necessity: Anti-Necessitarian Social Theory in the Service of Radical Democracy*, Cambridge: Cambridge University Press.

Urry, J. (2003) *Global Complexity*. Cambridge: Polity Press.

Udayagiri, M. and Walton, J. (2002) 'Global Transformation and Local Counter Movements: The Prospects for Democracy Under Neoliberalism', paper presented at 'The Next Great Transformation? Karl Polanyi and the Critique of Globalisation' conference, University of California, Davis, April 12–13.

Van der Linden, M. (2003) 'The ICFTU at the Crossroads: An Historical Interpretation', (mimeo), International Institute of Social History, Amsterdam.

Van der Pijl, K. (1998) *International Classes and International Relations*, London: Routledge.

Wallerstein, I. (1996) *Open the Social Sciences: Report of the Gulbenkian Commission on the Restructuring of the Social Sciences*, Stanford, CA: Stanford University Press.

Waterman, P. (1998) *Globalisation, Social Movements and the New Internationalisms*, London: Mansell.

Wills, J. (2001) 'Uneven Geographies of Capital and Labour: The Lessons of the European Works Councils', in P. Waterman and J. Wills (eds) *Place, Space and the New Labour Internationalisms*, Oxford: Blackwell.

— (2003) 'Rescaling Trade Union Organisation: Lessons From the European Frontline', in R. Munck (ed.) *Labour and Globalisation: Results and Prospects*, Liverpool: Liverpool University Press.

Wood, E.M. (ed.) (1997) 'Rising From the Ashes? Labour in the Age of Global Capitalism', *Monthly Review* 49(3).

Workshop on Methodological Nationalism (2002) *Draft Report. Seminar at the Centre for the Study of Global Governance*, LSE, London, at www.lse.ac.uk/Depts/global/Yearbook/methnatreport.htm.

PETER WATERMAN

Trade Unions, NGOs and Global Social Justice: Another Tale to Tell

Deborah Eade and Alan Leather (eds) (2005) *Trade Union and NGO Relations in Development and Social Justice*, Bloomfield, CT: Kumarian. ISBN: 1–56549–196–3.

Here we have an original and substantial collection on a relationship (more crucial than most involved may realise) to the development of a meaningful civil society globally. This is because unions and non-governmental organisations (NGOs) are two considerable but evidently very different sets of socio-political institutions which can be seen as bearers, respectively, of the old internationalism and the new. And which, separately or jointly, have claimed – or have had claimed for them – that they represent a global civil society (GCS) in the making. What the collection actually represents, I think, is an exceptionally rich resource book but one that does not possess the language for, or even the intention of, looking at these phenomena from the outside nor the specific forest in which they stand.[1]

---

1   I ought to mention that I was invited to contribute to the volume by Deborah Eade, Editor of the journal. I have known personally, though to differing degrees, Alan Leather, its Guest Editor, and Dave Spooner, who makes the first major contribution. I concentrate upon their contributions and see this as a re-opening of an old debate, discussion or dialogue with them. I can't remember if I gave Deborah, who shares their union-cum-NGO background, a reason for not myself contributing to the collection and have even now mixed feelings about my failure to do so. The ambiguity may have to do with the fact that although my own career and commitments have overlapped with those of these major contributors, I have a radically different angle on the matter than theirs (Waterman 2001). This is not so much the difference between Development in Practice (them) and Development in Theory (me); there are plenty of academic contributors here. The difference is that, despite 27 years in an institute of

Content and Coverage

As with all such extensive collections the problem is how one does them any possible kind of justice, or, rather, on deciding and making explicit with what kind of injustice one is going to handle them. Given its size and scope, I will concentrate on the major introductory pieces and abandon the rest to the gnawing criticism of other reviewers. This cavalier attitude can only be justified on my side by stressing that any-one interested in the construction of some kind of global civil society really ought to read this collection.

To start with we have the *tone-setting* editorial item of Deborah Eades and the path-breaking *mode* of Alan Leather. The tone consists, in the Eades overview, of two major elements: firstly the explicit engagement of both editors and many contributors with both unions and NGOs; secondly an assertion of the significant differences be-tween these two forces, yet the necessity, given the growing ethos of the global market and consequently growing social divisions and poverty, of their collaboration. The differences are described in terms familiar to those who have ploughed this field: 1) the membership mandate but bureaucratic procedures of the unions as against the speed and flexibility of the NGOs (which may lead to them following their own noses regardless of others); 2) the ideological positions, or criticisms of each other: the unions castigating the NGOs for a con-centration on 'poverty-reduction' measures that may ignore or under-mine worker power and organisation; the NGOs criticising union recruitment, organisation and strategies as inadequate to the needs of the poor in a globalised economy.

The Alan Leather piece embodies and expresses these elements in an autobiographical piece – a mode I give high priority. This is be-cause of an increasing need or demand, amongst ever-wider publics, to see a connection, in would-be – even has-been? – leaders and leaderships, between the Professional, the Political and the Personal.

---

development studies, I never believed in 'development' even when I first joined it. Let's see what this development-scepticism might mean. If my style along the way is partly autobiographical, licence is given by Alan Leather's contribution.

From being a British printer and union activist, Alan moved into the new social movements of the 1960s (peace, anti-apartheid), to the state-sponsored Voluntary Service Overseas, then work with Oxfam and the British cooperative movement, and then the trade unions. These bodies were then originally busy with their own developmental or justice concerns, making occasional alliances, carrying out joint actions with others from what we now call civil society. During this time he worked in Botswana and India. Eventually he pioneered the Trade Union International Research and Education Group (TUIREG), which worked on unions and development cooperation. TUIREG balanced cautiously between the union-created Ruskin College (I studied there 1961–3), the national and international trade unions, and other British NGOs involved in development education and solidarity. In 1987 Alan became a union education officer with what is now called a Global Union Federation (GUF), the Public Services International (PSI), of which he is now the Deputy General Secretary. The PSI has, particularly since the mid–90s, developed an increasing variety of relations with development and justice NGOs.

Alan makes significant mention of the UK War on Want publication, subtitled *An Account of Trade Union Imperialism* (Thompson and Larson 1978). This, he records, caused major problems between this NGO and the inter/national union movement.[2] It was a wild and woolly collaboration, striking just one note on the piano, which actually has several more. It nonetheless threw – to switch metaphors – the kind of laser light on a West European union development paternalism that had previously been concentrated on the US ones.[3] I note, however, that Alan makes no mention at all of *International Labour Reports* (my archive runs 1984–89), which not only had a longer-lasting but a broader impact within the UK, and which was inspired by

2   Also, I seem to recall, with funding, since such activities were considered incompatible with its tax-advantageous charity status in the UK.

3   I collaborated enthusiastically with this effort, but with no success in taming the wild and woolly argumentation, layout or grammar – a matter of much frustration when it concerned my own research on Nigeria. Where Thompson and Larsen pioneered, others followed, with Wedin (1991) pouring criticism down on the AFL–CIO, the 'Christian' World Confederation of Labour – and the ICFTU.

notions less of trade union imperialism or development cooperation
than solidarity. It even started a difficult dialogue with at least one
international trade union leader of social-democratic plumage, one
which has continued, under other circumstances, till the present day.[4]

ILR, co-founded by Alan's co-contributor to this collection,
Dave Spooner, was a rubber-band and paper-clip operation (for the
computer bit see below), run by a changing team, partly by each
taking turns in switching between minimal pay and unemployment insurance. Born with the first wave of New Social Movements (NSMs)
and independent socialism from the 1970s, it was, for five years or
more, the coordinating principle of the 'new labour internationalism'
in Europe – exercising some influence in the USA, Europe and elsewhere. ILR clearly saw itself less as providing a service, or acting as a
pressure group within the existing inter/national union movement,
more as pioneering meaningful solidarity relations with and between
workers at company and shopfloor level. This was particularly so for
the outstanding 'social movement unions' of this moment – in South
Africa, Poland, the Philippines and South Korea (Waterman 2001:
chapter 5). ILR's path-breaking effort at moving beyond both the discourses of union development cooperation and union imperialism
eventually foundered on the customary rocks: no rocks (despite confidential backhanders from sympathetic funding agencies), high staff
turnover, and eventual burnout. There were also policy differences between those prominently involved. And, to my mind, a limiting territorial imperative, with sympathetic academics[5] making clear their role

---

4   This was with Dan Gallin, then General Secretary of the Food and Allied Union
     International, of whom more in Footnote 7. In case it should be thought I praise
     ILR too much, I would like to record that when I suggested, at its collapse, that
     I be given access to the files to write up the experience, and even seek accom-
     modation in the Netherlands for such, this was turned down by the editorial
     board on the grounds that such an account was being planned, and that a local
     archive was going to be sought for the files. There was and is no such book, or
     even a memoir, as far as I know. And I know neither where the archive might
     be, nor whether it might now be accessible to the interested researcher.

5   Well, OK, *this* activist academic, running his own shoestring *Newsletter of
     International Labour Studies*, c. 1980–90. Whilst I have no intention of com-
     paring my material base with theirs, this activity carried its own risks. I can
     state that I took every possible advantage of my job – formal, informal and very

was to be one of support *to* rather than cooperation and dialogue *with*. Two of its important additional legacies, however, were its understanding, explicit or implicit, that the new labour internationalism was going to be communications-dependent. I am referring here less to the magazine itself, since there had been forerunners, than to its enthusiastic commitment to what I seem to recall was not yet even called the Internet. 'International labour communication by computer' in the UK and internationally was largely pioneered by ILR.

Alliances and Tensions (Threats and Promises?)

Dave Spooner provides us with an outstanding geography of the collection's terrain, well structured, of wide coverage, relevantly illustrated. A whole course could be run on this foundation. The basis for cooperation between the unions and the NGOs lies, he starts, not so much with their differing histories and constituencies but their common concern for working people in general and their 'desire to advance and improve the human condition' (19). They are crucial components of a global civil society in formation. They have had specific and longstanding interests and collaboration in the areas of international development and human rights, and, increasingly, in new rights agendas that address the needs of both the unionisable and marginalised, buffeted by neoliberal globalisation. Obstacles to collaboration include the breadth and generality of the union agenda itself, the differences between *levels* of union organisation, those between unions North and South, East and West, the problem of a

---

informal – to further this commitment. This, amongst other hypothetical crimes or misdemeanours, led to my expulsion from the Labour Studies programme and near-expulsion from the institute. My skin was saved for me by more-democratic and tolerant colleagues elsewhere at the institute, one Marxist, some social-democratic, most liberal. The point of this all is to try to break down any possible binary opposition between risk-taking activists and cautious academics. Like the Colonel's Lady and Mrs O'Grady, we can – and should be – sisters/brothers under the skin. More on binaries below.

necessary European union address to both the European and global levels; and then the sexy ones – gender, culture/democracy/class. The list continues. Dave (with whom I have repeatedly tossed this argument over the decades) gives much stress to the C/D/C complex – the historical origins, internal governance and the class composition of the two types of body.

I quote here at length, and pointedly, from page 27:

Point A

While examples of autocratically run and bureaucratic trade unions, some well-known, exist in many countries, it remains true, nevertheless, that the trade union movement as a whole is by far and away the most democratic institution in every society and certainly the only major democratic international movement worldwide.

Point B

All trade unions have a clearly-defined leadership elected at regular intervals. [...] This leadership may lose the next election. [...] Union accounts are usually audited and available to the scrutiny of the membership and the general public. [...] In a democratic (i.e. typical) trade union, members are the 'citizens'.

Point C

By contrast, there are few NGOs with a membership that has a sense of 'citizenship' and ownership of the organisation. In many cases, NGOs are perceived by unions to have a self-appointed and co-opted leadership, with no accountability to a constituency other than public opinion and funding agencies.

Point D

The middle- or upper-class origins of NGO activists of staff members, especially in the UK context, are vividly obvious to working-class union representatives. Their apparent shared confidence and social and cultural affinity with the 'enemy' (corporate or governmental), and their frequently displayed academic training, can easily create distrust and animosity among unions. NGOs may be perceived as being populated by 'posh' people, perhaps with private incomes, and with no experience of the realities faced by working-class communities, whether in inner-city London or on the streets of Manila.

I have to here offer a series of energetic caveats.

Point A. Unions are here presented, naively, and without argument or example, as not only historical models of democracy (which they certainly once were) but as the contemporary vanguard of such internationally. This despite a century of intensive and continuing political and theoretical debate about the crisis of union *and now all other forms* of representative democracy.

Point B. 'Citizenship', also within unions, is a many-splendoured, and many-poison-prickled, thing. The ICFTU knows it has 157 million members, but how many of them know that they have *it*? (Or who leads it? Or what it does? Or doesn't? No one has *ever* asked them.)

Point C. The problem of NGO accountability has been a matter of increasing public debate within and around the NGO community. And inter/national unions may be dependent, for 70 percent of their 'development cooperation' expenses on *the self-same* funding agencies as the NGOs. Pots and kettles.

Point D. The image of the NGOs is marked by such polemical overkill as to raise the question of whether it really lies in the retina of the worker. Which workers? Where? When? To what extent? Are we thinking of *information workers*, now, on broad definition, a majority of at least the Western waged working classes? Or does this image rest in the imagination of the writer? As for the question of who is sleeping with the corporate or governmental enemy (not 'enemy'), well, this is, of course, the century-old critique of unions made less by the upper- and middle-classes than *by their own unruly members*[6] –

---

6   One national case in point. And hardly a marginal one for what is better called 'trade-union foreign policy'. It has taken 40 years, in the AFL–CIO, for left activists to move from pamphlet exposures of its relations with US MNCs and US imperial interventions, invasions and torturings, to a resolution by its largest state affiliate, in California, significantly entitled, 'Build Unity and Trust among Workers Worldwide' (Scipes 2004). This despite the energetic, not to say, devious and violent opposition to such protests by both the 'right' and the 'left' within what has to surely be called the West's most autocratic and bureaucratic trade union. Key in this campaign has been Fred Hirsch (1974). Whether he would consider this new and yet-to-be-won campaign a victory for liberal representative democracy or a campaigning radical democracy would be

as well, of course, of NGOs by *their own* unruly elements. And as for
'"posh people [...] with private incomes'! *Por favor, compañero!*
In so far as Dave himself has been long working for a range of labour-
oriented NGOs, nationally and internationally, this caricature can
hardly be intended to portray himself and his (commonly or universally university-educated) colleagues, either back in the ILR, or
around him today in the international worker and adult education
movement. It belongs, in fact, to a treasured epoch of socialist
caricature, with top-hatted capitalists on money bags crushing burly
but smouldering proletarians in cloth caps and hob-nailed boots. And I
fear it serves a purpose – hopefully unconscious – or at least has
another effect, that of preserving fences where Dave Spooner intends
to build bridges. Can this be why he attributes these images to others
rather than expressing them in the first person himself? Moving
beyond attitudes, impressions and mutual counter-accusations, Spooner
reports the increasingly central debate – under neoliberal globalisation –

---

interesting to know. I make this last point because the AFL–CIO has had,
during its century and more of history, fewer Presidents than the Catholic
Church has had Popes and the Communist Party of the Soviet Union had
General Secretaries.

Popes (since around the creation of the AFL): Leo XIII (1878–1903), St.
Pius X (1903–14), Benedict XV (1914–22), Pius XI (1922–39), Pius XII
(1939–58), Blessed John XXIII (1958–63), Paul VI (1963–78), John Paul I
(1978), John Paul II (1978–2005), Benedict XVI (2005–). Ten. But then
produced with no particular democratic charade and announced by puffs of
smoke from a conclave of cardinals.

General/First Secretaries: Stalin, Malenkov, Khruschev, Brezhnev, Andro-
pov, Chernenko, Gorbachov. Seven. If we throw in Lenin, who led the Party but
never had such a title, Eight. But over the period 1917–91, and produced by
'democratic centralism'.

Presidents (of the un- or merged body): Gompers (twice), McBride, Green,
Meany, Kirkland, Donahue, Sweeney. Seven since 1886, or eight if we count
Gompers twice. This is the outcome of processses in a 'democratic (i.e. typi-
cal)' trade union, of which its members are 'citizens'.

These things have to be said and, regrettably, still from the margins of the
labour, the socialist and even the global justice movement movement. This
because European union leaders, independent socialists and international
labour-support NGOs know well enough the crimes and misdemeanours of the
US trade union movement.

around unions, NGOs and the 'informal economy'. This took dramatic place at the International Labour Conference 2002. The chief protagonists here were the ICFTU and friends, on the one hand, and the feminist Women in Informal Employment Globalising and Organising (WIEGO, a highly-professional and effective Harvard-based NGO) on the other.[7] At issue here was the challenge to the trade unions, from the NGOs and from the ILO itself, over who does, should or could speak for this growing economic sector and its *growing* percentage of the world's workers.

On the one hand, the trade unions are part of the original tripartite 'social partnership', together with capital and state, that created the ILO in 1919 (Capital and State 75 percent, Unions 25 percent). On the other hand, balloons were being floated for a *quatripartite* ILO, with the NGOs being brought in to somehow represent the un-unionised/un-unionisable, often women, workers in what some outside, and inside, the unions see as a promising sector of a globalised, networked, flexible capitalist economy that will, by some social-reformist Houdini manipulation of a neoliberal economy, save, enrich, empower and – above all – pacify the increasing percentage of the poor living below some fat-cat technocrat's poverty line. Little surprise that the union response to this was one of extreme scepticism, often of downright hostility. The problem was not in any way reduced, in my opinion, by trade-union territoriality (the dog in the manger) and the movement's lack of any equivalent, or alternative, to a 19th-century socialist, socially-addressed and mobilising vocabulary, updated in recognition of the globalisation juggernaut.[8]

---

7   Weird and full of wonder is the brave new world of TU-NGO collaboration. An eminent, though less-cloth-capped, ex-international union leader has been a prominent consultant with the top-hatted Harvard feminists of WIEGO (Gallin 2001).

8   So who on earth floated this balloon? The secret lies with our union and NGO cardinals who, after some admittedly desultory enquiry by myself, are not going to tell a sinner such as I. My guess is Juan Somavia himself, since he obviously has both the innovatory bug and the political background. The latter includes, prominently, the 1995 Social Summit which he led. Maybe, however, this is not a floating balloon but a haunting spectre?

In a rather balanced and detailed account of this complex matter Dave Spooner suggests that there are and can be negotiated solutions between the parties concerned. There are, indeed, there can be, and there will be more. Unfortunately these will, within the dispensation of this collection, likely preserve an archaic institutional balance of power within the ILO – the highest international instance for managing international labour–capital discontent. This dispensation is also one that preserves an increasingly ineffective discourse of 'social partnership' between capital, state and unions – one in which the unions have always consciously or unconsciously accepted an inferior and dependent status. Most gravely of all, any defensive or territorial attitude of the unions prevents consideration of the extent to which the new pro-labour NGO networks might not provide the very model for an effective global labour solidarity movement in times of globalisation. Maybe not, but the matter is surely worthy of *investigation* (Waterman 2004).

The unions – and the NGOs for that matter – are also trapped within a discourse that should have been long dead, buried and forgotten. This is 'development', either in practice or theory, since what it has increasingly meant – out in the world beyond discourse, academies and grant-dependent NGOs – is the increase in every possible indicator of human misery and alienation, both within and between nation states and blocs. And this, now, at a moment of the crudest and most violent capitalist aggression/regression of living memory (I do not forget war, the sex and body-parts trade and 'natural disasters'). We are, after all, talking about the cancer stage of capitalism, in which the proletarianisation and commoditisation of everything provokes and even *facilitates* (through alternative web networks for one dramatic example) a common labour and social movement reassertion, this time on a global scale – with the global including, of course, Cyberia.

The Martians around the Corner

A book on one of the repeated indigenous invasions of the Andean capital, and parliament, of Ecuador is called *The Martian at the Corner*. The title suggests that the Martians are already both there and visible, and the book is about how the local bourgeois-*mestizo* Quito press responded to this rather earthly space/place war. In the present collection, unfortunately, the Martians are *here* alright, the citadel is in a condition of considerable apprehension. But the Martians are not yet visible. And they do not even have a metaphorical name of their own.

This is curious, since the general motivation/orientation of these invisible space-beings is partially hinted at in the subtitle of the collection under consideration. This movement called itself, around WSF2, 2002, the 'global justice and solidarity movement' (GJ&SM). This particular, if much-disputed, title will do quite well for the movement's present moment of self-realisation and for my present purposes. To leap metaphorically through both space and time, I think that what we have in this collection is 'Hamlet', though less without his Father's Ghost than the Prince himself, as well as Gertrude, Ophelia, Rosencrantz and Sundry Others, whether wearing swords or bearing skulls. The prince (a New Prince for Gramscians?) is not, repeat *not*, an NGO. It is not an *NGO*.

An NGO is, after all, a perfectly literal *non-entity*, in so far as it is negatively defined and therefore logically dependent on that which it is not (i.e. government). It is, moreover, as Dave Spooner suggests, a descendent of 19th-century church and charity good works – though also, of course, of democratic clubs (sometimes full, simultaneously, of both top hats and cloth caps), community organisations, producer and consumer cooperatives, schools, anti-slavery campaigns, feisty vote-seeking women, anti-alcohol, anti-imperial and peace movements. So unions and NGOs really need to be placed within the history and significant stages of capitalist development (this noun is acceptable to me when accompanied by that adjective), as well as that of resistance to and struggles beyond capitalism. I refer to our present stage as a globalised, networked finance and services capitalism, though I am quite happy to work with related understandings. As for Marx's 'real movement that transforms the present nature of things' (Arthur 1970: 56–7), this is now, *pace* Karl, the GJ&SM.

'Trade unions' and 'NGOs' are the names of trees in 1) the burning forest of capitalist hegemony and 2) the admittedly uneven, inchoate, but recognisably burgeoning, counter-hegemonic movements (armed with fire-fighting equipment). Within *such* a perspective, NGOs can be found, with research, to have as much in *common with* as *differences from* unions. The question is *what* in common, *what* in difference, and how might each, apart or together, contribute to this new wave of struggle for human emancipation.

There is, in Britain, a cloth-capped word, 'gobsmacked'. A top-hatted word for this might be 'somewhat surprised'. There appears, in this 2004 collection, to be no mention of the major or minor expressions of what might, in the 1990s, have been called the 'anti-globalisation movement' (I would need an index or a digital version of the collection to confirm this). The popular, if decade-late, launch-date and place for this is Chiapas 1994, and this *thing*, whatever it is, moves transversally, in network fashion, to Amsterdam, Seattle, Washington, Cochabamba, and a myriad other places of which, as Neville Chamberlain might have remarked, we know very little (he did not have web access to Indy Media Centre). It has frequent but movable feasts in the World Social Forum process. It is based in that South which knows what development isn't. And it is an event *in which the national and international union movement, and labour-oriented NGOs have been increasingly involved* (Waterman and Timms 2004). Yes, I think the word has to be 'gobsmacked'. And, to revert to Shakespeare, I am afraid that in the *absence* of all this, what we might have here is, possibly, a Wicked Uncle, an Angry if Indecisive Nephew but no play. The plot has not been lost; it has not yet been found.

Conclusion

Read this collection. What we have here is a significant stimulus to a serious dialogue about the new drama.[9] I do not feel it necessary to apologise for the passionate (polemical?) note I strike. And this for at least the following reasons.

Firstly, we are confronted with two very considerable world-scale socio-political-cultural actors. The GJ&SM could well do with the full commitment of the institutionalised unions mobilising, potentially, 150 million members (China and Whereveristan so far not included). And there is no single hope of turning round the continuing decline in union power internationally without a profound, open dialogue and dialectic between the old unions and the odd NGOs.

Secondly, we still have to consider, and then continually renegotiate, under public scrutiny, and with full worker control, the terms of engagement. At present, for example, it seems to me quite feasible that the two sets of leaders might settle for a new social (i.e. capitalist) partnership. This would be of Untransformed Unions (with shiny new logos and non-interactive websites), Reasonable Capital (bearing Greek gifts for limited workforces and periods of time), Friendly Statesmen (at WSF 3, Porto Alegre 2003, they were represented by or as President Lula) and Interstate Organisations (with ever-newer 'compacts', 'contracts', 'standards' and other shiny but disposable and infinitely replaceable trinkets). This might well even *deliver* on a Global Neo-Keynesianism that restores some new capitalist balance,

---

9   By significant coincidence, an overlapping collection on 'global labour rights' was produced, in English, on an international NGO website in Latin America around the same time. Access to this collection can be found at the following: http://www.choike.org/nuevo_eng/informes/1872.html. Being digital rather than printed, this one has the built-in possibility of being added to, which is what happened to a first draft of this paper! However, two compilations do not a dialogue make. But the electronic one has the possibility of developing into such. And then, hypothetically, in Spanish as well as English. Should this happen it might be the first time that an open international dialogue on fundamental labour questions, involving those from the world of trade unions and of social movements (and of social movement unions?) did take place.

much as did the Inter/national Keynesianism of the post-World War II years. I am myself inclined to consider this a necessary but also quite insufficient stage – and therefore hardly a recommendable project.

Here we must call again for all power to the imagination. Look at it like this. You have been seriously infected by one week's TV news. Can you trust your health to a system, in which there is 'no other nexus between man and man than naked self-interest' (Marx and Engels 1980/1848). Can you trust it to cure a complex and self-transforming virus, consisting of global warming, human hunger, HIV-AIDS, imperial wars and sub-imperial genocides, the epidemic of obesity, fear and loathing in the bursting cities, dumbed-down media, gun violence in the schools, farmers committing suicide (also in Blair's Booming Britain), the citizen-as-consumer, mad scientists and greasy CEOs producing Frankenstein foods (whilst 'consulting' 'stakeholders' or, at least steak-eaters), 'representative democratic' politicians fiddling while Iraq burns? And do the trade unions, confronted by this, want to be seen globally – as Prasad and Snell remind us in their late contribution to the book – bearing the shield of vested interest or wielding the sword of social justice?[10]

References

Arthur, C. (ed.) (1970) *Karl Marx and Frederick Engels: The German Ideology*, London: Lawrence and Wishart.

Flanders, A. (1970) *Management and Unions*, London: Faber.

Gallin, D. (2001) 'Propositions on Trade Unions and Informal Employment in Times of Globalisation', in P. Waterman and J. Wills (eds) *Place, Space and the New Internationalisms*, Oxford: Blackwell.

---

10   Prasad and Snell have borrowed this metaphor from Richard Hyman (2000), who himself borrows it from Alan Flanders (1970). This has its own particular significance for our argument, given that Flanders was some kind of social-democrat and Hyman an independent socialist but only the quietest of fire-brands.

Hirsch, F. (1974) *Analysis of Our AFL-CIO Role in Latin America: Or Under the Covers with the CIA*, San Jose, CA: no publisher..

Hyman, R. (2000) 'An Emerging Agenda for Trade Unions?', at www.-labournet.de/diskussion/gewerkschaft/hyman.html.

Marx, K. and Engels, F. (1980) 'Manifesto of the Communist Party', in Marx and Engels, *Marx/Engels Selected Works in One Volume*, London: Lawrence and Wishart.

Scipes, K. (2004) 'CAL STATE AFL-CIO – "Immediate" End to U.S. Occupation of Iraq', Email received July 15.

Waterman, P. (2001) *Globalisation, Social Movements and the New Internationalisms*, London: Continuum.

— (2004) 'Research Project Outline: The Internationalisms of Labour's Others: Shall the Last be the First?'.

— and Timms, J. (2004) 'Trade Union Internationalism and the Challenge of Globalisation: The Beginning of the End or the End of the Beginning?', in M. Kaldor, H. Anheier and M. Glasius (eds) *Global Civil Society 2004/5*, London: Sage.

Wedin, A. (1991) *La 'Solidaridad' Sindical Internacional y Sus Victimas: Tres Estudios de Case Latinoamericanos* (International Trade Union 'Solidarity' and its Victims: Three Latin American Case Studies), Stockholm: Institute of Latin American Studies.

ROB LAMBERT

An Early Phase of Transition:
Global Corporations and the
Reconfiguration of Trade Union Power

Introduction

There is evidence that we are now entering an early phase of transition in the structure, form and mode of operation of trade unionism. Certain unions are exploring ways of broadening their horizon from a national industrial focus to a new civil society and global orientation that is distinctive from traditional labour internationalism. These experiments are the first signs that a global social movement unionism (GSMU) is in the making. This is occurring because there is a growing recognition that before all else, the movement's future hinges on its capacity to block the public and private restructuring agendas of global corporations, case by case, company by company, until there is power in civil society movements to redefine the nature and role of corporations and politics and thereby articulate the character of a just, participatory, democratic society. Failure to challenge restructuring and present an alternative vision will doom organised labour to a peripheral existence as workers abandon unionism, recognising that these organisations can no longer defend their most vital interests. This sense of crisis was captured in a speech by the Vice President of the Korean Confederation of Trade Unions (KCTU) to the 7th Congress of the Southern Initiative on Globalisation and Trade Union Rights (SIGTUR) in Bangkok in June 2005 when he argued that the union movement needs to embrace a bold phase of experimentation if it is to survive the restructuring onslaught.

We need to fundamentally transform ourselves. We cannot rely on traditional
methods of organizing and struggle. If unions fail in this we have no future. The
mission is to develop a new type of labour movement. This project is both
urgent and deadly serious (SIGTUR, October 2005).

Moody (1997) identified this crisis, arguing that unions are
'paralyzed' by restructuring. He contends that GSMU is a means to
challenge this corporate agenda. However, his book is vague on two
fronts: firstly, the precise form of GSMU is never specified; secondly,
the organising strategies essential to such a venture are not clarified,
nor are the obstacles to realising this new form analysed. This chapter
will address these issues.

Given GSMU's embryonic nature, the analysis is in part an
exercise in sociological imagination, one that moves beyond the
connection between personal problems and social issues described by
C. Wright Mills (1970). In the GSMU project we imagine what does
not yet fully exist to provoke debate and stimulate new organisational
initiatives. This is not purely speculative as there are already responses
to restructuring that carry the seeds of something new. However, these
initiatives have ended in failure more often than success, and at best
they are incomplete and partial. Most importantly, they are often
constrained by existing patterns of unionism that produce institutional
inertia and an aversion to experimentation, where rhetoric substitutes
for change and where congress resolutions are never implemented.

This chapter seeks to advance the debate on union alternatives to
an accommodation with restructuring through a case study of Australian responses to global restructuring imposed by the Swedish
multi-national corporation (MNC), Electrolux, the world's second
largest producer of household appliances such as cookers, washing
machines, dishwashers and dryers. The first section explores the
demise of local Australian white goods corporations following deregulation, which created conditions conducive to their acquisition by
the Swedish giant. The power shift is analysed in the context of the
dynamic of this global industry. This section concludes by highlighting
the need for a critical discourse on the role of global corporations to
stimulate a repositioning on restructuring. Based on a longitudinal
research project in Australia, the second section highlights the social

and psychological impacts of restructuring in two Electrolux factories. A transnational comparison is provided by considering a similar experience at an Electrolux factory in Michigan. This reveals how structural change creates objective conditions conducive to the emergence of GSMU by linking geographically distant workforces in MNCs, which impose the same form of restructuring across the geographic landscape. Union responses to these conditions are considered in section three. The question is: can the leaderships of existing unions seize this opportunity?

Power Shift: Deregulation, the Demise of Local Corporations and the Attack on Unionism in Australia

Each stage in the changing structure of Australian manufacturing reconfigures and consolidates corporate power and undercuts union strength. There are three phases in this power shift: the protection and nurturing of local companies by the state and the recognition of unions gave rise to a strong collective bargaining oriented trade unionism (1904–1986); economic deregulation and the de-protection of these companies was marked by unions becoming restructuring agents and declining in power (1986–2002); finally, global integration through MNC acquisition of local companies has forced unions to re-evaluate their role and search for new ways to rebuild their power.

The creation of the Australian Federal State at the turn of the last century gave rise to a social contract which protected local manufacturing, provided these companies bargained with unions and paid fair and reasonable wages. Industry protection and relatively high wages nurtured the growth of a diverse manufacturing sector in which the union role in collective bargaining was clearly defined. This recognition led to the rapid growth of unionism with the total membership of Australian trade unions increasing to one half million by 1914, one million by 1941 and 2.8 million by 1978 (Martin 1975: 2).

This system facilitated the development of white goods manufacturing in Australia with stoves, refrigerators and washing machines first being manufactured in the 1920s (Clark 1983: 29). During this golden era some forty factories came into existence, thriving on industry assistance and infrastructure development that reduced risk and encouraged local investment (Clarke 1983: 35). The leaders were Kelvinator Australia and Simpson and Pope Industries which were established in Adelaide, whilst another firm, Email, set up in New South Wales in 1934. Email became Australia's top producer. It built a refrigeration plant in Orange in 1946, and it expanded its total workforce from 400 in 1946 to 2150 by 1974.

Beginning in the 1970s, deregulation and the flow of cheaper imports transformed white goods manufacturing through accelerating acquisitions, mergers and closures. The Whitlam government cut tariffs 25 percent in 1974, which reduced forty corporations to seven. When the Hawke Labour Government slashed tariffs to negligible levels in the early 1990s only two producers survived, Southcorp and Email. In 2000 Email acquired its competitor before it was itself taken over by Electrolux in 2001. This pattern of global economic integration flows inevitably from deregulation.

This process had implications for the union movement, which initially sought a strategic partnership role in restructuring (Lambert 2000). In the late 1980s the state intervened to decentralise bargaining and link wage outcomes to lean production restructuring, thereby circumscribing the role of the union. Pressured by both state and capital, unions bargained away conditions, jobs and security in an effort to maintain wages. Once unions embraced this role, capital's demands became more radical. Despite their cooperative stance, unions were viewed as an obstacle to restructuring, hence the need for further labour market deregulation, which further marginalised unions.

In 1993 the Labour Prime Minister Keating argued, 'Completing industrial relations reform is another link in the chain of reform which began a decade ago. It is important now that we accelerate the reform so that all the other elements of flexibility in the economy can work in harmony'.[1] Keating's Industrial Relations Minister, Brereton enthused that a 'new, all encompassing concept of industrial relations was in the process of emerging in Australia' in which flexibility, team building and consultation would be maximised, in contrast to the old adversarial system centred on strikes and lockouts.[2] Keating then amended the 1988 Industrial Relations Act to give formal recognition to direct bargaining for the first time, allowing companies to bargain with workers without union involvement. When the Conservative Coalition government came to power in 1996, Prime Minister Howard lost no time in further advancing this process by introducing individual workplace agreements as the centrepiece of the industrial relations system. The 1996 Workplace Relations Act is now being further amended to drive down wages and strip away virtually all conditions. In future, workers will have to bargain individually for meal breaks and other taken for granted conditions. The amendments attack basic union rights, thereby contravening ILO conventions: right of entry will be restricted; companies will have access to common law courts to fine unions; and union officials and strikes will be restricted.

The introduction of these repressive anti-union laws in democratic Australia is justified in terms of maintaining global competitiveness. Howard contends that failure to meet these demands will lead to the decline of the Australian economy in that the country would fail to attract new investment. The white goods case study unveils the hidden logic of these 'reforms' and the process of union marginalisation. The research uncovers the global dimension and logic to this ceaseless attack on Australian unionism.

The acceleration of acquisitions, mergers and closures is a global process, which imposes itself nationally as countries integrate through deregulation. Thus, for example, Electrolux has swallowed up 450 companies in 30 years on its way to becoming the second largest MNC in the industry (Nichols and Cam 2005: 39). As the following tables show, the five largest corporations in the industry control 30 percent of the market with a combined turnover of US$45 billion in

---

1   Speech to the Institute of Company Directors, Melbourne, 21 April 1993.
2   Speech to the British Chamber of Industries, May 1993.

domestic appliance revenues in 2002. The top two white goods corporations alone controlled 15 percent of global volume sales while the ten largest corporations account for 44 percent of the global market. The developed world's MNCs dominate. The five European and North American MNCs account for just over one-third of world sales (35.6 percent). The four Japanese MNCs achieved 14 percent of world sales, with the emergent MNCs from China and Korea rapidly expanding their market share.

In 1982 350 corporations produced white goods in Europe. A mere decade later, this was slashed by two-thirds to 100 companies. By the late 1990s 15 companies controlled 80 percent of the European market (Segal-Horn et al. 1998: 105).

Table 1   Ten Largest Whitegoods Corporations 2001 and 2002
            (by share of total global volume sales)

% volume

		2001	2002
Whirlpool	(USA)	7.9	7.9
Electrolux	(Sweden)	7.3	7.1
Bosch-Siemens Hausgeräte	(Germany)	5.8	5.7
General Electric (Appliances)	(USA)	5.3	5.4
Haier Group	(China)	3.2	3.8
Matsushita	(Japan)	3.1	3.2
Maytag	(USA)	3.0	3.1
LG Group	(Korea)	2.4	2.6
Sharp	(Japan)	2.6	2.6
Merloni	(Italy)	2.3	2.5

Source: *Euromonitor: Global Market Information Database*, 'The world market for domestic electrical appliances', November 2003.

Table 2   Ranking of ten largest corporations by revenues
             (US$ million) 2001-2002

	2001	2002
Whirlpool	10,343	11,016
Electrolux	8,935	9,763
Matsushita	10,829	9,395
Haier Group	7,271	8,587
General Electric (Appliances)	5,810	6,072
Bosch-Siemens Hausgeräte	5,439	5,933
LG Group	3,844	4,829
Maytag	3,955	4,421
Samsung Electronics	2,965	3,678
Merloni	1,760	2,340

Source: *Euromonitor: Global Market Information Database*, 'The world
           market for domestic electrical appliances', November 2003.

There is a spatial dimension to this evolving industry structure, with serious consequences for unionism. The competitive war between these big corporations is being waged through lean production restructuring and geographic shifts to cheap labour zones, most notably Eastern Europe, Mexico and China. Electrolux has acquired factories in these areas and has identified its new plant in the Hunan province of China as its 'global production platform', signalling that the future of its factories in other countries could not be guaranteed. A key facet of General Electric Appliances (GEA) restructuring is the relocation of production from six unionised plants in the USA that employ 11,500 workers, to non-unionised factories in Mexico and Latin America. GEA developed a 48.5 percent stake in Mabe, a Mexican company, which has since become one of the most important producers of white goods in the region, employing an estimated 18,000 workers who annually produce over 4.5 million appliances.

Similarly, a significant feature of Whirlpool's global strategy is taking advantage of NAFTA to relocate a substantial volume of manufacturing to Mexico's 'maquiladora' free trade zone, where production costs are subsidised and where labour is cheap, defenceless and more exploitable. In 1997 Whirlpool began shifting production of small refrigerators from a US-based plant to Mexico. Whirlpool and GEA's relocation strategies led to the development of four 'appliance' production clusters (Monterrey, San Luis Potosi, Puebla, Queretaro). The underlying reason for the growth of these clusters was obvious; workers at the GE/Mabe cooker plant in Mexico were reported to be receiving US$15 per day, equivalent to the hourly wage received by US-based GE workers making the same products.[3] By 2002 Whirlpool had bought out its local joint venture partner (Grupo Vitro) to become Mexico's second largest white goods manufacturer. In the same year, combined appliance exports from Whirlpool and GE/Mabe in Mexico were thought to total more than US$1 billion, a tenfold increase from the year in which NAFTA came into effect.[4] It was not only 'Anglo-American' corporations that drove the growth of the appliance industry in Mexico. Korean-based LG Electronics (LGE) announced its ambitions by constructing a new Mexican plant to act as a 'regional production base' for white goods. LGE was said to have invested US$100 million in the plant, built on a 30,000-square metre site in Monterrey in the northeast.[5]

The threat of relocation forced unions into concession bargaining. For instance, in 1999 GEA workers at a Louisville (USA) plant agreed to assist in finding US$80 million in cost reductions in order to prevent the company shifting all refrigerator production to Mexico. Similarly, GEA workers in a unionised plant based in Indiana were

---

3   Millman, J. (1999) 'Mexico Builds a Home-Appliance Bonanza: GE, Whirlpool
     Shift Production, Boost Exports to U.S.', *Wall Street Journal*, 23 August.
4   Millman, J. (2002) 'Grupo Vitro Will Sell Unit to Whirlpool for $540 Million',
     Wall Street Journal, 26 February.
5   LGE Media Release, 7 July 2000, 'LGE to Build Consumer Electronics Plant in
     Mexico', accessed at www.lge.nl/nieuws/globaal/2000/mexico on 25 January
     2002.

confronted with a stark choice: slash costs by US$95 million or face the loss of 1400 jobs.[6]

If Mexico was the fulcrum of new investments in the late 1990s, it was only a matter of time before the disciplinary power of unconstrained capital mobility impacted even Mexican conditions. By late 2002 the business press signalled that Mexico was losing its 'magic' for restless investors seeking ever-greater reductions in labour costs and increases in profits.[7] According to one report, industries in the maquiladora zone were confronting new competitive threats from even lower wage production in China, with the CEO of Mabe announcing that he was 'worried' about this threat and expressing doubt as to the region's ability to attract new investments. Alluding to the possibility of relocation to China, executives in other industries castigated the Mexican government for failing to provide adequate infrastructure, attractive tax incentives, and more 'flexible' labour markets.[8] The competitive 'threat' from China, however, resulted in relatively few cases of relocation, while the lay-off of hundreds of thousands of workers in the maquiladora zone in 2001–02 was clearly related to a slowdown in US consumer demand. In this way, the mere threat of relocation to Asia was thought to provide an effective tactical means of creating a climate of 'fear' in order to suppress rising real wages, erode employee benefits, allow for 'flexibility' in replacing permanent staff with casual employees, and advance demands for regulatory restructuring.[9]

Under pressure from this global restructure, Electrolux sought to arrest its declining rate of profit through an aggressive global shift to these cheap labour zones. It set a target of 6 to 7 percent for its operating margin and around 15 percent for its rate of return on equity.[10] The company lifted its operating margin from 4.0 percent in

6   Murray, M. (1999) 'Will the New Repairman Be Able to Fix GE's Appliances Division?', *Wall Street Journal*, 15 November.
7   Smith, G. (2001) 'Is the Magic Starting to Fade for Manufacturing in Mexico?', *BusinessWeek*, 6 August.
8   Ibid.
9   Bacon, D. (2003) 'Anti-China Campaign Hides Maquiladora Wage Cuts', *ZNet*, 3 February (available at http://www.zmag.org/).
10   Electrolux, Annual Report 1997, p.7.

1997 to 5.2 percent in 1998, and thereafter reported an operating margin of 6.2 percent in 1999 and 6.5 percent in 2000. As Electrolux's report for the year 2000 shows, these results were achieved by a zealous strategy of closures, downsizing and relocations that led to sharply rising stock market values between 1997 and 1999.[11] Its annual reports reveal the significance of geographic relocation. During 2002 the company closed cooker factories in Sweden, Italy and Germany, relocating production to Romania and it has shifted some production capacity from a Spanish refrigeration plant to one in Hungary. The wave of rationalisations continued through 2003. An air-conditioning plant in New Jersey in the US was closed, resulting in the loss of over 1300 jobs. In Europe, the company announced its plans to close three facilities, a refrigeration plant and a cooking hob factory in Germany and a cooker plant in Norway.[12] In 2004 it closed a vacuum cleaner plant in Vastervik, Sweden, resulting in the loss of 600 jobs, and it threatened to close a refrigeration plant in Greenville, Michigan, where it employs 2700 workers. A new refrigeration plant is planned for Mexico. Its most recent announcement is the establishment of a global factory in the Hunan province of China. Electrolux's strategy with regard to these relocations has been labelled 'regime shopping'. When it enters into a bargaining process with unions in a particular country, it leverages agreements to restructure (intensify labour, downsize and casualise) by threatening closure and relocation to a place where labour costs are lower. Its bargaining agreements at national level are of short duration, forcing unions to bargain away conditions in the hope that this might influence the company's future 'regime shopping' decisions. This strategy had its genesis with Nike; the Asian producers contracted to Nike constantly competed for short term contracts. The difference is that Electrolux has inserted this system within its own companies.

Electrolux's acquisition of Email in Australia has had a crucial bearing on the nature of the most recent attacks on unionism in that country. There is a simple logical sequence in its strategy. Setting up factories in cheap labour zones enables the corporation to threaten

---

11   Tatge, M. (2000) 'How Swede It Is', *Forbes*, 24 July: 56–7.
12   *Electrolux Annual Report 2002*: 17–18.

closure in unionised zones unless unions intensify production and bargain away conditions. This strategic positioning has meant that Electrolux is an active agent in shaping the anti-union agenda of the Conservative Government's industrial relations reforms.

An example will illustrate the *lead* role of Electrolux in the negation of historically bargained labour rights and standards. Australian industrial relations evolved as a system of industry-based awards, which were the product of a bargaining process. Historically, these awards (legal agreements) covered a wide range of conditions. In the course of 2001 and 2002, soon after the multi-national had acquired Email, Electrolux went to the Federal Court of Australia to argue that terms in an agreement should be limited to issues that pertain to 'the relationship between employer and employee', this being narrowly defined. The Federal Court ruled in the company's favour, only for its decision to be overturned by the Full Court of the Federal Court. Electrolux then appealed to the High Court, which ruled in its favour. The company spent a lot of money to traverse this long legal process. The ruling was that agreements could not contain 'non-pertaining' subject matter, which includes the following range of issues: the deduction of union dues; the entitlement of union delegates to attend trade union training; the encouragement and facilitation of union membership; union right of entry; limitations on the use of contractors and the role of labour hire agencies; and the use of Australian-made goods. As a consequence of the decision, if unions take industrial action in support of any of these claims, they will be exposed to legal proceedings. In line with the legal precedent that Electrolux established, the current wave of industrial change introduced by the Federal Government restricts the content of agreements even further. These changes have led to mass protest rallies across Australia in which civil society united against the state's market driven agenda. As will be seen, Electrolux has not only changed the industrial relations system, it has been active in implementing the anti-union provisions of the 1996 Workplace Relations Act.

Electrolux presents an image of corporate social responsibility, which contradicts these Australian interventions and its implementation of restructuring. As a leading Swedish MNC, the company has developed corporate policies consistent with the values of Swedish social democracy. It is a member of the United Nations Global Compact, which states, 'Businesses should uphold the freedom of association and the effective recognition of the right to collective bargaining' (Section Three). In early 2002 its Group Management adopted a Workplace Code of Conduct. The Code defines minimum acceptable work standards and is based on internationally recognised treaties and agreements, such as the core conventions of the International Labor Organization and the OECD Guidelines for Multinational Enterprises. The Code includes a commitment to freedom of association and the company states that its suppliers are required to comply with the code.

The following analysis of restructuring in three Electrolux factories captures the contradiction between this image of social responsibility and the consequences of management decisions. The human impacts and union response to three decisions of the Electrolux Board are examined: the closure of the Chef cooker plant in Melbourne, Australia; the demise of the fridge factory in Orange, New South Wales, Australia; and the planned closure of a fridge factory in Greenville, Michigan. The neglected psychological and social dimension of market ideology that legitimates restructuring is highlighted through ethnographic research in the two Australian companies.[13] Based on participant observation and qualitative interviews, the study is longitudinal so that the full impact over time can be assessed.[14] Capturing the experience of victims is crucial to the GSMU project. Can anger be channelled into a new movement-building project, or will victims simply slide into fatalism? Will these closures be fought, or viewed as inevitable? Polanyi contends that the embrace of market ideology creates a counter movement against its destructive power.

---

13   We are planning to develop a similar project in Greenville.
14   Research at the Chef factory was conducted between 1995 and its closure in 2001. Since then, contact has been maintained with management and workers to assess the impact of the event on their lives. A similar method has been adopted in Orange since 2003. Here I have had to meet workers outside of the factory as the Electrolux management stated that I am 'not a friend of Electrolux'. Doubtlessly, they have read my article 2004 article on Chef.

The process is more complex. Resistance possibilities exist alongside passivity before global corporate power.

The Closure of Chef

The Chef cooker plant in inner-city Melbourne reflected the essence of the social contract described in the previous section. Protection provided stability and predictability, whilst wage increases stimulated market demand for the stoves the plant produced. The workforce was fully unionised and collective bargaining was accepted (Lambert 2004). Economically, the company was a paragon of success, capturing 39 percent of the Australian cooker market by the early 1980s when Chef became the leading Australian brand. By the 1990s profits averaged around A\$28 million per annum, high compared to similar-size manufacturing ventures in Australia. Because of its success, Chef was a prime target for acquisition. In the early 1990s Southcorp, a leading Australian winery acquired the iconic company, utilising the profits to further advance its wine interests instead of reinvesting in the factory. Late in the decade, the cooker producer's major Australian competitor, Email, acquired Chef. Two years later, Email itself succumbed to a bid by Electrolux, and part of the deal was the closure of Chef.

The story of Chef could end here. Economic deregulation, free trade, restructuring, closure – the market is the final arbiter. However, Polanyi (1957) offers a different perspective when he reflects on the human and social cost of self regulating markets. A seven-year ethnographic project in the factory (1995 to the 2001 closure) provided a unique vantage point to assess this negated dimension of restructuring. These are the voices that are absent in the Boardroom where fateful decisions are made.

Mick:

I came here as a young kid. It's as if someone's taken your home away from you – it hurts. I was brought up here. I learnt everything here. For someone to come in here and just close the place down – what a pack of fucking hypocrites these people are. They spit in your face. They treat you like shit. They have never set foot in this place. Do they know what they have done to us?

We were called into the boardroom and we all sat there waiting for the decision to be made by the board of directors in Sydney. Deep in my heart, deep in my heart, I never ever, ever thought they would close us down. I said, no they can't close us down. We're making profits, were making money, we've got good product, we've got the market – they can't close us down. It's impossible, it's impossible. It would take a brave man to try to close us down because it just does not make any sense – why would they want to close down such a great company?

Then we heard the announcement that they were going to close us down. I was sitting in the boardroom with my legs crossed. It must have been the nerves in my legs – I just kicked the bloody table. I got hot and flustered. I really wanted to reach over and grab this person by the throat. I wanted to climb over the table and punch his lights out.

I was very, very bitter and I said, NO I'm going to fight this. I rang up and joined the union and organised rallies at Brunswick town hall.

Politicians haven't got the guts to try and save manufacturing in Australia. We're just heading towards becoming just another third world country.

Ross:

It was the end of the world for me. I came here thirty five years ago. This was my first job. All of a sudden, someone makes a decision and it's all over. I cried. I had to go home and break the news to my wife and my family.

Ron:

It's just unbelievable to think that something like this could happen here. Just gone. What have we done wrong for it to come to this? Who would have believed that this could happen? Everyone is just in a state of shock. No one spoke – it's too painful to mention – it's like a death in the family. What do you say, what do you feel when faced with a death?

Luli, an assembly line woman worker, who had migrated from Greece:

> Where we go now? Even young people can't find jobs. My mind still fast. My hands still fast, but they close the factory. You can't forget. They take it from you.

Jeff, a young male assembly line worker:

> Electrolux is run by the rich. Personally, I don't like the rich people. All they do is think about their money. They don't give a shit, all they think about is their pocket and the ways that they can spend their money. That's the biggest issue, right?
>
> There are people starving, and these Electrolux people, they've got so much money, they don't know what to do with it, right? Like the boss from Electrolux, whoever he is that makes this shit decision.
>
> This is why the world is turning out to be such a terrible place to live in, because it's only good for the rich, so the days of Robin Hood when you pinch from the rich, them were the good days – them days – perfect!

Stan, an elderly assembly line worker:

> Politicians are scum. They forget about working people. When they want our vote, they come to us. After the vote, they change their story. Look at how many factories have just closed in Victoria – Dunlop, Arnotts, Ansett.

Frank, a middle aged male press shop worker:

> Politicians are big bludgers. They get money for do nothing. I work hard and get paid peanuts. Politicians try to sell us policies like they sell cigarettes, like they selling soap. When are they going to create something different? When are they going to get down to the people and understand our situation? Politicians don't listen to us. They need to represent us. They just represent themselves and forget why they are there.

Shock, pain, depression, a sense of class injustice and anger against the corporate leadership of Electrolux and Australian politicians – how is this experience 'measured' against Electrolux's profit? Will these feelings trigger a counter movement? Whatever opportunity may have existed within this emotional turmoil was missed. The Australian Workers Union (AWU) branch that was present in the factory was a weak, company-orientated, bureaucratic union that competed for membership in the metals sector with the left wing Australian Manufacturing Workers Union (AMWU), which had no presence in Chef. The AWU organised a town hall protest meeting together with several street protests outside the plant. At the time of the closure, the Victorian Branch of the AWU was led by Bill Shorten, a relatively young State Secretary who aspired to a career in politics and has been touted as a future Labour Prime Minister. SIGTUR (the Southern Initiative on Globalisation and Trade Union Rights), a campaign-orientated, global social movement in the South, approached Shorten and suggested the local campaign should be globalised. He appeared interested and the following plan, involving both the AWU and the AMWU, was partially implemented.

The AWU contacted the International Metal Federation (IMF) and requested that the Global Union Federation (GUF) set up meetings with the Swedish unions in Electrolux, with a view to forcing the Chef issue onto the corporate agenda. The initial request (stage one) was a simple one; the IMF should organise a meeting between Electrolux worker leaders from Australia and Sweden to fully brief Swedish leaders on the plight of Australian workers. Since Electrolux was also rationalising its European operations, it was felt that Swedish workers would not be indifferent. Australian workers had videotaped interviews with factory workers expressing their outrage at the closure that could be used in educational forums in Stockholm. The AWU sent a formal request to the IMF that global restructuring be challenged through globalising unionism. The purpose of the cross-border worker meetings was not only to raise consciousness but also to endorse the following action plan.

In phase two of the plan, the Electrolux union in Sweden would request a meeting with CEO Michael Treschow and his board members in order to personally deliver a statement opposing the Australian closure and demanding that the board reverse the decision. Rejection would be a predictable outcome, since the Board has made it clear that restructuring is a managerial prerogative. In anticipation of such a response, the following proposal was presented to the IMF. The international should draw the International Transport Federation (ITF) into the process. Electrolux's container movements should be identified and mapped. Relevant stevedoring and shipping unions would be briefed and won over. Electrolux would be threatened with zero movement of its commodities; just-in-time supply chains would be disrupted until the MNC agreed to negotiate.

This initiative never got off the ground for two reasons. Firstly, the IMF eventually responded negatively, arguing that such a course of action was not feasible because, 'The IMF is not a campaign oriented body'.[15] Fredericks contended that the IMF simply did not have the resources and the personnel to engage in a campaign with this level of detail, which required persistence and follow up. Furthermore he argued that Swedish workers, like other European workers, were self-preoccupied and were unlikely to commit to the plight of Australian workers. The global initiative lost its momentum when Shorten's interest waned. He had acquired a political modus operandi and moved swiftly between issues in his effort to maintain a high media profile.

Subsequent interviews with unemployed Chef workers reveal their profound sense of abandonment. Who is concerned about their plight? Not the AWU, not politicians, not church leaders, not the media. These workers are the forgotten remnant, alone with their personal pain, their waves of depression, their family breakdowns, and their isolation. They are persons on the scrapheap, at best mere survivors with memories of a life that was; a sense of existence that is a premature daily dying; time without spirit, will, hope, a mechanical functioning through seemingly endless days. They view themselves as the forgotten victims of corporate restructuring. In the reality of their commodity status, being nothing more than a 'factor of production', emotion holds no currency; feelings are worth nothing in the tough world of market efficiency.

---

15 Statement by Assistant General Secretary of the IMF, Brian Fredericks, September 2000.

The Fridge Factory in Orange

Orange is a country town approximately 500 km inland from Sydney. A large munitions factory was built in the town during World War II. The town was 'seething with anger' when the state government announced the factory would be closed immediately after the war. A meeting resolved, 'If the government can't run the factory then we workers will organise and run it ourselves'. The threat led to a sit-in strike in the factory (Edwards 1996: 1, 7). The government conceded and provided incentives to secure a commitment from Email, an Australian company, to establish a fridge factory in the town. To ensure that the factory prospered, the government subsidised the costs of decentralising production by offering freight concessions and financial incentives. They also expanded a housing program in Orange, thereby rendering the locale attractive to workers (Clarke 1983: 33).

> Trade unionism was strong in the town and unions were unafraid to take strike action. A union delegate reflected on the culture of solidarity that shaped work and life in the town.
>   In the past they couldn't put it over you. They knew you were not going to back down. In the past if they tried to push us we would have all been out on the grass for weeks. We used to organise a barbeque out in the front – sort of in their faces you know.[16]

Social contract capitalism was the bedrock of this assertive culture. Through the bargaining process established by the industrial relations system unions fought for 'reasonable working conditions' and won a 38-hour week, holiday leave, pensions and equal pay for women (Edwards 1996: 61). As a result of these gains, workers regarded the factory as 'a reasonably humane place to work'.[17]

As was the case with Chef, these local corporate histories count for little in the Stockholm boardroom, where the Orange factory, like all others on the global map, is measured only by its contribution to the MNC's shareholder value. Once it had acquired the plant, Electro-

---

16   Interview, union delegate, September 2003.
17   Interview, 26 April 2005.

lux immediately initiated a restructure, marginalised unionism, and set about changing the workplace culture. It applied simple and effective pressure to fast track these changes: the threat of closure. Workers were made aware of the new mega-factory it had built in China. The meaning of the term 'global production platform' was obvious. The threat sent a shock wave through the workforce, for it threatened the lifestyle choice workers had made decades earlier. Most had left the cities of Melbourne and Sydney to create a new life for their families in the rural setting of Orange.

The restructure was a classic lean production initiative: down-sizing, work intensification (increased line speed), outsourcing, and a new despotic managerialism reminiscent of Henry Ford's first factories, where talking to workmates on the line was forbidden. Over the past two years the workforce has been cut from 1800 to just 400. Management set a target of increasing output by 50 percent through investing in new technology. This also required a leap forward in productivity through radical downsizing. Electrolux's Director of Australian Manufacturing, Leon Andrewartha stated that the Orange plant benchmarked against the LG factory in Korea. He argued that the Koreans were 'light years' ahead in productivity:

> We are basically now using very similar plant equipment. But they run at 10 products per person per day. We're running at 2.2–2.3. [It is] because of work tempo, they've got the volume; they're running a fridge every 12 seconds. I mean those people, when I say work, they work. They're doing exercise in the morning not to feel good, it's so they can work flat out for 8–10 hours a day for six days a week. How do I create an environment that lets us work at the same rate and tempo that they do?

The work tempo had to increase, according to Andrewartha. His problem is simple: how much work can a person do in a five-minute period? The answer hinges on a renewed focus on Taylorist principles. The shift to work teams 'was the biggest balls up of all time', because it neglected real productivity gains through scientific management. A consequence of the dramatic increase in line speed is repetitive stress syndrome (RSI). 96 percent of those interviewed between June 2003 and June 2005 suffer body damage as a result of this work intensification.

Management was able to impose this new work regime because they broke the independent power base the unions had established in the factory over the past sixty years. They achieved this goal through skilfully applying the provisions of the 1996 Workplace Relations Act. Their strategy mirrored that of the Coalition Government. On the surface it seemed as if little had changed. Union delegates are still recognised in the factory and they have company phone access to union organisers. What has changed under Swedish ownership is that these organisers are denied access to the factory under the provisions of the new act; delegates are not allowed to engage in union activity during working hours (and this includes talking to workers), and union meetings in the plant are forbidden. When a new enterprise agreement was being negotiated the company applied the ballot provisions of the Act on key issues. The union narrowly lost these votes because they had no opportunity to present their case. This reveals how Electrolux operates in a manner not dissimilar to the Australian government. It claims consistency with the United Nations Social Compact and its own Workplace Code on collective bargaining rights by not banning unions, whilst at the same time severely restricting unions inside the factory to a degree where they are rendered relatively ineffective. In the short space of three years, the union became a shadow of its former self with the remaining delegates contending that workers 'no longer gave a shit', believing that the factory would close anyway. This is the iron fist behind the velvet glove. The company appears to act consistently with the corporate social responsibility principles it has adopted, whilst subtly marginalising organised opposition.

Union organisers in the town appear bereft of ideas other than upholding their role as redundancy negotiators. Like the AMU at Chef, they conducted a mass meeting in the town hall in June 2003 when the first major wave of downsizing was announced. At this meeting the union leadership expressed anger against Electrolux and the exploitative attitude of MNCs, but it advanced no resistance strategy. Not surprisingly, fatalism pervades the town.

Electrolux in Greenville, Michigan

The similarities between the factories in Orange and Greenville, a country town in Michigan, are striking. Both are converted munitions factories; the viability of both is tied to the plant; and the plants in both have been bought by Electrolux and then threatened with closure. The factory in Greenville is large, employing 2700 workers who produce 1.3 million fridges a year. 21 October 2003 was the fateful day when company executives met with the local leadership of the United Auto Workers (UAW) and announced that the factory would close and relocate to Mexico where they would save US$81 million a year through lower wage and environmental costs. The executives outlined that the wages and benefits package cost the company US$22.99 an hour in the United States (US$15 base wage), whereas they could hire labour for US$3.60 an hour in Mexico (US$1.57 base wage). Furthermore, the company will escape environmental regulation. In the US it is required to switch to environmentally friendly foam for the fridges that would raise costs by US$8 per unit, whereas Mexico does not impose this obligation. It claimed that these wages and environmental costs meant that it had 'no choice' but to relocate. The Greenville plant would continue operating through 2005 and possibly into 2006, whilst Electrolux set up production in Mexico.

For shareholders, relocation is positive since it signals Electrolux's commitment to profit maximisation, whilst for the workers, the decision had, in an instant, devastated their lives. Their feelings were identical to the displaced workers of Chef and Orange. They were 'stunned, devastated'. They experienced 'shock' and feelings of 'agony' that would not go away. Understandably, consequences for their families were of primary concern. Teenage children spoke at public meetings and shared fears of the loss of home and possessions. As was the case at Chef and Orange, employment is based on extended family networks with husbands, wives and relatives working at the factory, thereby magnifying the proposed closure's impact. Once the factory closed, the only option is accepting low wages and an anti-union environment at Wal-Mart. Most feared losing their medical insurance.

The prevailing sentiment is that 'the community is going to fall apart' because of the impact of closure on the life and the viability of families.[18] Closure will drain Greenville of US$437,000 in tax revenue each year.[19] As management statements rejecting the plan to save the plant reveal, Electrolux is indifferent to these human costs. When it devastates the community, when it exploits Mexican workers, it is not making ethical decisions. These are rational, economic choices; they are simply an application of 'the best interests of the corporation' principle (Bakan 2004: 36).

Over the past fifteen months, UAW Local 137 has been fighting the closure. A critical discourse emerged: 'Corporations aren't about heart, they're about profits'; this was 'a cold blooded corporate decision'; the company had 'chalked up another win for corporate greed'.[20] The union linked with the state government and tried conces-sion bargaining. They offered contract concessions of more than US$32 million a year through a sacrifice of wages and conditions, whilst local government formulated a raft of tax breaks. These included US$83 million in tax credits over the next 20 years; US$31 million over 15 years for a tax free renaissance zone credit; a community development grant of US$2 million for public works at the site; US$3.9 million over 15 years in education tax credits; and finally, a US$65,883 cut in local property taxes for the next 12 years. Electrolux's stance was uncompromising. It rejected the offer out of hand, pointing out that it was well short of the US$81 million that it would save by relocating to Mexico.

Whilst concession bargaining was the primary focus of UAW strategy, the union also mobilised the community, organising an American jobs rally that linked workers across the US. Workers spoke out against 'accountant like economic restructuring' that failed to recognise people and their families. They were 'waking up from the

---

18   UAW Local 137, online, January/February, 2004.
19   Online *Holland Sentinal*, 12 August 2004.
20   Comments of UAW Local 137 posted on the UAW web site, *Solidarity*. See January/February and March/April 2004.

American dream' since losing jobs also meant losing health insurance. Despite the anger a sense of fatalism seems to pervade. Workers spoke of 'constant feelings of powerlessness and paralysis'.[21] A fatalistic acceptance of closure is captured in the statement by one of the local union leaders, 'I have my resume out. I have one daughter in college and two more kids who will be going in the next couple of years. I don't know where I'm going to be able to find a good paying job, especially one with health care insurance and a real pension. But I'm out there looking'. He fears losing a job that pays US$15 an hour with health care, dental insurance and a defined pension plan, and he faces a future with a Wal-Mart-type job, if he can find one, that will pay US$8 an hour with virtually no benefits.[22]

These three examples of restructuring by a powerful global corporation such as Electrolux serve to confirm the unilateral character of these changes. When the company cooperated in establishing a European Works Council, they asserted that restructuring was off the agenda and could never be negotiated. These cases also reveal the paralysis of unions when confronted by these impositions. In the final section of this chapter a GSMU alternative is considered.

Global Social Movement Unionism

The response of the trade unions involved in these factories is traditional: a mass protest rally, concession bargaining, the search for state financial support, and inevitably, the negotiation of redundancies. Research into the response in the Australian factories reveals the deep

---

21   UAW Local 137, web site posting, 3 August 2004.

22   Senate Policy Committee Hearing: 'Shipping American Jobs Overseas: A Hearing on the Bush Administration's Claim that Outsourcing is Good for the US Economy', record of the presentation by David Doolittle, Greenville, Michigan, 5 March 2004.

pessimism of organisers, who are dubious that global corporations can be resisted. Pessimism is the death knell of a movement response to restructuring, reinforcing the view that there is indeed no alternative. If such an attitude is maintained, unions will become increasingly insignificant. The KCTU statement quoted in the introduction recognises the failure of traditional methods of organisation and struggle. If unions are to secure a future as civil society actors, a new phase of experimentation is essential.

The opportunity to experiment resides in the fact that there is a one to two year stay of execution for the two remaining factories as Electrolux fine tunes its Mexican and Chinese operations. My participant observation of one mass meeting at Orange in June 2003 revealed that these events stimulate a movement potential, for it was here that workers shared their trauma and their anger, and here that deeper, more organic social bonds were in the making. This is where they gained a sense of unity built on a common experience since restructuring had left none unscathed. Yet the meeting also showed that traditional unionism appeared bereft of ideas and as a consequence the energy of these meetings dissipated. No strategic plan of resistance was presented to those who participated. However, the story does not end here.

At this apparent dead end, SIGTUR intervened with an alternative plan, which reflected many features of the earlier failed intervention when Chef was shut down. SIGTUR grew out of a 'thought experiment' (Harvey 2000, 117) and the movement is based on a culture of bold experimentation to which the KCTU alluded. From its origins in 1990, it was a conscious attempt to build a counter movement to the power of global corporations (Waterman and Wills 2001; Sandbrook 2003; Taylor 2004). Following the June 2003 rally in Orange, SIGTUR entered into discussions with local union delegates, local organisers and national officials, asserting that Electrolux's plans to close the Orange plant could be countered. An alternative strategy had to be imagined, debated and then translated into union policy. The following account presents a brief summary of policy decisions that arose out of this process.

An action group is being formed in Orange comprising union delegates and community leaders. The June rally garnered strong community support for the workers' cause from local fruit farmers, small shopkeepers and citizens more generally who are concerned about the likely impact of the factory closure on the town. Apple farmers in the area were engaged in their own intense struggle against free trade, fearing that imports could introduce fire blight disease into Australia for the first time. These farmers had already organised a protest in the town centre where they threw petrol over a container load of apples and burnt them to a cinder to symbolise what would happen to their orchards if they were contaminated. The group plans to link the farmers' concerns about the future security of their industry with the predicament of workers. Broadening the social base in this way provides scope for building a social movement in the area.

The action group plans to create a web site and establish communications with the Greenville workers. The initial aim is to share experiences as victims of Electrolux restructuring, which may lead to exchange visits. Decisions taken at the national level complemented this local initiative. The Australian Manufacturing Workers Union (AMWU) has proposed that a modified version of a World Company Council (WCC) be created. The formation of WCCs was a policy initiative of the International Metal Workers Federation (IMF), which endorsed the creation of such a body for Electrolux in the mid 1970s. This was a paper tiger as the IMF never actually established an Electrolux WCC. In reacting to the present crisis in Orange, AMWU leaders believe the IMF initiative was stillborn because proposed councils were too large. Hence they argue for a lean WCC that will not drain scarce resources. The revised WCC could play a vital role in coordinating action against Electrolux along the lines originally proposed in the Chef case. The AMWU national leadership also argued for the creation of a research group linked to both the WCC and the local action groups. The research group would monitor Electrolux and provide information that would provide a foundation for a critical discourse on restructuring.

These new complementary structures in the making are the essential support mechanisms for the creation of a GSMU, which may be defined as the cyberspace for linking local social movements that have emerged in opposition to restructuring. In this way, GSMU is triggered by existing national unions and is dependent on their commitment. Thus traditional and new forms of unionism continue to coexist in a complementary commitment. GSMU will not come into being without the commitment and imagination of traditional collective bargaining unionism.

Conclusion

The potential of this emerging new form of unionism resides in the fact that it addresses the geography of corporate power. Corporations use space and scale to strengthen their power against the state and civil society. As the Orange case illustrates, unions have the potential to reconfigure their own power through networking across the geographical sites of global corporations. Here the first tentative step is contact with the Greenville workers.

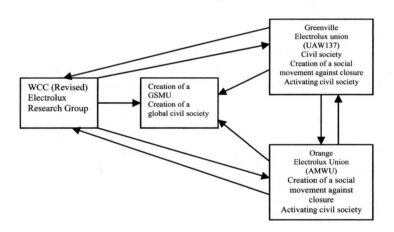

The acid test of this initiative is whether or not the fatalism engendered by restructuring can be transformed. The longitudinal research in Orange over the past 3 years reveals a complex and contradictory picture. There are activists from the shop floor who have become disillusioned by the union's inability to fight the waves of downsizing and work intensification. They 'don't give a shit anymore'. Some union organisers are now cynical and just go through the motions. However, despite this quite pervasive negative spirit, there remains a core of committed activists determined to fight the company's plans to the last. They form the nucleus capable of building the action group. Success in this endeavour is possible because of the commitment of the national leadership of the AMWU, who have vision, imagination and long term political commitment to the working class.

This chapter has analysed the power of global corporations through the Electrolux case study. This power was augmented when the Australian national state deregulated its economy, thereby accelerating acquisitions and mergers. Local companies were no match for the global players and their demise was paralleled by industrial 'reform', which has marginalised trade unions. Corporations describe restructuring in the language of market economics: efficiency, flexibility, competitiveness. Ethnographic research in the two Australian companies sought to reclaim the human and social dimensions of this process. The final section considered whether or not these impacts could be channelled into a GSMU with the capacity to eventually resist the unending restructuring agenda of global corporations. The experiment in the country town of Orange may contribute to a necessary debate on the reconfiguration of trade union power.

References

Bakan, J. (2004) *The Corporation: The Pathological Pursuit of Profit and Power*, London: Constable.

Bamber, G., Lansbury, R. and Wailes, N. (2004) *International and Comparative Employment Relations: Globalisation and the Developed Market Economies*, Sydney: Allen and Unwin.

Batliwala, S. (2002) 'Grassroots Movement as Transnational Actors: Implications for Global Civil Society', *Voluntas* 13(4): 393–410.

Calland, C. and Sil, R. (eds) (2001) *The Politics of Labour in a Global Age: Continuity and Change in Late-Industrialising and Post-Socialist Economies*, Oxford: Oxford University Press.

Centre of Indian Trade Unions (CITU) (2003) *United Struggles and the Organizational Consolidation of the Trade Union Movement*, Calcutta: CITU.

— (2005) 'The Attack on Labour Rights in India', paper presented to the 7th Congress of SIGTUR, Bangkok, June 2005.

Clark, L. (1983) 'Restructuring in the Whitegoods Industry: 1973–1983', Bachelor of Science Honours Degree thesis, School of Earth Sciences, Macquarie University.

Cobble, D. (2001) 'Lost Ways of Unionism: Historical Perspectives on Reinventing the labor Movement', in L. Turner, H.C. Katz and R.W. Hurd (eds) *Rekindling the Movement: Labor's Quest for Relevance in the 21st Century*, Ithaca NY: ILR Press.

Edwards, E. (1996) *Weapons to Whitegoods: Celebrating Email's 50 Years in Orange*, Orange: Orange City Council.

Gallin, D. (2001) 'Propositions on Trade Unions and Informal Employment in Times of Globalization', in P. Waterman and J. Wills (eds) *Place, Space and the New Labour Internationalism*, London: Blackwell.

— (2004) 'Political Education and Globalisation', paper presented to the International Federation of Worker Education Associations Seminar, Eastbourne, 9 October.

Harvey, D. (1996) *Justice, Nature and the Geography of Difference*, Oxford: Blackwell.

— (2000) *Spaces of Hope*, Edinburgh: Edinburgh University Press.

Hathaway, D. (2000) *Allies across the Border: Mexico's 'Authentic Labor Front' and Global Solidarity*, Boston: South End Press.

Haworth, N. and Ramsay, H. (1986) 'Workers of the World Untied: A Critical Analysis of the Labor Response to the Internationalization of Capital', *International Journal of the Sociology of Law and Social Policy*, 6(2): 55–82.

Herod, A. (2001) 'Labor Internationalism and the Contradictions of Globalization: Or, Why the Local is Sometimes Still Important in a Global Economy', in P. Waterman and J. Wills (eds) *Place, Space and the New Labour Internationalism*, London: Blackwell.

— (2001) *Labor Geographies*, London: The Guilford Press.

— (2003) 'The Geographies of Labor Internationalism', *Social Science History* 27(4): 501-23.

— and Wright, M. (2002) *Geographies of Power: Placing Scale*, Oxford: Blackwell.

Kelly, P. (1992) *The End of Certainty: The Story of the 1980s*, Sydney: Allen and Unwin.

KCTU (Korean Confederation of Trade Unions), 'KCTU Report on the Recent Situation of Labour Law and Industrial Relations', paper presented to the 7th Congress of SIGTUR, Bangkok, June 2005.

Johnston, P. (2001) 'Organize for What? The Resurgence of Labor as a Citizenship Movement', in L. Turner, H.C. Katz and R.W. Hurd (eds) *Rekindling the Movement: Labor's Quest for Relevance in the 21st Century*, Ithaca NY: ILR Press.

Lambert, R. and Webster, E. (1988) 'The Re-Emergence of Political Unionism in Contemporary South Africa', in W. Cobbet and R. Cohen (eds) *Popular Struggles in South Africa*, Trenton, NJ: Africa World Press.

Lambert, R. (1990) 'Kilusang Mayo Uno and the Rise of Social Movement Unionism in the Philippines', *Labor & Industry* 2 and 3.

— (1996) 'Asian Trade and Australian Labour Market Restructuring', in R. Robison (ed.) *Pathways to Asia*, Sydney: Allen & Unwin.

— (1997) *State and Labor in New Order Indonesia*. Perth: University of Western Australia Press.

— (1998) 'Asian Labour Markets and International Competitiveness: Australian Transformations', *International Review of Comparative Public Policy*, 10(special issue, Labour Markets in Transition: International Dimensions): 271–96.

— (1999) 'Australia's Historic Industrial Relations Transition', in P. Leisink (ed.) *Globalisation and Labour Relations*, London: Edward Elgar.

— (2000) 'Globalisation and the Erosion of Class Compromise in Contemporary Australia', *Politics and Society* 28(1): 93–118.

— (2003) 'Transnational Union Strategies: Civilizing Labour Standards', in R. Sandbrook (ed.) *Civilizing Globalisation: A Survival Guide*, Albany: State University of New York Press.

— (2004) 'Death of a Factory: An Ethnography of Market Rationalism's Hidden Abode in Inner-City Melbourne', *Anthropological Forum* 14(3): 297–313.

Martin, R. (1975) *Trade Unions in Australia*, Harmondsworth: Penguin.

Marx, K. (1976) *Capital Volume One*, London: Penguin.

Meszaros, I. (1979) *The Work of Sartre: The Search for Freedom*, Brighton: Harvester Press.

Moody, K. (1997) *Workers in a Lean World: Unions in the International Economy*, London: Verso.

Munck, R. (1988) *The New International Labor Studies: An Introduction*, London: Zed Books.

Munck, R. (2002) *Globalization and Labour: The New 'Great Transformation'*, London: Zed Books.

Nichols, T. and Cam, S. (2005) *Labour in a Global World: The Case of White Goods*, London: Palgrave.

O'Brien, R. (2000) 'Workers and the World Order: The Tentative Transformation of the International Union Movement', *Review of International Studies* 26: 533–55.

OECD, (2004) *OECD Economic Surveys: Australia*, Paris: OECD.

Ogden, M. (1992) *The Future of Unionism in Australia*, Australian Council of Trade Unions (ACTU), typescript.

Olle, W. and Schoeller, W. (1977) 'World Market Competition and Restrictions on International Trade Union Policies', *Capital and Class* 2: 56–75.

Peetz, D. (1998) *Unions in a Contrary World: The Future of the Australian Trade Union Movement*, Cambridge: Cambridge University Press.

Polanyi, K. (1957) *The Great Transformation: The Political and Economic Origins of Our Time*, Boston: Beacon Press.

Ramsay, H. (1999) 'In Search of International Union Theory', in J. Waddington (ed.) *Globalization and Patterns of Labour Resistance*, London: Mansell.

Rickard, J. (1984) *H. B. Higgins: A Rebel Judge*, Sydney: Allen and Unwin.

Sadler, D. and Fagan, B. (2004) 'Australian Trade Unions and the Politics of Scale: Reconstructing the Spatiality of Industrial Relations', *Economic Geography* 80(1): 23–43.

Sandbrook, R. (ed.) (2003) *Civilizing Globalization: A Survival Guide*, Albany: State University of New York Press.

Sassoon, D. (1996) *One Hundred Years of Socialism: the West European Left in the Twentieth Century*, London: I.B. Tauris.

Segal-Horn S., Asch D. and Suneja V. (1998) 'The Globalization of the European White Goods Industry', *European Management Journal* 16(1), 101–09.

SIGTUR (2005) 'Keynote Address of the Vice President of the Korean Confederation of Trade Unions (KCTU) to the 7th Congress of the

Southern Initiative on Globalisation and Trade Union Rights', Bangkok, June.

Silver, B. (2003) *Forces of Labor: Workers Movements and Globalization since 1870*, Cambridge: Cambridge University Press.

— and Arrighi, G. (2001) 'Workers North and South', in L. Panitch and C. Leys (eds) *Socialist Register 2001: Working Classes, Global Realities*, London: Merlin Press.

Taylor, R. (2004) *Creating a Better World: Interpreting Global Civil Society*, Bloomfield, CT: Kumarian Press.

Turner, L., Katz, H. and Hurd, R. (eds) (2001) *Rekindling the Movement: Labor's Quest for Relevance in the 21st Century*, Ithaca, NY: ILR Press.

Von Holdt, K. (2002) 'Social Movement Unionism: The South African Case', *Work, Employment and Society* 16(2): 283–304.

Voss, K. and Sherman, R. (2000) 'Breaking the Iron Law of Oligarchy: Union Revitalization in the American Labor Movement', *American Journal of Sociology*, 106(2): 303–49.

Waterman, P. (1984) *For a New Labor Internationalism*, The Hague: Institute of Social Studies.

— (1998) *Globalization, Social Movements and the New Internationalisms*, London: Mansell.

— and Wills, J. (eds). (2001) *Place, Space and the New Labour Internationalisms*, Oxford: Blackwell.

Webster, E. (1988) 'The Rise of Social Movement Unionism: The Two Faces of the Black Trade Union Movement in South Africa', in P. Frankel, N. Pines and M. Swilling (eds) *State, Resistance and Change in South Africa*, London: Croom Helm.

— and Adler, G. (1999) 'Towards a Class Compromise in South Africa's Double Transition', *Politics and Society* 27(2): 347–85.

Wright Mills, C. (1959) *The Sociological Imagination*, Harmondsworth: Pelican.

STEVE JEFFERYS

Forward to the Past?
Ideology and Trade Unionism in France and Britain

Introduction

For those still concerned with modernity's underlying emphasis on the progress of human freedom and with trade unionism's role in such progress, our present vantage point, 60 years from the changes to the labour–capital power balance provoked by the Second World War, is a good one for looking back, looking at the present and querying the future.

In this chapter we focus on two major trade union movements in 'old' Europe, those of France and Britain. These are countries whose populations are almost identical. The UK grew from 57.3 to 59.2 million in the decade from 1994 to 2003, and France grew from 56.1 to 59.8 million. They are both very wealthy G8 European Union economies with broadly similar GDPs (fourth or fifth largest in the world) and they have only slightly different industrial structures.[1]

This focus allows us to compare trade unionism in two EU neighbours that face similar pressures from globalisation yet exhibit quite distinct dominant trade union ideologies and behaviours, with different histories of struggle. To this extent it allows us to distinguish the significance of what can broadly be described as 'political' factors in the same global economic context. As we shall argue, while the different experiences of struggle are important in explaining different

---

1   In 2003 total UK employment (29.8 million) was higher than in France (24.9 million), and the UK service sector employed a higher proportion of workers (80.4 percent compared to 74.3 percent); the UK's industrial sector employed a lower share (18.7 percent compared to 21.6 percent) (European Commission 2004: 263, 246).

trade union behaviours, ideology also plays a key part. This chapter first looks back at the movements' roller-coaster last sixty years; it then sketches some selected features of their contemporary situations; and next it reviews the background influence of contrasting ideologies concerning human freedom. Finally, it contrasts two possible futures.

Back to the Past

In the late 1940s both trade union movements attracted nearly the same proportions of members among the ranks of the employed labour force, between one third and 40 percent, and represented around 80 percent of all skilled and unskilled manual industrial workers. In what were always diverse movements, each had close political links with mass political parties committed to one form or another of socialism. Both movements played a major role in influencing the terms of Western Europe's post-war 'compromise' between capital and labour. At work, this strong balance of forces essentially institutionalised forms of representative pluralism, while outside work the compromise led to nearly universal collective welfare provisions for workers' health, education and old age in both countries by the mid-1970s. Since then many of these achievements have been under attack, and both movements have been increasingly on the defensive.

The Second World War had a huge effect on the balance of forces between capital and labour in both France and Britain. In both countries the unions emerged in a much more powerful organisational and political condition than they had ever been before. This situation did not last long, but it was long enough to insert many of labour's demands onto the national agendas.

In France this was the result of most of the employers and right-wing political forces being tarred with collaboration with the German occupiers. The French Communist Party (PCF) was a major force within France, largely as a result of its role in the Resistance, being widely spoken of with respect as the 'party of 75,000 shot members', but also because of its role in the wartime underground trade union movement. In October 1945 the PCF attracted 26.1 percent of the vote for the First Constituent Assembly. This compared to 23 percent for the Socialists and 24 percent for a progressive Catholic party close to De Gaulle, who remained head of government until January 1946. At the end of 1945 the PCF had 785,000 members to the Socialist Party's (SFIO) 335,000, and its members dominated the re-unified *Confédération générale du travail* (CGT) that virtually overnight sold membership cards to one in three of all salaried employees.[2] For the first time the PCF participated in government with two ministers in De Gaulle's provisional government leading into the October 1945 elections and five or six ministers from then until 4 May 1947 (Dreyfus 1995: 216–24). Even after the Cold War pushed France's largest working class party out of government for 34 years and in 1948 once again split the CGT, coalitions of socialists and radicals continued to dominate French governments almost continuously until De Gaulle's return to power with the military rebellion in Algeria in 1958. Among the permanent legal rights introduced during the early post-war years were those to elect personnel and works committee delegates, to the 40 hour week with a 20 hours' ceiling on overtime, health and safety committees, legally binding collective bargaining agreements, and a national minimum wage (Jefferys 2003: 99).

The impact of the anti-Communist split away from the CGT by *Force Ouvrière* (FO-CGT) in 1947, the toeing of the Russian Cold War political line by the CGT in the 1950s, and Marshall Aid, all helped renew the confidence of the French employers and confirmed them in their vehemently anti-trade union stance. Despite having made early concessions in the immediate aftermath of the Second World War they then drew a line. From 1958 until the 1969 departure of De Gaulle, the political dominance of the right and union divisions ensured that little further progress was made. The welfare state moved slowly forward with an unemployment insurance (1958) and a redundancy payments scheme (1967), but in the workplace the outcome for French workers is traced in the bottom trend line in Figure 1: French

---

2   32 percent of the working population in 1946 was still working in agriculture (Jefferys 2003: 33).

trade union density collapses to a low point in the mid-1950s where it more or less stayed until the explosion of 1968.

Figure 1   Trade union density in the UK and France, 1947–2004
(membership as a percent of number of employees)

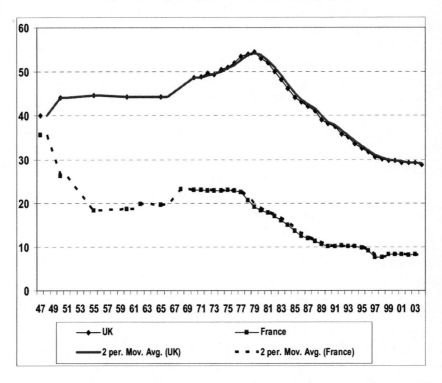

Sources: OECD trade union membership data for 1979–2001; For France and UK, Visser (1983) for 1947–79; For the UK, DTI data for 2002–4 (Grainger and Holt 2005); for France, for 1996–2003, Amossé (2004).

Note: The UK density figure from 1995 is the Labour Force Survey calculation of the density of union membership among employees in paid employment.

The ten years from 1968 to 1977 decisively marked a whole generation of French trade union activists. They had seen the collective strength of the workers' movement in practice and drew – in many instances – lifelong inspiration from it. This show of industrial strength severely frightened both employers and the state. So even though the political complexion of the Pompidou and Giscard presidencies remained right-wing, they were forced to introduce several social concessions, and the employers raised wage levels. Under the pressure of a huge continuing strike movement through the 1970s and of a PCF which still attracted 22 percent of the vote in the 1973 National Assembly elections, right-wing governments tried to 'normalise' workplace industrial relations and to moderate worker demands. After 1968 the unions were finally allowed within French workplaces to organise a legal presence and elect a 'senior representative'. In 1969 four week's annual holiday was enacted and in 1972 an equal pay law. In 1975 a law required all redundancies to be approved by a government Labour Inspector and in 1977 large firms were required to publish a 'social audit' in their annual reports.

Under the influence of the mobilisations from 1969 to 1976, the trade union activist core underwent dramatic changes. Until then French union activists had been broadly divided between the staid and often bureaucratic Communist-line followers of the CGT, the still more bureaucratic and secretive anti-Communists of FO-CGT, the politically centre Catholics of the CFTC,[3] the politically centre/left-wing Christians of the CFDT,[4] the politically centre/right-wing managers of the CGC,[5] and the politically left-wing and Communist-leaning teachers of the FEN.[6] 1968 radicalised most parts of this movement. It brought with it a major renewal of commitment and beliefs in democratic, bottom-up trade unionism that would consistently challenge the employers. Some 1.5 million new members were recruited. This spirit renewed the CGT, touched FO and largely transformed the CFDT, which even adopted a policy advocating workers' control. Politically, the astute François Mitterrand created a Common Programme with the PCF to build on this radical fervour, and had

---

3   Confédération française des travailleurs chrétiens.
4   Confédération française démocratique du travail.
5   Confédération générale des cadres.
6   Fédération de l'éducation nationale.

achieved considerable results. The CFDT and CGT worked closely and effectively together over a whole range of issues but of greater concern to the PCF was the fact that in 1976 Mitterrand's Socialist Party secured more votes in the National Assembly elections than had the Communists. In 1977 the PCF broke from the Common Programme and introduced a much more divisive line within the trade union movement. From that point French trade union density entered a new period of decline that ended only around 1990.

In Britain the Second World War boost to the movement's punching power occurred two or three years earlier than in France, and was not reversed nearly as dramatically by the resurrection of the Conservative right in the 1950s. As early as 1942 British capital began to make promises of significant reforms in the post-war years. The 1945 General Election confirmed the sea-change. The Labour Party received 48 percent of the vote in 1945, up 10 percent on its pre-war share, while the tiny British Communist Party at the peak of its membership even won two parliamentary seats. Six of the 20 members of the Attlee cabinet were directly sponsored by the trade unions, and one of them, Ernest Bevin, had previously been the boss of Britain's biggest union, the Transport and General Workers' Union. In 1951 when the Attlee government was defeated, it actually increased its share to 49 percent on an 83 percent turnout. The government had run out of steam and lost to Churchill's Conservatives who had a slightly lower share of the poll only because of the collapse of the Liberal vote and the vagaries of Britain's first-past-the-post electoral system.

By 1951 a free National Health Service had been introduced and a broad swathe of industries taken under state control with the consequent generalisation of union recognition and collective bargaining. The state sector represented about 20 percent of the national economy with a workforce of over 2 million people. In 1946 Labour repealed the anti-trade union law passed by the Conservatives in the aftermath of the 1926 General Strike. Although they never demanded the extensive protective intervention of the state for membership and representation rights that had been conceded in France, British trade unions entered a lengthy period of influence on government, whether Labour or Conservative, that was only to end in 1979. By then union workplace representatives had legal rights to paid time off work for trade union training, and health and safety committees had become a legal requirement.

The different class experiences of French and British workers in the 1950s – and one of the principal factors stoking the French fires of 1968 – can be measured by their respective shares of GDP going to wages and pensions. In 1960 the 'compensation' paid to French workers only made up 45 percent of GDP, while in the UK it was 59 percent. However, by 1982 French employee compensation levels were comparable to those of the UK, at about 57 percent of GDP (OECD 1998). While the British decline followed four years of incomes policy under Labour and three years of Thatcher's hostility to trade unionism, the French recovery was due partly to the wage settlements that followed the 1968 mass strike, and to the subsequent ten years of high strike levels and of higher union density levels that forced the right-wing governments of the 1970s to pass several significant welfare reforms. But the timing of the French achievement of parity in 1982 was also the result of the victory of the left in the 1981 elections which led to a substantial increase in the national minimum wage, as well as to Communist ministers returning to government.

The late 1970s and early 1980s were turning points for both countries. Slower growth rates, intensified competition, accelerated de-industrialisation and first the growing dominance of and then the hegemony of monetarism, deregulation and privatisation over national economic policy, shifted the trends for employee compensation in both countries downwards. Simultaneously, the GDP share of capital's operating surpluses turned upwards. By 1996 the GDP share made up of wages and pensions in the UK was 54 percent and in France 52 percent: virtually all the gains workers had made in the 1970s had been reversed. By 1996 UK capital's operating surplus had recovered its 1960 share of GDP (22 percent) and was joined at that level by French capital, which had improved its share by four percent since 1982 (OECD 1998).

With the benefit of hindsight we can see that there was nothing pre-determined about these trends. Although making labour pay for the crisis was capital's agenda it was only successful after imposing key turning points on the unions.

In the UK, trade union membership had already declined sharply from a reported peak of 13.2 million members in 1979 back to its 1970 level of 11.1 million by 1984. The unions lost the icing on the cake created by the successes of two miners' strikes and by the return of a reforming Labour government in 1974. But the impact of the major defeat of the heroic year-long miners' strike of 1984–5 cannot be underestimated. The breaking of the workers who had used industrial action to successfully challenge the government in 1972 and 1974 routed the combative left within both the whole trade union movement and within the Labour Party. It shifted the balance between left and right within the trade unions decisively towards the right. It also gave the employers a major confidence boost. Thus although the discourse of 'partnership' and 'social dialogue' with management came to dominate the national trade union agenda in the later 1980s and in the 1990s, the employers were powerful enough to pick and choose the issues and moments they would 'share' any 'problems' with the unions.

From 1984 to 1997 and the return of the Blair New Labour government, the decline was inexorable: down 3.3 million members to 7.8 million. The average number of working days lost per year that had been 12.9 million in the contested 1970s fell from 7.2 million in the 1980s to just 660,000 in the 1990s. The legal difficulties in taking strike action and the lack of confidence of British trade unionists in its success since the 1985 defeat can be seen in Figure 2.

The 1971, 1974 and 1984–5 UK strike peaks were all years of national miners' strikes, while the 1979 strike peak was the result of the breakdown of the Callaghan Labour Government's attempt to persevere with a fourth year of incomes policies that had operated largely against low-paid public sector workers. The election of New Labour in 1997 had little effect on the sense of powerlessness experienced by a trade union movement that had physically and legally been rolled over during the Thatcher years. Blair refused to include an election pledge to repeal the Conservative's anti-union laws and did not do so after his second (2001) or third (2005) election successes.

Figure 2   Working days on strike in the UK and France, 1951–2004 (millions)

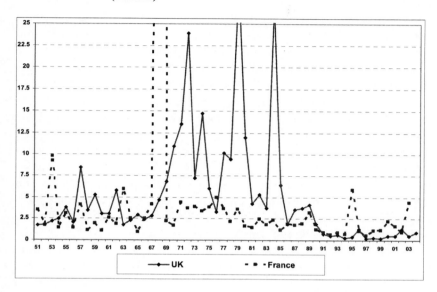

Sources: For the UK: National Statistics Office (various years); for France: Jefferys (1996), Merlier (2002) and Carlier and De Oliveira (2005), where the latest series omits strikes in the hospitals, local authorities and, from 1996, those in *La Poste* and *France Télécom*. If these last were included then the 2003 strike wave appears to have been even larger than that of the strike wave of 1995.

Notes: In France the mass strike of 1968 is estimated to have lost 180 million days; in the UK the year of the 1979 'winter of discontent' of public service strikes saw 29 million days lost and in 1984, the year the miners' strike began, there were 27 million striker-days.

In France, two different and more 'political' set-backs appeared to have triggered an equivalent decline in membership and combativity. In the fifteen years from 1976, French trade union density plummeted from 23 percent to ten percent. By then total membership had more than halved from a peak of 4.2 million to just under two million members. In terms of strike activity Figure 2 shows that strike levels also fell. It was only in the huge strike waves against unpopular government policies in 1995 and 2003 that strike levels recovered.

These declines can initially be explained by the disenchantment of many French workers with the new climate of hostility that broke out between the CGT and the CFDT in 1977 after the Communists walked out of the Common Programme. When asked, many French workers systematically report that trade union disunity inhibits them from joining. Then, a second bout of political infighting broke out in 1983–4. A huge wave of disillusion swept the combative trade union left, dashing hopes and expectations, when Mitterrand abandoned Keynesianism and opted for monetarist solutions to rising unemployment. As a result the French Communists pulled out of the government coalition, whose unpopularity among trade unionists and workers generally began to rise. Another indicator of the scale of the political defeat in 1984 was the election success of the re-badged French fascists of the *Front National*. This racist party came from nowhere to make its first significant public mark that June, winning ten Euro MPs with 10.95 percent of the vote (2.2 million electors).

As ever, the unions felt highly uneasy about trying to mobilise against a 'socialist' government, even when it was implementing clearly non-socialist measures. Thus when small strike upturns occurred, in the election years of 1986 and 1988, and particularly in 1989, grass roots strike action more or less by-passed the official unions. The activists formed rank and file 'coordination' committees involving strikers from several different unions and different areas and even non-unionists to give themselves momentum with greater 'legitimacy' than could be claimed by any single official union centre.

The durability and scale of this continuous union membership decline point also to other problems. Partly these reflect the French unions' activist culture. Historically they have welcomed active rather than passive members, creating an expectation that membership implies participation. Yet as the risks of victimisation increased in the 1980s the likelihood that trade union sympathisers would actually want to participate shrank.

Another part of the explanation relates to the French 'free-rider' problem. The national labour code governs the vast bulk of employment conditions with legally-extended sector collective agreements and a few thousand individual company-level agreements governing the rest. In this context the protected legal status of the five chosen 'representative' trade union confederations means they can bargain and sign agreements whether or not they have substantial numbers of members in a particular firm or sector. The corollary is that most workers find they are automatically covered by a trade union – and will be defended by them whether or not they are members. They can and even do, in large numbers, vote for the unions that most nearly represent their industrial views in five-yearly elections for workers' representatives to sit on employment tribunals, and every two years in elections for representatives to works councils in medium and large-sized firms.[7] So there is no particular logic to paying a subscription unless a worker feels particularly committed.

It was thus these non-member sympathisers who reacted when a particularly arrogant right-wing French government proposed a blunt pension reform in 1995. The unions first created a more or less coherent show of unity and then called for a widespread mobilisation that was followed on a mass scale by the public sector workers whose pension rights (as well as salaries) were being directly attacked. The 1995 mass strike movement can be seen as leading in 1997 to the defeat of the existing right-wing government and the election of a Socialist coalition government that again included the Communists as well as the Greens (Jefferys 2000). In 2003, when a further, even broader national strike wave against the new right-wing government was being defeated through inter-union divisions and some astute government tactical footwork, the CGT, the major union representing the combative forces, opted not to formalise a call for a 'national general strike', thereby avoiding the risk of a total defeat.

---

7   In 2002, for example, 65 percent of those eligible in firms that held works council elections participated. Of the three million who voted 78 percent voted for a trade union list. See Le Moigne and Jacod 2005.

The ten years of a continuous worker revolt in France from 1995 and the ending in 1997 of the near daily Conservative harassment of the unions in the UK more or less stabilised their membership levels after the earlier disastrous 15-year periods. But what were the organisational and political repercussions of survival through such a hostile period?

Back to the Present

Midway through the first decade of the 21st century, French and British movements remain on the defensive.

Organisational weaknesses mean that there are quite clearly fewer trade unionists and perhaps even more important, fewer volunteer trade union activists, on the ground in the workplaces and localities of France and Britain. Despite the major increase in the total working population over the last sixty years the numbers of members claimed by the unions is now slightly (the UK) or considerably below (France) the levels achieved in 1945–1947 as shown in Figure 3.[8]

---

8   In France the most accurate way of estimating trade union membership is via a yearly 8000-strong household sample survey that only started in 1996. Its latest data suggests there were nearly 1.9 million trade unionists at work in 2003 (Amossé 2004). This estimate for France is much closer to the actual trade union membership claims after unemployed and retired members are taken into account than is the equivalent Labour Force Survey (LFS) in the UK. In the UK it is probable that the true number of people who report themselves to the LFS as trade unionists is considerably lower than the figures reported by the unions to the Trade Union Certification Officer, and graphed in Figure 3. The explanation is that trade unions report their membership to the Certification Officer on the basis of the total numbers of members they are aware of at any one time. This total will include many who will consider themselves to have left the union, deliberately or through changing employment, and will include some members who pay union dues through the 'check-off' system or through bankers' orders, but who are not aware of this. It will also include retired or unemployed members. If the LFS is used as a source instead, the UK total of

Figure 3   Union membership in the UK and France, 1947–2003 (millions)

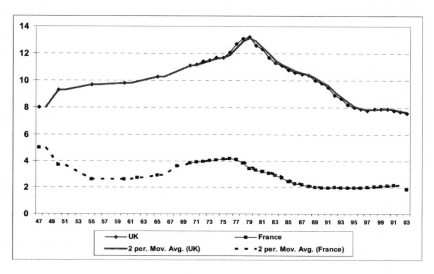

Sources: For France as Figure 1; for the UK the data since 1979 is based on
the annual reports of the Trade Union Certification Officer; before
1979 it is based on Visser (1983).

However, union organisational weakness has not just meant
having fewer members. Trade unionism is also becoming much more
closely identified with the public sector than it has been in most of the
post-Second World War period. In the UK, while public sector trade
unionists represented 39 percent of total union membership in 1948,
and 44 percent in 1979, by 2004, despite the shrinkage of total public
sector employment under both Thatcher and Blair, they made up 57
percent of all trade unionists. Of the 6.5 million just 2.79 million
worked for private sector employers. Although it too is declining,
trade union density is thus 3.4 times higher in the UK public sector
(58.8 percent) than in the private sector (17.2 percent) (Grainger
and Holt 2005: 3, 14). In France, the public-private differences are of

6.5 million self-reporting trade union members in paid employment appears
closer to French levels.

similar proportions. In the nationalised firms and social security system (15.6 percent) union density is exactly three times higher and in local and national government (15.1 percent) it is 2.9 times higher than in private firms (5.2 percent) (Amossé 2004: 3).

Trade unionism in both countries has nearly become extinct in small firms. In French private firms with fewer than 50 workers trade union density is just 3.5 percent, and in only one in five of these small firms do workers report there being even one trade union rep present. At the other end of the company size spectrum, 8.7 percent of employees in private establishments with 500 or more workers are unionised, and trade unionists are reported present in 92 percent of these large firms (Amossé 2004: 4). While the data is not directly comparable, in UK workplaces with fewer than 50 employees, union density averages just 18.3 percent, compared to over twice that level (38.5 percent) in workplaces with more than 50 workers. In small, sub-50, workplaces there is also a UK union presence in more than one in four firms (29 percent). This compares to the 65 percent average reported 'union presence' in firms with more than 50 workers (Grainger and Holt 2005: 37).

In both countries the combination of trade unionism's survival in the public sector and in larger organisations has seen trade unionism slowly mutate from its predominantly manual worker origins into a majority white collar and/or professional membership. In France in 2003 trade union density was highest among teachers, researchers and doctors (25.5 percent) and among civil service professionals and managers (25 percent). Overall 513,000 managers and professionals (14.5 percent) and 560,000 intermediate professional workers were unionised compared to 404,000 clerical (5.5 percent) and 389,000 manual workers (6.1 percent) (Amossé 2004: 4). In the UK in 2004 trade union density was highest among the 'professional occupations' (48.6 percent) and 'associate professional and technical occupations' (42.5 percent). Among the 'skilled trades occupations' at the origins of trade unionism, density was just 31.2 percent, while among the semi-skilled 'process, plant and machine operatives' and the unskilled 'elementary occupations', whose workers made up the bulk of the post-war mass unionism, density was 38.4 and 26.6 percent respectively (Grainger and Holt 2005: 17). Britain's unionised workers are also largely concentrated in the public sector or the formerly nationalised industries such as British Telecommunications, the railway and electricity, gas and water companies. Figure 4 shows how public administration, education, electricity, gas and water supply, health and transport and communication, the industries in which the state either plays or used to play a major role as employer, still dominate the union density levels of the UK:

Figure 4   UK trade union density (percent) by industry, 1995–2004

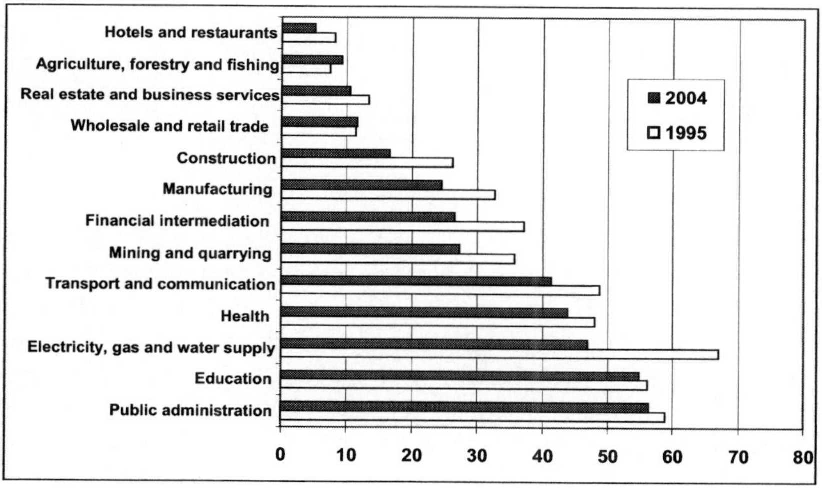

Source: Grainger and Holt (2005: 18)

One consequence of the greater resilience of public sector trade union density is that while women still are very far from having equal representation among the unions' senior appointed, elected or seconded officials, they are increasing as a proportion of total union membership. In France, the 890,000 women trade unionists has risen to make up 46 percent of the total number of working trade unionists, and the head of one of the five national representative trade unions was a woman between 1993 and 2002. In the UK women made up 29 percent of all trade unionists in 1980, but twenty-five years later make up just over 50 percent of all salaried trade unionists. Thus in 2004, for the first time, trade union density among women employees in paid work in the UK overtook that of male trade union density, as shown in Table 1.

Table 1   UK trade union membership and density among employees, 1995–2004

	People		Density (%)	
Autumn	Membership (000s)	Density (%)	Men	Women
1995	6,791	32.6	35.3	29.9
2004	6,513	28.8	28.5	29.1

Source: Grainger and Holt (2005: 12)

Union organisational responses to their reducing influence and membership density crises in the two countries have followed national traditions. In the UK the full-time officials have done their best to ensure that their unions remain financially viable through cost reduction programmes and mergers. There has been a nearly continuous process of trade union mergers, with a collapse in the number of certified unions from 482 to 296 between 1981 and March 2005. But in the last two years this process has accelerated. In March 2004 there were 15 trade unions with more than 100,000 members. But since then one of these has merged with the largest private sector union, Amicus, and three others are now in or actively considering negotiations on mergers, including the third and fourth and tenth largest unions, the TGWU, the GMB and the Communication Workers Union. If these negotiations are successful it appears as if within the next few years there will be one very large predominantly private sector union, Amicus, with about 2 million members and one very large public sector union, UNISON, with about 1.5 million members. Outside these two huge formations, there will probably still be three competing teachers unions with about 750,000 members all told, one or two

100,000-strong industrial or occupational unions and nearly another 500,000 in two occupationally distinct health professionals' associations representing nurses and doctors.

In the UK, then, protecting union funds and viability from slow strangulation by falling membership revenues, has become the major part of the union response to decline. Over the last ten years, too, a secondary refrain, but one that has still not won over the bulk of the trade union officials, has been the need to develop an 'organising' perspective, on the lines of those pioneered in the United States. The key problem with this perspective is that it often runs counter to the main political sales pitch of the trade unions towards the Labour government: this is to argue that trade unionism is good for business, improving productivity and profitability through improving employee commitment and participation in their work.

In France, where union membership revenues are very low indeed by comparison with the British levels, trade union officials have only very rarely been salaried by the union. Instead, since the trade union reforms of the 1980s confirmed a range of legal rights for elected representatives to take time off work on trade union business, those that there are (and there are significantly fewer of them than in the UK) are almost all seconded staff who are still on the payroll of their former employer. This continuous legal pressure on (generally larger and generally public sector) employers to effectively subsidise most full-time union leaders, means that the falling income from union members paying their cards, plays a much less determining role on French trade unions. There are no structural pressures forcing them to strategically try and save their bacon by either merging or organising for growth or both.

Instead, the experiences of diminishing influence in the face of more aggressive and sophisticated management, has tended to sharpen political differences between the different components of French trade unionism, and has caused greater fragmentation of any already divided movement. Entering the period of decline with five nationally representative confederations and one large teaching federation, the picture today is much more fragmented along continuing political-strategic lines. In 1989, after a small group of Post Office and France Télécom CFDT activists were expelled for helping organise a strike (under a Socialist government that the national CFDT leadership supported), a new union called SUD was set up. This later joined the 'Group of Ten' independent unions, and then in 2004 established itself as a 90,000-strong new trade union centre called *Union Syndicale Solidaires*. In 1992 there was a major split in the officially-recognised teachers' federation, FEN.[9] This was partly on political grounds, with the left challenging the centre, and partly on occupational grounds, with the interests of primary school teachers diverging from those in secondary schools. The result was a much smaller FEN, centred on primary school teachers, and a larger, more left-wing FSU[10] based mainly in secondary education. The FEN, however, quickly moved to create a larger right-of-centre independent union centre called UNSA.[11] Set up in 1993, today this grouping of autonomous unions has a considerable claimed membership of about 350,000 and is affiliated to the European TUC. Table 2 represents these new trade union lines as a political spectrum, from the combative 'left' to the political 'centre-right'.

Both movements, in reality, have the same political continuum of views within them. But one major difference is that in France the industrial relations structure allows and indeed encourages political disagreements to be played out by distinct politically-identifiable trade union organisations. In Britain, the political differences are usually always contained within the same organisation, and whose leadership often alternates between 'left' and 'right' according to the internal trade union election process.

An important common experience is that the last 25 years' dominance of monetarism, and, most notably the collapse of the so-called 'socialist' alternative in Russia and Eastern Europe, has ruptured the earlier clear union identification with any clear socialist project. The clearest consequence of this is in France, where the CGT

---

9   Fédération de l'éducation nationale.
10   Fédération synidcale unitaire.
11   Union nationale des syndicates autonomes.

Table 2   Heuristic left-centre/right political continuum of French trade union positions, c. 2005[12]

| | Combative Left | | | | | | Centre-Right | |
Election share %	Soli-daires	FSU	CGT	FO	CGC	CFDT	CFTC	UNSA
Industrial Tribunals[a]	1.51	0.15	32.13	18.28	7.01	25.23	9.65	4.99
Public sector[b]	5.0?	7.7	15.4	12.3	1.3	13.2	2.2	8.0
Works Councils[c]			24.3	12.4	5.6	22.1	5.5	
Works Councils[d]			22.6	13.1	6.1	22.8	6.0	
Working members (000s)[e]	90	130	400	250	140	450	160	250

a) In the December 2002 Prud'hommes industrial tribunal elections, 5.4 million employees (32.7 percent) of the private sector and nationalised company workers eligible to vote did so.

b) Share of internal elections in the government sector in the three year election cycle between 1996 and 1999 in which 3.6 million workers were eligible to vote (Andolfatto 2001).

c) Share of 2002 Works Council Elections. Non-union slates received 21.7 percent of the vote. The participation rate was 64.7 percent (Le Moigne and Jacod 2005).

d) The other half of French companies hold their Works Council elections in odd calendar years. In 2001 the shares of the 1.7 million workers who voted were as shown. The same point about UNSA and Solidaires holds for this year as for 2002 (Le Moigne 2003).

e) These rough estimates of the numbers of working members in 2005 are derived from Jefferys (2003: 216), Amossé (2004) and by reconciling these estimates with the most recent confederation membership claims or reports.

---

12   Although this has to be something of a caricature, those located on the right of the table are more likely to seek accommodation with government and good relations with the employers in order to negotiate improvements in working conditions. Those unions placed on the left are more likely to seek to mobilise pressure on whichever government is in power to force it to act in support of the workers, and although they may make detailed proposals for improving work organisation and productivity they essentially remain sceptical as to how far good relations with the employers can ever permanently guarantee better working conditions.

has formally broken its links to the PCF.[13] However, even in Britain, where the unions still provide substantial funding to the Labour Party, the New Labour leadership sees itself as no longer having any particular obligations to the trade unions. Even when they were apparently in a strong bargaining position, a year before the May 2005 general election when Blair was still highly unpopular for having taken the UK into an unjustifiable war, the unions secured only the very mildest of promises from the government to consider a reform programme if it were re-elected.

The July 2004 Warwick Agreement between the Labour government and the leading unions was the mildest possible series of proposals. In it, the government promised merely 'to work with unions and employers' to develop a voluntary 'good employment standard', to 'radically improve enforcement, advice, guidance and support for workers' and to 'review' the 'issue of reinstatement' at employment tribunals. It 'recognised the value of facility time for union reps' and promised 'discussions between government and unions on this issue'. Within the public sector it promised to give contracted-out workers 'protection' and to keep Royal Mail as a nationalised institution. In return for these promises the unions sent 6 million pieces of direct mail to their members urging them to vote for the Labour Party, 1.8 million of these in the 100 most marginal seats. The private sector union, Amicus, even sent out a personalised DVD to all its members in the key marginal constituencies. It is too early at the time of writing to predict how many of the Warwick promises will be met in full. But already the signs are not positive, and government ministers are telling the unions not to expect too much. What, however, was not on the 2004 trade union agenda was any hint of policies that were once a cornerstone of trade unionism:

---

13   One upshot of this has been the collapse of the union's monolithic apparatus that always delivered the vote for the leadership. In the debate over the EU Constitution referendum in 2005 this collapse was revealed when the union's General Secretary was publicly defeated by the union's National Executive when he wished to placate the ETUC (to which the CGT was allowed to affiliate to in 2002) by not making a public (hostile) recommendation on the issue.

measures aimed at redistributing wealth and power at work towards working people.

This total absence of any clear socialist project is largely true also of the contemporary French trade union movement. But in France there remains a much stronger, although hazy anti-capitalist discourse. There, for example, the tiny Solidaires still stands for a 'counter-power trade unionism that links the daily defence of workers to the transformation of society'. [14] But much more significantly, the union with most national support in elections, the CGT, still systematically seeks to mobilise under the slogans like 'Let's Build Collective Action to Win' in defence of 'workers' demands, jobs and the defence of public services'. [15] The CGT remains by far the union that initiates most strikes in France, being responsible for a quarter of all stoppages in 2002 and 2003, far in advance of the CFDT (10 percent) or FO (2 percent) (Carlier and De Oliveira 2005: 5). The continuing presence of its politically 'left' discourse within the trade union movement is the second major political difference between the France and the UK.

A comparison of responses to the actuality and threat of closure helps demonstrate the political significance of these differences in discourse. In April 2005 the Phoenix car assembly operation at Longbridge, Birmingham collapsed. Within a month 5,300 jobs were lost. In 2000 the British trade unions organised a protest march to pressure the government as well as BMW to find a solution to that year's Rover crisis, but this time, despite the proximity of the May 2005 British parliamentary general election, the unions made no attempt at all to mount a collective mobilisation. Not even to try and ensure the workers would receive their full occupational pension rights. [16] By comparison, it took 19 months of intermittent strikes and protest marches before, in May 2005, Nestlé finally broke the

---

14   See the summary presentation of Solidaires on www.solidaires.org/article215.-html

15   See the CGT's daily news bulletin for 29 August on http://www.cgt.fr/internet/

16   This is not so surprising. Out of the fifteen years 1990–2004 only three years experienced higher strike losses than occurred in the first full year of the Second World War. That year, 1940, had itself been a record low since UK strike records began at the end of the 19th century.

resistance of the biggest union at its Perrier water Vergèze bottling plant. The conflict there was about a reorganisation involving the loss of a third of the factory's workforce through early retirements. The local Confédération générale du travail (CGT) representative finally signed the early retirement and work reorganisation agreement alongside the Nestlé Waters Supply director and human resource director at the Nîmes prefecture in the presence of the Gard prefect (the most senior regional representative of the French state).

In both cases the unions and more directly the workers lost. Yet in the British example both the unions and the Longbridge workers entered the conflict already ideologically defeated. More outrage was expressed at the huge amounts pocketed by their 'partners' in Phoenix's management than at the brutality of a system that over-night deprived thousands of families of their livelihoods. In France, in contrast, union suspicion of Nestlé management remained so acute, that even in defeat the unions insisted that the agreement was witnessed by a senior French state official. Any future reneging on its agreement by Nestlé will automatically see the state having to concede legitimacy to any union protest. It thus directly raises the issue of government's role in the defence of workers' rights not to be lied to or otherwise brutally exploited. The origins of these different political approaches may be traced to core trade union values concerning their understanding of freedom and human liberty to which we turn now.

Locke, Rousseau and Trade Union Ideologies

Ideologies help frame human action. They give people a sense of direction, a sense of history and an understanding of their place and contribution in the world. Often, for better or for worse, they have the capacity to become a decisive actor in the unfolding of the human story. Yet they are still all too often overlooked when it comes to understanding labour-capital relationships and the institutions these relationships create.

One significant institutional form that emerged during the first hundred years after the American and French Revolutions were the trade unions. Building on the supplanting of god-given birth rights to political governance by the notions of democratic and participative rights, voluntary associations of workers began to challenge unilateral employer rights to determine wages and working conditions. As these collective associations became more long-lasting trade union ideologies emerged to help frame how individual members or supporters of these associations should view and respond to employer and government actions, and issues such as accident and sickness insurance.

By the early twentieth century these worker associations had become the object of both political and academic analysis and debate. Marx and Engels had approved of trade unions as 'schools of war' against capital. Lenin argued that they were essentially 'economistic', inevitably raising demands that could be resolved without a fundamental challenge to capital. Luxemburg suggested they could be transformed during a mass strike into a political weapon against the capitalist state. The Webbs proposed a threefold analysis of trade union purpose in terms of mutual insurance, collective bargaining and political action but also explored the concept of 'industrial democracy'. From the United States came the competing concepts of 'business' and 'revolutionary' unionism and later, born out of the Parsonian anti-Communism of the 1950s, that of a superior American 'pluralism'. This involved unions negotiating collectively for the mutual benefit of the firm and its employees, an encompassing ideal that was contrasted in the 1960s by Fox with 'unitarism' and 'class' as approaches shaping employment relations. In Italy, Germany and Sweden the importance of unions as permanent institutional actors increasingly came to be stressed as part of a 'generalised political exchange' involving political parties, the state and the employers. Yet as the full employment of the '30 glorious years' of growth following the Second World War began to dissolve, other academics began to take a broader focus. In particular a group of mainly French scholars jumped to a systemic level of analysis that virtually denied the significance of industrial relations actors. They argued that as a production system advanced capitalism was in the process of changing from a 'Fordist' form to a 'post' or 'neo-Fordist' one. It was only as it became clear at the conceptual level, that contemporary capitalism's mix of continuities and discontinuities and of the old with the new provides a context recognisable to trade unionists for at least 150 years, that greater attention is again being paid to what and how trade unionists think. Thus Hyman recently developed a triangular model explaining British, Italian and German trade union ideological differences in terms of the extent of their organisational attachments to pairs of the three key competing values he argued were present in all Western European trade union movements: class, social integration and the market (Hyman 2001).

While most of these positions help categorise, explain or predict trade union behaviours, the day-to-day differences between French and British trade unions also touch another layer of ideology. This concerns beliefs that are both at the very core of trade union association and at the cornerstone of modernity. This ideology is all about 'liberty' or *liberté*. In English or, rather, in the dominant American English usage in the world today, 'liberty' is quite simply a synonym for 'freedom'. If we were to directly translate the French term *liberté,* however, the best literal translation of its meaning in English when referring to society would be something like 'freedom with civil democracy'.[17] Although this French term is thus somewhat broader than the English/American, in both the Anglo-American and French trade union traditions there is scope for a discussion about the elements of liberty/*liberté* that still need to be extended. Trade union beliefs, value systems and world views, however, are profoundly influenced by the available national understandings of what this *liberté* actually includes. This is for a quite simple reason: at its heart

---

17   The *Dictionnaire Hachette Encyclopédique Illustré* (Paris: Hachette Livre, 1998: 1087) suggests four French language meanings: freedom as opposed to slavery or imprisonment; 'the possibility guaranteed by law or by the political and social system of being able to act as you want, provided you don't harm anyone else's rights or public safety'; as opposed to any constraint; and philosophically, being able to act autonomously without submission to any fatalism or determinism.

it is a concept that can embody a profound challenge to capitalist property.

The argument can be stated quite briefly. While the 18th-century Enlightenment's contribution to modernity may be likened to an exceptionally long pregnancy, the real birth pangs of modernity occurred in two formative 18th-century revolutions, those of 1776–1783 in America and of 1789–1794 in France. Together they rang the Liberty Bell of Freedom against the colonialism, royal dictatorships and corruption of their *ancien régimes*. Together they forged the edifice of contemporary democratic society. They exalted rational thought over superstition, confirmed that all those bound by social rules should participate in the framing of those rules, and underlined that the purpose of rule-making was to secure freedom, equality and solidarity for all. Freedom, human solidarity and equality meant a rational world in which access to power was no longer to be the exclusive privilege of high birth, and power was no longer to be exclusively used for self-interest.

This common revolutionary discourse was celebrated in 1889 by the donation of the Statue of Liberty to the American people from the 'people of France'. But the same word, liberty/*liberté,* the two peoples then celebrated had significantly different underlying meanings arising out of the materially different revolutionary contexts and from different core philosophies.

The 1776 Declaration of Independence was essentially a taxpayers' revolt by dissident propertied colonials against the additional taxes imposed by a foreign British King whose coffers had just been emptied by the Seven Years' War with France. To succeed it required huge amounts of courage and significant unifying organisational skills, and for both it required ideological conviction. While the formal individualism preached by the Protestant sects contributed one part of the necessary revolutionary certitude, another was found in the followers of the English philosopher John Locke, who had died in 1704. In his writings they found the justification for property owners to unite against absentee landlords and aristocratic rule. In 1690 Locke had proclaimed that 'The Liberty of Man, in Society, is to be under no other Legislative Power, but that established by Consent in the Commonwealth'. Revolution was permissible where government subverts the natural rights of life, liberty and property of the people. Locke wrote in 1691 that the *'Freedom of Men under Government,* is, to have a standing Rule to live by, common to every one of that Society, and made by the Legislative Power erected in it'. Yet Locke himself had invested in the slave trade and drafted the *Fundamental Constitutions of Carolina* (1669), which granted absolute power over slaves. Thus his work also legitimated the limitation by 'Legislative Power' of revolutionary American freedom, equality and solidarity to the voting property owners. The American Constitution specifically excluded those at the bottom of the pile, the slaves. After all, slaves were property, and the American Revolution was in defence of individual property owners against the random, absolute power of the state. Lockean liberty was a radical ideology for the *individual* property owner, who could only be taxed if represented in some local democratic structure. But his ideology justified the 'freedom' of property owners to oppress and exploit others. Equality among property-owners was one thing. Equality with property was something different. And, most critically, the American revolutionaries did not need a close alliance with the poor to achieve their independence. The King's armies they were fighting were foreigners or conscripts and the King's coffers were already bare.

In France, a successful revolution required a different, more radical and collective ideology. This was because, even if the 1789 upsurge was led – as in America – by privileged dissidents, from the start France's revolutionary lawyers and merchants were forced to be more inclusive. France's aristocrats, tax collectors and clerics occupied the same physical space as those leading the struggle for change. The enemy in France were not absentee kings and lords. In France the *Ancien Régime* was the local tax collectors, soldiers, large propertied landowners and priests. They lived in the local castles, fortified mansions, religious and large houses that dominated France's small towns and villages. They had access to troops living in local barracks. To defeat this much stronger conservative force, the revolutionary middle classes were forced to seek alliances with ordinary workers and peasants and they embraced the philosophy of the Protestant-turned-Catholic Jean-Jacques Rousseau. He had denounced the stranglehold of vested interests over civil society, and in 1762 attacked birth-derived privileges and exalted the rationality of governance through a social contract between equal individuals. The 1789, 1793 and 1795 Declarations of the Rights of Man and of the Citizen that followed the Revolution established the principles of equality before the law, respect for property and freedom of expression. On February 4 1794 this broader, collective logic of *liberté* as freedom and equality led to the National Convention abolishing slavery.[18]

To secure its victory over feudal and semi-feudal France, the French revolutionary agenda had had to be more radical than in America. In the towns, French landless workers were promised real freedom and equality; in the country, a significant chunk of the rural peasantry was won over through their acquiring some of the vast divided Church lands. Meanwhile the highly centralised French state bequeathed from the Bourbons had to be maintained since the enemy was both internal and at its borders. A strong state was necessary to defend the Republic against home-grown aristocrats, against the royal families of the rest of Europe and against the Catholic Church. The Church's resistance to a revolution and a republic that encouraged free trade, outlawed the Guilds (and trade unions) and imposed modernisation in the name of a 'golden' collective-corporate past left several legacies. Today, in what nominally is a largely Roman Catholic country, the 'good republican' of both left and right remains as staunchly secular as ever.[19] Large swathes of French Catholic employers ruled their employees through paternalistic corporatism and in the 1980s embraced the new discourse of 'human resource' management more rapidly than did their British counterparts. While the Church's long-standing opposition to the state form of bourgeois capitalism created in France could lead the major 20th-century French historian Fernand Braudel to ask: 'Is it perhaps both France's tragedy

---

18   Reinstated by Napoleon in 1802 after his Consulate had seized power in 1799 and shortly before he inaugurated the 1804–1814 First Empire.

19   Illustrated in 2004 by the lack of political opposition to legislation explicitly outlawing the hijab and other signs of religious commitment worn or carried by pupils in all French public schools.

and the secret of its charm that it has never really been won over to capitalism?'

The philosophical differences between Rousseau and Locke and between the social basis of the French and the property basis of the American Revolutions have had a long reach. And a reach that still marks certain differences between France and Britain, where Locke's empiricism was also hugely influential. Thus in France, universal manhood suffrage was established permanently in 1848. In Britain a property qualification for male voters survived until 1918.

The trade unions in both countries were effectively fully legalised at about the same time in the 1880s. In France this came after the major revolutions of 1830, 1848 and 1871 had each posed more socialistic ways of restructuring capital–labour relations. If achieving *liberté* through social justice was the goal, the methods used were forms of political solidarity, operating against the state. In Britain at the same time many unions were already building up funds and property in order to provide workers with 'mutual insurance' within the contemporary capitalist order. Making up a much larger proportion of the total population than in France, and working in larger units in a much more urbanised environment, there was a natural stress on 'organic', industrial solidarity in Britain in which social justice could be achieved within the trade or industry.

Trade union ideologies in the two countries thus developed with quite different emphases. In France the trade unions were understood as vehicles for mobilising the workers to influence the terms of the social contract between the state and its citizens; to do this required leaders and activists who could read accurately what the masses of workers felt. In Britain the unions were understood as vehicles for sustaining workers in their attempts to influence the terms of the labour-capital contract; to do this required a mass membership and negotiating skills. In France, the unions thus represent and advise all workers, whether members of a trade union or not. In Britain, the unions generally only represent those workers who are up to date with payments of their subscriptions.

This is, necessarily, a very clipped comparative account. In France, trade unions also negotiated with their employers when the latter agreed to do so; and in Britain, union leaders and activists often attempted to mobilise their memberships to challenge individual employers and even, although very rarely and with little confidence, as in the 1926 General Strike, the British state. Equally, if the British trade unions largely left mediation with the state to the Labour Party founded in 1900, in France union activists were also generally also active in the different pre-First World War socialist groups and the later Communist and Socialist Parties, which were also significant players at both local and national levels within the French state.

In both countries trade union ideologies include visions of social justice, a better world and of the dignity of labour. Both recognise the importance of collective action in achieving these goals. In both, union ideologies challenge the 'commodification' of workers' labour power and for this reason, however 'cooperative' they might be in their relationships with the employers, the employers of both countries consistently saw and see them as actively or potentially 'subversive' (see the argument in Contrepois 2005).

Yet the accumulated weight of one hundred and fifty years of different ideological roots and different economic, social and political histories has had a marked impact. The ILO's World Labour Report 2000 produces data showing a significant difference in the overall income distribution between France and Britain, with Britain's richest 20 percent of earners taking just over half of all income compared to 40 percent in France, as shown in Table 3.

Table 3   Income distribution in France and the UK[20]

	France, 1989	United Kingdom, 1995
Richest 10 percent	24.9	35.0
Richest 20 percent	40.1	50.4
Poorest 20 percent	7.2	6.9
Poorest 10 percent	2.5	2.6

---

20   ILO 2000: 291.

If we take just the group most likely to be affected by trade union activities, those workers who are aged between 25 and 54, we find their distribution of earnings in France is significantly more egalitarian than in the UK (which is very close to the inequality levels of the US). In 1996 a mere nine percent of French workers earned more than one-and-a-half times the national median wage, compared to the 22 percent of UK wage earners, as shown in Table 4.

Table 4   Employment–Population rates and prevalence of low and high earnings in France, the UK and the USA, 1996[21]

	Percent of age group employed	Percent in earnings category		
		Earn less than two thirds of Median wage	Earn near Median wage	Earn more than one and a half time of Median wage
France	77	7	61	9
UK	78	13	43	22
USA	80	14	42	24

And at the other end of the distribution just seven percent of French workers earned less than two-thirds of the median wage, compared to a figure nearly double that, of 13 percent, in the UK. Of course, this data reflects realities before the introduction of the National Minimum Wage by the Labour Government in the UK. But since that was deliberately set so low (35–39 percent of average national hourly earnings if bonuses and overtime are excluded) as to only benefit between one million and 1.5 million people, perhaps a maximum of 5 percent of the labour force, this inequality gap is certain to remain.

---

21   Burtless 2003: 22. If we go on to consider the consequences of such a wage distribution (in the context of much higher proportions of French two-parent families), after taxes and social security transfers the proportions of under 16-year-olds living in poverty (on less than one-half of median wage) in 1993–4 was just 7 percent, compared to 21 percent in the UK and 25 percent in the USA (Burtless 2003: 28).

What these different outcomes suggest is that while both the UK and France are profoundly capitalist countries, societal and trade union priorities have reflected different understandings of freedom and *liberté*, and, of course, different histories. They imply too that these two countries may well also have different futures.

Looking Forwards

Looking into the future, nothing is certain. Will the next thirty years see a further decline or renewed growth and influence for French and British trade unionism?

Clearly the global context will have a major impact on the kinds of choices available to voluntary workers' self-organisation. If the American model of managerial capitalism with its key themes of the primacy of property rights and 'shareholder value' and of 'transparent' or 'democratic' governance by those property-owners and shareholders continues to dominate, then one future would almost certainly be a further decline in workers' collective influence. Workers' organisations could also be increasingly intimidated from advocating any significant or coherent political interventions aimed at extending economic democracy. In this scenario, nearly all of the new generation of 21st-century workers, especially those in the most dynamic knowledge-intensive service industries, will have working lives outside the reach, protection and mobilising power of trade unions. Outside the place of work the political protection afforded by the mobilisation of trade union pressure on the state would also weaken, and collective welfare rights could gradually be dissolved in the generalisation of the anti-egalitarian property-based notion of individual responsibility. Trade unions might survive in the tiny remnants of the state sector and in the very largest firms, cushioned from acute global competition, where they would be tolerated as well-intentioned moralisers. They would have lost most, if not all, their mobilising power as the independent voice of a significant section of civil society.

Yet it is also possible to foresee a different future. In this vision, the contradictions that the generalisation of the American model generates in inequalities, social injustices, intolerance, growing environmental hazards and even military aggression fuel a huge global reservoir of anger and organising potential to feed union regeneration. Younger knowledge-intensive workers, women, black and migrant workers in the expanding retail and personal services areas, professionals who find their expertise being increasingly commodified, all find themselves increasingly alienated by the model's blatant denial of non-property-based freedoms. The current passive resistance, measured and reflected by many of today's unions, turns. It becomes more aware, more active. It takes on new technologies, new tactics, new alliances and new politics. New mobilisations occur that snowball up to the point where they inscribe the extension of human freedom and democracy at work as well as in society on the 21st-century agenda.

Looking back in 30 years' time, academics will trace this new movement of the broad working classes back to the major resistance to pension 'reforms' offered by the French, the Italians and the Spanish workers between 1995 and 2003, and to the huge demonstrations challenging the new American imperialism that took place in Britain, Germany and Spain in the early 21st century. Uplifted by this 'new' unionism, the future could take us forward to the past. Will it be towards modernity's unfinished agenda of economic and social freedoms and *liberté*?

References

Amossé, T. (2004) 'Mythes et réalités de la syndicalisation en France', *Premières Syntheses* 44(2): 1–5.

Andolfatto, D. (2001) 'La représentativité syndicale en débat', *Regards sur l'actualité* 267(janvier): 35–49.

Burtless, G. (2003) 'Social Policy for the Working Poor: US Reform in a Cross-National Perspective', in N. Gilbert and A. Parent (eds) *Welfare Reform: A Comparative Assessment of the French and US Experiences*, New York: Transaction Publishers.

Carlier, A. and De Oliveira, V. (2005) 'Les conflits du travail en 2002 et 2003', *Premières Syntheses* 18(4): 1–6.

Contrepois, S. (2005) 'Trade Unionism: Roads to Renewal', *Labor History* 46(3): 362–368.

Dreyfus, M. (1995) *Histoire de la c.g.t.*, Paris: Éditions complexe.

European Commission (2004) *Employment in Europe 2004: Recent Trends and Prospects*, Luxembourg: Office for Official Publications of the European Commission.

Grainger, H. and Holt, H. (2005) *Trade Union Membership 2004*, London: Department of Trade and Industry.

Hyman, R. (2001) *Understanding European Trade Unionism: Between Market, Class and Society*, London: Sage.

International Labour Organisation (2000) *World Labour Report 2000*, Geneva: ILO.

Jefferys, S. (2003) *Liberté, Égalité and Fraternité at Eork: Changing French Employment Relations and Management*, Basingstoke: Palgrave Macmillan.

— (2000) 'A 'Copernican Revolution' in French Industrial Relations: Are the Times a' Changing?', *British Journal of Industrial Relations* 38(2): 241–260.

— (1996) 'Down But Not Out: French Unions after Chirac', *Work, Employment & Society* 10(3): 509–527.

Le Moigne, C. (2003) 'Les élections aux comités d'entreprise en 2001', *Premières Synthèses* 43(2).

— and Jacod, O. (2005) 'Les elections aux comités d'entreprise en 2002', *Premières Synthèses* 3(2): 1–7.

Merlier, R. (2002) 'Les conflits en 2000: le regain se confirme', *Premières Synthèses* 9(1): 1–8.

OECD (1998) *National Accounts, Main Aggregates, 1960–1996*, 2 vols., vol. I, Paris: OECD.

Visser, J. (1983) *Trade Unions 1950–1980: A Quantitative Assessment of the Development of Union Membership and Union Density in 10 West European Countries*, Amsterdam: University of Amsterdam, Sociology of Organisation Research Unit.

DAN CLAWSON

US Labour and the Neoliberal Challenge:
Destruction or a New Upsurge?

Introduction

On the opening day of the Democrats' 2004 convention, Andy Stern, president of SEIU, the largest, fastest-growing, and in some accounts most militant US union, said that organised labour 'might be better off in the long run if Senator John F. Kerry loses the election'. Stern told reporters that the labour movement is 'in deep crisis' (not exactly hot news), that reform was desperately needed, and that 'I don't know if [labour reform efforts] would survive with a Democratic president'. Saying he was not interested in becoming president of the AFL–CIO, Stern said that 'pressure is needed' to bring about real change. 'It was not enough to have Martin Luther King Jr.,' Stern said. 'You needed Stokely Carmichael to raise the threat of disruption unless demands were met.' Stern is exceptionally smart, and presumably these remarks were carefully calculated. Equally calculated, one presumes, was Stern's next day announcement that 'There's nothing I want more than a John Kerry victory [...] a Kerry victory is the biggest goal of our union right now' (Quoted in Broder 2004).

Stern's flip-flop is a good barometer of the current state of organised labour in the United States. On the one hand, there is a widespread recognition that labour's long decline cannot be reversed through small incremental changes. There's a general acceptance that John Sweeney and the New Voice team that took control of the AFL–CIO in 1995 have made many needed changes, but an equal agreement that Sweeney and company – who operate on a consensus model – are unwilling or unable to take the next steps. Historically US labour has not grown through small incremental steps, but rather through massive upsurges. Much is happening down below. This might lead to a new upsurge; if not, US labour might get effectively wiped out. The labour leadership knows the crisis is severe, but cannot decide how much risk it is willing to take, what actions to pursue, and to what degree it is willing to trust and involve the membership, as opposed to mobilising it from the top for goals and actions determined by the leadership. The US labour movement is now contesting over these possibilities. At the moment the debate is mostly conducted at the top levels, but there are signs that a widespread democratic debate is increasingly possible.

Labour's Long Decline

The decline of the US labour movement is not a recent phenomenon. As a percent of the (non-agricultural) labour force, union membership in the United States peaked in 1954 at 34.7 percent, also (coincidentally?) the time when the more conservative American Federation of Labor merged with the more militant Congress of Industrial Organizations to create the AFL–CIO. Although the absolute number of members continued to grow as the US labour force grew, as a percentage of the total labour force union membership dropped slowly but steadily, to 31.4 percent in 1960 and 27.4 percent in 1970, then somewhat more rapidly to 23.6 percent in 1978, 20.1 percent in 1983 (after Ronald Reagan took office and broke the PATCO strike of air traffic controllers), and 12.5 percent today. The drop in the private sector has been more severe, to 7.9 percent of the labour force; only the rise of public sector unions (almost non-existent in the 1950s) has helped mask the haemorrhaging in the private sector.[1]

The problem is much more than a drop in membership: union power dropped even faster. In order to maintain power, workers and unions have to demonstrate an ability to disrupt the smooth function-

---

1   US Census Bureau (2005): 444–445; most recent data from *New York Times* 29 January 2005.

ing of the economy and society. Historically, this has meant strikes above all. But in the 1980s, US workers largely lost the ability to win strikes. Prior to the late 1970s, employers rarely attempted to break strikes or unions; undoubtedly they wanted to do so, but any such attempt would have been met with a fierce reaction that could have crippled a company. In the 1970s a few employers began to break strikes; in 1981, Ronald Reagan gave that approach the official imprimatur of the US government, and in the 1980s the practice took off. From 1969 to 1979, strikes involved an average of more than a million workers a year; since 1986 they have never involved even half a million workers, despite a larger labour force (US Census Bureau 2005: Table 637).

In the United States workers have an official right to strike, and legally they cannot be fired simply for going on strike. But in practice this has become meaningless, as the courts have ruled that US employers do have the right to permanently replace striking workers. So workers cannot be fired, but they can be permanently replaced, and for most purposes there is little difference. If the union capitulates and orders members back to work, the 'permanent replacements' (or scabs, at they used to be called) keep their jobs; union members get re-hired only if and when the scabs quit or are fired. In the 1980s a set of long bitter strikes were fought by unions opposing employer demands for take-aways. Almost every one of those battles – Arizona copper mine workers, Minnesota meat cutters, Maine paper workers, Caterpillar and Staley workers in the Midwest – was lost by the workers, with their militant unions crushed. At first unions were caught by surprise, and mounted their responses too late and without enough systematic reach. A decade of such strikes taught unions how to fight back, and a combination of tactics enabled them to win some of these massive confrontations, but unions remain scared to strike (Clawson, Johnson and Schall 1982; Franklin 2001; Green 1990; Hage and Klauda 1989; Kingslover 1989; Rachleff 1993; Rosenblum 1995; Juravich and Bronfenbrenner 1999).

Although some unions fought hard and were broken, most unions simply made concessions. Prior to the mid 1970s, when union contracts were expiring the question was how much the company would have to give in order to maintain labour peace. From the late 1970s through the mid 1990s the question became how many concessions the union would need to make in order to prevent the company from going all-out to break the union. In some cases the concessions involved wage reductions for existing members, but more commonly the contracts provided a lower rate of pay for new hires (so that two people could be side-by-side doing the identical work, one at a much higher rate of pay than the other), an increase in non-benefited part-time employees, reductions in benefits (especially health care), work rule changes, and union permission for the company to contract out some of the work to (non-union) suppliers (Moody 1988).

A further factor, harder to document, has been the decline in rank-and-file power combined with a shrinking organised left. Both rank-and-file and left activism continue to exist, of course – they are almost inevitable accompaniments of capitalism – but my estimate would be that in the US today the organised left is weaker than it has been at any previous point in more than a century. During the 1930s the Communist Party and a variety of Trotskyist and socialist groups were the driving force behind many organising drives and militant actions. The Communist Party at that time had perhaps 100,000 members, with a high turnover and a large group of sympathisers; today the largest left party in the US has less than one-twentieth that number of members (despite a population twice that of the 1930s) and for the most part left parties have little presence in the working class. The most notable exceptions are Teamsters for a Democratic Union and a constellation of forces around the monthly newsletter Labor Notes (Cochran 1977; Stepan-Norris and Zeitlin 2003; LaBotz 1990). Similarly, in the 1950s and 1960s a substantial fraction of all strike activity consisted of 'wildcat' strikes initiated by workers outside of, and often in opposition to, official union leadership. Rick Fantasia, writing in the mid 1980s, argued that 'If the proportions found in the Mangum study are even roughly accurate for the general situation, then the majority of all strikes throughout the postwar period have been wildcats' (Fantasia 1988: 64). Today such strikes are almost invisible.[2]

---

2   But see *Labor Notes* January 2005 for an account of an auto worker wildcat strike opposing mandatory overtime.

Unions also suffered a decline in political power. The Republican Party has always depended on business for its campaign financing, but a generation ago Democrats received twice as much campaign money from unions as from business. Today the Democratic Party gets seven times as much money from business as from labour (see www.open-secrets.org). Not only is labour a proportionately less important player; it has also been ineffective in its efforts to influence the Democratic Party. In the 2004 election, for example, a majority of unions supported Richard Gephardt and a minority of the most active and politically sophisticated unions supported Howard Dean. Both candidates were effectively eliminated at the very beginning of the race. The eventual nominee, John Kerry, had almost no labour support until his nomination was a foregone conclusion.

Political leverage over the government is particularly important in the US where unions are tightly tied to the state. In the US, although this is changing somewhat, in almost all cases in order for unorganised workers to win union representation, the union must collect signed authorisation cards from at least 30 percent of the workforce, and then petition the National Labor Relations Board (NLRB) to schedule and hold an election. But the rules for who is and is not included in the unit – part-time workers? all job categories? – and the rules about what constitutes fair play in the election are decided by the NLRB. Although Democratic and Republican foreign policy may not differ much, appointments to the NLRB do differ significantly, one of many reasons that unions are preoccupied with the outcome of presidential elections.

Reasons for Decline

A bedrock principle of capitalism, agreed on by Marx, Schumpeter, and Milton Friedman, is that capitalism is constantly changing. In Marx's words of more than 150 years ago:

> The bourgeoisie cannot exist without constantly revolutionizing the instruments
> of production, and thereby the relations of production, and with them the whole
> relations of society. [...] Constant revolutionizing of production, uninterrupted
> disturbance of all social conditions, everlasting uncertainty and agitation
> distinguish the bourgeois epoch from all earlier ones. All fixed, fast-frozen
> relations, with their train of ancient and venerable prejudices and opinions, are
> swept away, all new-formed ones become antiquated before they can ossify. All
> that is solid melts into air, all that is holy is profaned [...]. (The Communist
> Manifesto in Marx 1970: 38).

As a consequence, any labour movement that attempts to stand still, to simply hold on to what it had, will be gradually – and sometimes not so gradually – displaced. If labour controls 100 percent of the horse-shoeing jobs, that is much less significant today than it would have been in 1890. When transportation shifts from teams of horses to trucks, the Teamsters have to adapt or the union will soon be irrelevant.

Labour can maintain its strength only through constant renewal. That means bringing in new demographic groups and organising new forms of work, including work that had not previously been thought of as appropriate to labour unions. Even if the will is there, each new group poses what seems like an insuperable challenge. Frequently those challenges can only be solved through new forms of organisation (a switch from craft to industrial unions, for example) and the use of new tactics (the sit-down strike). After the new organising succeeds analysts point to the (now obvious) vulnerabilities that provided workers leverage, explaining that therefore of course organising would succeed.

This bedrock reality has been the key to US labour's long slow decline, a decline that began well before globalisation had a major impact, and a decline that reaches well beyond the parts of the economy most directly affected by globalisation. This reality also remains crucial to any possibilities for renewal. If the world changes and some of the changes mean that unions lose members, then unions must make offsetting gains elsewhere. The problem is that the current rules in the US make it extraordinarily difficult to organise new members.

Union decline is due to multiple factors. The first is the declining importance of industries where unions were strong. Take coal and steel, two of the foundations of the 1930s labour upsurge. Even if the Steelworkers continue to represent the same proportion of all those employed in primary metal industries, employment in those industries dropped from 1.3 million in 1970 to just 0.7 million in 1999; employment in mining dropped even faster, from 1.0 million in 1980 to half that two decades later. Combined with that has been an explosion of growth in areas where unions were weak. From 1980 to 1999 more than 80 percent of the total growth in employment, an increase of more than 30 million workers, came in services and in wholesale-retail trade, two areas where labour represented few workers (US Census Bureau 2000: 428–9). Unions have improved their situation in some services, but not in wholesale or retail trade.

Second is a decline in union members due to a company's closing unionised plants and moving production elsewhere. 'Elsewhere' can be, and for many years was, somewhere else in the US; more recently it has frequently been to another country. Kochan, Katz and McKersie (1986: 263) argue that management's strategy has been to accept the union and operate within the collective bargaining agreement at established plants, but to operate on the principle that no plant which is unionised will be expanded onsite. Over time the unionised facilities become antiquated, with investment and employment growth directed to new plants that at least start out non-union, and which the company then works to keep non-union.

Third has been the contracting out of work that was formerly done by a unionised employer, who shifts to using a non-union supplier. Geographically employment does not need to shift very far (assuming the union shows little interest in organising the new plant, or is too weak to do so).

Fourth, a decline in union members can be the result of the rise of new, non-union employers. In the US auto industry this has meant the spread of US-based auto factories owned and operated by Japanese companies like Toyota and Nissan. But the non-union firm can be US-owned, as in meatpacking, and most recently and most spectacularly, Wal-Mart.

Fierce Employer Opposition

All those factors get their bite, however, from the fact that there are enormous obstacles to organising new workers. Given employer opposition, and given a set of regulatory agency and court decisions hamstringing workers and unions, it is expensive, time-consuming, and a major struggle to bring new workers into the labour movement. Assuming the employer is paying attention, and almost all of them are, only a very determined set of workers, backed by strong union support, have much chance of unionising.

In 1935, in the wake of militant worker actions, including general strikes in three major cities, Congress passed the National Labor Relations Act (also known as the Wagner Act). Comparatively speaking pro-worker, it provided ways for workers to bring in unions through government-supervised elections, rather than through general strikes and sit-in factory occupations. In 1947 Congress passed the Taft-Hartley Act, reducing or eliminating many of the pro worker-union provisions contained in the original legislation. Labour's problems are not based on just that one act, however, but on a subsequent long series of ever more restrictive decisions by courts and regulatory agencies (Bernstein 1969; Tomlins 1985; Gross 1995; Friedman et al. 1994).

In theory, here's how workers in the United States form a union: A group of workers decide they want a union, or an existing union decides to see if it can persuade workers to join. Workers are asked to sign statements saying they would like to be represented by a union. When 30 percent of the workforce has signed cards or a petition asking for a union, this information is presented to the National Labor Relations Board (NLRB), which schedules an election. The election is held promptly, no worker is rewarded or penalised for supporting or opposing the union, and the employer provides no assistance to workers who oppose forming a union. The NLRB guarantees fair play; if pro-union workers are fired or otherwise penalised the NLRB speedily intervenes to restore the worker(s) to their old job(s) and working conditions. A free and fair election is held, the NLRB counts the ballots, and if the union wins a majority of the votes it is officially recognised and the employer sits down to bargain a union contract.

In practice, none of that holds true in that form. Few unions are willing to file for an election unless at least 65 percent of the workers have signed that they want a union, because experience shows that in the face of a relentless employer campaign many workers will be intimidated into voting against the union. Employers have a variety of means of delaying the election, and using that delay to mount an anti-union campaign.

Perhaps most important, employers have been held to have a 'free speech' right to be equal participants, in fact more than equal participants, when workers make a decision about who and what they want to represent them. It is somewhat like the US government being a more-than-equal participant when Iraqi citizens decide who and what they want to represent them. There is an occupying army and a guerrilla war in both places (although a much higher level of violence in Iraq).

Consider just three of the mechanisms available to US employers fighting a group of workers who want to bring in a union. First, employers may hold 'captive audience' meetings. The employer can require every worker in the shop to attend a meeting, held during work hours, where the employer makes the case why workers should vote against the union. In the 1930s, if an employer held such a meeting it was considered an egregious violation and entitled the union to a new election (or, in extreme cases, to be certified without a new election). Then a change in the law legalised such meetings, but the NLRB held that when the employer held such a meeting the union had to be given equal time for its own meeting. Today employers may hold an unlimited number of such meetings, and the union has no right to any meeting – in fact, no right to set foot on the premises. Typically employers show videos (say about union violence or corruption), since they are more effective than a speech.

A second, even more coercive (but totally legal), employer tactic is the 'one-on-one' grilling of an employer by a supervisor. Vulnerable workers are called in, one at a time, to a private conference where their supervisor (or sometimes an entire group of supervisors) asks them what they think about the union, whether they intend to vote for it, why, are not they troubled by union corruption, do they realise a union might require them to go on strike, and so on.

Third, if a worker or set of workers are the visible leaders of the pro-union campaign, the employer can – and does – simply fire them. Doing so is not legal, but employers can delay any penalty for up to three years, during which time the worker stays fired; if and when the worker wins the job back, the only penalty to the employer is to re-instate the worker and compensate him/her for lost wages, minus whatever the worker earned in the interim. Kate Bronfenbrenner's research shows that in one out of four union organising campaigns, employers fire one or more workers. For these reasons among others, Human Rights Watch concluded that 'the reality of NLRA enforce-ment falls far short of its goals' with 'weak and often ineffective' remedies and enforcement 'often delayed to a point where it ceases to provide redress' (Human Rights Watch 2000; Bronfenbrenner 1994; Bronfenbrenner and Hickey 2002; Geoghegan 1991; Friedman et al. 1994; Weiler 1983; Carreiro 2005).

But Labour Is Still a Power

Despite all this, US unions and the labour movement remain a major force. The AFL–CIO claims to have more members than any other labour federation in the world except for China. US unions have 16 million members, including more than 6 million women, 2.5 million African Americans, and 1.6 million Latinos. Unions have more mem-bers than any other progressive group: more women members than the National Organization of Women, more black members than the NAACP, more environmentalists than the Sierra Club. Including union members' families, 40 million Americans are directly affected by union victories and defeats (Clawson 2003: 15).

Politically, unions are still the most powerful progressive force. It is not just that they spent more than US $100 million on the 2004 presidential election. Much more important were direct communica-tions with members, and the ability to influence member voting. 'For example, gun owners favoured Bush by a 63–36 margin, but union members who own guns supported Kerry by 55–43%, according to an AFL–CIO survey. Bush won among white men by a 62–37% margin, but Kerry carried white men in unions by a 59–38% margin' (Dreier 2004: 5). If unions had represented the same percentage of the workforce as in 1980, the Democrats would have won decisive victories in both 2000 and 2004.

Precisely because of labour's remaining power, during Bush's second term unions will be in the cross-hairs. It is payback time. That is true not only for the AFL–CIO, but also for unions outside the federation. Bush's Secretary of Education labelled the leading teachers union, the (non AFL–CIO) National Education Association, a 'terrorist' organisation. Andy Stern, head of SEIU, the largest US union, has his wish: the political situation is as bad as that for organising, and it is hard to challenge the conclusion that unless something drastic is done, labour will at least decline, and perhaps disappear. But before examining the responses of top labour leadership, and the current discussions about restructuring labour, it is important to look at some positive signs at the grassroots: victories won, innovative strategies, new alliances, and impressive levels of militancy.

Driving Labour to Militancy

A standard Marxist argument is that employers' solution to one crisis becomes the factor that drives them into the next crisis. The mass production of Fordism leads to over-production, which in turn creates an economic collapse and crisis. The strong unions and welfare state policies of the 1930s and 1940s provide a social wage and resistance to wage cuts which in turn creates an economic underpinning that prevents a crisis of over-production. But the social wage, and the rising real wages unions won, in turn created a crisis that led to Reaganism and Thatcherism.

In the same way, the labour solutions of one period create the conditions that drive the next crisis. In the late 19th century, the problem employers faced was that workers knew more than management about the technical details of production and about the time and methods needed to accomplish a task; to a considerable degree, workers controlled production. This made it difficult for employers to impose speed-up. The solution to this, from employers' point of view, was the emergence of Taylorism and Fordism, processes whereby management came to understand production and control the speed at which employees worked. But the tightly interlinked top-down systems they created were vulnerable to stoppages at key points, and the routinised high-speed production led to resentful workers eager for revolt. In the 1930s that led to sit-down strikes where a single plant, or a small part of a plant, could shut down a company's entire operations. The result was industrial unions and seniority systems to limit managerial discretion (Clawson 1980; Taylor 1947; Ehrenreich and Ehrenreich 1980; Montgomery 1976).[3]

In the period after World War II, strong US unions forced US companies to provide substantial wage increases. Using constant 1999 US dollars, from 1949 to 1973 average family income more than doubled, from US \$19,515 to US \$41,935; moreover, incomes during this period became more equal, so those at the bottom benefited even more. This was not a simple result of corporate benevolence: 'From the late 1940s through the early 1970s [exactly the period of rapid income increases], strike levels in the United States stood higher than at any time, before or since' (Lichtenstein 2002: 136).

The strength of unions, and workers' willingness to fight for wage increases, squeezed corporate profits. As US world dominance declined, both because of the rise of economic competitors in Europe and Japan, and because of Vietnamese resistance to US imperialism, the US and world economies entered a slow crisis. Although this period was very different from the 1930s, employers had a sense that drastic action was necessary. In 1971, David Rockefeller, chairman of Chase Manhattan Bank, wrote in its Annual Report: 'It is clear to me that the entire structure of our society is being challenged' (MacLean 1999: 43). At meetings of top US business executives in 1973,

---

3   For a brilliant account of changes in the labour process in response to worker militancy around the world over the course of a century, see Silver 2003.

executives articulated this vulnerability: 'We are fighting for our lives', 'We are fighting a delaying action'. As one said, 'If we don't take action now, we will see our own demise. We will evolve into another social democracy' (Silk and Vogel 1976: 44, 45, 72).

Part of the employer action was a political mobilisation that led to Ronald Reagan, Republican political dominance, increased military spending, attacks on the welfare state, and a host of tax cuts. But equally important, though less reported, was a war on labour. The rules themselves were gradually changed to give employers additional weapons and to further restrict what unions could do, but more important than rules changes were the on-the-ground steps that employers took, sometimes within the law and often outside it. In 1962 46.1 percent of all NLRB elections were consent elections, meaning that the employer did not dispute or attempt to delay the union's request for an election. By 1977 only 8.6 percent of elections were consent elections (Prosten 1979: 39). Union busting became big business, involving billions of dollars. Many union-busting firms offered money-back guarantees: if workers successfully unionised, the union buster would stay to fight them, and the company would pay no fee (Levitt 1993).

The employer offensive was highly successful, both in its attack on unions per se and in its more general ability to re-shape the economy, society, and politics. From the mid 1970s to the mid 1990s and beyond, employers largely had it their own way and unions were slow to respond, often not recognising that the rules had changed. Employers had ended the accord, but labour had not responded, had not really accepted that the accord was over.

For a labour regulatory regime to succeed, it must channel activity within accepted limits; to do so it must provide rewards for accepting the regime. The employer offensive altered the de facto rules of the system to provide workers and unions much less hope of winning within the rules. Unions made two responses to that. Most unions simply stopped trying to organise, or to engage in militant action, figuring that it was not possible to win. But some unions took the opposite approach: if playing within the stacked and unfair rules led to failure, why play within the rules? Why not try new and innovative tactics, create new forms and new alliances?

If workers and unions stop worrying about what the rules say, they come up with very different kinds of unions, just as workers did in the 1930s. Under NLRB rules, the only mandatory subjects of bargaining are wages and hours and working conditions. Unions can raise other issues, but the employer can refuse to bargain about them, and the union may not legally go on strike over them. If the company is dumping pollutants in the community's drinking water, inside the NLRB rules the union cannot do much about it. Even attempting to raise the issue thus becomes a distraction, something that dilutes the union's inside-the-rules power.

But if the model is 'forget the NLRB and win by mobilising community power' then unions need community allies. Dealing with a women's issue, or immigration, or the environment, or global justice is not a distraction. It is a way to take on the issues that matter to workers AND it's a way to build strong relations with community allies. These days if people think something is 'just' a union issue, it is often hard to build public support or get media attention. But almost all union issues are also about family, and the environment, and equal rights for all; making that clear, and building those connections, creates a stronger labour movement that does not have to rely on the NLRB or the courts. Instead of expecting the government (through the NLRB) to guarantee fair play, increasingly unions mobilise community support and public pressure. The company avoids anti-union actions not because of their fear of NLRB penalties – which are minimal, delayed, and ineffective – but rather because anti-worker actions will bring public condemnation and potentially hurt business. In effect, this is a quasi-anarchist approach, substituting the community for the state. Needless to say, the unions adopting this approach are not intending to be anarchists or radicals – they are just trying to find some way to win.[4]

---

4   For a superior analysis addressing labour-community interactions in South Africa, see von Holdt 2003.

Ground Level Stirrings

If labour is to revive, and a new upsurge is to restore labour power, this will not happen simply because national leaders re-shuffle existing unions or increase organising expenditures by ten percent. A burst of growth depends on labour using new tactics and creating new organisational forms that enable unions (or other groups) to reach new constituencies around new issues. Fortunately, a great deal is already happening. Here I will briefly describe a few of these initiatives: anti-sweatshop organising, workers centres, living wage campaigns, Justice for Janitors, a multi-union coalition of low-wage service workers, graduate student unions, cross-border alliances, and anti-war organising.

Anti-sweatshop activity

Sweatshops – garment factories that pay less than minimum wage, or fail to pay for overtime, or fail to pay wages at all – are common not just in the Global South but in the US as well. Awareness of the issue took off in 1996, both through an anti-Nike publicity campaign, and through the exposure of the way clothing was manufactured for a line of clothing carrying the name of Kathie Lee Gifford, a popular television host, whose clothing was featured at Wal-Mart stores. Wendy Diaz, a fifteen-year-old Guatemalan worker who had been employed making Kathie Lee clothing since she was thirteen, testified before the US Congressional Democratic Policy Committee that she had to work from 8:00 a.m. to 9:00 p.m., and sometimes was forced to work all night (Shaw 1999: 99–113; Ross 1997: especially 51–77).

Growing out of this, and from an AFL–CIO program to employ student interns in the summer, college students formed United Students Against Sweatshops. Students used their leverage as consumers, but did so as collective consumers pressuring their colleges and universities to pledge to buy only sweat-free goods. Students said they could feel no pride in wearing a college-logo article unless they could be sure that no workers were exploited in making the cap or sweatshirt. College-logo goods are a US $2.5 billion a year business. Through a series of sit-ins on college campuses around the country, colleges and universities were forced to adopt Codes of Conduct pledging to use only those goods that could be shown to have been produced without exploiting workers. Collectively these campaigns revived what had largely disappeared as a tactic, the consumer boycott, and in doing so created an alliance of college students and ultra-low-income workers. The campaigns had to struggle against possible paternalism – privileged students doing something for workers, rather than in solidarity with workers – but they definitely raised public and student awareness of worker exploitation (Bonacich and Appelbaum 2000; Needleman 1998; Louie 2001).

Workers centres

Workers centres are a new form of organisation, targeted especially to immigrant low-wage workers. Many of these workers do not have a regular employer, and they may switch frequently from one to another kind of low-wage work. Rather than organising around a particular workplace, as unions do, workers centres are community organisations, often structured largely around an appeal to immigrants from one or another continent (Latinos, Asians), but focused on workplace issues. One out of eight workers in America today is a first-generation immigrant, and that figure rises to one in four for low-wage workers (Fine 2005, 2006).

    One typical form of action is helping workers recover wages they are owed, perhaps because an employer paid less than minimum wage, or did not pay the legally required time-and-a-half for overtime, or because the employer simply refused to pay wages at all (which marginal employers often do prior to closing one factory, moving across town, and opening under a new name). Lost-wages activity can be done either through a servicing approach – a workers centre staff member helps file charges and follows the case through the bureaucracy – or through collective organising, with a group of workers going to confront the boss and threaten exposure and legal action. Workers centres also organise day labourers, providing some kind of hiring hall, or organising on street corners so that no one will accept employment for less than a fixed dollar figure, say US $70 a day instead of the US $50 they had been receiving. There were only five workers centres in 1992, but by 2004 there were 133, an indication that this kind of organisation meets a real need – and also an indication that foundations have been willing to put money into these efforts, since almost none of them are self-financing (Gordon 1995; Gordon 2001: especially 88–9).

Living wage campaigns

In the US today, the minimum wage is US $5.15 an hour. Someone who worked at that wage full time all year round, never missing a day, would earn US $10,712 a year – but the poverty line for a family of four is US $19,311 a year. The concept of a 'living wage' is that a full-time worker should be able to earn enough to support a family of four at the poverty line – hardly a munificent level. That requires a wage of at least US $9.66 an hour.

Living wage campaigns have been conducted almost entirely in the public sector, focusing on winning a city or county ordinance specifying that all government employees, and all the employees of contractors working directly on providing services to the city, and all companies benefiting directly from city subsidies, must be paid a living wage. Most of the ordinances have been narrowly drawn. Because they cover a comparatively small number of people, they are relatively cheap to implement. A few campaigns have involved much broader coverage, sometimes becoming a new minimum wage ordinance, applying in a limited geographic region.

Living wage campaigns have also burgeoned. More than 125 cities (or other governmental units) have passed ordinances. New ordinances have continued to be added steadily; even the events of 9–11 seem to have done nothing to slow the living wage movement. The campaigns almost always involve a coalition of labour and community groups, and a high proportion of the campaigns win, although sometimes not until after a prolonged effort (Luce 2001, 2004).

Justice for Janitors

One of the first campaigns in the revival of innovative organising was an early 1990s effort to organise janitors in Los Angeles. In the 1980s unionisation rates and wages for janitors fell precipitously. Instead of the building owner providing cleaning directly, building owners gave contracts, often short-term contracts, to cleaning companies. Legally an organising campaign conducted under NLRB rules could only target the employer of record, the cleaning company. But if a campaign successfully unionised the cleaning company, the building owner could refuse to renew the (30 day) cleaning contract, hiring another (non-union) contractor instead. Therefore unionising one cleaning contractor was a recipe for unemployment.

The union responded by saying: Fine, we'll organise outside the NLRB process. We won't ask for a government supervised election. We will target the building owners, not the cleaning companies, and we will mobilise a minority of workers, but workers who are militant enough that they are willing and able to disrupt the building's normal operations. We will create enough disruption that building owners will decide it is better to accept the union and settle the contract rather than to face continuing demonstrations and inconvenience to tenants. The union's campaign lasted two years. At the end of the first year the union (SEIU) had spent a million dollars but not a single worker had (formally) joined the union; by the end of the second year the downtown office buildings were almost entirely unionised, with significant improvements in wages and benefits (Waldinger et al. 1998; Fisk, Mitchell and Erickson 2000). The Los Angeles campaign became a model for others, not only for janitors elsewhere, but for the labour movement more generally. As Steve Lerner, organiser for the campaign notes, this is so much so that now he frequently hears people say 'It's easy to organise janitors', to which he replies, 'Of course it is. It's easy to organise high turnover, minimum wage workers, most of them undocumented immigrants, working for independent contractors with short-term contracts. Of course.' (Lerner 2003).

Multi-union coalition

In Stamford, Connecticut, a remote suburb of New York City that is headquarters to many large corporations, the AFL–CIO helped bring together a coalition of unions all of which organised low-wage service sector workers, workers who are overwhelmingly women and people of colour. As the unions began to organise, they found that the issue that mattered most to workers was housing. Stamford has a very high median income – in the late 1990s over US $100,000 per year – and equally high housing prices. Workers earning US $25,000 a year could not afford to live in town, and the city was gradually replacing its public housing, displacing the existing tenants and converting low-income units into 'middle income' units for families with incomes up to US $71,000 a year.

The union coalition began to organise around the issue. Union researchers found out in advance about the city's plans to gentrify a complex, then went door-to-door talking to tenants. When the city held its meeting on the plans they expected the usual turn out, something like four or five people. Instead over 200 people came, and demanded that no changes be made that would displace existing tenants. The tenants and unions continued to organise and agitate, winning that battle, and several more, eventually winning an ordinance that the city cannot close down public housing unless it is replaced by an equivalent number of units at the same level of affordability.

Some might argue that unions cannot afford to use their scarce resources for this sort of campaign, that doing so means it is less possible to enrol new members and increase union power. But the coalition argued, and had the evidence to show, that these campaigns built the unions' reputations, and made it much easier for them to organise other workers. Many of the workers they subsequently organised had worked with the union staff in one or another tenant campaign (Clawson 2003: 110–130).

Graduate student unions

Twenty years ago, almost no graduate students were members of unions. In the US, a high proportion of doctoral students are supported by working twenty hours a week as Teaching Assistants grading papers and leading discussion sections, or as Research Assistants doing research in laboratories or on grant projects. In the last decade graduate student employees have successfully unionised at numerous public universities and at one private university, bringing tens of thousands of new members into labour unions.[5] Graduate student unions would win at several other private universities, but the Bush National Labor Relations Board, on a straight party-line vote, decided that the fact of being a graduate student at a private university means that the person cannot legally be an employee, even if he or she works twenty hours a week for pay. Graduate student unions are important not simply because of the number of members they enrol, but also because of the vitality and fresh viewpoint they bring to labour, and because of their effect on the consciousness of large numbers of people who are union members for at least a few years of their lives.

Cross border alliances

Much of the discussion of cross-border alliances assumes that workers in a country like the United States will offer aid and support to workers in a country like Guatemala. But equally significant are campaigns that bring together workers and unions most of whom are in advanced industrial societies. In preparation for the 1997 UPS strike in the US, for example, the Teamsters union reached out to UPS workers in Europe and to the unions that represent them. The US

---

5   Unionised public universities include the University of California system, the University of Wisconsin, the University of Massachusetts, Michigan State, the University of Michigan, the City University of New York, and several others. The one private university is New York University. For a full list of universities with recognised graduate student unions, as well as a list of campaigns in progress, go to: www.cgeu.org/contacts.html.

Teamsters represent two-thirds of UPS's world wide workforce, but UPS has employees in sixteen European countries, including 18,000 workers in Germany. A little over two months before the strike, an international working group of unions organised 150 job actions and demonstrations at UPS facilities worldwide. A world council of unions representing UPS workers was formed, and the council met in Washington the day US negotiations began. Representatives from around the world came to negotiations and were introduced to the UPS management negotiators, with the implicit threat of coordinated job actions. During the US strike, a variety of job actions took place at UPS sites around the world. What better time for unions in other countries to find UPS vulnerable? These coordinated actions had a material effect during the US strike, and they show the potential for other such actions. SEIU, for example, which represents building service workers, faces fierce opposition by European-owned companies that accept unions in Europe but resist them in the US. SEIU is building alliances with European trade unions, with the aim of pressuring the European companies to give US workers a level playing field.[6]

Anti-war organising

Historically, US unions have strongly supported US foreign policy. When John Sweeney took office in 1995, he replaced the old AFL–CIO international relations department head with Barbara Shailor, who openly referred to the previous policy as the AFL–CIA policy. During the Vietnam War an anti-war resolution was brought to a vote at the AFL–CIO national convention. The vote was 6 in favour and 2000 against. For the Iraq war the story was substantially different. Prior to the war the AFL–CIO as a whole adopted a weak resolution calling on the US not to go to war unless the United Nations voted to

---

6   For UPS, Russo and Banks 1999. For US unions working with Latin American workers and unions, Frundt 1988 and 1999, as well as Moberg 1988. See also Gordon and Turner 2000; Cohen and Early 1999; Seidman 2002; Bandy and Mendez 2002.

support military action; in effect that was an anti-war resolution, but not a full and open one. Since then unions representing about 40 percent of total AFL–CIO membership have adopted much stronger anti-war resolutions.

The 1960s and Today: Understanding the New Initiatives

Each of those sorts of campaign is significant enough in and of itself, but they are the more so because of their commonalities and what they indicate about the base for significant social change. At least two points need to be stressed: the relation of these activities to movements of the 1960s, and the character of the new forms that are emerging.

In order to flourish, and perhaps in order to simply survive, labour must constantly be adapting, incorporating new groups and taking up new issues. The world of today is very different from the world at the time of labour's last US upsurge (the 1930s and 1940s). Some of the crucial changes are:[7]

- The number of women working for pay has increased dramatically, with the most pronounced shift among white married women. In 1940, more than two-thirds of all families had employed husbands and stay-at-home wives; today less than 1 in 5 US families fit that pattern.
- An economy, and a labour movement, focused on manufacturing have given way to an economy dominated by a service sector. In 1940, the number of manual workers exceeded the number of white-collar workers by more than 25 percent; in 1998 there were more than twice as many white-collar workers as manual workers. This change interacts with the previous one, since women are much more likely than men to be white-

7   For a more complete discussion of these changes and their effects on unions see Clawson 2003.

collar workers. Among US men today, there are almost as many blue-collar as white-collar workers; among women, there are seven times as many white-collar as blue-collar workers.

- African Americans used to be overwhelmingly concentrated in the rural South; now they are more urban than the general population and substantial numbers live in every geographic region.
- Immigration had been reduced to a trickle, and what immigration there was came from Europe. As recently as 1960 only 6 percent of children were in immigrant families, and more than two-thirds of those immigrants came from Canada or Europe. Today, more than 20 percent of children are in immigrant families, and three-quarters of them come from Latin America and Asia.
- The US economy was largely self-sufficient and its foreign policy avoided foreign entanglements except in Latin America and the Caribbean; although the US traded with the rest of the world, that trade was a tiny fraction of the total economy. For example, up to 1963 the import content of finished manufacture was never more than 3 percent.

The social movements of the 1960s were centrally concerned with the changes listed above. And in turn the movements of the 1960s were themselves the forces driving those changes forward in all kinds of ways. But for the most part the labour movement did not connect with those movements, even though they were taking up exactly the concerns that should have been central to a vibrant labour movement. The future course of labour would have been sharply different had unions taken up race and gender issues. Perhaps the single greatest failure of the US Left in the past fifty years is the lack of connection between labour and the movements of the 1960s. This drastically weakened and limited both labour and the Black, feminist, environmental, student, public interest, and anti-intervention movements, contributing to the class-biased nature of 1960s movements and to the ossification and insularity of labour.

If the Sweeney era of the AFL–CIO (1995 on) can take credit for one thing, it is the widespread efforts to re-connect labour with the successors to the movements of the 1960s, and the significant successes in those efforts. There is a very long way to go, and the situation is extremely uneven, but significant parts of the labour movement are not only taking good positions on women's issues, immigration, war, and globalisation, but also are forging connections with those movements and working with them. The AFL–CIO sponsored an Immigrant Workers Freedom Ride; labour helped fight for and win parental leave in California and the Family and Medical Leave Act nationally; living wage campaigns unite labour and low income community groups; important unions have taken strong anti-war positions; and labour has endorsed and participated in many anti-globalisation activities. To put this in crude terms, if the labour movement of the 1930s was the thesis, and the movements of the 1960s were the antithesis, there are indications that labour today has the potential to create a new synthesis that incorporates both of the previous movements as it transcends them both.

The second major point about the grassroots labour initiatives discussed above is that each of them, in different ways, breaks down the barrier between unions and other kinds of movements. All of these are labour initiatives, but none of them are traditional union initiatives. Sweatshops, living wage campaigns, union coalitions focused on housing, anti-war activities all address labour issues, but do so through forms and in ways that do not fit comfortably within the unions that have dominated the US scene for at least fifty years.

Struggle at the Top and Its Impact

The AFL–CIO seems to respond more to political crises, which come suddenly and decisively, than to union decline, which has been a slower and seemingly more inexorable process. Thus the first 'revitalisation' of labour came in 1995 with the election of John Sweeney and the 'New Voice' leadership. Although labour's decline had been underway for many years, and the seriousness of the situation had been evident for some time, it was the sweeping Republican victories in the 1994 Congressional elections which precipitated the crisis. It seemed – incorrectly for the short run, as it turned out – that Republicans were on the brink of assuming a firm political control on all branches of government.

This time around the political situation is also crucial, as Andy Stern's remarks (quoted in the chapter's opening) make clear, although there is also recognition that the crisis is profound, and band-aids – even a lot of band-aids – will not provide a solution. The election of Bush to a second term, together with Republican majorities in both houses of Congress and control of most state governments, means that the terrain of struggle will become more difficult, in what was already an extremely challenging situation.

Consider one example: in the past decade, many of labour's most innovative campaigns have avoided National Labor Relations Board elections, instead collecting signed cards from a majority of the workers. Under US law, the employer does not have to accept that as evidence that workers prefer a union, but the employer may do so. As a consequence, unions have mounted pressure campaigns to force the employer to agree in advance to accept 'card check' recognition. Now the Bush National Labor Relations Board may rule that 'card check' elections are unacceptable under any circumstances, even if the employer voluntarily agrees to them. A second example: unions have been strongest in the public sector, since it is politically difficult to use some of the most coercive tactics or to prohibit union supporters from entering a public building. The Republican response has been legal changes that rule large categories of public sector workers can no longer be represented by unions. In combination, these attacks are intended to eliminate whatever pockets of union strength remain.

Whether provoked by political reversal or the long decline in union numbers and strength, this situation has generated more discussion of major change than has been heard for at least fifty years. The internal precipitating factor was the spring of 2004 emergence of the New Unity Partnership, a strange coalition of five unions. Three of the unions – the Service Employees International Union, the Hotel Employees and Restaurant Employees, and UNITE (the garment workers union) – are among the most progressive and vibrant in the labour movement. One, the labourers union (also known as LIUNA) represents some of the less skilled construction workers, and has had some progressive organising campaigns. The final union, the Carpenters, had left the AFL–CIO earlier, after an extended period of not paying its dues. On the one hand the Carpenters have emphasised organising; on the other, the Carpenters' president has provided political support to Republican candidates, including appearing with President Bush. All five unions come out of the AFL wing of the labour movement; none are CIO industrial unions in manufacturing. Three of the five unions (SEIU, HERE, the labourers) have had recent problems with internal corruption, although all now have leaderships actively working to root out any remaining corruption.

The New Unity Partnership (NUP) aggressively pushed for a change in labour, specifically that the AFL–CIO should merge and consolidate from 64 unions to something more like 20, and in the process should re-organise and re-structure, so that each union represented workers in a defined sector, and all the workers in that sector were in one union. This would involve drastic re-shuffling, since many US unions are in effect conglomerates, representing pockets of workers in many different industries, and some kinds of workers are divided among many different unions – nurses, for example, are to be found in eighteen different unions. The NUP also emphasised the need to put more money into organising, and to be more politically effective, both goals that are verbally endorsed by almost all unions, but acted on by comparatively few. Although NUP claimed to be no more than a voluntary grouping of unions committed to these goals, its members simultaneously threatened to leave the AFL–CIO unless major changes were made.

The New Unity Partnership itself never gained traction, but its actions have led to turmoil, debate, and the likelihood of significant change of some sort. As I write, in February 2005, three possibilities are actively being discussed, but the situation is fluid, and the specifics are less important than the range of possibilities being actively considered and the fact that many actors seem insistent that there must be some change.

The first possibility is a contested election for president of the AFL–CIO, an election that will take place later this year. When John Sweeney was first elected he had said he would not serve more than ten years, in which case he would retire at the end of his current term, but in response to NUP Sweeney announced he would run for another term. There are persistent rumours that John Wilhelm, head of HERE (now merged with UNITE), will oppose Sweeney, and Rich Trumka, the number two leader of the AFL–CIO, has publicly said that if Sweeney should choose to retire then he, Trumka, would expect to run. New leadership, by itself, would lead to only minimal change, but perhaps a leadership contest would pose alternatives and force structural transformation.

A second possibility is to further weaken the AFL–CIO, the central union federation. In the fall of 2004 the Teamsters union proposed that unions that invested a substantial fraction of their dues into organising new members should be permitted to cut their AFL–CIO dues payments by 50 percent. This proposal quickly gained support; even John Sweeney, president of the AFL–CIO, has come out in support of some version of the measure. The AFL–CIO receives only a small fraction of the total amount of money collected by unions, so this change is estimated to involve only about US $35 million, out of total labour revenues of nearly US $7 billion. It is difficult to imagine this would lead to a substantial increase in organising. It might lead to a significant weakening of the central labour federation, but by itself that will solve little or nothing.

The third possibility, and the one posing both the greatest dangers and the greatest opportunities, would be a split in the AFL–CIO leading to rival labour federations. On the one hand this might lead to internecine warfare that weakened both sides and left employers the big winners. On the other hand, union rivalry might force all unions (those that stayed in the federation as well as those that broke away) to be more responsive to members. US labour's greatest growth came at a time when the AFL and CIO unions opposed each other. Sometimes one union would undercut another by cutting a deal with the employer, but often unions were forced to be more militant and effective in order to keep workers from switching to the rival federation. A crucial difference this time around, however, is that at least so far there is no difference in ideology or orientation between the potential federations, as there was between the industrial unionism of the CIO and the craft unionism of the AFL.

References

Bandy, J. and Mendez J.B. (2002) 'A Place of Their Own? Women Organizers Negotiating National and Transnational Civil Society in the Maquilas of Nicaragua and Mexico', American Sociological Association Meetings, Chicago IL, August 18.

Bernstein, Irving (1969) *Turbulent Years: A History of the American Worker, 1933–1941*, Boston: Houghton Mifflin.

Bonacich, E. and Appelbaum, R. (2000) *Behind the Label: Inequality in the Los Angeles Apparel Industry*, Berkeley: University of California Press.

Broder, D.S. (2004) 'SEIU Chief Says the Democrats Lack Fresh Ideas', *Washington Post*, July 27.

Bronfenbrenner, K. (1994) 'Employer Behavior in Certification Elections and First-Contract Campaigns: Implications for Labor Law Reform', in S. Friedman et al. (eds) *Restoring the Promise of American Labor Law*, Ithaca, NY: ILR Press.

— (2001) 'Organizing Women Workers in the Global Economy: Findings from NLRB Certification Election Campaigns 1998–1999', paper presentation at the Los Angeles AFL–CIO International Women's Day, March 8.

— (2002) and Hickey, R. 'Changing to Organize: A National Assessment of Union Organizing Strategies', paper presented at the ILE Research Conference on Union Organizing, May 17.

Carreiro, J. (2005) 'The Political Economy of the News Media: A Study of the Extent of Labor Movement Coverage in U.S. Newspapers', photocopy.

Clawson, D. (1980) *Bureaucracy and the Labor Process: The Transformation of U.S. Industry, 1860–1920*, New York: Monthly Review Press.

— (2003) *The Next Upsurge: Labor and the New Social Movements*, Ithaca, NY: Cornell University Press.

— Johnson, K. and Schall J. (1982) 'Fighting Union Busting in the 80's', *Radical America* 16(4–5): 45–62.

Cochran, B. (1977) *Labor and Communism: The Conflict That Shaped American Unions*, Princeton: Princeton University Press.

Cohen, L. and Early S. (1999) 'Defending Workers' Rights in the Global Economy: The CWA Experience', in B. Nissen (ed.) *Which Direction for Organized Labor*, Detroit: Wayne State University Press.

Dreier, P. (2004) 'Labor in the Bush Era', *In Critical Solidarity* 4(1): 1, 5.

Ehrenreich, J. and Ehrenreich, B. (1980) 'The Professional-Managerial Class', in Pat Walker (ed.) *Between Labor and Capital*, Boston: South End Press.

Fantasia, R. (1988) *Cultures of Solidarity: Consciousness, Action, and Contemporary American Workers*, Berkeley: University of California Press.

Fine, J. (2005) 'Low Wage Workers, Faith-Based Organizing, Immigrant Worker Centers and "One Big Movement" in Dan Clawson's *The Next Upsurge*', *Critical Sociology* 31(3): 401–10.

— (2006) *Worker Centers: Organizing Communities at the Edge of the Dream*, Ithaca, NY: Cornell University Press.

Fisk, C.L., Mitchell, D.J.B. and Erickson, C.L. (2000) 'Union Representation of Immigrant Janitors in Southern California: Economic and Legal Challenges', in R. Milkman (ed.) *Organizing Immigrants: The Challenge for Unions in Contemporary California*, Ithaca, NY: ILR Press.

Franklin, S. (2001) *Three Strikes: Labor's Heartland Losses and What They Mean for Working Americans*, New York: Guilford Press.

Friedman, Sheldon, Hurd, R., Oswald, R.A. and Seeber, R.L. (eds) (1994) *Restoring the Promise of American Labor Law*, Ithaca, NY: ILR Press.

Frundt, H. (1999) 'Cross-Border Organizing in the Apparel Industry: Lessons from Central America and the Caribbean', *Labor Studies Journal* 24(1): 89–106.

— (1988) *Trade Conditions and Labor Rights*, Gainesville: University Press of Florida.

Geoghegan, T. (1991) *Which Side Are You On? Trying to be for Labor when it's Flat on Its Back*, New York: Farrar, Strauss, & Giroux.

Gordon, J. (1995) 'We Make the Road by Walking: Immigrant Workers, The Workplace Project, and the Struggle for Social Change', *Harvard Civil Rights-Civil Liberties Law Review* 30: 132–151.

— (2001) 'Organizing Low-Wage Immigrants – The Workplace Project', *WorkingUSA* 5 (1): 87–102.

Gordon, M. and Turner, L. (eds) (2000) *Transnational Cooperation Among Labor Unions*, Ithaca, NY: Cornell/ILR Press.

Green, H. (1990) *On Strike at Hormel: The Struggle for a Democratic Labor Movement*, Philadelphia: Temple University Press.

Gross, J.A. (1995) *Broken Promise: The Subversion of U.S. Labor Relations Policy, 1947–1994*, Philadelphia: Temple University Press.

Hage, D. and Klauda, P. (1989) *No Retreat, No Surrender: Labor's War at Hormel*, New York: Morrow.

Human Rights Watch (Lance Compa) (2000) *Unfair Advantage: Workers' Freedom of Association in the United States under International Human Rights Standards*, New York: Human Rights Watch.

Juravich, T. and Bronfenbrenner, K. (1999) *Ravenswood: The Steelworkers' Victory and the Revival of American Labor*, Ithaca, NY: Cornell University Press.

Kingsolver, B. (1989) *Holding the Line: Women in the Great Arizona Mine Strike of 1983*, Ithaca, NY: ILR/Cornell University Press.

Kochan, T.A., Katz, H.C. and McKersie, R.B. (1986) *The Transformation of American Industrial Relations*, New York: Basic Books.

LaBotz, D. (1990) *Rank and File Rebellion: Teamsters for a Democratic Union*, London: Verso.

Lerner, S. (2003) 'Labour's Future', paper presentation at the University of California, Berkeley; 29 October.

Levitt, M.J. (1993) *Confessions of a Union Buster*, New York: Crown.

Lichtenstein, N. (2002) *State of the Union: A Century of American Labor*, Princeton: Princeton University Press.

Louie, M.C.Y. (2001) *Sweatshop Warriors: Immigrant Women Workers Take on the Global Factory*, Cambridge, MA: South End Press.

Luce, S. (2001) 'Building Political Power and Community Coalitions: The Role of Central Labor Councils in the Living Wage Movement', in I. Ness and S. Eimer, (eds) *Central Labor Councils and the Revival of American Unionism,* New York: M.E. Sharpe.

— (2004) *Fighting for a Living Wage*, Ithaca, NY: Cornell University Press.

MacLean, N. (1999) 'The Hidden History of Affirmative Action: Working Women's Struggles in the 1970s and the Gender of Class', *Feminist Studies* 25(1): 43–78.

Marx, K. (1970) *Selected Works*, Moscow: Progress Publisher.

Moberg, D. (1998) 'Lessons from the Victory at Phillips Van Heusen', *WorkingUSA* 1(2): 39–49.

Montgomery, D. (1976) 'Workers' Control of Machine Production in the Nineteenth Century', *Labor History* 17(3): 485–509.

Moody, K. (1988) *An Injury to All: The Decline of American Unionism*, London: Verso.

Needleman, R. (1998) 'Building Relationships for the Long Haul: Unions and Community-Based Groups Working Together to Organize Low-Wage Workers', in K. Bronfenbrenner et al. (eds) *Organizing to Win: New Research on Union Strategies*, Ithaca, NY: ILR Press.

Pollin, R. and Luce, S. (1998) *The Living Wage: Building a Fair Economy*, New York: New Press.

Prosten, R. (1979) 'The Rise in NLRB Election Delays: Measuring Business' New Resistance', *Monthly Labor Review* 102(2): 38–40.

Rachleff, P. (1993) *Hard Pressed in the Heartland: The Hormel Strike and the Future of the Labor Movement*, Boston: South End Press.

Reynolds, D. (1999) 'The Living Wage Movement Sweeps the Nation', *WorkingUSA* 3(3): 61–80.

Ross, A. (ed.) (1997) *No Sweat: Fashion, Free Trade, and the Rights of Garment Workers*, London: Verso.

Rosenblum, J.D. (1995) *Copper Crucible: How the Arizona Miners' Strike of 1983 Recast Labor-Management Relations in America*, Ithaca, NY: ILR Press.

Russo J. and Banks, A. (1999) 'How Teamsters Took the UPS Strike Overseas', *WorkingUSA* 3(3): 75–87.

Seidman, G. (2002) 'Deflated Citizenship: Labor Rights in a Global Era', paper presented at the American Sociological Association Meetings, Chicago IL, August 18.

Shaw, R. (1999) *Reclaiming America: Nike, Clean Air, and the New National Activism*, Berkeley: University of California Press.

Silk, L. and Vogel, D. (1976) *Ethics and Profits*, New York: Simon and Schuster.

Silver, B. (2003) *Forces of Labor: Workers' Movements and Globalization since 1870*, New York: Cambridge University Press.

Stepan-Norris, J. and Zeitlin, M. (2003) *Left Out: Reds and America's Industrial Unions*, New York: Cambridge University Press.

Taylor, F.W. (1947) *Shop Management* [orig. 1903], and *The Principles of Scientific Management* [orig. 1911], reprinted in *Scientific Management*, New York: Harper and Brothers.

Tomlins, C. (1985) *The State and the Unions: Labor Relations, Law, and the Organized Labor Movement in America, 1880–1960*, New York: Cambridge University Press.

U.S. Census Bureau (1975) *Historical Statistics of the United States*, Washington, DC: U.S. Government Printing Office.

— (1980) *Statistical Abstract of the United States: 1980*, Washington, DC: U.S. Government Printing Office.

— (2000) *Statistical Abstract of the United States: 2000*, Washington, DC: U.S. Government Printing Office.

— (2005) *Statistical Abstract of the United States: 2004–05*, Washington, DC: U.S. Government Printing Office.

von Holdt, K. (2003) *Transition from Below: Forging Trade Unionism and Workplace Change in South Africa*, Pietermaritzburg: University of Natal Press.

Waldinger, R., Erickson, C., Milkman, R., Mitchell, D.J.B. and Valenzuela, A. (1998) 'Helots No More: A Case Study of the Justice for Janitors Campaign in Los Angeles', in K. Bronfenbrenner et al. (eds) *Organizing to Win*, Ithaca, NY: ILR Press, 1998.

Weiler, P. (1983) 'Promises to Keep: Securing Workers' Rights to Self-Organization under the NLRA', *Harvard Law Review* 96: 1769–1827.

ANITA CHAN

Realities and Possibilities for Chinese Trade Unionism

Introduction

In the past few years China has become the focus of international attention as it emerges as an important economic power. Injecting tens of millions of workers into the world labour market in the past two decades, the China labour issue and, related to it, the All China Federation of Trade Unions (ACFTU), China's only official trade union federation, have aroused emotive and heated debates within the international trade union circle. China is feared as a gigantic competitor snatching jobs from developed and developing countries alike. Trade unions of the developed world criticise the ACFTU as an arm of the Chinese state and refuse to recognise it as a trade union. The International Confederation of Free Trade Unions (ICFTU) does not accept the ACFTU as a member.

Underlying this criticism that the ACFTU is not a real trade union and is hopelessly ineffectual is the wish that if only independent trade unions were allowed to exist, Chinese labour standards would rise and somehow in the distant future there would be a better world internationally for workers. Will this scenario come true, or is it wishful thinking? Readers who have read the earlier chapters of this book may have doubts about any optimistic expectation. Neoliberal globalisation, new technologies and fast movement of capital are eroding the gains that workers and their trade unions have made. This is particularly obvious in the developed world, and is preventing those who had never previously enjoyed these benefits from sharing any of them. The domination of the market over social justice seems unstoppable. Workers desperate for jobs and security are engaged in a race to the bottom. According to Andréia Galvão (in this volume), even the rare labour success story of a trade union leader popularly elected as president of Brazil paradoxically required that one of the two major union federations compromise by retreating to a less combative 'citizen unionism' model.

In this chapter on the official Chinese trade union, I want to underline the fact that Chinese workers and the ACFTU are subject to the same anti-labour forces, even though right now, on the surface, China and Chinese workers seem to be winning in the global competition for foreign direct investment (FDI) and employment. There are two main forces at work today shaping the ACFTU. The first is internal: its nature as an organisation, which is a product of Maoist socialism and a one-party state system; and the second is the growing influence of external global economic forces ever since the Chinese economy was integrated into the international economy a quarter century ago. The chapter will take these two factors into account, including the historical and contemporary dimensions, when discussing the present and future of Chinese trade unionism.

The ACFTU under Maoist Authoritarianism

One issue in studies of trade unions is a union's ideological and strategic relationship with the state. At one end of the spectrum is a system where the trade union has a weak relationship with the government. At the other, a union can be under absolute state domination. This latter was the case in Leninist one-party states, where the trade union was an integral organ of the party-state. Even within Communist systems there were variations, and China had occupied the extreme end of the spectrum in terms of the trade union's incorporation into, and subjugation to, the party-state and management during the Maoist period (1949–76). According to a comparative study conducted by a Soviet specialist, even in the Soviet Union in the 1950s and 1960s enterprise-level trade unions had played a bigger role than did Chinese trade unions in the 1980s. In the USSR, 'some 3 to 10 percent of the Soviet industrial labour force was involved each year as plaintiffs in one or another aspect of the grievance procedure, whereas the Chinese enterprise trade unions appear to be involved almost exclusively with matters of worker welfare' (Granick 1990: 238). As will be observed, this tradition of government control has left an imprint on present-day union capacities and workers' abilities to mobilise.

Despite the controls – and indeed in reaction to them – there have been several episodes in which workers and/or the ACFTU publicly asserted themselves in Maoist times. The ACFTU or some of its leaders had tried unsuccessfully to play a more independent role from the party-state on four separate occasions: first, immediately after Liberation resulting in the purge of the union chair; in 1956–67 at the time of the Hungarian Uprising, also resulting in another union chair stepping down; in 1966–67 during the Cultural Revolution; and the fourth time, shortly after Mao's death in 1976 (Chan 1993; Sheehan 1998). The wish of some trade union officials to shake off tight Party control was always there, strategically surfacing at times when state authority was under challenge from social upheavals usually instigated or led by other social groups (such as the Red Guards, students or intellectuals).

In this history of sporadic Chinese working-class movements and their recurrent alliance with Communist trade unions, sceptics would surely question whether workers and the official Communist trade unions ever actually shared similar goals. Very often, plainly, the trade unions and their cadres have acted ineffectually or against workers' interests, and they function at times merely as an arm of enterprise administration. However, this does not alter the fact that the political structure of a one-party Communist state is not totally monistic, and that, just as in a pluralistic structure, a bureaucratic organisation within the state may seek sometimes to assume its own separate identity. It can act in accordance with the institution's collective interests and/or its members' individual interests. But once crushed by the Communist Party in 1957–58, the ACFTU was not able to re-emerge as a bureaucratic interest for more than twenty years.

1980s: In Search of a Role
in the Transition to a New Economic Order

During the 1980s, the ACFTU was allowed to re-organise itself. The party-state even granted the ACFTU a certain measure of authority to protect workers' rights from being violated by the party-state itself. One reason was that during 1980–81, not long after Deng Xiaoping and his team took power, a wave of strikes and agitation for the formation of autonomous trade unions swept China (Wilson 1990). Whether by coincidence, by convergence or by contagion, this unrest emerged around the same time as the Solidarity movement in Poland, the first successful workers' revolution in a workers' state and one which aroused great consternation in the socialist world. Thereafter, China's Party leaders sought to forestall any possible re-enactment of such a movement on Chinese soil. One of the leadership's strategies in the 1980s was to reinvigorate the ACFTU and to give it somewhat greater latitude to act as a representative of its constituency, so as to lobby on the workforce's behalf from inside the state and to act as a means to mediate workers' interests within enterprises.

Once allowed to re-establish itself, the ACFTU immediately launched a programme of trade union reforms. Since then, 'trade union reform' has been discussed incessantly in trade union publications to this very day. It first tried to assert itself by publicising the rehabilitation of Li Lisan, the trade union chair purged in the 1950s for challenging the Party. Second, it worked from the grassroots upward by reviving the Staff and Workers Representative Congress (SWRC) system in enterprises, first created in 1957 as a version of the Hungarian workers' councils. The enterprise-level trade union committee was to act as the standing administrative body of the Congress (Sheehan 1998: 72–5, 176). Because the Congress was endowed on paper with much power, the ACFTU placed building up the SWRC system on its priority list. It had hoped that the SWRC system could become the vehicle by which the union could share power with the Party (Jiang 1996: 127).[1] Unfortunately, for a variety of reasons, the SWRC system was unable to take off.

The blue-collar workforce increasingly needed a means of defence, at a time when the workers' situation was increasingly under threat. The second half of the 1980s witnessed revolutionary changes in China on all fronts – with entrance to the world market, industrial restructuring, the emergence of private domestic capital and foreign capital, the separation of Party and management in state enterprises, the leasing out of state enterprises to managers, and related changes. China embarked on a programme to dismantle the state enterprise structure and, with it, the status of workers, eroding job security. It marked the beginning of a decentralised system of employment of a contractual nature and a new industrial relations system (You 1998; Tomba 2002). Whereas under the planned economy system wage-setting was determined by the central government and the same levels of pay applied nationwide, it was now determined increasingly at the enterprise level, so that it would be necessary to have genuine collective bargaining if workers' wages were to keep up with the expanding economy.

In the face of such monumental changes, abetted by an increasingly vibrant atmosphere of intellectual debate and a gathering rebellious social mood that would erupt by the end of the decade, notably as the social upheaval of 1989, the ACFTU seized the opportunity to become relevant in the new political and economic configuration, trying to shake off the control of the party-state.[2] For

---

1   Kevin Jiang's article is an unusual piece of writing on the ACFTU. It was based on an insider's knowledge and from an insider's perspective, as Jiang was a former trade union historian. The piece was written and published after he left China, and therefore contains an enormous amount of rare insider's information that could not have seen the light of day inside China. The title of the article, 'The Conflicts between Trade Unions and the Party-State: The Reform of the Chinese Trade Unions in the Eighties', was most challenging, since the official discourse has always been that the party-state and the union have a hierarchical relationship and unified goal, and so are not supposed to be in 'conflict'.

2   *Zhongguo Quanzong Lilun Taolunhui Lunwn Xuanbian* (Selected Essays from a Workshop on Trade Union Theoretical Issues), *Gonghui Lilun Wenti Tantao* (Exploring Trade Union Theoretical Questions) (1988), vol. 3, Beijing: Workers Press. It is possible to detect restiveness among the authors in this

instance, it demanded the right to 'participate and discuss politics' (*canzheng yizheng*) at all levels of the government, especially on occasions when the issues related to workers' welfare were affected. The ACFTU was fighting to be included in policy-making. In 1986, top ACFTU leadership initiated a 'dialogue' with the government, setting an example for lower-level unions to follow suit. It issued a series of documents expressing the ACFTU's opinion over a range of issues: occupational health and safety, retirement, indexing retirees' pensions to the rising cost of living, etc. Although the SWRC system had not been particularly successful, it continued incessantly to push for its legalisation in the course of drafting the Enterprise Law. It fought to insert articles to prevent drafts that sidelined trade union and workers' rights. It demanded that a new chapter be devoted solely to the trade union, or that articles such as 'No one is allowed to eliminate or amalgamate a trade union organisation, or use the excuse of restructuring to replace the trade union chair' be inserted (Jiang 1996: 129–131). These aggressive activities ultimately served to change the thrust of several important Chinese labour laws, making them more inclusive of rights for workers and the trade union.

According to an internal document released by the Beijing Municipal Committee Research Office in 1988,[3] during some thirty forums organised by the city and the city-level unions there were suggestions by union cadres that they should be rid of such duties as overseeing the social welfare of workers on behalf of the enterprise management, in order to free them up to concentrate on protecting workers' rights. Some suggested that union membership should be voluntary instead of automatic, to strengthen workers' sense of identity with the union. Some union cadres even wanted to dissociate

---

collected volume of some 30 short articles written by trade union officials and teachers from various parts of China. The term 'democratic management' appeared repeatedly. One subheading read, for instance: 'To reform the system of management of trade union cadres, I think the trade union has the capacity to organize this management work' (112). Reading between the lines this meant the trade union could manage its own cadres, and it did not need to be managed by the Party.

3   The Chinese Communist Party's Beijing Municipal Committee Research Office (1988) *Diaocha yu Janjiu* (Investigate and Research) 5(3): August.

themselves from the state's administrative structure, and in view of the rapid erosion of Party authority in enterprises this would have meant a completely new ACFTU, an independent union reliant upon voluntary membership.

When calls for political liberalisation from other social quarters became louder and louder in 1988, influenced by all these discussions at its grassroots, the ACFTU leadership drew up the most daring document ever, 'Thoughts Related to Trade Union Reform'.[4] For the first time it openly asked for smoothing (*lishun*) the relationship between the party and the union, implying the relationship had been strained. The document re-prioritised the unions' functions. It down-played its social welfare and education roles and added two new func-tions: protection of workers' rights and interests, and participation in state and enterprise management (Jiang 1996: 133). After extensive internal discussion of the document at different levels within the ACFTU, it was presented to the government.

By early 1989, taking advantage of the calls for political liberal-isation from society, the ACFTU's call for a new structure of strength-ened industrial unions and trade-wide unions would have weakened the local party-state control over trade unions at various regional levels. The ACFTU's determination to reform reached new heights during the Tiananmen protest movement. It lent moral and monetary support to the protesting students on Tiananmen Square, and some union officials participated in the demonstrations. But the ACFTU was also confronted for the first time by the appearance of an independent trade union on the Square (Jiang 1996: 135–6; Walder and Gong 1993: 1–29). When the government crushed the protest movement, there began a few years of tightened political control in which the workers suffered more than the students even though the students had occupied the centre stage in the movement. Like other social groups, the ACFTU retreated back to its usual timid self.

In 1989, as in previous times, the ACFTU took advantage of social upheaval to assert its independence, while struggling to find a new role. But trade unions in socialist systems have great difficulty reforming themselves, constrained by their own limitations. Imbued

---

4   In Chinese the document is called 'guanyu gonghui gaige de shexiang'.

for some decades with a unitarian collectivist ideology and unwilling to relinquish its relationship of dependency on the party-state, the ACFTU's desire to be a workers' representative could not progress far. There were two possible routes: to work within the power structure and share in some of the power, or to work outside the power structure and struggle for power. The latter would mean outright rebellion and revolution, which the ACFTU was of course unwilling to do. At a self-interested individual level, most trade union officials of all ranks preferred after all to continue to work within the nomenklatura structure and to enjoy all the associated employment benefits of state civil servants. The enterprise-level trade union chairperson, in particular, having been elevated to the same status and salary scale as a deputy manager of state enterprises in the early 1980s, often preferred to enjoy the status and privileges (minus the power) that went with the position. The original intention of this policy was to grant the enterprise trade union more power, but with devolution of decision-making from the government to enterprise managers, the outcome was obvious – the trade union chair could be quickly co-opted. As a result of all these self-limitations, the ACFTU's rebelliousness quickly dissipated with the June 4th crackdown. The retreat, though, was little different from that of many other social groups, organisations and individuals, cowed when faced with violent suppression.

1990s: ACFTU Overwhelmed by Neoliberalism

The decade of the 1990s was different from the 1980s. Neoliberal capitalism took root and flourished in China. The surge came from two fronts: internally by a massive industrial restructuring programme; and externally, from the penetration of foreign capital, particularly first from Hong Kong, and then from Taiwan, that brought with it capitalism's 'sweated' employment system.

In 1992 during his so-called 'Southern Tour' of Guangdong province, Deng Xiaoping gave the green light for accelerated mercantilism and privatisation. This began with a quickened 'reform' of state-owned enterprises, many of which were already under strain from market competition and were losing money. A programme of downsizing led to rapidly growing urban unemployment, exacerbated by an erosion of entitlements. On paper, state and collective enterprises were supposed to continue to take care of their employees by contributing to newly-pooled medical, social security and unemployment benefit funds. But in reality only money-making enterprises could shoulder these responsibilities, leaving those workers laid off in unhealthy enterprises with little means of livelihood (Solinger 2003; Kernen and Rocca 2000). By the early 21st century the government was beginning to sketch out blueprints for more centralised urban welfare and safety-net measures, but while these were being built many millions were excluded.

The dismantling of the state industrial structure and the Maoist employment system was accompanied by the rapid rise of the non-state-owned industrial sector, beginning in the late 1980s with a surge of foreign direct investment (FDI) from Hong Kong and Taiwan, concentrated in the southern provinces of Guangdong and Fujian. Together with Singaporean FDI, these Asian sources of investment accounted for half the FDI flows to China in 2004,[5] cumulatively totalling about US$500 billion, surpassing the United States as the world's number one FDI destination. The factories that they and Korean corporations own and manage are the principal suppliers of the 'Made in China' goods to Western brand-name multinational corporations and to retailers of the developed world. In other words, much of the FDI in China is invested in these Asian-owned factories that constitute a link in the global production chain. This has added one more player in the chain to extract surplus value, i.e., the Chinese local governments where these factories are located. They cream off portions of the money that should have gone to the workers. For

---

5   Including Japanese and South Korean FDI, it was 60 percent between 2000–02
     (Martin 2005: 60).

supplier factory owners, product costs decreased many times after relocating to China, because wages were much lower.

The influx of Asian-funded capital has had a serious impact on China's new employment relationships because investors from these Asian nations or territories brought with them a fiercely coercive, exploitative and even physically violent variant of management behaviour (Pun 2005a; Chan 2001). In their own home territories they operated in an environment of weak trade unionism. One of the motivations to relocate to China, apart from the cheap labour needed to survive in the competitive global market (Lee 2004), was to escape from better regulated industrial systems in their own home territories. Compounded by a Chinese neo-apartheid household registration system (Alexander and Chan 2004) that has denied China's migrant workers citizenship rights in urban areas (Solinger 1999),[6] China today has become the world's choice destination and haven for neoliberal globalisation.

Rural factories were originally set up by rural collectives. For more than a decade, under local public ownership, the sector expanded very rapidly, and by 1996 these rural factories employed some 130 million people (China News Analysis 1997). But during the past decade, with central government encouragement, many have been transformed into private enterprises (Zou 2003; Hendrishke 2005). The union has rarely been represented in these rural enterprises, either under collective or private management.

In both the private foreign-invested export industries and the rural enterprises, Tayloristic management techniques, originally designed for relatively unskilled labour-intensive work, today readily find their way into these labour-intensive factories in China. That is to say, the most exploitative kind of management practices in China are most commonly found in the small and medium-sized factories that are either collectively or privately owned. In both the export industries and the rural enterprises, most employees are former peasants – first-

---

6   As of two years ago the central government has issued policies that make it easier for richer and better-educated migrants to stay in the cities. But it will be some time before the rural-urban residential divide totally disappears.

generation workers – who have travelled from the poorer regions of China and are employed on a temporary basis. The sweatshops in which they labour evoke thoughts of a 19th-century Dickensian industrial revolution.[7] Nothing illustrates the exploitative nature of this export sector better than the Chinese government's announcement that 'Studies show the salary of migrant workers in the Pearl River Delta area has grown by a mere RMB 68 (US$8.2) over the last 12 years, far behind the increase in living expenses, and in real terms, wages are declining. Nevertheless, wildcat strikes and other less confrontational forms of resistance have erupted in an increasing number of these factories'.[8] Given their precarious, temporary situations working in districts where they are vulnerable outsiders, they are in a weak position to mount protests. Nevertheless, wildcat strikes and other less confrontational forms of resistance have erupted in an increasing number of these factories.

China's industrial restructuring is unquestionably the largest in human history in terms of the number of people affected. The ACFTU had no means to respond, nor had it the ideological underpinning to do so. In the developed world, in times of mass layoffs, strong, active and competent trade unions can at best negotiate better severance pay packages for laid-off employees. Mired in a corporatist mentality, the ACFTU could only play a minor role in helping to soften the blow for workers, and this is exactly the role the party-state wants the ACFTU to play in this period of monumental change.

By the 2000s, therefore, the ACFTU was confronted by an industrial and employment structure very different from that of a decade earlier. As state enterprises continued either to collapse or to be transformed into other ownership forms, union membership declined. Under the planned economy, since the workplace trade union was considered as an administrative department of management, it was allocated a budget like other departments. But once enterprise-

---

7   My thanks to Zhu Xiaoyang for this information. Zhu helped direct an investigative survey (1987–89) of 135 county enterprises. Also see the description in Forster (1990–1) of Wenzhou, the region in China hailed as a model for private entrepreneurship.

8   MOLSS report, http://www.molss.gov.cn/new2004/0908a.htm.

level decision-making power had been devolved to management, there was little the ACFTU could do if management decided not to allocate the union staff a budget. Restructured state enterprises under new management even use the excuse of 'efficiency' to rid themselves of the trade union chair or to collapse the position of the trade union chair into a shared administrative position (Jiang, 1996).[9] Faced with a financial and membership crisis, the ACFTU has had to establish branches in enterprises from the booming private sector (Gallagher 2004a; Ng and Warner 1998: 95–123).

But this has been a mission impossible. At a time of frantic economic activity, with foreign and private enterprises mushrooming and the entire nation caught in the frenzy of 'integrating with the global economy', there were concerted efforts by local governments to sideline the trade unions. My fieldwork in the mid-1990s in a newly industrialising zone, Pudong District outside Shanghai, showed how difficult it was for the union to set up union branches inside the private foreign-funded enterprises. First, the local government was more interested in attracting FDI, and allocated only a few trade union staff to the new Pudong District Trade Union. How can a few union officials go about organising thousands of new factories to fulfil a unionisation quota allocated by upper level trade unions? The only way was to do it in a top-down fashion. Never having been exposed to the idea of grassroots organising from the bottom, their top-down bureaucratic mentality prompted them to call a meeting of factory owners and managers to persuade them to let the union set up workplace unions. In the meetings, the union allayed the managers' and owners' fears, telling them that the new union branches would be docile and helpful, and of course, they did not mention anything about collective 'negotiation'. Even with such assurances it was not easy. Japanese and European managers tended to be more amenable. But the Taiwanese, Hong Kong Chinese and Koreans, according to the Pudong union staff, were always resistant. If allowed to set up union branches, the local union went to the factories to identify a couple of middle-management staff members and asked them to serve as the union chair and deputy chair (Chan 1998: 134–140).

---

9   *Gongren ribao* (Workers' Daily), 9 March 1998; 21 March 2001.

This, unfortunately, is how most of the union branches in the foreign-funded sector have also been established in the foreign Asian-funded enterprises I have visited in Guangdong and Fujian provinces. As can be expected, these union branches are virtually impotent. At worst, they are totally inactive, to the extent that workers do not even know of their existence. At best, management pays the union the union activities fees, which by statute are supposed to be equivalent to 2 percent of the total payroll. This allows the enterprise union to run some social activities for the workers, which at least can liven up the workers' grinding existence or buy a present for everyone during a festival. Some of the higher-level union officials saw the absurdity of this way of organising, but had no alternatives. Their reasoning is to get a foot in the door of these foreign enterprises first and then try to turn the unions into regular unions later.

Other new efforts to organise union members are also dictated by the weakness of the unions' situation as the state enterprise sector shrinks. This became clear when I visited a county in Jilin province in 2000, where about half of the state-enterprise industrial work force had been laid off, some 10,000 people in all. Without jobs, these former workers could no longer be trade union members, causing a sudden drop in union membership in the county. Simultaneously the county was encountering a budget crisis, and the trade union staff – who were on the county government payroll – had not been paid for some months. The local trade unions' role became twofold: helping laid-off workers to register for the various government programmes set up for the unemployed; and arranging for some way to make a living by setting themselves up in business peddling delivery tricycles and the like, and organising them into 'a trade union for the self-employed'. The purpose of this 'trade union' was to help the members ward off other predatory bureaucracies that came to collect all types of fees. To claim jurisdiction over these laid-off workers and collect 'union' dues, the local union competed with the local government Labour Bureau in a turf war. From the union's vantage point, it was helping laid-off workers while making up for declining union finances. Ironically, the trade union in this same county had earlier received national publicity from the ACFTU for taking an unusual initiative in 1984 to implement open nominations and elections for trade union heads. In fact, even today, the county continued to be well known in China for its democratic election of village committees.

There was a marked shift in attitude within the ACFTU from the early 1980s to the late 1990s. The 1989 crackdown against the Tiananmen protests had sapped the organisation's momentum, and it now faced rapid industrial restructuring that undercut the union's traditional base in the state enterprises. The national political leadership increasingly accepted privatisation and private ownership, flexibility of labour and integration with the global market, and gave priority to economic development over equity. The ACFTU was on the defensive. The union's zeal for reform in the 1980s had dissipated, and a mood of accepting reality prevailed within the higher and middle ranks of the organisation. Lower-level trade union cadres had no concept of activist trade unionism. Their corporatist, unitarian, bureaucratic, top-down understanding of trade unionism was geared toward their own survival and, at times, a secondary concern for workers' interests. External constraints were overwhelming and seemed insurmountable. At no other time in its history has the ACFTU been regarded with more disdain by workers than at present, when both the state and the non-state sector workers need help more than ever before.

2000s: Emergence of an Industrial Relations Legal Framework

The ACFTU and workers' advocates channelled a lot of energy into fighting for input in the drafting of legislation. The 1980s saw the promulgation of a whole series of laws in response to the new economic situation. Intervention in the legislative process at that juncture was deemed crucial if workers and unions were not to lose out in the redistribution of power and resources. In this one area the ACFTU can claim to have achieved a measure of success: since the late 1980s, as a branch of the government, it was able to lobby successfully to include a number of pro-worker and pro-union clauses in key labour legislation – the Enterprise Law passed in 1988, the Trade Union Law of 1992 (this law, revised in 2001, gives the union more authority, at least on paper) and the Labour Law of 1994 (Ngok 2000). These laws constitute the legal framework that regulates China's new industrial relations. Critics are quick to point out that the biggest problem is the absence of the right to organise. But the laws contain clauses that have the potential to empower workers. In the Trade Union Law, 'work stoppages' and 'slowdowns' are legal even though 'strike' is not mentioned, and one of the core international labour rights, the right to bargain collectively, is guaranteed by the Labour Law (Taylor, Chang and Li 2003: 176–8, 182–206). The laws stipulate a maximum number of work hours and a minimum age for entering the work force, establish industrial labour dispute procedures, and include clauses on the right to a democratically elected workplace union committee that are on a par with international standards. Establishing a new workplace trade union branch is, by law, surprisingly easy: 'A basic-level trade union committee shall be set up in an enterprise, an institution or a government department with a membership of twenty-five or more; where the membership is less than twenty-five, a basic-level trade union committee may be separately set up' (Chinese Trade Union Law, Article 10). The new union committee has to register with the district trade union. This step pre-empts independence. We shall return to discuss the implication of this important article later.

Enforcement is a problem. The weakness of trade unions at all levels and the absence, in practice, of collective bargaining means that labour relations are individuated. But a growing number of labour disputes and workers' increasing resort to the arbitration committees stipulated in the laws reflect rising workers' labour rights awareness, suggesting that these laws have laid a very important foundation. Labour arbitration leapt from 19,000 cases in 1994 to 184,000 cases in 2002 (Fu & Choy 2004: 17–22) and became more collective in nature (Gallagher 2005: 98–132). Unfortunately, the majority of these cases involve serious abuses, such as non-payment of wages (both in state and non-state enterprises), improper layoffs of state workers and loss of guaranteed entitlements, irregularity in pension payments, exces-sively long work hours, a lack of compensation for industrial injuries, and the incidence of work-related diseases (Chen 2004; Gallagher

2004b; Thireau and Hua 2003). These are thus reactive claims, employing spaces provided by the legal system to redress injustices. They are not proactive collective claims, to rights such as forming an autonomous union, or demanding that management collectively bargain, or against trade union officials for not protecting workers' rights.[10] In fact, the legal options may even serve to avert a crisis situation where desperate workers might actively seek to set up alternative trade unions or engage in mass protests, which is precisely the reason behind the government's policy of regulating industrial relations through legal channels.

Although the ACFTU at the top fought hard for the passage of these laws, the local unions at the bottom play only minor roles in helping workers in litigation.[11] An encouraging side effect is the rise of a nascent civil society in the labour arena – a handful of labour NGOs and a substantial number of labour lawyers and paralegals – to fill in the gaps by offering services to workers. Filing lawsuits to seek compensation for industrial injuries is increasingly common. But this rising frequency is also built on a shocking reality, illustrated by some 40,000 crushed or severed fingers a year in Guangdong Province's Pearl River Delta, one of China's main export-manufacturing regions (Zheng Gang and Dong Wei 2005). Litigation is a drawn-out and costly process for workers, and the number of cases, though high, represents a tiny proportion of serious grievances.

More promising is the ACFTU's success in strengthening the position of the union's legal status and power as embodied in the revised Trade Union Law of 2001,[12] though this does not promote the

---

10   The first lawsuit by an employee against his trade union for not protecting his labour rights was described in *Nanfang Zhoumo* (Southern Weekly), 4 September 2003, p. A3.

11   Shanghai General Trade Unions, recognised generally in China's labour circle as the most active trade union in China, seems to play a more active role in this (Chen 2004).

12   In the couple of years before, during and after the law was revised, I observed the great amount of effort trade union officials and labour lawyers in Beijing had exerted to get the law through. After the law was passed, the union also held a big campaign publicising the law within the trade union structure and in the mass media for the general public. On the front page of the *Workers' Daily*

union's independence from the party-state. As one expert comments: 'Nonetheless, the 2001 amendments to the Trade Union Law offer limited, but important, new space in which Chinese trade unions might act to improve working conditions. [...] There are some indications that the Chinese state may now be countenancing a more active union movement.' (Cooney 2004: 8–9). Laws that are on the books often subsequently have an impact on the path-dependency of a nation's employment relations.

Seeds for Workplace Representation

One particular instrument that could potentially be of importance is the Staff and Workers Representative Congress (SWRC) system. Although the system has not been successful, it is enshrined in the Enterprise Law. In some respects the SWRCs resemble Germany's works councils, though in Germany the works council operates as a separate institution parallel to the trade union at the workplace (Luthje 2004), whereas the SWRC is institutionally directly linked to the workplace trade union. It is the union that is charged with the task of convening the Congress and then to oversee the decisions passed by the Congress. Like the German system, the SWRC has some powers of co-determination and has a role in monitoring management compliance with the laws. In theory, the SWRC has the power to elect factory managers and the power to 'exercise democratic management'. Other powers of the SWRC include the legal right to be informed of enterprise matters, a veto power over workplace labour standards, power to decide on policies related to workers' welfare, in particular the distribution of housing, and a power to monitor, evaluate, penalise and reward factory officials (Zhu and Chan 2005). These are unusual powers to be given to employees at any workplace in any industrial relations system. If a Chinese union and Chinese

---

the old law and the new law were placed side by side, with the new changes highlighted in bold print. The ACFTU saw the new law as a big achievement.

workers were to exploit this SWRC power, they could act as a countervailing force to management. This could be the driving force behind the ACFTU investing so much energy into legalising the power of the SWRC. Thus, at the end of the 1990s when privatisation of medium and small state and collective enterprises was at its height, the ACFTU President, Wei Jianxing reasserted his support for the SWRC, to the displeasure of some high-level Party colleagues (Chan 2002: 57). In 2004, the ACFTU even wanted to extend the SWRC into non-state enterprise workplaces by issuing a directive instructing union branches in the non-state sector to set up SWRCs.[13] Regardless of what exists in Chinese law, however, under the present circumstances the SWRCs' powers are only very rarely used.

Nonetheless, there have been reports in the Chinese press of workers themselves occasionally seizing the initiative to transform into practice what has been written into law.[14] Such initiatives can be distinguished into two main types. The first occurs at workplaces where the trade union and the SWRC are allowed to function and have some say in major decisions on the enterprises' strategic plans or on housing and welfare policies, as stipulated in the laws. At one state enterprise which I have researched in depth, the SWRC was convened during the mid-1990s to determine the terms on which more than 500 new enterprise-owned apartments should be sold to managers and workers. The SWRC provided workers there with a strong opportunity to seize the moral high ground and press their case. After lengthy deliberations by the SWRC and meetings in all of the enterprise's workshops, the SWRC determined that the largest apartments should go to veteran employees, who were largely blue-collar workers, with a 2 percent deduction in price for every year they had worked at the

---

13   The directive issued in September 2004 is called, 'Announcement to further strengthen democratic management work in non-state enterprises' (guanyu jinyibu jiaqiang feigongyouzhi jiye zhigong minzhu guangli gongzuo de tongzhi), in '2004 nien quanguo gonghui weihu zhigong hefa quanyi nannishu (quanwen),' (2004 Blue Book on Chinese Union Protecting Workers' Legal Rights), 13 September 2005 www.acftu.net/template/10001/file.jsp?cid=21&aid=23945.

14   A nation-wide survey conducted by the ACFTU revealed that, in those enterprises where the SWRCs were evaluated by the workers as functioning well, work conditions tended to be better (Zhu and Chan 2005).

enterprise. They rather than the managers received priority (Unger and Chan 2004). Egalitarian ideals are not entirely dead in Chinese enterprises like this one, albeit it is one of a dwindling minority.

A second category consists of state and collective enterprises that are going downhill and are financially in the red. This can be due to a variety of reasons, but often is related to mismanagement, corruption and asset-stripping, sometimes with the connivance of local government officials (Ding 2000a, 2000b). A point is reached when workers' wages are in arrears, benefits are in jeopardy, production lines are not running normally, and workers are being laid off or pushed into early retirement, depriving them of their livelihoods and leaving them feeling cheated. Occasionally such workers 'discover' the SWRC, exploit the normal procedures guaranteed on paper, elect their own SWRC representatives and elect their own trade union chair to replace an old one appointed by management. For instance, in a well-publicised case in the city of Zhengzhou, workers at a paper factory used the SWRC to claim back ownership of the factory after it was privatised by management and the local government. They occupied the factory, and the struggle lasted for several years until they prevailed. Since this precedent, workers at about twenty other enterprises in the city have used the same method to regain ownership rights (Tong 2005; Zhu 2005).

In another case, in 1998 a group of taxi drivers in Beijing formed their own democratically elected SWRC and trade union to replace the ones appointed by management when the taxi company, which was a city bureaucracy, tried to eliminate privately-owned taxies. The leader of the group had been 'given a copy of the Labour Law and the Collective Ownership Regulation by a local trade union comrade'. Only then did they become aware that the highest level of decision-making power legally rests in the hands of the SWRC: 'Even the manager is to be elected by the Council. So we are the real masters!' *Workers' Daily*, the official ACFTU newspaper, publicly supported their campaign, but their effort has been plunged into a legal battle. Today, the group still has not been able to elect its own SWRC representatives, but its leader 'has not lost his freedom. On the contrary, he is in the forefront of protecting the legal rights of Beijing taxi drivers'.[15]

These are isolated incidents used to illustrate the point that, despite the cynicism directed both within and from outside China against the SWRC system, its very existence in legal statutes provides a wedge that might someday have an impact on industrial relations in China's still-large state-owned industrial sector. To the extent that representatives of the factory staff have any genuine say in the SWRC, employees are provided with a means not only to influence company policies but also to influence what the enterprise union is supposed to implement.

Thus far, our discussion has mainly focused on China's internal developments and on domestic pressures on the ACFTU. As China became more and more integrated within the world economy, forces were at work affecting standards in China's export industries. On the one hand, workers' wages in the export sector were low and declining in real terms, to compete with other southern countries; on the other hand, the corporate social responsibility (CSR) movement began to penetrate China in the mid-1990s, putting direct pressure on the ACFTU.

In the developed world, the multinational Western corporations had been criticised by the anti-sweatshop movement for the horrific conditions under which products bearing their brand-name were produced in China. In response, many of the multinationals began monitoring, auditing and verifying that their supplier factories complied with 'codes of conduct' that the multinationals drew up (Pun 2005b).[16] When CSR was first pressed upon China's supplier factories in the 1990s, this meant that factory managers came under pressure to have safer and cleaner shopfloors and dormitories, comply with the codes or China's labour law in terms of wages and work hours,

---

15   There are a series of reports on the case. The most comprehensive is 'Beijing zui nui de dige' (The Most Difficult Taxi Driver in Beijing), *Nanfangchuang* (South Wind Window), 20 January 2005, <news.sohu.com>, accessed 9 June 2005.

16   The definition of CSR can be very broad, including corporations' responsibility for the environment and to society (Blowfield and Frynas, 2005: 499–513).

establish better occupational and health programmes, etc. But the supplier-factory managers soon learned how to resist these impositions and to hide transgressions from the monitors and auditors.[17] Having invested resources in improving their corporate image but reaping little gain, some of the Western corporations turned in frustration to the idea of 'workers' training' and even to democratic elections for workers' committees or workplace trade-union branches.[18] The rationale is that workers are the best monitors of their own conditions. 'Training' involves informing workers of the Chinese Labour Law, the official minimum wage, occupational health and safety measures, or even international labour standards. Many thousands of migrant workers have participated in these training programmes. As for the democratic elections of workers' committees and workplace trade unions, they are only pilot programmes in a few supplier factories that try to make use of the space provided by the Chinese Trade Union Law allowing democratic elections for workplace unions and workers' committees. Such elections are legal as long as the trade unions are not proclaimed to be independent.

Obviously such solutions – in-factory training sessions by outsiders, or, far less often, elections – pose a challenge to the ACFTU. But if Western capitalists insist on raising labour standards and on compliance with Chinese laws, how can China's trade union say no to improvement of worker's conditions? China had to react. To resolve the dilemma, in 2005 China drew up its own CSR standard (initially only for the textile industry, CSC9000T),[19] which is rather similar to

---

17 'Why Ethical Sourcing Means Show and Tell', *Financial Times*, 22 April 2005.

18 Usually the corporations pay NGOs and commercial firms from outside China to conduct the programmes. If these NGOs can get their own funding from bigger funders they can go into factories to carry out training independently, but it still requires the consent of the corporation and factory management. Some PRC NGOs are also beginning to conduct this kind of in-factory training. I am currently involved in one of these training and election programmes.

19 The Chinese Textile and Apparel Council drew up the 'CSC9000T, China Social Compliance for Textile and Apparel Industry, Principles and Guideline, 2005', CSC9000T ENG 2005 ed.pdf.

the internationally accepted SA8000 standard.[20] China is telling the world that it can handle its own labour standards compliance (Zeng Yuan 2005).

The ACFTU also reacted to the CSR movement by suddenly declaring at the end of 2003 that in Zhejiang Province more than 300 factories have had direct elections for workplace trade union officials (Xie Chuanlei et al 2003; Zhong Guodong 2000), and that the ACFTU would roll out the programme nationwide.[21] The implicit claim is that 'direct' elections are equivalent to 'democratic' elections, though it is unclear how democratic they are. Nevertheless, in view of the fact that village leadership elections in China, originally a top-down government policy, have become widespread since their inception more than two decades ago and are today sometimes hotly contested (Liu 2000; Schuter 2003), this new ACFTU policy may mark the first step to workers' representation at the workplace. In other words, both in using the legal power of SWRC and in workplace representational elections, the space provided by the industrial relations legal framework is critical

Conclusions and Prognosis

We have presented a more complex picture of the ACFTU than the commonly held image of an ACFTU that is monolithic and unchanging, stuck in the Maoist era. It has been shown that, trapped by its own history, political and institutional arrangements of a one-party 'socialist' system, it had tried to change but was not capable of breaking through. With the Chinese economy and labour market incorporated into global capitalism in the past two decades, the ACFTU is encountering new challenges and problems. The state has allocated to

---

20   Caijing Cankaobao (Financial & Economic Reference News) 1 June 2005, http://finance.sina.com.cn.

21   'China Trade Union to Allow Direct Election of Shop Leaders', Associated Press, 26 September 2003.

it the bureaucratic function of protecting the labour rights of a massive number of laid-off workers and first generation migrant workers in the context of a scale of economic industrial restructuring unprecedented in human history. It is also at a historical juncture where the global labour market has never been more competitive and flexible, driving down global wages in both the North and the South. In setting the ACFTU in this context my intention is not to be uncritical of the ACFTU's incapacity to defend the labour rights of Chinese workers, of its timidity, absence of will, its self-serving motive, its bureaucratic mentality, its subservience to the party-state or any of its other defects. The point is, given this objective conundrum, what can be done? Is there no hope for Chinese labour?

There could be two possible developments in the next one or two decades. One is peaceful evolution. Labour and management could gradually come to accept the legal framework as a regulatory mechanism, while the ACFTU acts as a mediator rather than as a labour representative. Labour would continue to be dominated by capital, but not suppressed so far as to lead to social instability. For instance, the urban unemployed would need not be totally destitute but able to scrape an existence in a minimal welfare system. In the urban state sector and large enterprises, the core workers who survive downsizing and remain employed may have the capacity and consciousness to utilise the SWRC system to gain a limited amount of workers' representation at the workplace level. The industrial relations system may stabilise into a more corporatist variant closer to the Japanese and German systems. The enterprise-level trade union too would be operating within the limited space available engaging in a weak form of collective bargaining. Grievance procedures would go through formal institutional channels. The direct workplace union election programme that has just begun may, two decades from now, democratise the trade union structure to some extent, just as has occurred in some village elections. This scenario is in fact what the Chinese government hopes to see. But this will hinge on the labour laws not being revised to disadvantage labour. In fact, any revision that could raise labour standards, strengthen labour rights and trade union rights and improve enforcement will be helpful.

The other scenario is large-scale social upheaval, a prospect the political elite is eager to avoid. To this end, they are presently instituting band-aid policies to improve the condition of the disadvantaged social groups to establish a so-called 'harmonious society' (Li 2005). But if gross social injustice continues to prevail, the workers, together with the peasantry, may have to resort to massive protest actions and even violence. Of the two main types of workers, it may be the migrant workers rather than the state workers who will be in the forefront of the struggle. By now, the downsizing of state enterprises has passed its peak. If the government is able to establish a workable social welfare system for the urban poor, it may be able to contain urban discontent. Yet the conditions of migrant workers who are still outside the welfare safety net have shown little improvement. On the other hand, their labour rights consciousness is soaring, ironically developing as a by-product of global capital's corporate social responsibility movement. As yet, the ACFTU has not shown the will to do anything for the migrant workers. This provides an opportunity for the growth of better organised collective protest action. An independent trade union movement could be sparked by any sudden downturn in the economy or a major social upheaval, initiated possibly by the peasantry. In 1989 the intellectuals and the students led the rebellion, but since then they have been co-opted by the state (Unger 2005). At that time migrant workers did not join in the protests, but this time around they may seize the opportunity to organise themselves. As in the past upheavals described earlier in the chapter, at least portions of the ACFTU will possibly come out on the side of workers.

Over the past half-century, predicting how Chinese history will develop has always proved a hazardous enterprise for scholars in China studies. These two scenarios have been drawn up based on how the current situation might logically develop. With China being such a vast country and enjoying such a dominating position in the global labour market, what role can the international labour movement play to help Chinese workers and in turn all workers in the world? The international trade union movement is keeping the ACFTU at arms length, while internally a debate on whether or not to engage with the ACFTU has been going on for some years (Quan 2005; Shailor 2005;

Wong 2005, 2004). As the debate goes on, in the past decade more and more trade union affiliates have established formal or informal relations with the ACFTU. It seems that trade unions or individual unionists who are willing to engage are from countries that have more corporatist structures, for instance, Germany, Denmark, Norway, Sweden, Japan and Singapore.[22] Certainly, external intervention in the form of helping the ACFTU is only marginal to China's labour development. These trade unions believe that only by engaging with the ACFTU can they hope to effect some changes in it. Technical assistance and capacity-building are seen as the first step in the right direction. Indeed, the ACFTU also tends to ask for technical assistance such as training programmes in building up knowledge on labour legislation, collective bargaining, the shop steward system and employee buyouts, areas in capitalist industrial relations systems that did not exist under the socialist system, and in occupational health and safety, particularly in mining.[23]

In this debate, a point that is missed is that a trade union that originated from a socialist system, though state-controlled, is different from a state-controlled official trade union in a capitalist system. The official socialist ideology nurtures a wish among the workers for the state to act out its socialist mission, and for the official union to play the assigned labour-protecting role. In practical terms, the legacy of the socialist system and its rhetoric preserve some space for both the workers and the union to manoeuvre by taking the moral high ground. I agree with Bill Taylor (2005) who also expresses some optimism in his paper entitled 'So the ACFTU is not a Trade Union, and does it Matter?':

---

22 This information has been accumulated in the past few years on the basis of personal communication via email, meetings and internal trade union documents.

23 A few of the trade unions that I know of include the Norwegian Confederation of Trade Unions, the Trade Union Congress (UK), the Union Network International and The Australian Construction, Forestry, Mining and Energy Union.

The Chinese government (including the ACFTU) is very keen to build up an image of the ACFTU as a union movement through its international links and propaganda. Behind this, however, are genuine desires for the ACFTU to 'behave' like a union – that is to set the promotion of worker interests as its 'primary goal'. Given the right encouragement and incentives, there is a good possibility that this can happen.

By isolating the ACFTU, the international trade union movement is inadvertently playing into the hands of global and Chinese capitalism and other anti-labour interests. In the past twenty years, all major actors – international organisations, businesses, educational institutions, NGOs and government departments such as labour bureaus, and even the military – have eagerly sought to establish relations with their counterparts in China, except for the international trade union movement. The business sector in particular (including the ubiquitous business schools) is having a profound influence on China, introducing neoliberal ideas and training a large crop of Chinese managers in the art of human resources management through an increasingly capitalist-style corporate structure. But sorely absent is an external countervailing presence to help build up an anti-neoliberal capability in China. The impact of the trade unions and the miniscule number of labour NGOs that run programmes in China is like David versus Goliath.

For the moment it seems most of the relationships with the ACFTU established by unions tend to remain at a formalistic level. With time, these relationships may become more substantive. The case of engagement with the Vietnamese General Confederation of Labour (VGCL) may serve as a precedent. After more than a decade of engagement with some foreign trade unions, the VGCL, like the ACFTU a trade union of a one-party socialist system, is today receptive to behaving more like a trade union[24] and is active in

---

24 Trade unions that have capacity-building programmes in Vietnam that I am aware of include the International Textile Garment and Leather Workers Federation (ITGWF), the Asia and Pacific Regional Organisation of the Union Network International, the Norwegian Conference of Trade Unions and quite a number of trade unions in Australia. The liaison personnel of some of the unions are quite positive about the results of their programmes.

protecting labour rights, at least compared to the ACFTU (Chan and Norlund 1999; Chan and Wang 2004).

There is urgency about engaging with China. Not only is the flood of FDI into China lowering labour standards all over the world, the space that is presently available through the legal system may disappear at any point when the socialist ideology officially gives way to capitalist ideology. Already capitalists are welcomed to join the Communist Party. The present industrial-relations legal framework is of utmost importance in the maintenance of a comparatively pro-labour system, not least because Chinese workers are now relying on it to protect their labour rights and seek social justice.

References

Alexander, P. and Chan A. (2004) 'Does China have an Apartheid Pass System?', *Journal of Ethnic and Migration Studies* 30(4): 609–629.

Blowfield, M. and Frynas, J.G. (2005) 'Setting New Agendas: Critical Perspectives on Corporate Social Responsibility in the Developing World', *International Affairs* 81(3): 499–513.

Chan, A. (1993) 'Revolution or Corporatism? Workers and Trade Unions in Post-Mao China', *The Australian Journal of Chinese Affairs* 29: 31–61.

— (1998) 'Labour Relations in Foreign-funded Ventures', in G. O'Leary (ed.) *Adjusting to Capitalism: Chinese Workers and the State*, Armonk, NY: M.E. Sharpe.

— (2001) *China's Workers under Assault: The Exploitation of Labour in a Globalizing Economy*, Armonk, NY: M.E. Sharpe.

— (2002) 'Labour in Waiting: The International Trade Union Movement and China', *New Labour Forum* 10(Fall/Winter): 54–59.

— and Norlund, I. (1999) 'Vietnamese and Chinese Labour Regimes: On the Road to Divergence', in A. Chan, B.T. Kerkvliet, and J. Unger (eds), *Transforming Socialism: China and Vietnam Compared*, Sydney: Allen and Unwin; Boulder: Rowman and Littlefield.

— and Wang, H. (2004) 'The Impact of the State on Workers' Conditions: Comparing Taiwanese Factories in China and Vietnam', *Pacific Affairs* 77(4): 629–646.

Chen Feng (2004) 'Legal Mobilization by Trade Unions: The Case of Shanghai', *The China Journal* 52(July): 27–45.

China News Analysis (1997) 'Rural Enterprises and the Law', 1 January: 1–10.

Cooney, S. (2004) 'Limitations and Possibilities', *International Union Rights* 11(4): 8–9.

Ding Xueliang (1999) 'Who Gets What, How? When Chinese State-Owned Enterprises Become Shareholding Companies', *Problems of Post-Communism* 46(3): 32–41.

— (2000) 'The Illicit Assent Stripping of Chinese State Firms', *The China Journal* 43(January): 1–28.

Forster, K. (1990–1) 'The Wenzhou Model for Economic Development', *China Information* 5(3): 53–64.

Fu Hualing and Choy, D.W. (2004) 'From Mediation to Adjudication: Settling Labour Disputes in China', *China Rights Forum* 3(September): 17–22.

Gallagher, M.E. (2004a) '"Time is Money, Efficiency is Life": The Transformation of Labour Relations in China', *Studies in Comparative International Development* 39(2): 11–44.

— (2004b) '"Hope for Protection and Hopeless Choices": Labour Legal Aid in the PRC', paper presentation at the Grassroots Political Reform in China Conference, Fairbank Center of East Asian Research, Harvard University, 29–30 October.

— (2005) *Contagious Capitalism: Globalization and the Politics of Labour in China*, Princeton: Princeton University Press.

Granick, D. (1990) *Chinese State Enterprises: A Regional Property Rights Analysis*, Chicago: University of Chicago Press.

Jiang, K. (1996) 'Gonghui yu dang-guojia de chongdu: bashi niandai yilai de zhongguo gonghui gaige' (The Conflicts between Trade Unions and the Party-State: The Reform of the Chinese Trade Unions in the Eighties), *Hong Kong Journal of Social Sciences* 8(3): 121–26.

Kernen, A. and Rocca, J-L. (2000) 'The Social Reponses to Unemployment. Case Study in Shenyang and Liaoning', *China Perspectives* 27(1): 35–51.

Lee, A. (2004) *In the Name of Harmony and Prosperity: Labour and Gender Politics in Taiwan's Economic Restructuring*, Albany: State University of New York Press.

Li, C. (2005) 'The New Bipartisanship within the Chinese Communist Party', *Orbis* 49(3): 387–400.

Liu, Y. (2000) 'Consequences of Village Committee Elections in China: Better Local Governance or More Consolidation of State Power', *China Perspectives* 31(3): 19–35.

Luthje, B. (2004) 'Co-Determination and Collective Bargaining in Germany-A Model under Stress', paper presented at the International labour Law Forum: Reform and Development, held at Beijing University, 26–28 February.

Martin, R. (2005) 'Opportunities in Higher Value Manufacturing and Other Collaborations', in Committee for Economic Development of Australia (ed), *China in Australia's Future*, Melbourne: Committee for Economic Development of Australia.

Ng, S.H. and Warner, M. (1998) *China's Trade Unions and Management*, New York: St Martin's Press.

Ngok, K. (2000) 'The Development of the Labour Law of the People's Republic of China', *Chinese Law and Government* 33(1): 1–94.

Pun, N. (2005a) *Made in China: Women Factory Workers in a Global Workplace*, Durham: Duke University Press, 2005.

— (2005b) 'Global Production, Company Codes of Conduct, and Labour Conditions in China: A Case Study of Two Factories', *The China Journal* 54: forthcoming.

Schuter, G. (2003) 'Democracy under One-Party Rule? A Fresh Look at Direct Village and Township Elections in the PRC', *China Perspectives* 46(2): 15–25.

Sheehan, J. (1998) *Chinese Workers: A New History*, London: Routledge.

Solinger, D.J. (2003) 'Chinese Urban Jobs and the WTO', *The China Journal* 49(January): 61–87.

Solinger, D.J. (1999) *Contesting Citizenship in Urban China: Peasant Migrants, the State, and the Logic of the Market*, Berkeley: University of California Press.

Taylor, B. (2005) 'Is the ACFTU a Union and Does it Matter?', paper presented at the conference on 'China, Trade Liberalization and Labour: Racing the Bottom or Building a Foundation for Labour Rights', organised by the Australian Council of Trade Unions, the New Zealand Council of Trade Unions and Monash Institute for the Study of Global Movement, 14–15 February.

— , Kai, C., and Li Qi (2003) *Industrial Relations in China*, Cheltenham UK: Edward Elgar.

Thireau, I. and Linshan, H. (2003) 'The Moral Universe of Aggrieved Chinese Workers: Workers' Appeals to Arbitration Committees and Letters and Visits Offices', *The China Journal* 50(July): 83–103.

Tomba, L. (2002) *Paradoxes of Labour Reform*, London: Routledge.

Tong Xin (2005) 'The Cultural Basis of Collective Action by Workers in a Traditional State-owned Enterprise during a Time of Transition', *Chinese Sociology and Anthropology* 38(1): forthcoming.

Unger, J. (2005) 'The Rise of a Conservative Chinese Middle Class', *The Diplomat* 4(3): forthcoming.

— and Chan, A. (2004) 'The Internal Politics of an Urban Chinese Work Community: A Case Study of Employee Influence on Decision-Making at a State Owned Factory', *The China Journal* 52(July): 1–24.

Walder, A.G. and Gong, X. (1993) 'Workers in the Tiananmen Protests: The Politics of the Beijing Workers' Autonomous Federation', *Australian Journal of Chinese Affairs* 29(1): 1–29.

Wilson, J.L. (1990) 'The Polish Lesson: China and Poland 1980-1990', *Studies in Comparative Communism* 23(4): 259–80.

Xie Chuanlei, Fu, J. and Wang, J. (2003) 'Direct Trade Union Elections as a Form of New Labor-Capital Relation to Compete in the New Rules of the Game', *Nanfang zhoumo* (Southern Weekly), 3 July.

You, J. (1998) *China's Enterprise Reform: Changing State/Society Relations after Mao*, London: Routledge.

Zeng, Yuan (2005) 'Cong SA8000 zhi CSC9000T: zhongguo qiye mangjingchu zhengchu zhudong diyibu,' (From SA8000 to CSC9000T: Chinese Enterprises Taking the First Step to Grab Back Initiative), in *Shanghaiqingbao fuwu pingtai* (Platform for Shanghai News Service), http://www.istis.sh.cn/list.asp?id=1823.

Zheng Gang, H.L. and Dong Wei (2005) '*Jiqi 'chi' re heshi liao?*' (When will the Man-eating Machine Ever Stop?), *Zhongguo anquan shengchanbao* (China's Safety Production News), 24 February.

Zhong, Guodong (2000) 'Pushing Ahead with Direct Elections of Trade Union Chairs in Non-Publicly Owned Enterprises', *Zhongguo guanli* (Chinese Management News), 17 March.

Zhu, X. and Chan, A. (2005) 'Staff and Workers' Representative Congress: An Institutionalized Channel for Expression of Employees' Interests', *Chinese Sociology and Anthropology*, 37(4): forthcoming.

— (2005) '"Misreading" of the Law and the "Imagined Homeland": A Case Study of a State-Owned Enterprise', *Chinese Sociology and Anthropology* 38(1): forthcoming.

Zou W. (2003) 'The Changing Face of Rural Enterprises', *China Perspectives* 5(December): 17–30.

DAVID OST

After Postcommunism:
Legacies and the Future of Unions in Eastern Europe

Introduction

Postcommunism is over. The grand effort to transform a state socialist economy into a market economy has been completed. Whether it will be a long-term success or failure is still unknown. But the transformation of the economy, the breakup of the state firms, the disciplining of labour, the creation of a class system – these grand historic projects have been completed. Postcommunism began to deteriorate around the beginning of the century, and died with the 2004 enlargement of the European Union. Postcommunism is dead. Globalisation is here.

The aim of this chapter is to explore what this means for labour in the manufacturing and industrial sectors. I will show that after fifteen years in which labour – both everyday workers in the workplace and organised trade unions – have been humbled and marginalised, often with their own conscious complicity, things are now beginning to change. A new generation of workers and of union officials is more eager than its predecessor to defend the interests of those on the job. But this is far from a return to, or a new embrace of, a recently radical past. Today's emerging unionism is much more elitist – male and 'producerist' – than East European unions in the past. It also faces severe obstacles to its growth. As in the past, the obstacles it faces are due to problems of legacy. But in a twist from the old story, today's obstacles are due to the legacy not of communism but of postcommunism, with the peculiar pro-capitalist sensibilities so central to unions in the postcommunist era.

Everyone knows that trade unions have fared poorly in post-communist Eastern Europe. Everything about them has declined: their membership, workplace authority, collective solidarity, sectoral diversity, enterprise responsibilities, and political influence. Of course, in the old regime, unions were essentially part of the state apparatus: one part of the triad of management, party cell, and trade union that governed the plant and represented its interests in relations with the central government. (Some referred to this as the 'Bermuda triangle' because of the way independent working-class representation ran aground on its shores.) Communist unions did not independently represent workers' interests, but insofar as they were responsible for maintaining stability in the plant by keeping employees content, their advice and opinion did count in shaping local and enterprise policy. Stark and Bruszt (1998: 113) call such mid-level post-Stalinist elites 'responsive responsibles' – officials who, precisely in order to maintain order, needed to be responsive to their constituents.

Postcommunism, basing its legitimacy on votes rather than popularity, jettisoned the informal social contract that gave the old unions their pocket of power. A decade after the postcommunist transformation began, unions had been largely marginalised in the workplace. Unions, moreover, played a key role in their own decline: most union officials believed in the necessity of market reform and believed, contrary to the West European experience of which they were largely unaware, that market economies work best without much union involvement (Kubicek 2004; Ost and Weinstein 1999).

If it never looked like unions would *completely* disappear, that was chiefly thanks to the continued existence of the public sector. In health and education, union membership has remained high. In manufacturing, most new private firms are indeed union-less, particularly the small ones. In privatised firms, unions hung on but barely. They survived due to inertia, to laws protecting union activists (and mandating their payment out of enterprise coffers), and to the desire for protection felt chiefly by the firm's least-skilled and thus most vulnerable employees. But as their clout disappeared, so did members. And poll numbers showing the unpopularity of unions, even as organisations defending workers' interests, suggest that mass numbers of workers are not going spontaneously to return.

Why did unionism decline so precipitously in manufacturing but not in the public sector? Standard objective economic reasons certainly apply. Large manufacturing firms radically reduced their workforce, competitive pressure pushed owners and managers to cut labour costs, and the plethora of small private firms in a time of high unemployment discouraged potential union organisers. But one of the most striking findings of all who have studied postcommunist unionism concerns the beliefs and attitudes of union officials in the manufacturing sector. Most of them simply did not believe that unions ought or needed to play much of a role in the private manufacturing sectors, and all manufacturing plants in the postcommunist era were either in the process of privatising or had been newly established as private firms. Unionism declined so dramatically in manufacturing because it did not have proponents committed to building it.

Unskilled rank-and-file workers liked unions because they wanted protection. But in postcommunist Eastern Europe it was almost entirely skilled and more highly educated workers who led unions in the large manufacturing plants. This was true for the former communist unions because the Party relied on moderately educated, middle management types to be union representatives. It was true for the independent, anti-communist unions because those activists tended to be skilled, ambitious workers angry at the nomenklatura system and wanting to be more upwardly mobile (Kurczewski 1993). None of the postcommunist unions, in other words, were created or run by the kinds of workers (unskilled) who most needed unions to protect them from the negative effects of market reform. Instead, they were run by those who believed they had an interest in reform, and who thought unions would be an obstacle every bit as much as the new elite did.

Much of my published work has documented this for the Polish case, but cross-national studies show it to be true throughout the region. The collected authors in the edited collection by Steve Crowley and me, or Paul Kubicek in his excellent new book on unions in Poland, Hungary, Russia, and Ukraine, all show postcommunist unionists in privatised industrial enterprises to be unenthusiastic about their union work. Unlike in the old industrialising west or in much of the developing world, unionists in the postcommunist world have not seen themselves as part of a labour *movement*, but simply as labour representatives whose job is not to push for benefits for their members but to teach members that benefits are no longer possible. (Leninist notions of 'representation', according to which leaders pursue the realisation of a group's 'historic interests', of which the rank-and-file may be unaware, thus persevered.) Postcommunist union officials inherited their positions, they did not fight for them, and the best evidence of their indifference to the union cause was their refusal even to try to organise unions in new private manufacturing plants. Indeed, the exception only confirms the rule: unionism has grown recently in the plants of *transnational* corporations, for it is precisely here that contacts with western labour both persuade easterners of the need for unions and provide them resources to help build them.

Recently, however, things are beginning to change. As just mentioned, there has some been foreign involvement in unionisation drives in transnational firms operating in eastern Europe. While unions were identified in the postcommunist period as stodgy, old-fashioned institutions, somewhat affiliated with the discredited system just passed, since about 2000 increasing numbers of younger workers are getting involved. In addition, union officials are more excited about their work. In industrial plants that I have visited in Poland since about 2000, I have seen unmistakable signs of a new kind of unionist, more committed to union work than in the past. Other observers report similar developments. Kubicek (2001: 125), for example, mentions a Russian metallurgical plant he visited in 2001 in which the union had finally broken free of ties with management and the leadership began taking an unusually tough stand defending its employees.

The aim of this chapter is not just to explain these changes but to suggest what they mean for the future. My argument is that while there are signs of real changes today, the legacies of the recent past will probably prevent unions from maximising their advantages. What we will see is a double irony. First, the reasons why unionists did *not* want to be unionists a short while ago are what make them want to be unionists today. Yet, second, it is precisely their behaviour as unionists a short while ago that makes it difficult to *be* successful unionists today. In other words, while the communist legacy was the main problem facing unions in the postcommunist period, it is the *post-*

communist legacy that is the chief obstacle to the development of unionism today.

Postcommunism and the Decline of Labour

Contrary to what traditional western leftists argue, the main obstacle facing East European unionism after the fall of the old regimes in 1989 was not the spectre of capitalism but the legacy of communism.

In the early 1990s, most market reformers in the region felt that the introduction of capitalism would spur the emergence of a militant labour movement. After all, market logic would mean attacks on labour, the introduction of unemployment, and tightening labour discipline. The desired creation and empowerment of a new propertied class would require the disempowerment of workers, and reformers widely feared an imminent 'social explosion'. But while attacks on labour proceeded apace, nowhere in the region did labour leaders offer a militant response. And this was not because they were shell-shocked and disoriented, unable to come up with a response to such a frontal assault. In fact, the assault was not so 'frontal'. Because the elite was so afraid of a social explosion, it tried to mitigate the potential damage. The new market-oriented governments often consulted with organised labour, and set up tripartite councils to symbolically include labour representatives. When they eliminated economic subsidies and drove firms to lay off workers, they ensured that this be done, at least initially, through attrition or advantageous new early retirement laws.

Union leaders were certainly not deluded about what was going on. No sweetening measures could hide the fact that a grand systemic transformation was underway and that the new elites wished to marginalise the power and authority of organised labour. What the elites did not understand, however, is that labour leaders did not oppose these developments. Far from being militant representatives of a radical labour movement committed to defending one set of particular interests against another, union leaders in the postcommunist era were every bit as reformist as the new governmental leaders. They supported privatisation efforts, and often tried to accelerate them. They accepted that new managers would have to lay off many and tighten labour discipline on the rest. 'Employees will have to learn', wrote a leading Solidarity activist in Poland, just days after market reformers came to power, 'that their salaries are a function of the talents and capabilities of the managers, economists, and engineers, and that the general state of the our factories depends on the level of the cadre governing the firm' (Arkuszewski 1998). They went along contentedly with symbolic tripartite councils, allowing market reformers the veneer of social approval that made their plans go smoother (Ost 2000). So accepting were union leaders of a new system opposed to organised labour that they often refrained from trying to organise unions even in foreign firms that expected them.

As to why that was so, we can be brief: postcommunist unions tended to be pro-capitalist chiefly because they were anti-communist, and came to believe that the enemy of their enemy was their friend. This was particularly true in countries where opposition union movements emerged before 1989, fighting against communist rule. But even in those countries where the old official unions stayed dominant, post-1989 leaders were anxious to dissociate themselves from the past, and proclaimed their support for new market principles. Postcommunist union leaders thus embraced two central tenets: that private employers are better for workers than state employers are, and that unions had common interests with employers in getting rid of the excess workers of communist-era firms. Unions were so quiescent in the postcommunist era, despite the staggering cutbacks inflicted on their members, precisely because union leaders largely agreed with the architects of shock therapy.

Unions thus became weak not because they were attacked by capitalism and not because they were mollified by capitalism. They became weak because union leaders largely agreed with the policies aimed at weakening them.

Trade unions in the postcommunist era are thus different kind of creatures than trade unions sociologists and industrial relations specialists are used to. Seemingly straightforward definitions about unions being organs for the defence of labour's interests in the workplace and the advancement of their interests in society at large do not work for postcommunist society. That is what unions are when they are formed within capitalist society, when activists are taking risks simply by being involved in unions. But that's not what unions were about in the communist era, and since the activists largely remained the same, not what they were about in the immediate postcommunist era either.

Communist legacies are thus of crucial importance. They were responsible for the decline in the prestige of labour, helped legitimate the collapse of union resources and of union power, and led to the ideological incoherence of the labour movement that has been the source of its greatest weakness since 1989.

The decline in prestige was perhaps the first major consequence of postcommunism. For communism's strong association with labour – less by its formal glorification than its commitment to large, sprawling, early-20th-century style industrial factories – made everything connected with it seem passé after 1989. The new elites promoted new ideologies championing individual achievement, entrepreneurial freedom, white-collar over blue-collar work, and the importance of creating a propertied class, while the media unremittingly promoted this new paradigm. First to go was the communist-era cult of the proletariat. That of course had long been on the wane, jettisoned by late communist elites who tried to legitimise themselves according to their technical expertise rather than class origins (Konrad and Szelenyi 1971). But it had persevered symbolically to the extent of making labour protests the most powerful way political oppositionists could express themselves. Trade union activism thus figured prominently in the 1989 anti-regime mobilisations in Poland, Hungary, Bulgaria, and Russia, and performed the *coup de grace* in Czechoslovakia. For the same reasons, 'defending the achievements of the working class' served as the symbolic way for the regime to condemn oppositionists and defend its own rule in the crunch. When Poland's leaders declared martial law in 1981, and the plotters against Gorbachev briefly seized power in the abortive Soviet coup ten years later, they each claimed they would rescue 'working people' from the tribulations brought on by their reform-minded predecessors.

The new regimes after 1989 denigrated the cult of labour any chance they got. Newspapers now taught 'free market' ideas and business etiquette, lauded individual entrepreneurs who had quit their companies and struck out on their own, approvingly quoted economic neoliberals and foreign advisers on the need to break up the 'socialist factory' system through massive layoffs and the introduction of individualised pay and bonus systems. Virtually overnight, trade unions began to be seen by the new dominant culture as something retrograde, an obstacle on the road to a healthy 'transition' that would bring prosperity on its own provided that those at the bottom *refrained* from making any class-based demands. ('Class' itself did not become a bad word, only 'working class'. 'Middle class', in contrast, now gained a discursive sparkle, signifying wealth creation, entrepreneurial *chutzpah* and consumerism all in one.)

As noted above, organised labour generally supported these developments. Anti-communist trade union leaders in Poland, Hungary, and Bulgaria were mostly skilled, educated, ambitious potential-professionals, who supported the breakup of the old-style factories with their archaic *faux* collectivism that stifled technological advancement and thereby stifled their own advancement. Former communist trade union officials, meanwhile, had been reared in acceptance of political authority, and also raised no objections. Moreover, as classical 'organisation men' with some higher education, they had reason to believe they too would do better in the new system. Without any prominent unions run by and for the unskilled and under-educated that would clearly be the victims of the new economic developments, and would thus have a clear interest in challenging the new consensus, East European labour went along with the post-communist assault on blue-collar prestige.

Trade unions thus became associated with the past, and this allowed the attack on union resources to proceed quickly. Resources refer to the material or cultural assets that an organisation disposes, or the various kinds of capital – economic, social, and cultural – that it can deploy to its advantage. High membership, automatic dues payments, enterprise payment of union activists and bureaus, factory newsletters, trained activists, links with political and intellectual circles: these are some examples of resources that have been adversely affected by postcommunism. High membership with firm-collected dues payment has everywhere been abolished. Some countries, such as Poland, still mandate company payment of a small number of union officials, provided the union surpasses a threshold membership level, but this too is under increasing attack. Unions can still publish a factory newsletter, but because they now have to pay for it themselves, they do so less, with membership decline likely to accelerate this trend. As for capable union activists, only the independent and thus oppositionist unions ever really had these, as the former official ones were staffed with administrators charged with maintaining firm discipline and helping fulfil the plan. The opposition unions, however, quickly lost these activists after 1989, when many went off to government and business posts, with those staying usually more intent on selling market reform to their members than defending members in the face of such reform.

Communist legacies also bear the brunt of responsibility for the rapid decline of union power. For as already noted, postcommunist unions put up much less of a fight than the reformers anticipated. They did not react strongly against perhaps the worst peacetime recession in history. They accepted increasingly authoritarian and secretive management styles, without collective bargaining, transparent wage or bonus policies, or even basic observation of labour law (Gaciarz 1999; Kubicek 2004). They tolerated new 'human resources management' practices that ignored rank-and-file input, even when the latter knew such practices were often hurting the firm. (On the inefficiency of many new postcommunist labour practices, see Dunn 2004). Management consultation with unions was either routinely ignored, even where mandated by law, or routinised in such a way that management preferences prevailed regardless of what unions thought. Indeed, an official of a transnational corporation that took over a firm in Poland once told me how management was unable to find any unions ready to speak on behalf of the workforce even though the management *sought* such representation. Early postcommunist union officials believed so much that private property worked best with weak unions that they would not revive their activity even when management solicited it. It is hard to see what else to attribute this to *except* legacies. In terms of workplace participation, rights on the job, and broad systemic outcomes, communist legacies smoothed the way for the postcommunist shift toward empowering management and marginalising labour.

These legacy issues entailed a comprehensive crisis of ideological coherence. Labour simply no longer knew what its role ought to be. It sought to contribute to the development of a democratic market economy, which it understood to mean cooperation with the new authorities. But how to defend workers when cooperating with a new regime that wanted to create a new, subordinate working class? Those who took their union role seriously – almost certainly a minority of union officials – resolved the problem for themselves by positing a notion of long-term interests, which is what labour movements have always done at times of systemic transformation (including East Europe's ruling communist parties during the early days): we defend labour's interests in the long-term by joining with the new government in the short-term, and even by trying to get ourselves into positions of power within it.

This is a difficult strategy at any time, but in the postcommunist era it was compounded by what can be called the 'Cold War syndrome', or the historically inaccurate views about the role of organised labour in market society cultivated by both sides of the Cold War. According to the dominant western Cold War view, workers benefit in capitalist society when moderate unions work closely with owners and managers; according to the official Soviet view, capitalist society entails the exploitation of workers and the marginalisation and endless harassment of unions. Both sides, in other words, presented unions as weak. It is understandable, then, how East European unionists came to believe that the higher standards of living prevalent in the West came about through weak unions. Neither side in the Cold War had an interest in presenting the historic evolution of this higher standard of living, which resulted when strong unions enforced a postwar 'class compromise' in order to ensure social peace.[1] Thus, even sincere East European labour leaders came to believe in the postcommunist era that weak unions were in workers' long-term interests. Not only did neither union officials nor labour rank-and-files

---

1   Of course, business had an interest in promoting Keynesian social democratic policies too. See Swenson 2002.

believe in a historic mission for a labour movement, they didn't even believe in the importance of resisting day-to-day encroachments on their power, influence, and livelihoods. As Crowley and I wrote (2001: 230), 'East European labour seems to believe that weak unions are precisely what capitalism is all about. They tend to see unions as rearguard institutions for the weak, relevant chiefly for obsolescent state-sectors, rather than as vital representatives of labour against capital, let alone agents of expanded citizenship'.

Factors Favouring Unionism after Postcommunism

It is then, we might say, the subjective factor – or as Gorbachev used to say, the 'human factor' – where legacies proved so destructive to postcommunist trade unionism. *Unions didn't mobilise on behalf of workers because they didn't believe in unionism.* A counterargument claiming that they did believe in unionism but recognised that reforms were necessary in the short-term, or that they 'recognised' that protest would do no good at the present time, would be beside the point. For survival, organisations need to engage in self-promoting symbolic activity all the time. Entrenched trade unions regularly speak up even for lost causes, or for causes that their members believe in even when their leaders do not, in order to keep the organisations thriving and members mobilised. Indeed, Polish Solidarity survived to the extent that it did occasionally recognise this: particularly at the local level, union leaders did sometimes 'lead' protests for causes in which they did not believe (Ost 2005: 88). Even in Poland, though, national leaders usually did their best to stifle union activism, despite the fact that this worked *against* their own interests as leaders of trade unions. But in the first postcommunist decade, most union officials didn't care first of all about their own interests (though perhaps some miscalculated into believing that overeager cooperation would earn them privileges from employers). Legacies were crucial precisely here.

Why then are things beginning to change, since about the beginning of the new century? There seem to be five key factors: survival needs of the union bureaucracy, incorporation into the European Union, emerging international labour solidarity, a new generation of labourers, and the end of postcommunism in the firm, creating new challenges for unionists. These last two factors, due to generational and temporal changes as postcommunist experiences replace communist ones, lead to a new subjectivity that is perhaps the most important part of the story. Let's look at each of these factors in turn.

The first factor is the survival needs of the union bureaucracy. Put simply, today's union officials simply *cannot afford* the ideological beliefs of their predecessors. Unlike those in the immediate postcommunist period, today's union leaders cannot easily move from union office into business or government. Those jobs are now filled with people who know the rules of a market economy, and no longer need the ideologues they did in the past. The period of rapid mobility is over, meaning that union leaders no longer have a safe cushion. They can no longer believe, as their predecessors did, that promoting market reform from within the ranks of trade unions would yield them a better-paying job in management or government instead. If today's union officials are going to maintain their relatively good jobs, they need to do so *as union officials*. Thus it is now in their interest to promote union expansion. Their own survival requires it. Moreover, this is true not just for old anti-communist unionists with good political credentials. Officials from the surviving ex-communist unions also used to feel, in the postcommunist years, that they did not need to be active in order to survive in their jobs. They believed the state would maintain union subsidies and that companies would continue to pay them. It was only when the demise of postcommunism made old unionists realise they had to fend for themselves and new unionists realise they were still unionists, that both groups saw the need to try to organise new members. Maintaining their own livelihoods now requires union officials to be more committed to union building. They no longer have any obvious exits into a better life.

Second, there is the role of the European Union. While some reformers and even some unionists might have *wanted* unions to fade away, EU integration guaranteed that would not happen. The EU of course explicitly recognises unions as a key part of the European political economy, an essential actor in the 'social partnership' regime that EU rules mandate. Even while EU leaders have tried to eliminate some of the prerogatives of western trade unions, they have provided both money and personnel to promote union education programs in the east, and to facilitate contacts of eastern unionists with their western counterparts. The EU aid program PHARE, for example, financed 'Project "Social Dialogue"', instructing postcommunist states on the details of west European social partnership, and training trade unionists to take part (Pliszkiewicz 1996). Incorporation into the EU seems to mean that unions in the east are condemned not only to survive but to be at least somewhat active.

Third, emerging labour solidarity. While unions in the West of different ideological stripes – whether the conservative old AFL–CIO, socialist French unions, or communist Italian unions – used to aid oppositionist East European unions on ideological grounds, as labour and civil society groups fighting against dictatorship, recently western trade unions have begun to get involved in the east because of globalisation. That is, labour leaders in the West see the need to follow capital as it moves abroad, and they have far greater possibilities of doing so in East Europe than in East Asia. Consequently, labour aid has moved beyond the work done, say, by the Friedrich Ebert Foundation in publishing books and sponsoring labour-related research and conferences. In the early 1990s, the AFL–CIO's Service Employees International Union (SEIU), which made its reputation in the US by its aggressive commitment to organising, began conducting recruitment seminars in Poland, and funnelled more money into it when SEIU leader John Sweeney became president of the AFL–CIO. Solidarity officials were not very interested in this activity when they were still deeply involved in politics, but by 1999, when their political arm was declining and symptoms of union weakness seemed to endanger long-term union survival, they followed through and created a Union Development Office aimed at organising in new industries. Western trade unions also, as mentioned, began following trans-national corporations abroad. German unions have been particularly helpful in assisting auto workers in eastern Volkswagen and Opel plants to establish and manage successful unions. Foreign retail workers' unions, meanwhile, have been helping new organising drives in East European 'hypermarkets'.

The fourth factor pushing towards union revival in Eastern Europe is the emergence of a new generation of workers. By the beginning of the new millennium, young workers began getting interested in unionism for the first time since the fall of communism. This was a big turnabout, for unions, as noted earlier, had completely dropped out of fashion after 1989. Central to the pageantry and iconography of communism, from May Day rallies to productivity campaigns, trade unions were associated with the system that had just passed, not the new one to be created. Young workers deserted unions in droves, new labour market entries simply declined to join. Besides the image problem, the 'aging' process of trade unions stemmed from two other factors: the availability of the bulk of the new jobs in the new private sector, which were non-union and went to younger workers, and the economic crisis which kept established unionised firms from making new hires, causing more youth to move into the informal sector, travel abroad for work, or seek higher education.

Of course, the patterns were different in different places. Unions were particularly unpopular among youth in the Central European countries where small-scale privatisation came quickly, for this took many of the basic services unions provided – from consumer-goods procurement to summer vacations to housing – out of union hands. Where such privatisation did not occur fast, such as Russia and Ukraine, union membership stayed higher even among youth, since unions remained at least a potential provider of important services. But even in Central Europe, things began to change by the end of the 1990s, as young workers now had experiences shaped not by actually-existing socialism but by actually-existing capitalism. The private sector lost the glitter and gleam that swathed it earlier. Harsh discipline and long hours, violation of labour law with impunity, low pay for all except for a relatively small number of elite manufacturing jobs – these conditions quickly became more real to young workers than the fading memories of the past, stoked only by aging parents and an increasingly out-of-touch political class. Youth who, in the late communist period, believed capitalism to be a meritocratic system, soon found that it was as perfectly compatible with cronyism, toadyism, and nepotism as the old system had ever been. And so young people started seeing unions in a different light: not as a dismal remnant of the past but as a possible protector in the future. Youth who had travelled and lived in EU countries picked up the more favourable impressions of unions common in the west. They began to see unions not as a *traditional* provider but as a *potential* provider.

Finally, the fifth factor driving new interest in unionism in eastern Europe today is the end of postcommunism in the firm. As management and the state have finally privatised, restructured, and downsized the myriad old state firms they inherited in 1989, union leaders are finding that they are no longer responsible for the unskilled workers for whom they never had much respect. Indeed, this is probably the most important development of all. For the key reason union leaders were barely committed to 'doing their job' in postcommunist Eastern Europe was that they agreed with the reformers that the socialist factory need to be fundamentally overhauled. The skilled workers who headed the unions did not want to lead organisations of the unskilled, which trade unions in the postcommunist era had overwhelmingly become. But precisely as the factories give up their old state socialist character, they become more open to union mobilisation.

Skilled workers tended to treat communist-era over-employment in the factories as a threat to their chances after communism, since it meant that firms that might otherwise be healthy were weighted down with excess labour costs. Communist governments had hired massive numbers of workers not needed in the production process in order to maintain order, secure popularity, provide social welfare benefits, and maintain discipline, and managers were happy to have these superfluous workers as insurance to fulfil the plan. But when the old regime was toppled, and firm survival came to depend on profit-making, not plan fulfilment, these workers were needed to no one but themselves. They figured this out pretty quickly, and looked to the trade unions to defend them. With professionals leaving unions to go into management, and many skilled workers leaving the old state factories to go into (non-unionised) private-sector jobs, the unskilled suddenly became the mainstay of the trade union movement (Gardawski et.al. 1999). For trade union *leaders*, this was a blow. For they believed in the need to move toward a 'normal' market economy – one where firms needed to make a profit in order to survive and prosper – and thus saw their members not as a valuable resource but as a problem they wished to overcome. Trade union leaders, in other words, did not want the rank-and-file that they had.

My long discussions with Polish unionists from 1992–1995 first made me aware of the depths of anti-union sentiment among union activists. For example, Solidarity officials in the large aircraft manu-facturing plant in Mielec, often considered a hotbed of militancy because of a strike and City Hall demonstration that took place in 1992 after months of non-payment of wages, told me they were not very proud either of their members or their unions. The local vice-president, a 44-year old skilled worker, said union work in the 1990s was about 'the protection of losers':

> Most people in the plant don't want to work, they want the state to take care of them. They complain to the union that they're not making enough money, basically they complain about everything, but in the end most of the problem is their own. The ones who are good workers, they are only a handful.[2]

The ones who ran the unions were largely skilled workers who felt degraded by the old regime's commitment to use factories less as a site of production than as a site of social control. Indeed, the socialist firm's perennial woes stemmed precisely from it being the place where benefits were delivered and order maintained – which were, of course, the very characteristics that prevented reform. Reformers in the Soviet Union, after all, had identified the economic problems of the socialist factory already in the 1960s. But plans to deal with them always ran aground, since any real effort to do so would challenge the social contract on which the system was based – the contract that gave workers jobs, welfare benefits, and loose on-the-job discipline in return for acceptance of party control (Schroeder 1979). So instead of tackling the problems, the party maintained the arrangement of employing virtually the entire citizenry (except, as is now clear, for those in non-urban areas in the non-Slavic republics) in

---

2   These and other quotes below from my conversations in Mielec, May 1994.

factories that administered housing, maintained cultural institutions, and provided basic social welfare.

The point, as far as our skilled workers are concerned, is that under the old regime, *cultivating craftsmanship took a back seat to maintaining order.* The system worked well for low-skilled and un-motivated workers, as it provided them work, certain social guarantees, and a sense of inclusion. Comparisons with contemporary Russia, where such people have seen their lives so degraded and impover-ished, make this starkly clear. For skilled workers, however, the communist system became a humiliating one, depriving them of their job satisfaction, ambition, drive, and the chance to fully use their skills. The old communist-era complaint that 'they pretend to pay us and we pretend to work' has often been misinterpreted as a boast. In fact it was a lament, on the part of skilled workers who resented that they had to 'pretend to work'. (Sensitive military work constituted the only real exception, in the 'closed cities' of the former Soviet Union [Zaslavsky, 1982] or in top defence-producing plants in eastern Europe, such as the Mielec plant I visited. By 1989, due to the crisis of the Soviet state, such work quickly disappeared.)

These workers, who largely ran the unions particularly after the professionals had left for better positions outside the factory, looked to postcommunism to change all that. That is why they did not oppose unemployment. They thought the socialist enterprise was too large, employing too many people doing unnecessary work. They wanted the numerous 'fictitious' employees to be fired – which is why they wanted most of the women fired too, as women were more likely, because of educational patterns, to have been hired doing makeshift deskwork – 'unproductive work', in the view of the craftsmen. When I spoke with the Mielec Solidarity president in 1993, he noted that the plant now employed only 11,000 people, down from 21,000 at its peak. Instead of complaining about the high number of layoffs, however, he complained that they weren't high enough: 'there's still only room for 7 or 8 thousand at the most'. Indeed, one reason he was concerned about the Social Democratic government that had just come to power was because he thought they might discontinue unemploy-ment in response to public pressure. 'They have the word "social" in

their name, so let's see how it will relate to the factory. Will it be
"social" or will it be a factory?'

When I visited Mielec in 2001, however, the scene was quite
different: I found a new union president interested in protecting his
members and *excited* to do union work. In fact, this seemed increasingly to be the case everywhere I went. A unionist at the
Lucchini Steel Mill in Warsaw, privatised just a few years earlier,
spoke to me in 2000 about his pride in being a unionist, about the
recent course he took on labour law and his close monitoring of the
situation in his firm. He was aware that he was a new type of unionist,
on the one hand less militant – 'we can't just walk in here and call a
strike anymore' – yet on the other hand more assertive – 'we have to
know the legal rules inside and out, because management is always
trying to use them against us'. In the past, he said, Solidarity had been
militant chiefly over political issues; now it needed to be assertive
over workplace issues. Glaringly absent in his comments was the
scornful disapproval of the rank-and-file, an attitude widespread
among Polish union leaders in 1994.[3] Instead, the new leaders took
union work more seriously, and saw it as their role as unionists to
protect workers against management.

What had changed? One simple thing: the excess labour force of
the earlier postcommunist period had all, finally, been dismissed.
*Unionists have become more engaged in union work in firms where
restructuring and privatisation have already done their damage.* By
1999, the Warsaw steel works had been through the wringer: its
workforce was perhaps 30 percent of its previous size, the firm had
jettisoned most of its social welfare apparatus, and the Italian owners
had already weathered several tough confrontations with its unusually
militant workforce and unions. The plant in Mielec, meanwhile, had
been through an even tougher time: in 2000, in fact, the firm had gone
officially bankrupt, victim not just of continuing tough economic

---

3   In a 1994 survey of unionists in nearly 100 Polish industrial enterprises
     conducted by Marc Weinstein and myself, we found that union leaders
     generally feared greater workforce participation because they did not trust their
     members, and saying that one of the reasons they were involved in unionism
     was to explain the need for market reform to their members. See Ost and
     Weinstein 1999.

times but of insider corruption. The new workers now represented by the unionists I spoke with had all been hired *after* bankruptcy – after, in other words, bankruptcy had wiped out all rights and privileges to remaining employees, leaving those who previous union leaders had derided as 'unproductive' labourers now out of a job.

Once communist-era 'add-on' workers are let go, it seems, unionists don't mind being unionists anymore. Unionism, in other words, is likely to experience a revival because postcommunism is over. As postcommunism ends, and a more 'normal' capitalism begins – 'normal' in the sense that firms do not have large numbers of non-productive workers on their payrolls – labour can begin to move on too. As it comes to see the workplace as a place where interests clash, it comes to see that unions might be important after all. We shall see in the conclusion, however, that this has important consequences for the *kind* of union that will arise.

Obstacles to Union Revival

And yet, the question is whether all this really makes a difference. Will the labour weakness of the postcommunist era, brought about in large part through self-inflicted blows, prevent it from re-arising now, just when it seems increasingly possible? Will labour now be impeded by *postcommunist legacies* just as it was earlier impeded by communist legacies? Much evidence suggests that it will.

There seem to be three chief obstacles to union development today, all due to postcommunist legacies. These can be categorised as ideological, organisational, and structural. Together, they indicate why labour in the east is likely to remain weaker, more marginalised, and less class-based than in the west even after a revival of union activity.

The ideological obstacles refer to what I have been discussing above: the general distrust of unions, their association with the old regime, the sense that they are inadequate and ineffective and perhaps not really necessary. As noted, there are signs that this is changing.

But there are still very few people *writing* about this, helping change social expectations, for postcommunism pushed away most of the people who might have been able to do so. The Gramscian organic intellectuals are sorely missing. The irony is great: precisely at the moment when class became a relevant matter, when the new elites openly proclaimed their intentions of creating a 'normal' class society, journalists and scholars largely turned their attentions away from the situation at the bottom. Opposition activists who regularly bemoaned the hardships of labourers during communist times treated the hardship of labourers during postcommunist times as a sign of 'normality'. Scholarship dealing with class, meanwhile, focused chiefly on the question of identifying the new elite, with the marginalisation of labour seen as a fundamental, and therefore not troublesome, feature of a 'normal' society. There has been little study of the western experience, and little interest in the long line of neocorporatist theory that shows it matters greatly for a society's economic and political health *how* workers are incorporated into a market economy. (It is indicative that the few who did do such research often had difficulties publishing. A great deal of Polish publications on labour matters has been subsidised or published by the Friedrich Ebert Foundation. And when I asked a Hungarian colleague why he didn't publish locally, in a single volume, his many different articles on labour and postcommunist industrial relations presented at international conferences and frequently published abroad, he replied simply that no publishers were interested.)[4] The ideological legacy of postcommunism, in other words, makes difficult overcoming the anti-labour tendencies so dominant in that period.

By 'organisational' obstacles, I mean the plethora of small firms that have taken the place of the large, unified enterprises of the past. Such firms are difficult to organise in any environment, but are particularly difficult in the postcommunist context since unions in general now serve so poorly as a model. The new types of union officials would like to change this, but they now have a problem simply getting their foot in the door. Unions were terribly weakened even in the old state-owned firms, for when these firms were privatised and

---

4   Conversation with Laszlo Neumann, Budapest, 2003. For some of his articles, see references.

restructured, they created a host of spin-off firms as entirely new entities. Yet union membership did not go automatically with it, and few employees rejoined. Having lost their base in the old state firms, never having had one in new private firms, and now confronting myriad small firms with managements predisposed against unions and workforces inexperienced with them, unions will find it extremely tough to create that base now.

Structural obstacles to union revival refer to the new political economy that has taken shape in the postcommunist era. In a rich empirical article with a comparative and historical framework, Böhle and Greskovits (2004) argue that not all types of production processes are equally hospitable to successful unionisation, and that what has taken hold in eastern Europe since 1989 are those industries that are least hospitable to it. Analysing eight discrete variables of production and the degree to which they facilitate or impede labour strength, and presenting data on international investment, they show how eastern Europe has precisely the kind of labour-intensive capital goods industries that are least conducive to successful unionism (as opposed to the capital-intensive consumer goods industries that are most conducive to unionism). So while international capital has indeed transformed and even 'modernised' eastern Europe, this is unlikely to result in the union power, not to mention the social democratic neocorporatism, that came to the West. As Böhle and Greskovits sum up, 'Unlike in Western Europe, where industrial structure appeared to facilitate the historical compromise, in Eastern Europe it is becoming a serious constraint on the eastward extension of the European social model. [...] The social model [of the West] has not traveled to the East because its socio-economic foundations [...] have not travelled either'. The post-communist industrialisation of the east, in other words, creates its own structural legacy that hinders labour revitalisation.[5]

---

5   It is of course possible that one or two eastern countries will eventually succeed in moving from the periphery to the core, bringing labour-friendly capital-intensive consumer goods industries with it. Poland, with its large domestic market, and Hungary, with its proximity to Germany and Austria and very favorable policies on foreign ownership, are probably in the best position to do so. But that is still a ways off, and whether it would even then benefit organised labour as such is far from clear.

The Rise of Aristocratic Unionism, or
Is Mexico Again the Model?

While discussing obvious 'objective' obstacles to unionisation, I have emphasised here the 'subjective' ones: whether union leaders have a clear sense of what unions are supposed to do, whether they really believe in the importance of unions, and how regular workers perceive the role and effectiveness of unions. In short, the overall ideological and discursive milieu surrounding unions and unionisation is critical in a given society, since without that there will not be the activists willing to do the work, and the work won't be effective enough to make others eager to follow. The subjective dimension of trade union success has received little theoretical attention since most social scientists, having studied the problem from a western perspective, simply assume that there will always be workers ready to fight for the economic and workplace-based interests of labour, and that unions that exist are committed to doing exactly that.

Postcommunism has taught us that these are erroneous assumptions. Eastern Europe after 1989 was filled with trade unions that were not accustomed to fighting for labour interests, and with trade union activists that did not see such a fight as their major role. The official unions had been created to work *with* the company and the political authorities, not to defend labour's interests against them. And the *new* unionists, who rebelled against the old ones on the grounds that they were not defending workers, were even less concerned with fighting for workers' economic interests. For their gripe with the old unions was a political one – that the old unions served as a buttress for communist rule. These activists formed new unions because they wanted to topple communist rule, and they chose unionism as their form of opposition precisely because it struck the ruling party where it was most vulnerable: on its ideological claim that it represented the working class. They objected to the way communist ideology proclaimed its adoration of the working class, and saw unionism as a way to upend that claim. But class ways of thinking did not come naturally to them (Meardi 1996; Ost, 2005). Once the dictatorship fell, they were stuck with being unionists but did not much know what to do *as* unionists.

I argue above that the end of postcommunism changes that. As the relevant work experiences of younger workers change, and as the skilled workers that are the union officials finally embrace union tasks now that privatisation and restructuring have jettisoned the old workforce, those who lead unions have new incentives to involve themselves actively in union work. But even if they do succeed, against the obstacles I list above, we should note that this would be a very new kind of unionism. It would not mean a return to the past. Instead of large industrial unions representing all workers in the enterprise – the communist model which postcommunist unions all inherited – the new ones are emerging as *small unions of skilled, elite workers,* a kind of unionism for a new labour aristocracy.

For unionism seems to be re-arising now in the industrial sphere on the grounds of a *producerist* identity, rather than a more modern notion of class. Victoria Hattam draws the distinction between the two in a discussion of late nineteenth-century American working class movements: 'The primary cleavage for many workers', she writes, 'was not between labour and capital, or workers and employers, but rather between the producing and nonproducing classes' (Hattam 1993: 18). 'Producers' refer both to skilled labourers and to employers intimately involved in the production process, but excludes non-skilled workers who are seen as cheapening and degrading the 'manly' process of production. New East European unionists seem to be producerists *par excellence.* They are becoming proud to be unionists, for the first time since the fall of communism, precisely because the firm seems increasingly a place only for 'producers', and not for the motley collection of citizens that the old regime threw together.

As the firms become more 'productive' and more male, both desirable – and usually seen as identical – values for union officials in the industrialising manufacturing sectors, these unionists can be unionists again. Whereas postcommunist leaders found themselves ashamed of their organisations – the central reason, after all, they so widely supported systemic reform – these new union leaders, almost all skilled male workers, see themselves as representing an entirely different breed of worker. They are finally free to turn the union into the 'producer organisation' they wished it had been before. When the factory bottoms out and dispenses with the old employees, becoming a factory in the 'proper' economic sense, then, it seems, unionists can feel proud of their organisations again. In other words, after the layoffs, asset-divestment, structural adjustment, streamlining, and sometimes even bankruptcy, unions may well re-emerge in privatised manufacturing firms more determined to act as trade unions – as the representative of one discrete social group against another – than they were during the postcommunist period.

These new unions will thus be based on a *disavowal* of class solidarity. Whereas unions in the West often moved from their origins as craft unions of skilled workers to becoming vehicles for the advancement of broad class interests, newly reviving East European unions are likely to stay focused on being protectors only of skilled workers for a long time to come. They are likely to *embrace* an identity as a labour aristocracy rather than flee from it. They are not likely to articulate the interests of 'the working class' precisely because they've spent the last fifteen years running away from such a responsibility. And as much as outsiders might have wished they had not done so, the communist legacy that devalued work and made slogans like 'defending the working class' nothing more than a cynical phrase justifying party rule perhaps meant that nothing else was possible.

The future in this regard may thus look like Mexico or Venezuela, where unions chiefly represent skilled workers in the leading economic sectors, and the poorest labourers are not much involved in unions.[6] Labourers in marginalised sectors may try to form their own unions, but they're not likely to go far without substantial foreign involvement, since veteran domestic activists not only are not too interested in them, but have been strengthening themselves precisely by separating from them. Labour organising among un-skilled retail workers in the hypermarkets has been possible in large

---

6   Melvin Croan has written before about Mexico as a model for East European development, hypothesising already in the 1970s that its authoritarian but not totalitarian model might be the way the region develops. For his later reflections on that idea, see Croan et al. 1993.

part thanks to international union involvement, and still faces strong obstacles. Existing domestic union leaders are unlikely to seriously focus on this group in the foreseeable future, even if they occasionally pretend otherwise in order to look good to their western colleagues.

In the end, then, we can understand the future of trade unionism in the east by understanding the different *meanings* of trade unionism east and west. And if we do so, perhaps observers can be less harsh about East European unions, too. In a sense, it has been perhaps too easy to criticise postcommunist unions in the past. (I have certainly been one of those to do so.) But they have been in an exceedingly difficult position, not economically but situationally. It's tough to be a good union in a market economy after being a union in a state socialist one. On the one hand, there was nothing to do *except* to accept cutbacks. Making a new market economy competitive required the new elite to cut back on the formal privileges that the old system granted labour. If unions could have maintained all the privileges the old system granted, they would have been stronger than almost all unions in the advanced capitalist world as well. However much union supporters on the outside wished they would have pursued this path, whatever good theoretical arguments can be made to demonstrate that union power does not clash with economic competitiveness, union leaders in the postcommunist world knew intuitively that it didn't make sense. You can have strong unions only if leaders and rank-and-file alike believe in the need for them. But market ideology was so strong during postcommunism that few did believe in them. Unions were compromised by communism just like democratic socialism was. It is no surprise that the few unionists who did believe that unions should fight for extensive participation in enterprise affairs and high wages too found even fewer in the workplace going along with them. Time had to pass before unions could be reconstructed.

Even with their limited aims, new 'elite' unions will not find it easy. This, again, is due to the legacy not of communism but of post-communism. Local activists may now finally be ready to do their jobs seriously. Some are even eager to be trade unionists again. But fifteen years of postcommunism means that few are eager to join. Union officials spent so long being distant and disdainful to the workers they did represent that few of those they would now *like* to represent see them as competent representatives. Workers have seen what unions do and most of them believe they are better off representing themselves, or looking elsewhere for representation. At the very moment when unions are able to recreate themselves, then, they are not likely to find it easy to do so.

So, the paradox is that it is precisely why unionists did not want to be unionists a short while ago that make them want to be unionists today. Yet it is precisely their behaviour as unionists a short while ago that makes it so difficult to be successful unionists today. The post-communist legacy may be more of a burden than the communist one.

References

Arkuszewski, W. (1989) 'Od góry do dolu,' *Tygodnik Solidarnosc*, Warsaw, September 22.

Böhle, D. and Greskovits, B. (2004) 'Capital, Labor, and the Prospects of the European Social Model in the East', Working Paper No. 58 in Program on Central and Eastern European Working Paper Series, Cambridge, Mass.: Harvard University.

Croan, M., Skidmore, T., Ost, D., Graham, L. and Hershberg, E. (1993) 'Is Latin America the Future of Eastern Europe?', *Problems of Communism* (May–June): 44–57.

Crowley, S. and Ost, D. (2001) *Workers After Workers' States: Labor and Politics in Postcommunist Eastern Europe*, Boulder, Colo: Rowman & Littlefield.

Dunn, E. (2004) *Privatizing Poland: Baby Food, Big Business, and the Remaking of the Polish Working Class*, Ithaca: Cornell University Press.

Gaciarz, B. (1999) 'Dynamika zbiorowych stosunkow pracy,' in J. Gardawski et.al. *Rozpad Bastionu?: Zwiazki Zawodowe w gospodarce prywatyzowanej*, Warsaw: Institute of Public Affairs.

Gardawski, J. et al. (eds) (1999) *Rozpad Bastionu?: Zwiazki Zawodowe w gospodarce prywatyzowane*, Warsaw: Institute of Public Affairs.

Konrad, G. and Szelenyi, I. (1971) *The Intellectuals on the Road to Class Power*, San Diego: Harcourt Brace Jovanovich.

Kubicek, P. (2004) *Organized Labor in Postcommunist States*, Pittsburgh: University of Pittsburgh Press.

Kurczewski, J. (1993) *The Resurrection of Rights in Poland*, Oxford: Oxford University Press.

Meardi, G. (1996) 'Trade Union Consciousness, East and West: A Comparison of Fiat Factories in Poland and Italy', *European Journal of Industrial Relations* 2(3): 275–302.

Neumann, L. (1997) 'Circumventing Trade Unions in Hungary: Old and New Channels of Wage Bargaining', *European Journal of Industrial Relations* 3(2).

— (1997–98) 'The Phenomenon of Relocation: "Movement of Jobs" from Western Europe to Eastern Europe', *Acta Oeconomica* 49.

— (2000) 'Decentralised Collective Bargaining in Hungary', *International Journal of Comparative Labour Law and Industrial Relations* 16(2).

Ost, D. (2000) 'Illusory Corporatism in Eastern Europe: Neoliberal Tripartism and Postcommunist Class Identities,' *Politics and Society* 28(4).

— (2005) *The Defeat of Solidarity: Anger and Politics in Postcommunist Europe*, Ithaca: Cornell University Press.

— and Weinstein, M. (1999) 'Unionists Against Unions: Towards Hierarchical Management in Post-Communist Poland', *East European Politics and Societies* 13(1): 503–30.

Pliszkiewicz, M. (1996) 'Trójstronność w krajach Europy Środkowej i Wschodniej,' in *Syndykalizm Współczesny i jego Przyszłość*, Łódź: Wyd. Uniwersytetu Łódzkiego.

Schroeder, G. (1979) 'Soviet regional policy and CMEA integration', in U.S. Congress, *Soviet Economy in a Time of Change*, Washington, D.C.: Government Printing Office.

Stark, D. and Bruszt, L. (1998) *Postsocialist Pathways: Transforming Politics and Property in East Central Europe*, New York: Cambridge University Press.

Swenson, P. (2002) *Capitalists Against Markets: The Making of Labor Markets and Welfare States in the United States and Sweden*, Oxford: Oxford University Press.

Zaslavsky, V. (1982) *Neo-Stalinist State: Class, Ethnicity and Consensus in Soviet Society*, White Plains, NY: M.E. Sharpe.

ANDRÉIA GALVÃO

Trade Unions and Neoliberal Politics in Brazil

Introduction

The aim of this chapter is to assess the impact of neoliberalism on Brazilian trade unionism. Thus the implementation of neoliberal politics in Brazil and some of the reforms carried out from 1990 onwards will be considered before attention is turned to assessing the current status and future prospects of trade unionism in this pivotal South American country.

After describing the political context in which union activity takes place in the first and second sections, the third section will focus on the impact of neoliberalism. The performance of the two most important Brazilian labour federations, the CUT (*Central Única dos Trabalhadores*) and the FS (*Força Sindical*) will be analysed, highlighting both their differences and similarities.[1] These two federations represent distinct traditions in Brazilian trade unionism: the former exhibits a more combative approach and the latter represents what is often referred to as *results unionism*, and which can be described as a Brazilian variant of business unionism. The rise of neoliberalism has significantly impacted the practice of both federations, particularly so in the case of CUT.

---

1   In the Brazilian Trade Union model, federation membership is not obligatory. Only 38 percent of Brazilian labour unions are members of a federation. Most of the eight existing federations are poorly represented. The CUT and the FS, however, represent the most important unions and the greatest number of workers. It is estimated that the former represents approximately 22 million workers at its grassroots (of which around one third are members); the latter represents approximately 12 million workers at its grassroots (of which around one quarter are members).

In the fourth section, the recent strategic convergence between the two federations will be examined, revealing why and how both are moving towards a model of *citizen unionism*. In the final section, more recent developments will be addressed, including the impact of the Lula Government, a government run by the Labour Party (PT), on the union movement. In this section, the activities of the CUT, whose link with the PT is historically well known, will be the primary focus.

Neoliberal Politics in Brazil

Compared to many countries, neoliberal practices came late to Brazil. Since the 1980s, key financial institutions (the IMF and World Bank) have been pressurising Brazilian governments to adopt so-called 'structural' reforms as a pre-condition for re-establishing capital flows – suspended due to the external debt crisis – as well as a way of controlling inflation and stabilising the economy (Cruz 1998). Neoliberal ideas have also gained favour among the dominant classes and the principal employer organisations since 1980, with the help of economists who wield significant influence in the universities, the media and the political sphere (Galvão 2003). Nevertheless, neo-liberalism was not introduced at the level of policy until the beginning of the 1990s. Even at that time it was impossible to know whether neoliberalism would prevail, since the 1989 presidential elections were polarized between the candidacies of Fernando Collor de Mello and Luiz Inácio Lula da Silva, the latter representing a 'desenvolvi-mentista' popular-democratic project.

The divisions within the electorate during that presidential campaign and resistance from certain sectors of the union movement forced Collor to implement the neoliberal programme slowly. The first measures his government introduced were the opening of financial markets and privatisation. The former was seen as a means to increase the competitiveness of Brazilian companies, while the latter was deemed necessary to combat the state's fiscal crisis. The opening of financial markets started only in 1991 and had a dual role: to attract external resources in order to spur economic growth; and to augment international reserves as a way to compensate for increased imports.

Apart from promoting the opening of the markets and initiating the privatisation process, Collor took on the civil servants, whose number was considered excessive and whose rights were seen as exorbitant.[2] Yet his government did little in terms of fiscal, administrative, social security, and labour reforms, frustrating the expectations of many who championed the adoption of free market reforms. Collor inaugurated a decade of neoliberal rule in Brazil, but it was during Fernando Henrique Cardoso's government that neoliberalism was consolidated.

The success of the *Plano Real* in stabilising the currency provided for the continuity of the neoliberal project. It guaranteed victory for Fernando Henrique Cardoso, who was Minister of Finance when the *Plano Real* was implemented, in the first round of the 1994 presidential elections (Novelli and Galvão 2001). Helping to achieve monetary stability handed Cardoso not only electoral victory, but it also gave him the political capital to push through various other reforms he desired.

The *Plano Real* is the mainstay of neoliberal hegemony within Brazilian society, the basis from which neoliberal ideas began to penetrate the middle class, some urban trade unionists, and the general public (Sallum Jr. 2000: 32). The popular appeal of neoliberalism was demonstrated in many ways: 1) the election of neoliberal governments; 2) the relatively easy passage of some constitutional reforms in the National Congress in 1995 (the break up of public monopolies, elimination of differences between companies with national capital and those with foreign capital, and the concession of public services to private companies); 3) and the wide support for privatisation of telecommunication companies. Brazilians believed that the sale of these public companies would lead to a reduction in tariffs and an expansion in services. Not even the socially negative results of neoliberalism (Singer, 1998 and 1999; Lesbaupin and Mineiro 2002) or popular dis-

---

2   Collor's campaign exploited popular dissatisfaction with salary distortions between the private and public sector in an effort to obtain support from low-income voters. Once in office, Collor closed 22 public agencies and removed 160,000 civil servants.

satisfaction with the quality of the privatised public services (Cardoso 2003: 46) were enough to eliminate this support. Cardoso was re-elected in 1998.

Why do the Brazilian working classes support a political programme that apparently does not benefit them? Saes (2001) believes that popular support for neoliberalism stems from the fact that

> State interventionism in Latin America provoked the concentration of national income; and which was not followed up by the implementation of a Welfare State. In this context, the neoliberal proposal that the 'government' dismantle the 'State' can take on an apparently progressive facet of a redistributional fight, notwithstanding that the subsequent facts (it is important to say: the concrete results of the neoliberal governments) deny this (Saes 2001: 79).

In this way, the appeal of neoliberalism lies less in material advantages and more in the popularity of certain ideas. According to the author, neoliberal ideology employs some of the claims of popular movements that demand autonomy in relation to the state, and moreover, it exploits the general dissatisfaction towards inequalities generated by the Brazilian state. It is this incorporation that has allowed neoliberalism to become the dominant ideology and extend its influence to the working classes.

Although propaganda played a role in the propagation of the neoliberal ideology, the success of neoliberalism also has an objective basis in the dualities in the Brazilian labour market. Neoliberal rhetoric champions the fight against 'privileges' and opposition to state intervention in the labour market (Boito Jr. 1999). There is inequality of working conditions for and the work benefits of those with and without work permits, rural and city workers, public and private sector workers. As a result many working people are predisposed to anti-statist rhetoric, which is based on the fight against civil servants, on the criticism of waste and consequently on the 'necessity' to reduce the state. In its place, a consensus emerges around the 'opportunities' provided by the private sector. However, acceptance of neoliberalism remains difficult to understand without also recognising that it followed 'a defeat of the workers' movement' (Boito Jr. 1999: 222), evidenced by Lula's defeat in 1989, and the resulting crisis in socialist thought and practice.

Neoliberal Reforms:
Social Security, Administrative and Labour Reforms

In his first year in office President Cardoso proposed various constitutional amendments aimed at tax, administrative and social security reforms. Justified by the increase in life expectancy and by the chronic deficits created by the public pension system, the proposals to reform Brazilian social security follow, on the whole, reforms in other countries. These include increasing workers' contributions and reducing benefit levels paid by the state, and opening the door to private pension systems.[3]

Social security reform, initiated in 1995 but not approved until 1998, principally impacted those with private sector pensions.[4] The reform modified retirement calculations, substituting contributions to the Social Security National Institute (INSS) for years worked (as demonstrated by work permits, documentation, and witnesses). This measure penalises workers from the informal sector who do not contribute to the INSS, and it disadvantages those whose employers withhold contributions to social security.

Social security reform was not completed under the Cardoso government. Lula's government continued the process by making further alterations to the social security system for the public sector, taking on arguments and proposals that had previously been criticized by the PT. Calling attention to the social security deficit, the Lula government advocated taxation of retired civil servants and elimination of their generous full-pay benefits. Thus the push to harmonise the public and private sector meant hardship since the rights of public

---

3   In Latin America, between 1981 and 1998, Chile, Peru, Columbia, Argentina, Uruguay, Mexico, El Salvador, Bolivia and Venezuela followed the recommendations of the World Bank. 'The pensions would be based on defined contributions and the benefits would depend on the accumulation of resources, without a previous guarantee of the values to be received' (Dieese 2001: 248).

4   The retirement plans for the public and private sector (the so-called General Social Security Plan) are distinct. One principal difference is the value of benefits to be received.

workers were weakened and pensions in the private sector were not improved.

The constitutional amendment on social security, adopted in December 2003, established a maximum limit for benefits, and matched the pensions of new civil servants with those from the private sector. New civil servants would not have the right to full-pay benefits (the calculation of the pension would be based on the average of the contributions and not on the last salary) or equality with more experienced civil servants. Full-pay benefits would be maintained only for civil servants who fulfilled the following conditions: minimum age of 60 years for men (55 years for women); 35 years of contribution (30 years for women); 20 years of public service; 10 years of career and five years in the position. Civil servants retiring before meeting these requirements have their benefits calculated by the average of contributions. The reform also reduced benefits of retired civil servants (the so-called contribution of the inactive), as well as on the pensions of their dependents (Galvão and Novelli 2004).

Administrative reform received much government attention beginning in 1995, with resulting legislation passed in 1998. Its main objectives were to undercut the job security of civil servants eliminate their differentiated hiring status (Novelli and Galvão 2001). As in the sphere of social security, government objectives were not completely realised since the reform did not fully eliminate civil servant job stability (guaranteed after three years of work, albeit with the possibility of loss of position due to a negative periodical performance evaluation).

Labour reform did not at first receive the same priority as social security or administrative reform. Although critical for employers' interest in reducing labour costs, labour reform began only in 1998, when the sharp rise in unemployment was used as a pretext to intensify the fight against labour protection laws and justify the implementation of more flexible contracts. [5]

---

5   According to the Employment and Unemployment Research, for the metropolitan region of São Paulo, unemployment stood at 13.2 percent in 1995 (the first year of the Cardoso government), reaching 18.2 percent in 1998 and 19.3 percent in 1999.

The government and employer organisations advocate flexible labour contracts as a stimulus to employment. They frequently cite the Clinton, Thatcher and Blair administrations as examples of success in the fight against unemployment, after having of course loosened the official controls on the labour market. There are however substantial differences between Brazilian and Anglo-American deregulation, particularly with regard to the British experience: the Thatcher government promoted deregulation through legislation and union repression, as illustrated by the miners strike in 1984–85. In Brazil, where labour law is more extensive, deregulation was carried out not only through legislation but also through collective bargaining, with the support of the unions. The reason why this was possible will be discussed further on.

Labour reform in Brazil was codified in the following laws: Law 9.601/98, which establishes a flexible work week; [6] Provisional Measure 1.709–4/98 which regulates part-time hiring, allowing the replacement of part-time with full-time contracts, with the corresponding reduction of salary, social charges and workers' benefits; and Provisional Measure 1.726/98, which allows the suspension of labour contracts for a period of up to five months, after which the worker can either be fired or rehired by the company.

In his second term, President Cardoso altered the laws governing civil servants, introducing various measures to make it easier to dismiss these workers and to modify the hiring process, laws that were based on the objectives of administrative reform. Among the measures taken, Law 9.801/99, stands out as it enables the dismissal of civil servants upon payment of a bonus but without the need to replace them; Law 9.849/99, provides for renewable short-term contract hiring in the public sector; Law 9.962/2000 establishes the principle that public sector hirings are to be based on the same criteria as private sector hirings (as described in the Labour Code, the CLT); and Law

---

6   The 'hours bank' was designed to harmonize production and the fluctuations of the market. In times of expansion, workers would work beyond the legal limit, without receiving overtime; during market retraction, they would work less than that stipulated by law, without loss of salary. Time worked was either credited or debited in an individual account and adjusted throughout the year.

10.331/2001 links the revision of civil servant salaries to budget forecasts and proof of financial viability.

The government also instituted changes in labour-capital conciliation procedures. Law 9.958/2000, authorising preliminary conciliation committees, is a response to the growing tendency to privatise mediation and arbitration. Composed of representatives of both employers and employees, these committees seek to resolve individual work conflicts and have already produced favourable results for employers. Since committees can be installed in the workplace, where the asymmetry of power between capital and labour is evident, employers are in a position to pressurize employees to give up their rights. Moreover, there have been accusations of fraud in committee proceedings, and there are cases in which trade unions are involved in the 'selling of rights', whereby unions encourage workers to accept benefits inferior to those prescribed by law (Galvão 2003).

The Ministry of Labour has also sought to redefine labour rights, seeking to renegotiate what has been legislated. The ministry first wanted to deregulate Article 7 of the Constitution, a cornerstone of both urban and rural workers' rights, including unemployment compensation, FGTS,[7] minimum wages, wage levels, extra pay for hazardous work, mandatory annual bonuses equivalent to one month of salary, night shift premiums, the 44–hour work week, paid overtime and holidays, pensions, maternity and paternity leave, and other basic features of the Brazilian labour relations system.

Deregulation of Article 7 required an addendum to the Constitution stating that the rights therein could be altered through collective bargaining. But since alterations of the Constitution require a three-fifths majority among both representatives and senators in two voting sessions in each house, the attempt to deregulate Article 7 stalled in the National Congress. The executive sought to circumvent this resistance by means of a relatively simple ploy: rather than a constitutional

---

7   This is a form of social security, available to workers in the private sector, in
     which eight percent of the employee's salary is deposited monthly by the
     employer. In the case of unjustified dismissal, another 40 percent is added to
     the total amount. This sum can be used for various purposes, such as
     unemployment or the purchase of a house.

amendment, the desired objectives were to be achieved through ordinary legislation. Although the impact would be less incisive, the results would be the same. Thus law project 5.483/01 authorises collective bargaining agreements that are flexible when applying legal norms, as long as the agreements do not openly violate the Federal Constitution or worker safety and health legislation.

After three consecutive defeats in national elections, Lula's victory in 2002 brought hope that the process of deregulation would be suspended and labour rights upheld. Such hopes were soon dashed. Labour reform remains very much on the agenda and is under discussion in tripartite forums established by the government to pursue its aims. While it is true that the PT government has suspended law project 5.483/01, the then Minister of Labour, Jacques Wagner, insisted on the government's ability to 'revise' labour rights, including the forty percent fine levied in cases of unjustified dismissal.

In various pronouncements, President Lula himself has offered glimpses of the future flexibilization in work rules:

> It is necessary to adapt not only the union structure but also the labour law to the time we live in. [...] [N]owadays, in the great majority of the workers' categories of this country, union leaders go to the factory doors to call for assemblies and many times come across more ex-workers selling things at the doors of the factory than workers going to work in the factory. [...] I always say to my union friends: the time of being merely a contesting union has gone, and I possibly have become known for this. But now History is demanding from both workers and employers another way of thinking. There is another way to act. In other words, the solution to the problems of the Brazilian society is a question of you all understanding each other. Discussing, from the generation of job positions to labour rights that have to be maintained. Others have to be rethought [...]. (Lula's speech at the beginning of the National Labour Forum 2003).

Later on, Lula agreed to review the 40 percent fine on the FGTS in unjustified dismissals and to divide the mandatory annual bonus, stating that 'the only non-negotiable rights are 30 day paid holidays' (Cantanhêde and Alencar 2004: A9). The push for flexibilisation, it should be noted, has been slowed by Ricardo Berzoini, who took over from Jacques Wagner in the Ministry of Labour.[8]

> The government has the opinion that Brazil does not necessarily have an excess of rights. There is an excess of bureaucracy as how to apply these rights. [...] The important thing is not to mix up the work of reform that modernizes and democratises with that which the previous government proposed, the focus of which was the removal of rights (Sofia 2004).

Despite statements such as these, some union members feel that labour reforms negotiated during the tripartite National Labour Forum pave the way for the principle of negotiation above of what has been legislated, as will be seen below.

The Unions Confront Neoliberalism: Between Accommodation and Resistance

The two biggest Brazilian labour federations, the CUT and the FS, responded to neoliberal politics in different ways. The FS's approach evidences support for neoliberalism, although its support is selective rather than unlimited (Trópia, 2002 2004). The CUT's course is more complex, fluctuating between adoption of some elements of neoliberal discourse to resistance toward actual neoliberal policies. The majority wing of the federation, the so-called *Articulação Sindical*, has since the beginning of the 1990s been more inclined to accept the rhetoric and policies of neoliberalism and has advanced a *propositive* agenda. But there is a minority wing in the CUT, identified with its left wing, which defends the combative trade unions practices that have been a hallmark of the federation since its birth in 1983 (Galvão 2002).[9]

---

8   Both are ex-union members of the CUT. Wagner was in charge of the Chemical Union (Bahia) and Berzoini of the São Paulo Bank Employees Union.
9   Propositive unionism is marked by concessions, conciliation and negotiations with the government and capital, while combative unionism is marked by grass-roots organising and mobilising, by the fight for extending workers' rights

The FS was founded in 1991 with the objective of presenting itself as a legitimate and trustworthy interlocutor for both the government and the employer, strongly contrasting with the confrontational unionism that until then was identified with the CUT. Embodying *results unionism*, a variation of business unionism, the FS regards confrontation as a last resort, encourages conciliation with the state and employers, and acts pragmatically when pressing for the immediate economic interests of workers (Rodrigues and Cardoso 1993; Trópia 2002, 2004; Cardoso 2003).

Accordingly, the FS at first supported the opening of the financial markets as a means to modernise the economy and labour relations, a step toward establishing Brazil's proper place in the global economy. The social costs of the attendant restructuring, especially for industrial workers in the private sector, forced the federation to review its position on this vital question.

The FS did support civil servant pension reform, but balked at aspects of private sector social security reform, including the new calculations for determining pensions. The FS focused on disparities between rights enjoyed by private and public sector workers, which the federation rightly noted led to the animosity of private sector workers against the 'privileges' of those in the public sector. The federation also supported a reduced role for the state and the idea that the state should operate according to market-defined criteria, such as performance evaluations and an end to permanent tenure for civil servants.[10] In addition to supporting privatisation, the FS leadership encouraged the establishment of investment funds and the purchase of state shares by its members. They articulated a 'worker-entrepreneur' ideology in which privatisation would not only benefit consumers, but through the wide distribution of shares the public estate would become democratic (Trópia 2004).

(when on the offensive) and by resistance of these rights (when on the defensive).

10 The FS expected that its loyalty to the government would be politically rewarded and at the same time would 'bombard the social bases of the CUT' (Cardoso 2003: 66), since civil servants were a significant element in the CUT.

The FS looks favourably on labour market deregulation, arguing that it represents the best course of action against unemployment and casual labour.[11] Indeed, many recent laws aimed at creating a more flexible labour force (such as laws enabling short-term contracts and suspension of existing labour contracts), were originally proposed by the FS. Thus in 1992, one of its most important unions, the São Paulo Metal Worker's Union, proposed a flexible working day. Based on its proposal, companies could increase working hours up to twenty percent in the first six months of the contract (Trópia 2002: 179). In 1996 the FS sponsored a 'special' work contract that allowed a temporary reduction of employers' social charges for new employees. In 1997 the federation presented a proposal to the Ministry of Labour suggesting a 30–hour work week, coupled with a ten percent wage reduction, and tax reductions for corporations – 37.3 percent in corporate tax and 7.18 percent in social tax. The FS justified this proposal on the grounds that all parties would benefit: more jobs and leisure time for workers; higher productivity and competitiveness for corporations; and ultimately greater tax revenues for the state since increased employment would more than compensate for the decrease in corporate tax rates. As the president of the federation stated:

> The loss of 10 percent of workers' salaries will definitely be compensated by the increase in the family income, and the entrance of someone unemployed into the labour market adds another salary to the family's income. And more: with the reduction to a 30 hour week, the workers can dedicate themselves to other activities, to increase the family income, improve studies and prepare themselves, or even dedicate themselves more to the family, improving the quality of life (Pereira da Silva 1997).

The FS was one of the most vehement defenders of the law project intended to privilege negotiation over legislation. During the voting session on law project 5.483/01 in the House of Representatives, the leaders of the FS 'had privileged access to the Congressional Areas' and

---

11   FS leaders regard unemployment as a relentless (due to technological innovation) and individual problem (due to workers' poor qualifications). They therefore advocate job training and professional qualification courses to increase the 'employability' of workers.

FS president Paulo Pereira da Silva, 'remained in Brasilia to pressure the representatives to vote favourably' (Trópia 2004: 79).

In order to demonstrate to the Senate that workers were in favour of this project, the São Paulo Metal Workers' Union and the FS held an assembly to make some articles of the CLT flexible 'in practice'. They adopted a proposal that established a staggering of the holiday period throughout the year, division of the obligatory annual bonus into ten payments, division of profit-sharing in up to four payments, the selling of paternity leave, and a reduction of lunch breaks from one hour to thirty minutes (Rolli 2002). This was justified as a means of 'putting more money in the workers' pockets, creating jobs and giving the workers more options to chose from' (Trópia 2004: 189). Finally, the federation supported the creation of conciliation committees that signed various agreements that undercut labour rights (Galvão 2003).

The FS strategy has caused problems. Support for neoliberal policies has not been popular with its members, who are of course deeply concerned with high unemployment and the precarious nature of informal labour. With unemployment rising and working conditions worsening, the FS has begun to backtrack, opposing the government occasionally, and joining hands with the CUT in various initiatives that have led to strikes and joint campaigns for wage increases. For example, in 1996 the FS supported a general strike organised by the CUT and the *Confederação Geral dos Trabalhadores* (CGT). These three labour federations attributed unemployment to the government's high interest rate policy and the disorderly opening of the financial markets, demanding a seventy percent index for the nationalisation of car components and the increase of import tax for the sector (Trópia 2004: 115). To be sure, in contrast to the other two federations, the FS continued to advocate administrative and social security reform, as well as continued deregulation of the labour market as a way to fight unemployment. The FS, together with the CUT, also reacted against the threat of the closing of a Ford plant in São Paulo which occurred with the opening of another plant in Bahia. The two federations even fought side by side for a national labour contract for the automobile sector to eliminate wage and benefit differentials between the different states (a difference that, combined with competitive state tax policies, had altered the automobile industry in Brazil). The two federations carried out various strikes in 1999 to pressure the car assembly factories to sign a national labour contract (Cardoso 2003; Trópia 2004).

These and other actions indicate that the FS commitment to neoliberalism is not without limits. But it is nevertheless true that the FS supported the majority of neoliberal reforms, leaving a minority in the Brazilian labour movement, primarily the left unions in the CUT, to challenge the new policy orientation. This minority strenuously resisted the dismantling of labour and social rights, although as we shall see, resistance was sporadic and rarely successful.

An appreciation of the low union mobilisation capacity in Brazil from 1990 onwards must begin with the divisions within the movement. With a dominant labour federation embracing neoliberal policies, the capacity of the working classes to resist the rising power of capital is certainly inhibited. Another reason for the weakness of resistance is that when a labour federation adopts aspects of the dominant neoliberal ideology, it has difficulty not only organising workers but simply expressing opposition to the government (taking on, at times, terms and practices that it intended to fight against). A third reason is repression, which is carried out either by physical force (such as the petrol workers strike in 1995) or by legal action (such as the civil servants strike in 2001) designed to discourage strikes and punish strikers.

Unlike the FS, the CUT opposed administrative and social security reforms, denounced the privatisation policies, the opening of the markets, the dismantling of the public services and the reduction of rights. However, the CUT's stand is multi-faceted and full of internal conflicts.

The beginning of the 1990s marks a change in the position taken by the CUT's main current, the *Articulação Sindical*, which is slowly abandoning the practice of resistance and giving in to negotiation. This change was brought about by various economic, political and ideological factors, and was resisted by a minority bloc that remains committed to a confrontational strategy (Galvão 2003). The creation of the FS also contributed to the CUT's positional shift, as competition with the new labour federation encouraged a friendlier stance towards government and employers. Thus the CUT played a role in negotiations for most of the reform agenda of President Cardoso's government.[12] In so doing, the CUT legitimised itself in the eyes of their opponents, showing themselves to be competent and 'mature', and overcoming criticism from the media, the government, and the FS that they were too 'radical' and 'antidemocratic' to negotiate. In terms of social security reform for example, the CUT at first vigorously opposed the Cardoso government plan, on the grounds that the plan insisted on retirement pensions based on years worked. However, Vicente Paulo da Silva, the CUT's president from 1994 to 2000, ultimately accepted the substitution of years worked for years of contribution and even changes in the public sector social security system, a step that generated opposition from both civil servants and left-wing unions in the CUT.

Throughout negotiations on social security reform, the CUT proved ready to negotiate on terms dictated by employers and the government, even incorporating elements of neoliberal discourse. The CUT was clearly on the defensive, and rather than formulating counter-proposals that demonstrated the conflict of interests between capital and the working classes, the federation made its demands flexible and compatible with corporate ideology and vocabulary.

The CUT's stance reveals the limits of its propositive strategy. For proposals to be taken seriously at the negotiating table, they needed to be regarded as 'realistic', in tune with the dominant ideology, of plausible interest to both the state and employers. Otherwise negotiations failed before they began. Thus the competence of the negotiator is based on the 'viability' of the proposal presented. In this ongoing propositive process, the CUT made ever-increasing concessions to capital, integrating itself in the logic of the market and taking on capitalist values demanded by neoliberalism, such as profitability, productivity, quality and efficiency. The propositive strategy is based on the proposition that it is possible to reconcile class differences at the bargaining table. It is no longer a question of organizing, mobilizing and defending the interests of the working class, but of improving (or preserving) the market conditions of

---

12 The one exception was administrative reform, probably due to the fact that the majority of unions representing civil servants are controlled by the left-wing opposition (Jard da Silva, 2001).

targeted economic sectors. In this way, the CUT acts as a 'partner' (even if it plays a secondary role) in the administration of capital (Boito Jr. 1999: 169).

Despite the ascension of propositive unionism during the 1990s, the CUT continues to oppose the deregulation of labour relations, questioning flexible contracts and defending the CLT. Existing workers' rights were the fruits of a hard-fought struggle and should be maintained, the CUT argues, especially during critical times economically for the working population. The CUT therefore appealed to the Supreme Court to declare unconstitutional an attempt to legislate short-term contracts. The federation also brought pressure to bear on representatives to uphold the principle of the law over negotiation of labour contracts, conducting a one-day national strike on 21 March 2002.[13]

Yet even in the arena of labour rights, not all CUT leaders are opposed to the idea of flexibility or the subverting of the law by negotiation. Some of its leaders and unions believe they are more capable of securing favourable work conditions through negotiation rather than through legislation.[14] Not only Luiz Marinho, but also another ex-president of the federation, Vicente Paulo da Silva, both from the ABC Metal Workers Union (one of the main proponents of propositive unionism), admitted to having negotiated labour rights in some situations (Galvão 2003). Thus like the São Paulo Metal Workers Union, the ABC Metal Workers Union worked like a 'laboratory' in labour relations, negotiating measures that led to flexibility of rights (Jácome Rodrigues 2001; Martins and Jácome Rodrigues 2000; Noronha 1999).

This process is evident in negotiations carried out in the automobile industry. In the second half of the 1990s, this sector was in serious difficulty, due to decline in both production and sales. In order

---

13   'CUT unites 1 million against the changes of CLT', *Folha de S. Paulo*, 22 March 2002. The left wing of the federation criticized what it perceived as a lack of dedication by the CUT leaders in the preparation of the strike, and for not making effective use of worker mobilization.

14   The ABC Metal Workers' Union was the first to adopt an hours' bank in 1995, creating a flexible work week in the car industry. However, there was always a division within the CUT and the *Articulação Sindical* in regard to this initiative.

to reduce stocks of unsold cars, assembly plants resorted to shutdowns and threats of layoffs. More often, assembly plants concocted a variety of plans to reduce labour costs, such as slashing overtime and night shift premiums, and cutting the obligatory annual bonuses and holiday bonuses. With apparently no viable alternative, workers accepted such cuts. To cite but one example, in December 1998, workers at the Volkswagen plant in São Bernardo do Campo accepted a four-day week, with a subsequent fifteen percent wage reduction.

Such negotiations of course represent a substantial loss of rights, and workers make significant concessions without receiving guarantees of job stability. Dismissals are postponed to the near future and workers, their position greatly weakened, are less and less able to resist. The 'surplus' in the car industry is a recurring argument used by automobile companies to threaten employees with dismissal, and thus promote flexibility of rights *with the mediation of the union acting as a 'partner' of the company.* In 2001 'surplus' was once more brandished by Volkswagen, which proposed a twenty percent reduction in wages and working hours. Workers ultimately accepted an agreement that brought them a fifteen percent reduction in wages and working hours and a 'voluntary' resignation programme. For each new 'decrease' in the work force, remaining employees face increasingly worse working conditions. They avoid mass dismissals by accepting fewer working hours and lower wages, yet dismissals are still carried out through monetary 'incentives' that encourage voluntary resignations and through various early retirement schemes.

Workers at Ford were also pressured to 'collaborate' with plans to revive company productivity and competitiveness. Dismissed by letters in the post in December 1998, workers were then given the option that instead of dismissal, they could either join a programme of 'voluntary' resignation or have their contract temporarily suspended as established by MP 1.726/98.

This type of agreement, however, causes dissatisfaction among union leaders opposed to the *Articulação Sindical.* For the president of the Campinas Metal Worker's Union, the first agreement with Volkswagen 'was a surrender, not an agreement, and it dismantled all the strategy of the resistance with regard to the policy of the Government in taking away workers' rights' (Beiguelman 2002a: 162). Workers themselves of course feel exploited: 'The workers work four days a week, but feel that they produce for five' (Beiguelman 2002b: 12). Thus contrary to the FS, which supported flexibility of labour relations, there was a lot of resistance against this measure within the CUT.

The CUT and the FS Move Towards Citizen Unionism

Despite their obvious differences, both the CUT and the FS have begun to show signs that they are converging on a model of *citizen unionism*. A principal characteristic of this new style of unionism is that it offers workers (whether or not they are members) services that until then had been the preserve of the state.

There are many justifications for this change. The future of the FS depends on its capacity to act not only in the direct interests workers (such as wages and working conditions), but also more broadly as a provider of solutions to social problems. For the CUT leadership in the *Articulação Sindical*, providing social services is a way of defending all aspects of workers' lives, rather than their work and financial situations alone. Citizen unionism implies that unions are transformed into a type of Non-Governmental Organisation (NGO), that they are certified by the state to carry out certain public services.

However, by taking on the role of 'non-state public sector', the federations not only collaborated with the privatisation of public policy but also promote the idea that the state is inefficient and civil servants are incompetent. While this attitude is consistent with the FS's approach, it represents a contradiction for the CUT. Public service unionism, camouflaged as citizen unionism, is part of the same process that has led to the dismantling of public services and established labour rights, steps the CUT has opposed.

Employers and government ministers tend to blame the increase of unemployment on the lack of adequate skills formation. Brazilian workers, it is argued, are not sufficiently 'employable'. By becoming an agent of employment policy, the CUT ends up authenticating the 'employability' rhetoric that blames the unemployed themselves for their situation. In the same way, when taking on tasks related to education and skill development, the CUT contradicts itself. At the same time that it criticizes neoliberal politics and the dismantling of public services, placing responsibility for unemployment and the deterioration of social services on the government, its practice ends up legitimising this same policy.

The consequences of the CUT's conversion to propositive and citizen unionism are clear. It has tempered its fight against industrial restructuring, which it now considers an unavoidable phenomenon, and it is jettisoning effective resistance movements in favour of quantitative negotiations over the elimination of jobs. The CUT's negotiations are never enough to stop the dismissals that follow one after another, because dismissal is only temporarily avoided. The federation's alternative is to send the dismissed workers to the skill development programmes it offers. Moreover, the new emphasis on the concept of citizenship has led by and large to the abandonment of the concept of class. When acting in the name of all citizens, the CUT moves further away from a class-based stance, as the concept of 'citizen' conceals class differences, uniting everyone in an abstract entity.

When opting for citizen unionism, unions help the neoliberal agenda and undermine labour rights. They undermine universal policies and encourage those of a limited and compensatory nature; and thus they promote the individualisation of the unemployment problem and blame unemployed workers for their own condition. The CUT exists therefore, between criticism of and accommodation to neoliberalism.

The FS was a pioneer when it set up an employment agency, the *Centro de Solidariedade ao Trabalhador*, in 1998. The centre, situated in São Paulo, offers unemployment benefits, an employment agency, professional education and job training, and finally, makes available to workers resources from the Income and Job Generation Public Programme. All these programmes are primarily financed by a public fund: the Worker's Support Fund (FAT). The CUT responded to the initiative of its rival by setting up the *Central de Trabalho e Renda* in 1999.

The FS now provides a wide range of services, including life and health insurance, a financial agency offering loans to working people, a pension fund, and even a football club (Trópia 2004: 84, 136). The CUT is equally active. It encourages the proliferation of small businesses and the setting up of cooperatives, many of which are also supported by NGOs. In order to coordinate these activities, the CUT set up in 1999 the *Agência de Desenvolvimento Solidário* (ADS), with the intention of organizing and assisting cooperatives, offering them qualifications and credit (Zarpelon 2002). Contrary to the FS, however, the use of the resources from FAT for such public services has caused intense controversy within the CUT.

Providing service is justified by the CUT as a means for it to compete for financial resources offered by state institutions. The *Articulação Sindical* holds that the CUT should explore all avenues that will take full advantage of FAT funds. Its leaders argue that the federation cannot allow FAT to be used by the government, employers or labour federations that are not committed to workers' interests. They argue that with these steps, the CUT can build an alternative, propositive project of public policies. The left wing in the CUT has of course criticised federation policies in this regard, despite the fact that many left-wing unions have themselves set up job training projects. But the left wing remains highly critical of the type of public service carried out by the CUT.

FAT resources are a way for unions to overcome economic difficulties. They make new initiatives possible. But there is a price to be paid. Although maintaining a combative rhetoric, the CUT unions slowly altered their conceptions and activities. Thus the choice of propositive and citizen unionism has a political price. The CUT unions have not become enamoured with capital or the government, but they have started to make growing concessions to them. These concessions are not exclusively the result of neoliberalism and industrial restructuring, which certainly hinders union activity, but does not explain everything. The change in the CUT union practice also had an ideological component. That is, CUT resists but is also affected by neoliberalism. Unlike the FS that adhered to neoliberalism from the outset, the CUT follows a tortuous path, full of ambiguities and contradictions.

These ambiguities and contradictions are directly linked to the internal composition of the federation, whose factions play differing roles, provoking disparities between speech – that praises citizenship but has not yet eliminated class references – and practice. This hybrid speech seems a way to settle internal disputes, uniting the various groups that comprise the CUT. Nevertheless, it is a rather feeble speech, as the predominance of a propositive and citizenship stance has ideologically disarmed the federation in its fight against neo-liberalism, compromising its capacity to resist the deterioration of social rights and especially the deregulation or labour relations.

As mentioned earlier, deregulation in Brazil has been carried out with the support or at least the consent of the unions. Unions supported the process largely because results unionism does not threaten the interests of the dominant class. On the contrary, unions become a partner of the dominant class, helping in the process of deregulation of rights, as in industrial restructuring. The same can be said about propositive unionism. This type of unionism assists both the government and employers, since it hinges on 'realistic' negotiations and thereby limits the range of possibilities. In this way, Brazilian trade unions can collaborate with neoliberal reforms that continue to be implemented in the Lula government.

Trade Unions and the Lula Government

The victory for Lula in 2002 was the result of a social upsurge that gained increasing intensity after the exchange rate crisis of 1999 that undermined support for neoliberal reforms. Having supported Cardoso during his two terms, the FS moved away from him during this election year. Indeed, the FS president, Paulo Pereira da Silva, became the vice–presidential running mate for Ciro Gomes.[15] In the case of the

---

15 Despite his criticisms of Lula during the campaign, Gomes was named Minister of National Integration in Lula's government.

CUT, despite its internal divisions, this federation had by and large remained critical of Cardoso. The CUT had historic links to the PT, played an important role in its 2002 victory, and afterward various ministers and their teams were recruited from the ranks of the federation (Galvão and Novelli 2004).

Paradoxically, the CUT's difficulties actually increased with the election of President Lula. The expectation that the new government would break away from neoliberalism was frustrated. Instead of fighting this model, the PT government maintained its fundamentals and even intensified the reforms introduced by the Cardoso government in areas such as social security reform. Thus rather than strengthening trade unionism and increasing social and workers' rights, the rise to power of the PT has led to a further erosion of these rights. In this new context, the CUT's capacity to resist has diminished. The historic relationship between *Articulação Sindical* and the dominant wing of PT, which includes Lula himself and the top-ranking members of his government, has inhibited the CUT from aggressive criticism of the government, even when government action threatens social and labour rights. In general, the CUT accepts the argument that the 'medicine' to be administered to the Brazilian economy in the first year of the PT mandate will be bitter, due to the inheritance of the Cardoso government.

The CUT's capacity to resist has also been affected by its change in leadership. President Lula used his influence to guarantee the election of Luiz Marinho, the former president of the ABC Metal Workers' Union, as the new president of the federation. Thwarting the re-election of João Felício was a defining moment for the CUT. Despite belonging to the same current (*Articulação Sindical*) as Marinho, Felício is a civil servant, a category adversely affected by neoliberal politics, whereas Marinho is a metal worker and is one of the main leaders of propositive unionism. And while Felício is critical of the government, Marinho tends to minimize criticisms made against the PT by union members and workers. Thus the CUT fulfils a role for the PT government comparable to that played by the FS for the Cardoso administration. Rather than organising the resistance of workers and mobilizing them in defence of their rights, the CUT dampens anti-government protests, urging the grassroots to adopt a more tolerant and patient approach to a government that it elected.

The CUT's tolerance of government policy is clearest in the area of social security reform. This reform caused great dissatisfaction among the civil servants who opposed taxation of their retired colleagues, the elimination of full-pay pensions, and the creation of pension funds. Federation leaders, however, while critical of some points in the reform package, worked hard to spare the government the full wrath of the civil servants. They actively opposed a strike planned by civil servants and their allies (many of whom are affiliated with the CUT), and sought instead to negotiate all points at issue. Yet leadership caution was not enough on this occasion to squelch anti-government sentiment. A civil servant strike took place, during which 50,000 demonstrators took to the streets in Brasilia. Some strike leaders threatened to secede from the CUT, and indeed a Civil Servant Federation was created, although this federation does not have the backing of unions affiliated with the CUT.

Factors other than leadership have generated a sense of crisis within the CUT. Firstly, its main current, the *Articulação Sindical*, has produced opposition by its appeasement of the government's small increases in the minimum wage and its apparent unwillingness to pursue the social objectives it had itself established. Secondly, the *Articulação Sindical* has sought on several occasions to block strike action by its constituent unions. And thirdly, the CUT leadership opted to participate in government-organised tripartite bodies to discuss intended reforms.

The National Labour Forum's discussions on labour reform have caused considerable disquiet in the CUT. Many affiliates and opposition leaders see the talks as a means to bolster CUT leaders, weaken rank-and-file input, and pave the way for greater flexibility of labour laws. The report of the National Labour Forum supports the idea of legalising federations (they are currently not recognised under Brazilian law) and recognising their right to sign collective bargaining agreements. The report also endorses a new multi-level collective bargaining system, possibly one in which terms accepted by the federations could not be altered by agreements made by affiliated unions. Although the same report also proposes that, in case of conflict between agreements negotiated by the federation and the unions, the most favourable terms for the affected workers would apply, local leaders worry that this clause may not pass in Congress. If their fears are realised, the federations could negotiate agreements harmful to worker interests – a very common practice in the case of the FS – or agreements that undermine existing labour legislation. Despite the CUT's track record during the Cardoso government of opposition to the idea of allowing negotiation to supersede legislation, it seems to have done so more as opposition to the government rather than a position of principle. In the Lula government, the CUT has found it easier to support this idea, inasmuch as its stronger and more organised unions have the means to negotiate agreements that stipulate more advantageous norms than those set by legislation. Unions controlled by the left strongly resist the principle that bargaining agreements could supersede labour law, but these unions may well have no choice but to follow the dictates of the majority.

The CUT's internal conflicts were evident during the September 2004 strike of workers in the banking industry. On that occasion, the grassroots rejected an agreement negotiated by the CUT's National Bank Employees Union, led by the *Articulação Sindical*, and employers. Defying the leadership, the rank-and-file voted to strike rather than accept what it regarded as an unacceptable pay package negotiated by the union's leaders. Rising discontent with the CUT's leadership has also led to the disaffiliation of some important unions such as the São José dos Campos and Region Metal Workers.[16] The dissident unions organised themselves around the National Fight Co-ordination (*Conlutas*), a diverse body of organisations linked to various social movements, the objective of which is to fight reforms adopted by the government. *Conlutas* also relies on the participation of unions that criticise the CUT yet remain affiliated to it.

Conlutas has organised a variety of protests against reform initiated by the Lula government. More specifically, *Conlutas* has mobilised against trade union, labour and university reforms. Its protests have not as yet generated widespread enthusiasm, but they are nevertheless an important indication of social movement activism against government policy.

---

16   Approximately 23 unions have already disaffiliated the CUT. One estimate suggests that this number would grow to 100 in January 2005. See Gomes Batista 2004.

Final Considerations

Lula's election profoundly impacted the Brazilian trade union scene. If the intensification of the social conflicts at the end of the 1990s seemed to indicate a reactivation of combative unionism, the PT government's decision to pursue the model of neoliberalism has undermined the critical capacity of its allies, since the party that represented robust opposition market-oriented reforms has now embraced them. While the PT was in opposition, conflicts between the various CUT factions were camouflaged by united criticism of the Cardoso government. Numerous attempts by the *Articulação Sindical* to negotiate with the government and employers were frustrated by opposition leaders and factions, and confrontation was once again on the rise. With the PT's victory, the internal divisions of the CUT have become increasingly apparent. While a vocal minority continues to resist neoliberalism, the majority is prepared to make only superficial criticisms of the government. Like the government itself, the majority element within the CUT seems to have surrendered to neoliberalism.

If the CUT faces serious questions about its independence from the Lula government, the FS is going through an identity crisis. Having had the ear of governments since its inception, the FS has now lost this position of influence to CUT. The FS criticizes interest rate increases and some other measures that it had previously defended, presenting itself as an opposition. But this criticism is much more an attempt to differentiate itself from the CUT rather than a political conviction. And some unions linked to the FS, uncomfortable in the role of opposition, have now affiliated with the CUT to get closer to the government.

The dramatic changes in both the CUT and the FS represent a significant challenge to Brazilian unionism. Some unions have opted to break away from the CUT, while others have chosen to continue fighting within it, in an attempt to change the course of the federation. Both options are difficult and risky. Disaffiliation implies intensive mobilisation at the grassroots level and a new organisational structure to replace the CUT as the vanguard of combative Brazilian unionism.

Remaining inside the CUT entails fighting an increasingly powerful majority faction that is supported by the government.

Those within the CUT who resist neoliberalism have been disarmed. They gambled that the Lula government would initiate a more progressive project of social change and they lost. Some of these currents do not consider either the CUT or the PT as any longer representative of workers' interests. Nevertheless they hesitate to abandon these organisations because they believe there is no alternative. For workers themselves, there remains the possibility *Conlutas* might continue to grow and offer a more effective way of resisting neoliberalism.

References

Beiguelman, P. (2002a) 'Os companheiros de São Paulo – flashes contemporâneos', in P. Beiguelman (ed.) *Os companheiros de São Paulo: ontem e hoje*, São Paulo: Cortez.
— (2002b) 'A nova investida da Volks', *Debate Sindical* 41(December–February): 12–13.
Boito Jr., A. (1999) *Política neoliberal e sindicalismo no Brasil*, São Paulo: Xamã.
Cantanhêde, E. and Alencar, K. (2004) 'Lula wants flexibility of the CLT in 2005', *Folha de S. Paulo*, 13 February.
Cardoso, A.M. (2003) *A década neoliberal e a crise dos sindicatos no Brasil*, São Paulo: Boitempo.
Cruz, S.V. (1998) 'Alguns argumentos sobre reformas para o mercado', *Lua Nova, Revista de Cultura e Política* 45: 5–27.
Dieese (2001) *A situação do trabalho no Brasil*, São Paulo: Dieese.
Galvão, A. (2002) 'A CUT na encruzilhada: dilemas do movimento sindical combativo', *Idéias, Campinas* 9(1): 105–154.
— (2003) *Neoliberalismo e reforma trabalhista no Brasil*, Tese de Doutorado em Ciências Sociais, Unicamp/Instituto de Filosofia e Ciências Humanas.
— (2004) 'A reforma sindical no governo Lula: mudança ou continuidade?', in A. Borges (ed.) *A reforma sindical e trabalhista no governo Lula*, São Paulo: Anita Garibladi.

— and Novelli, J.M.N. (2004) 'Het eerste jaar van de regering-Lula: de angst heeft de hoop overwoonen', *Vlaams Marxistisch Tijdschrift* 38(3): 24–42.

Gomes Batista, H. (2004) 'PT Government alters situation of federations', *Jornal Valor Econômico*, 20 July.

Jácome Rodrigues, I. (2001) 'Um laboratório das relações de trabalho no Brasil: ABC paulista nos anos 90', paper presented at the XXV Encontro Anual da Anpocs, Caxambu.

Jard da Silva, S. (2001) 'Companheiros servidores: o avanço do sindicalismo do setor público na CUT', *Revista Brasileira de Ciências Sociais* 16(46): 130–46.

Lesbaupin, I. and Mineiro, A. (2002) *O desmonte da nação em dados*, Petrópolis: Vozes.

Martins, H. de S. and Jácome Rodrigues, I. (2002) 'O sindicalismo brasileiro na segunda metade dos anos 90', *Tempo Social, Revista de Sociologia da USP* 11(2): 155–82.

Noronha, E. (1999) *Entre a lei e a arbitrariedade: mercados e relações de trabalho no Brasil*, São Paulo: LTr.

Novelli, J.M.N. and Galvão, A. (2001–2) 'The Political Economy of Neoliberalism in Brazil in the 1990s', *International Journal of Political Economy* 31(4): 3–52.

Pereira da Silva, P. (1997) 'A solution for unemployment', *Folha de S. Paulo*, 25 May.

Rodrigues, L. and Cardoso A.M. (1993) *Força Sindical: uma análise sóciopolítica*, Rio de Janeiro: Paz e Terra.

Rolli, C. (2002) 'FS forces flexibility for CLT', *Folha de S. Paulo*, 18 March.

Saes, D. (2001) *República do capital*, São Paulo: Boitempo.

Sallum Jr., B. (2002) 'O Brasil sob Cardoso: neoliberalismo e desenvolvimentismo', *Tempo Social, Revista de Sociologia da USP* 11(2): 23–47.

Singer, P. (1998) 'Um imenso equívoco', *Praga – estudos marxistas* 6, São Paulo: Hucitec.

— (1999) 'A raiz do desastre social: a política econômica de FHC', in I. Lesbaupin (ed.) *O desmonte da nação: balanço do governo FHC*. Petrópolis: Vozes.

Sofia, J. (2004) 'Work reform may not occur until 2006', *Folha de S. Paulo*, 31 October.

Trópia, P. (2002) 'A adesão da Força Sindical ao neoliberalismo', *Idéias* 9(1): 155–202.

— (2004) *O impacto da ideologia neoliberal no meio operário: um estudo sobre os metalúrgicos da cidade de São Paulo e a Força Sindical*, Tese de Doutorado, IFCH/Unicamp.

Zarpelon, S.R. (2002) 'ONGs, movimento sindical e o novo socialismo utópico', *Idéias* 9(1): 203–244.

PIET KONINGS

African Trade Unions and the Challenge of Globalisation: A Comparative Study of Ghana and Cameroon[1]

Introduction

The far-reaching economic and political reforms in Africa as a result of neoliberal globalisation have been the focus of a growing body of literature in the last decades. Surprisingly, the response of certain civil-society organisations to the challenge of economic and political liberalisation appears to have been understudied (Buijtenhuijs and Thiriot 1995). This study attempts to fill this lacuna by examining the role of African trade unions in these reforms.

African trade unions had first to respond to the challenge of economic liberalisation. From the 1980s onwards and faced with a deep and prolonged economic crisis, virtually all African governments have been required by the International Monetary Fund (IMF), the World Bank and western donors to implement a neoliberal reform package in the form of Structural Adjustment Programmes (SAPs). The aim of these SAPs has been to reduce the government's role in the economy, to establish free markets and a secure environment for private capital, and to enhance Africa's competitiveness in the global economic order. Their central demands include drastic cuts in public expenditure, such as the elimination of subsidies, the dismantling of

1   An earlier version of this article entitled 'Organised Labour and Neo-Liberal Economic and Political Reforms in West and Central Africa' appeared as (2003) *Journal of Contemporary African Studies* 21(3): 447-71. For this journal's website, see http://www.tandf.co.uk/journals. The author would like to thank Taylor & Francis for granting permission allowing the reproduction of a substantial proportion of the earlier version.

price controls, rationalisation in the public sector through privatisation, lay-offs, wage cuts and closures, liberalisation of the economy
guided by market forces domestically and comparative advantage
internationally, promotion of commodity exports and foreign investment, and currency devaluation. In terms of macroeconomic performance, structural adjustment has produced widely diverging results in
Africa but the social cost of SAPs has been more uniformly negative.
It is now generally recognised that wage workers have been among
the most seriously affected by the economic crisis and structural
adjustment. They are being confronted with retrenchments and job
insecurity, wage restraints and the suspension of benefits, soaring
consumer prices and user charges for public services, flexible
management practices and subcontracting, and an intensification of
managerial efforts to increase labour productivity.

World Bank reports have often attempted to justify these anti-
labour measures, both in economic and political terms (Bangura and
Beckman 1993; Adesina 1994; Gibbon 1995; World Bank 1995). The
economic justification for structural adjustment is that workers are
'too many and too costly'. This is attributed to misconceived policies,
including the development of an overprotected and oversized import-
substituting industrial sector. Another problem is the growth of over-
staffed state enterprises and public services, with wage bills out of
proportion to their carrying capacity and deficits paid by state
subsidies due to a combination of budgetary laxity and the influence
of corrupt and clientelistic modes of labour recruitment. Such policies
have worked against the development of the private sector and
increased competition in the global market.

The political justification for structural adjustment is that
workers are 'powerful and selfish'. The World Bank argues that
organised labour has been a major beneficiary of pre-adjustment
policies, stressing that the historical influence of African trade unions
has led to excessive levels of wage employment, inflated wages and
pro-urban, pro-worker allocation of public funds. It is interesting to
observe that this argument comes close to earlier populist positions of
'labour aristocracy', 'urban bias' and 'urban coalition', which tended
to view workers as a privileged minority pursuing narrow self-
interests at the expense of the urban poor and peasantry, taking

advantage of better organisation, and being closely connected with the urban elite (Waterman 1975; Lipton 1977; Ferguson 1999). Jamal and Weeks (1993) presented a detailed refutation of the argument, showing that the so-called rural–urban gap was largely illusory and had in any case been closed before the harsh SAP measures were applied to correct it. These views have nevertheless often been used by African leaders, like Rawlings in Ghana (Kraus 1991), to legitimise the implementation of SAP measures and to suppress any trade union opposition.

Many labour specialists appear pessimistic about the ability of African trade unions to play any significant role in the defence of workers' interests during economic liberalisation (Isamah 1994; Mihyo and Schiphorst 1995; Simutanyi 1996). They stress that trade unions are usually small in Africa – organising only a tiny minority of the working population in predominantly agrarian societies – and that, in many instances, trade unions have been incorporated into the state in the aftermath of independence for the sake of national development, undermining their claims to represent workers and turning union leaders into a privileged and often corrupt labour aristocracy (Beckman 2002; Hutchful 2002). Above all, SAPs are interpreted as having further weakened the position of trade unions in African post-colonial states. Not only are they likely to operate in a hostile political environment, but the logic of structural adjustment also tends to constrain their ability to defend their members' rights effectively. With mass retrenchments of labour in the public and private sectors leading to substantial losses in union membership and revenues, government abolition of legislative provisions concerning job security, participatory rights or guaranteed collective bargaining rights, and outright government oppression of any opposition union action, trade unions find themselves with their backs to the wall. In these circumstances, there is little they can do for their members. Increasing job insecurity and falling real earnings have forced the rank and file to search for alternative sources of income, straddling the formal and informal sectors and subsistence farming, as well as engaging in illicit income-generating activities. The fusion of labour markets has ensured the survival of workers but, according to some authors (for example, Jamal and Weeks 1993), it also signifies the virtual collapse of the

wage-earning class as a distinct entity. As a result of these developments, trade unions are said to be facing a deep crisis of identity,
having not yet devised any new strategies to deal with these dramatic
changes.

While admitting that African trade unions show a number of
weaknesses, a few labour specialists still appear optimistic about the
unions' ability to intervene in defence of their members' interests
during neoliberal economic reforms (Kester and Sidibé 1997; Beckman 2002). They usually refer to certain specific factors that guarantee
trade unions an exceptional position among civil-society organisations. First, trade union members may account for only a small
proportion of the working population in Africa, but they are concentrated in the cities and active in strategically important sectors of the
economy. As such, they may exercise considerable political power,
being potentially capable of paralysing the economy and threatening
the regime in power. Second, trade unions are among the oldest civil-
society organisations, with a long history of struggles against oppression and exploitative regimes. On some occasions, they were even
able to mobilise support beyond their own membership. Small
producers and traders in the expanding informal sector, who usually
maintain close relations with workers, were particularly inclined
to support their actions. The trade unions, in turn, have tended to
represent the interests of these unorganised popular strata, serving as
their spokesmen (Sandbrook 1982; Freund 1988). They have also
played a leading role in establishing wider alliances in civil society for
economic gains and political changes, in particular with student and
academic staff unions and professional associations. Third, trade
unions often enjoy a higher degree of international solidarity than
other civil-society organisations. International trade union organisations and the International Labour Organisation (ILO) in Geneva have
frequently requested that authoritarian regimes release trade union
leaders from prison and ensure a basic minimum of trade union
liberties.

From the end of the 1980s, African trade unions have also had to
respond to the challenge of political liberalisation. There were several
reasons for the rapid spread of neoliberal reforms in Africa, notably
the global trend towards political liberalisation in the wake of the

collapse of the former communist states in Eastern Europe, the strong opposition of domestic civil-society organisations to corrupt and authoritarian African regimes, and the new standards of international financial institutions and western governments for capital accumulation, linking structural adjustment to liberal democracy. This latter linkage reflected the growing post-Cold War consensus that liberal-democratic regimes were more likely than authoritarian regimes to enhance efficient public management and the legitimisation of harsh structural adjustment measures. Remarkably, this new perspective assigned a vital role to civil-society organisations in the realisation of both economic growth and democratic sustainability.

Whereas the World Bank had previously looked upon trade unions as an obstacle to neoliberal economic reforms, it now argued that their participation in policy-making would ensure ownership, credibility and sustainability of the reform process (World Bank 1992, 1995; Rakner 2001). However, for the transitional governments that had to implement neoliberal economic and political reforms simultaneously, the new perspective created a political dilemma: to achieve a balance between, on the one hand, meeting popular demands, and implementing market-based reforms which spelt hardship and sacrifice on the other. In this study, I explore the role that African trade unions played in neoliberal political reforms. To what extent have they been involved in the political restructuring of the state? Has political liberalisation really enhanced their political influence and ability to defend their members' interests? And, above all, has the simultaneous occurrence of neoliberal economic and political reforms inspired them to devise new strategies that would augment their capacity to cope with the dramatic changes taking place in the national and international labour markets and to remain meaningful to their members and even to other social groups?

Recent research cautions against any easy generalisations about the response of African trade unions to the challenge of neoliberal globalisation. There actually appears to be a large variation in their performance (Konings 2000; Rakner 2001; Beckman and Sachikonye 2001). This article offers a comparative study of the role of trade unions in Ghana and Cameroon based on the author's long-term research on organised labour in these countries (see, for instance,

Konings 1977, 1986, 1993, 1998). Trade union responses to economic and political liberalisation appear to be quite different in these countries: generally positive in Ghana and clearly negative in Cameroon. It is argued that a range of factors are responsible for this situation, including differences in the impact of structural adjustment, the nature of the state and state-society relations, the organisational capacity of the unions, their relationship with political parties and other civil-society organisations, and their search for innovative ways to respond to neoliberal economic and political reforms and to champion the cause of the workers (Konings 2000: 169–70; Beckman 2002: 93–94). The Ghana case deserves most attention since there have been significant changes in state–trade union relations in Ghana during political liberalisation. The Cameroonian case, however, has been characterised by a remarkable degree of continuity in these relations, as was aptly observed by Nyamnjoh (1996: 20): 'Today Cameroonians have multi-partyism but the one-party logic persists.'

Ghana has earned the reputation among western donors for being one of the few relative success stories in Africa concerning economic and political liberalisation. Several authors (Rothchild 1991; Nugent 1995; Hutchful 2002) have highlighted the spectacular adoption in 1983 of a neoliberal economic reform package by the radical populist military regime, the Provisional National Defence Council (PNDC), albeit without abandoning its populist rhetoric altogether. Following the rigorous execution of its SAP, there was a relatively peaceful transition from the military PNDC regime to the civilian National Democratic Congress (NDC) government in 1992, with Flight-Lieutenant J.J. Rawlings being promoted from PNDC Chairman to President of Ghana's Fourth Republic. Not only has the Fourth Republic outlasted earlier democratic interludes, it has also spawned a fragile institutionalisation of some of the rules and procedures of the democratic game, manifest, among others, in a large degree of autonomy for the press and judiciary, and the resurgence of civil society (Sandbrook and Oelbaum 1997). Ghana, moreover, is said to have a relatively strong labour movement that, after having been subordinated to the state during the Convention People's Party (CPP) era, has been able to sustain a tenuous defence of labour rights and union autonomy in spite of repeated military interventions and impositions (Damachi 1974; Konings 1977; Jeffries 1978; Crisp 1984; Akwetey 1994; Panford 2001). Although Ghanaian trade union leaders tended to be strong advocates of neoliberal political reforms, they were nevertheless opposed to any alliances with opposition movements and parties. They regarded trade union autonomy as an essential prerequisite for the defence of workers' interests and the pursuit of creative responses to economic and political liberalisation.

In sharp contrast to Ghana, Cameroon has gained the reputation of being a disappointing 'adjuster' after the Biya government reluctantly agreed to implement an SAP in 1988–89. Several authors (Van de Walle 1993; Konings 1996; Gabriel 1999) have argued that the neo-patrimonial nature of the Cameroonian post-colonial state forms a clear obstacle to neoliberal economic and political reforms that threaten the ruling elite's control over state resources and rent-seeking activities. As a result, the process of economic and political liberalisation has been slow and erratic in Cameroon. The Cameroonian trade union movement, too, has less standing and influence than its Ghanaian counterpart, having been subdued and deactivated by the one-party state following independence and reunification in 1961, and with its leadership co-opted into the 'hegemonic alliance' (Bayart 1979). This proved to be the main reason for its blatant failure to defend workers' interests during economic liberalisation and to support the movement for political liberalisation. Autonomous trade unions that have emerged during political liberalisation are characterised by a high degree of militancy, thus posing a serious challenge to continuing state intervention in the unions.

The Ghanaian Trade Union Movement and Neoliberal Reforms

When the PNDC, under the leadership of Flight-Lieutenant Jerry Rawlings, seized power on 31 December 1981, the Ghanaian economy was in a state of prolonged recession, disinvestment and virtual collapse (Rothchild 1991). After an initial fifteen-month period of populist mobilisation and experimentation, during which Ghana's woes were attributed to 'imperialist' and 'neo-colonialist' forces, the PNDC was compelled to adopt a more pragmatic stance on economic issues. In the absence of a realistic alternative from the intellectual left and assistance from socialist countries, the technocratic faction convinced Rawlings in 1983 that the best possible solution to the challenges posed by the desperate economic situation was to seek help from the Bretton Woods institutions (Yeebo 1991). The persistent rhetoric of populism then became linked to a neoliberal reform package in the form of an SAP, which was designated in Ghana as the Economic Recovery Programme (ERP). The military-led populist regime had considerable leverage to manoeuvre, enabling it to impose a variety of harsh measures intended to rehabilitate the economy. By the end of the 1980s the IMF and the World Bank were in a state of euphoria about Ghana's performance. Indeed, from a macro-economic point of view structural adjustment has been more successful in Ghana than in most other African countries. However, from a labour-market perspective its effects have been as devastating in this country as elsewhere on the continent (Panford 2001).

Some analysts have puzzled over why and how the PNDC was able to 'implement a series of policies that apparently have resulted in significant income losses on the part of workers while suffering almost no popular unrest' (Herbst 1991: 173), particularly given the relatively well-organised and politicised character of trade unions in the country and their previous success in deterring what were seen as anti-labour reforms. The answer lies partly in the fact that the Ghanaian labour movement entered adjustment during a deep internal crisis and amid serious divisions (Hutchful 2002: 170).

When the PNDC seized power on 31 December 1981, the labour movement was in disarray. The leadership of the Ghana Trades Union Congress (GTUC) was severely compromised in the eyes of many of its members who accused it of bureaucracy, opportunism, the betrayal of workers' interests and self-perpetuation in office. Shortly after the coup, a group of militant trade unionists in the Accra-Tema area who were organised in the so-called Association of Local Unions (ALU) launched a *putsch* of their own, taking over power from the 'old guard'.

The new leadership expressed its objectives in terms of building a dynamic, revolutionary and democratic trade union movement (Adu-Amankwah 1990; Yeebo 1991). From the very start, the PNDC had supported the change of leadership which, it thought, would bring the trade union movement more in line with the regime's populist orientations. The new leaders were indeed more committed to the 'revolution' than their predecessors but they nevertheless continued to assert the independence of the labour movement and its right to represent the interests of workers. This latter claim became an immediate source of friction between the revamped trade union movement and the PNDC, since new and apparently competitive labour organisations had been created in the early days of the 'revolution', the so-called Workers' Defence Committees (WDCs) (Konings 1986; Hansen and Ninsin 1989; Yeebo 1991).

The installation of WDCs in the work place undoubtedly posed the greatest challenge in Ghanaian labour history to the existing power relations within enterprises. The WDCs had wide-ranging responsibilities including the propagation and defence of the revolution, the exposure of management malpractice and corruption, the distribution of essential commodities, supervision of promotions, demotions, transfers and dismissals, and – even though this was barely visible during the most radical phase of the populist regime – disciplining workers and raising productivity. Above all, the WDCs were supposed to secure an active role for workers in the decision-making process. Understandably, in the absence of any clear guidelines regarding relations between the newly formed WDCs and the trade unions, there were numerous power struggles between the two organisations. Most union leaders were inclined to perceive the WDCs as instruments of the PNDC's hidden agenda to either replace or control the unions. Given this situation, the GTUC leadership took the unprecedented step of calling on the International Labour Organisation (ILO) to help resolve the issue of who legitimately represented the workers (Gyimah-Boadi and Essuman-Johnson 1993: 202). Although the ILO proved incapable of resolving the dispute, the conflict between the two labour organisations was eventually more or less settled when the WDCs were abolished in late 1984, having become a threat to the successful implementation of the SAP and the regime itself (Konings

1986; Yeebo 1991), and were replaced by Committees for the Defence of the Revolution (CDRs). Placed under the strict control of the regime, one of the main roles of the CDRs was to check any resistance by the labour movement to structural adjustment. As a result, they rapidly lost the confidence of the rank and file (Ninsin 1989: 35–37). With the abolition of the WDCs, the GTUC was restored as the pre-eminent organisation of Ghanaian labour.

Although not yet fully recovered from these internal divisions and conflicts, the Ghanaian labour movement had to face another, even more formidable, problem for which it was ill-prepared: the presentation of the first SAP-inspired budget in April 1983. Its announcement of severe curtailments in public subsidies and price rises came as a shock to workers who had been the main supporters of Rawlings's 'revolution'. Strikingly, the ALU leaders of the GTUC had not been consulted in advance and deeply resented the perceived failure of the regime to shift the burden of adjustment from the shoulders of the poor to those of the rich, but they refused to mobilise angry workers against the anti-labour budget. Being still strongly committed to the revolution, they appealed to workers to exercise utmost restraint so as not to jeopardise the long-term goals of the workers' struggles (Herbst 1991: 186). Nevertheless, they expressed reservations about the budget as a whole and called for the suspension of some points, in particular increases in the price of petrol and the severe limits set on wage increases through collective bargaining. Their criticism provoked a violent WDC attack on the GTUC headquarters – no doubt with PNDC support.

The rank and file's loss of confidence in the ALU leadership of the GTUC became manifest at the end of the same year when the frequently postponed GTUC delegates' conference was finally held. The ALU leadership was then voted out of office, being generally seen as too subservient to the Rawlings regime (Yeebo 1991), and was replaced by the old guard. The newly elected Secretary-General, A.K. Yankey, had served on the ousted GTUC board as the General Secretary of the General Transport, Petroleum and Chemical Workers' Union. These old-guard leaders were not concerned with safeguarding the ideals of the revolution since they had been among its principal casualties in 1982. They were more worried about preserving trade union autonomy versus the state and upholding what they considered was the essential task of the unions, namely the defence of workers' interests, even if this brought them into conflict with the PNDC regime that was determined to implement successfully the harsh SAP measures.

Significantly, Rawlings's speech at the conference heralded future conflicts. He warned the delegates that the GTUC was viewed by the people as an organisation that had 'attempted to hold the rest of the community to ransom in order to extract benefits for its members'. This, he asserted, was untenable in the 'revolutionary situation, in which we are all working for the common good'. Yankey, in reply, said he hoped that the labour movement would be consulted on all future economic measures, and ended by maintaining that the GTUC was fully behind PNDC efforts to rebuild the country. This was immediately belied in PNDC eyes when the GTUC called for a minimum wage of 300 cedis a day at a time when the country's lowest paid workers could expect only 21–25 cedis. Rawlings greeted the demand with derision and anger: it was 'absolute rubbish – the outcome of ignorant minds. Are such people enemies?' (Adu-Amankwah 1990: 100). The division between the PNDC and the GTUC as to what was a reasonable wage remained.

The new GTUC leadership soon started attacking various SAP measures for their nefarious effects on workers' living and working conditions, leading to the development of increasingly antagonistic relations between the unions and the regime. For example, a resolution adopted by the GTUC Executive Board in 1984 noted:

> As a result of these IMF and World Bank conditions, the working people of Ghana now face unbearable conditions of life expressed in poor nutrition, high prices of goods and services, inadequate housing, continuing deterioration of social services and growing unemployment above all. [...] We caution government that the above conditions pose serious implications for the sharpening of class conflict in the society (quoted in Herbst 1991: 184).

The GTUC repeatedly demanded the withdrawal of the SAP 'as being imposed by the Bretton Woods institutions on Ghana', the restoration of collective bargaining procedures and union participation in the economic decision-making process (Adu-Amankwah 1990). However, while they continued to agitate against reforms, the new leaders clearly recognised that, given the autocratic nature of the PNDC, there were limits to the regime's patience when it came to confronting actual protests. The new Secretary-General, Yankey, therefore sought to operate cautiously, doubting the ability of the GTUC to survive a war of attrition. Consequently, he usually tried to make the GTUC position known by presenting memoranda to the government and press communications to the general public. This form of trade union protest appeared to have little impact on the government, which mostly ignored union demands. Only on rare occasions did the regime feel compelled to make concessions (Adu-Amankwah and Tutu 1997).

The GTUC's greatest victory during this period was in 1986 when the government unilaterally cancelled leave allowances for public-sector workers. The GTUC leadership told the government that lack of communication between the regime and the unions left it with no choice but to call a general strike. It exhorted workers to wave red flags and wear red armbands and headbands (the customary sign of mourning). The outrage expressed by ordinary workers, who perceived the allowances as a welcome addition to their meagre incomes, suggested that the strike enjoyed the overwhelming support of its members. The PNDC realised that it had gone too far and swiftly reinstated the allowances and soon also reactivated the existing tripartite institutions and created new bilateral forms of consultation. Subsequent government attempts to convene these fora on an *ad hoc* basis and to use them as instruments for compromising the unions (by having them accept already predetermined wage levels), created new sources of conflict between the PNDC and the GTUC. Workers, too, regularly expressed their dissatisfaction with the outcome of the tripartite negotiations. For example, at the May Day rally in 1991, they protested against low wages and waved banners, some of which accused their leaders of collaborating with the PNDC (Akwetey 2001: 92).

The PNDC effectively deployed a variety of strategies to contain trade union opposition. First, the government and its leading spokesmen, using the state-controlled media, continued to accuse the trade union movement of being selfish, of making unrealistic demands, misleading workers, and being engaged in subversive activities aimed at destabilising and derailing the revolution (Adu-Amankwah 1990; Gyimah-Boadi and Essuman-Johnson 1993). Second, the PNDC continued to use divide-and-rule tactics against organised labour, capitalising on the fact that the SAP had a differential impact on the various sectors of the economy. Thus the Ghana Private Road Transport Union, which generally endorsed the liberalisation measures (increased fares, imports of vehicles and spare parts), and the Railway Workers' Union, which had benefited from the rehabilitation of the railways, were easily pitted against the Industrial and Commercial Workers' Union (ICU) whose members were threatened with privatisation and job losses (Nugent 1995). Third, while radical trade union leaders were being hounded by the security agencies, the PNDC was careful to nurture its relationship with those it perceived as moderates. For example, due to the intimidating tactics used by the PNDC during the elections at the 1988 GTUC Congress in Cape Coast, the majority of the delegates refused to elect the radical General Secretary of the ICU and Acting Secretary-General of the GTUC, L.G. Ocloo, as the Secretary-General of the GTUC. Ocloo was later even forced to go into exile because of his outspoken and independent stand on trade union matters. Yankey, who was then re-elected with the support of the PNDC, became more or less co-opted into the regime. He was subsequently appointed a member of the National Commission for Democracy (NCD), an agency created by the PNDC to oversee the formulation of new political and constitutional arrangements for the country. Following this appointment, he regularly assured the PNDC of GTUC support for its economic policies (Adu-Amankwah 1990: 105) and was subsequently offered an ambassadorial post.

It is also beyond any doubt that some trade union members remained susceptible to the regime's continued use of populist rhetoric. Rawlings, with his apparent honesty and modest behaviour, seems not to have lost his charismatic appeal as the champion of the common man (Hutchful 2002: 175). As a result, there was the lingering belief that not he, but rather the IMF and the World Bank were to blame for the harsh SAP measures.

In the last instance, the PNDC did not hesitate to employ strong-arm tactics including coercion and repression. While the PNDC left workers some latitude in remoulding power relations in the workplace between 1982 and 1984, by the mid 1980s it appeared that the coercive apparatus of the state was being actively deployed on the side of management and employers in the event of a dispute. For example, when Cocobod (the former Ghana Cocoa Marketing Board) wanted to lay off over 20,000 workers in November 1985, the PNDC passed a special law (PNDC Law 125) that empowered the management to ignore the labour law regarding retrenchments. Protesting union leaders were summoned to the Bureau of National Investigations (the state security agency), were held for a couple of hours and then released with a warning to behave 'if they did not want to spend Christmas in detention'. Subsequently, the government was to deploy security forces at the GTUC headquarters to prevent its leadership from holding a mass meeting to protest against the method of retrenchment. It was a mark of the regime's ruthlessness in dealing with worker and union protests that relatively few strikes were recorded between 1983 and 1991, even though labour discontent was running high (Gyimah-Boadi and Essuman-Johnson 1993: 206).

Given these developments, it is not surprising that the GTUC joined the growing opposition of urban civil-society organisations to military rule, insisting upon the reintroduction of democracy and constitutional rule. The GTUC leadership strongly believed that democratic reforms would enable the labour movement to operate without fear of repressive military tactics and to influence structural adjustment decision-making. For example, the GTUC Secretary-General Yankey made the following observation at the 1991 Labour Day rally: 'Experience in Africa shows that SAPs fail if they are not based on a high degree of national consensus which depends on free and independent trade unions operating within a strengthened tripartite arrangement for the discussion of key policy issues' (quoted in Panford 2001: 94).

At its Third Quadrennial Delegates' Conference at Cape Coast in March 1988, the GTUC called for the convening of a democratic National Constituent Assembly to formulate a constitution that could be submitted to the people for approval and introduce a large measure of political liberalisation. It also took the lead in opposing the 1988 'no-party' district assembly elections (Ayee 1994), urging a boycott. Although its pro-democracy and pro-human rights position coincided with that of the Movement for Freedom and Justice (an opposition umbrella organisation created in 1990), the GTUC refused to join this organisation and support its struggle for the introduction of multi-partyism in Ghana. And even more significantly, around the time that the campaign for multi-party elections began in the autumn of 1992, the GTUC constitution was amended to prohibit the organisation from entering into an alliance with any political party for the purpose of winning elections. This amendment appears to have been partly motivated by the bitter lessons learnt by the GTUC in prior alliances with political parties such as the Convention People's Party (CPP) (from 1958 to 1966) and the Social Democratic Front (SDF) (from 1979 to 1981). A second reason was the lack of confidence in the alternative constituted by the opposition coalition to Rawlings. The labour movement also mistrusted a number of opposition leaders who, as members of the Progress Party government (1969–72), had dissolved the GTUC in 1971 for its allegedly 'unofficial opposition'. As a result, the GTUC concluded that it would be in a better position to defend workers' interests if it preserved its autonomy towards the political parties. Its conclusion seems to be justified by the generally negative experiences of trade union alliances in other African countries. The Zambian experience highlights the fact that union alliances with political parties to facilitate political transition cannot necessarily guarantee that the labour movement will become more influential in government circles. The influence of the Zambian trade unions declined when its ally, the Movement for Multiparty Democracy (MMD), committed itself to an ambitious economic liberalisation programme after electoral victory (Akwetey 2001; Rakner 2001). Union alliances with political parties that favour neoliberal economic reforms also appear problematic in other African countries such as South Africa and Zimbabwe (Webster and Adler 2001; Sachikonye 2001).

Confronted in the early 1990s with national and international pressures for neoliberal political reforms and rapidly expanding democratisation in Africa, the PNDC announced in 1991 that the country would return to a multi-party system. During the transition period, Rawlings formed his own party, the National Democratic Congress (NDC), which pledged to continue PNDC policies. Several

authors (Nugent 1995; Hutchful 2002) have already explained why
Rawlings and the NDC were able to win both the 1992 and 1996
presidential and parliamentary elections. What is of greater relevance
here is that it swiftly became clear that the NDC government would
find it harder than the PNDC to implement the harsh SAP measures.
Rawlings, who had never bothered to hide his dislike for neoliberal
political reform, immediately blamed democracy for undercutting the
adjustment process. To a certain extent, he was right. Political liberalisation and mobilisation by the pro-democracy forces now encouraged
a more open, articulate and better-organised resistance to adjustment
policies and rendered repression less feasible as an avenue for policy
reform. However, as Hutchful (2002: 220–23) aptly observes, internal
processes of regime transformation in response to the challenge of
competitive politics provide a second key to understanding the
apparent lack of government resolve to execute the harsh SAP
measures, which drew scorn from international donors. For example,
just before the 1992 presidential elections the regime tried to win the
support of civil servants by granting them salary increases of up to 70
percent. The price was an increase in the budget deficit from 1.5 to 4.8
percent of GDP. The regime's increasing concern with winning
elections was bringing about a shift in power from technocrats to
political brokers who were more interested in patronage than in
market rationality. Corruption by the ruling political elite became
increasingly blatant, eroding the ascetic image that had served the
regime so well during the earlier years of structural adjustment and
robbing it of the moral stature and ability to demand sacrifices.

One of the effects of political liberalisation on industrial relations
was renewed labour militancy. The civil and public services in particular were regularly paralysed by severe and protracted strike actions –
a manifestation of the workers' relative freedom to voice their long-
standing grievances about low real incomes, increasing retrenchments
and job insecurity, persistent government efforts to postpone or reduce
end-of-service benefits that prevented retrenched workers from setting
up in the informal sector, and flexible management practices. On
several occasions, workers invaded the office of the Minister of
Finance and Economic Planning, Dr Kwesi Botchwey, who had
occupied this post since 1982 and was generally perceived as one of

the main architects of structural adjustment in Ghana, and threatened to hurt him.

The mounting social discontent exploded in 1995. On 1 March, the NDC-dominated parliament approved a new value added tax (VAT) of 17.5 percent as part of the Bretton Woods institutions' strategy of enhancing public revenues. A few months later, on 11 May, a group of opposition leaders calling itself the Alliance for Change organised a massive demonstration by workers, youth, the unemployed and members of the general public to protest against the imposition of the new tax. The anti-VAT protests, which were supported by the GTUC, were initially restricted to Accra but spread later to other regional capitals as well. The demonstrators chanted in Akan '*Kume Preko*' ('You might as well kill me now') to express their willingness to die rather than live under structural adjustment. In many respects, these demonstrations resembled the previous anti-SAP uprisings in Zambia (from 1985 to 1987) and in Nigeria (in 1986 and 1988–89) where revolts by the urban masses protesting against the withdrawal of subsidies and concomitant price hikes forced their governments to withdraw SAPs temporarily (Simutanyi 1996; Bangura and Beckman 1993). Although the anti-VAT demonstrations in Ghana were of a peaceful nature, participants were nevertheless attacked by pro-government militia, resulting in the death of four demonstrators and numerous injuries, some critical. Faced with such a dangerous situation, President Rawlings recalled parliament from recess and, under a certificate of urgency, it reduced the rate of VAT to 15.5 percent, before dropping it completely on 11 June. The government also announced financial compensation for the deaths and injuries caused during the demonstrations.

Developments preceding the 2000 elections were reminiscent of events associated with the VAT debacle. After a lull, growing signs of public dissatisfaction with the effects of the SAP emerged that resulted in serious strikes, demonstrations and boycotts. There were various reasons for this renewed expression of mass discontent: there was the serious deterioration in the general economic situation as a result of a record fall of cocoa and gold prices on the world market coupled with a steep rise in imports of oil; a widening gap between the mass suffering of so many and the lavish lifestyles of NDC politicians and apparatchiks; and in addition the implementation of the Price Waterhouse Report. After expecting for several years that this report would finally resolve the thorny issue of wages and salary structures in the public service, it instead generated one of the stormiest labour responses in the country, almost leading to a nationwide strike (Panford 2001).

Political liberalisation also had important effects on the labour movement. The 1992 constitution for the first time recognised the right of workers to join any local, national or international union of their choice and to demonstrate against public policies without having to go through the cumbersome procedure of acquiring a police permit beforehand (Panford 2001). These constitutional provisions permitted workers to form and join trade unions and trade union federations that were not affiliated to the GTUC. With the registration in 1992 of the Textile, Garment and Leather Employees' Union (TGLEU), a breakaway ICU union, the first non-GTUC union was born in Ghana. In April 1999, the TGLEU and a few other relatively small unions and public servants' associations founded a new trade union federation, the Ghana Federation of Labour (GFL), to 'inject new blood and competition into union organisation to meet the challenges of the SAP' (GFL 1999). While the GTUC used the 1992 constitution to officially affiliate itself with the International Confederation of Free Trade Unions (ICFTU), the GFL opted to affiliate itself to the World Labour Congress (WLC). The GFL is still in its infancy and has not yet been able to challenge the dominant position of the much older and larger GTUC in the field of industrial relations.

Having achieved a larger measure of autonomy during political liberalisation, the GTUC began to reassert its right to promote the interests of workers through the pursuit of collective bargaining, participation in the national decision-making process, and other ways of representing the workers such as representations to parliament on issues that were considered of vital importance. Its newly elected leadership proved less reluctant to deploy the general-strike weapon to back its demands for higher wages and to denounce the NDC government's repeated attempts to violate collective agreements as well as decisions arrived at in the bilateral and tripartite fora. For instance, in January 1995 the GTUC threatened a general strike on these issues. Subsequently the government allowed the tripartite forum to negotiate a new national minimum wage and promised to implement the decisions of the tripartite meetings (Adu-Amankwah and Tutu 1997: 265–66). The GTUC also began to explore other ways of forcing the government to respect collective bargaining procedures. It has increasingly relied on the courts in Ghana and has filed two complaints with the ILO to prevent the government from rejecting conditions of work and lay-off benefits established through collective bargaining.

Interestingly, the GTUC began to assume a series of new initiatives to meet the challenges posed by economic and political liberalisation. At its Fifth Quadrennial Congress at the University of Cape Coast in August 1996, it adopted a number of policies that it has been implementing ever since (GTUC 1996).

The first was to strengthen the organisation. The GTUC has been confronted with a declining membership since the implementation of SAP. Estimated membership dropped from a peak of 708,000 in 1990 to 521,000 in 1996. In response to this painful development, the GTUC leadership decided to take a number of measures to stabilise and even increase its membership. To retain its members' loyalty, the GTUC has encouraged membership participation in trade union affairs through improving democratisation and communication within the organisation and expanding services to its rank and file, such as vocational training and retraining, counselling and other welfare services. In order to increase its membership, the GTUC started organising senior staff in the industrial and commercial sectors and intensifying its recruitment efforts among workers in the rapidly expanding informal sector. A few recent initiatives to bring informal-sector workers into the framework of the union organisation are the following. The Public Service Workers' Union has organised small-scale photographers into the Ghana Union of Professional Photographers, and the ICU assisted hairdressers and barbers to form the Ghana Hairdressers' and Beauticians' Association (Yanney 2000; Panford 2001). Another measure proposed to increase membership was to pay more attention to the organisation of women, who are more likely to lose their jobs during SAPs. Women will also be given more leadership positions within unions.

The second policy initiative taken at the Fifth Quadrennial Congress was the establishment of worker-owned enterprises. This initiative – not a completely new phenomenon in Ghanaian labour history (Konings 1977; Damachi 1974) – was an attempt to contribute to employment generation, to expand the base for union membership, and to improve and broaden the main sources of union finance. In 1996, the GTUC resolved to set up a Labour Enterprise Trust (LET) with a minimum share capital of 25 billion cedis. This was based on the assumption that an estimated 500,000 workers would contribute 50,000 cedis over a twenty-month period. However, at the end of the subscription period, it emerged that no more than 86,000 workers had contributed to LET, amounting to 5.5 billion cedis (only 22 percent of the expected share capital) (LET Company 2000). The LET board then started investing in projects such as the Accra City Car Project, an insurance project, as well as water tanker and radio taxi services. Excluding the Accra City Car Project, the projects created 90 jobs. Future projects will include the establishment of a commercial bank, security services, fuel service stations, waste management, estate management, and a supermarket (Yanney 2000). A historic moment in Ghanaian labour history occurred in January 1999 when the local branch of the Ghana Mine Workers' Union took over Prestea Goldfields from Barnex, a South African gold-mining company, by investing its members' one-million-dollar severance award in continued mining operations. Workers and management resolved to run as effectively as possible the first worker-owned mining company in Ghana, which was renamed Prestea Gold Resources Ltd. The 1473 miners took this radical measure to save their jobs and to forestall economic decline and social decay in the Prestea area (Yanney 2000; Panford 2001). It is still too early to assess the prospects for labour-owned enterprises in Ghana. Compared to South Africa (Iheduru 2001), 'labour capitalism' in Ghana is still in its infancy.

A third policy initiative taken at the Fifth Quadrennial Congress was the improvement of workers' representation and participation. While the GTUC had continued to oppose SAPs, its opposition was weakened by the lack of a clear and credible policy alternative. This can be mainly attributed to the fact that its research capabilities at present are too limited to intervene meaningfully in the policy debate

(Hutchful 2002: 173) and this is why the GTUC needs to expand its research activities and collaborate more closely with the country's research institutes. Besides its determination to improve workers' participation in the national decision-making process and collective bargaining, the GTUC has also decided to initiate a research programme on industrial democracy and educate the rank and file on workers' participation in enterprises. This drive for greater participation by workers is a clear indication that the trade unions are not only prepared to contribute to the development of a democratic culture in society but also to come to grips with forms of collective action that are supplementary to traditional collective bargaining, with its often confrontational nature (see Mihyo and Schiphorst 1995). Realising that many enterprises will need to restructure if they are to survive and meet global competition, the unions appear to be accepting responsibility for improving their efficiency and productivity in exchange for a greater say in decision-making.

A final policy initiative taken at the Fifth Quadrennial Congress was the intensification of relations with other civil-society organisations. Back in 1986, the GTUC had already mobilised the support of Ghana's most important public-service associations – the Ghana National Association of Teachers, the Ghana Registered Nurses' Association (GRNA) and the Ghana Civil Servants' Association – resulting in the formation of a common platform in defence of workers' interests, the so-called Ghana Consultative Labour Forum, but it unfortunately became virtually dormant during the 1990s. In 1999, the GRNA and a newly formed public-service association, the Judicial Services Staff Association, opted to join the new labour federation, the GFL. Besides the labour organisations, links to other civil-society organisations, such as the Ghana Bar Association, and the media were strengthened as well. In 1995 the GTUC requested that the government set up a national forum made up of the tripartite partners and important civil-society associations to discuss the state of the Ghanaian economy. This idea materialised in May 1996 when, under the auspices of the Tripartite Committee, labour, business and other civil-society groups such as the Bar and Journalist Associations met the government and political parties to discuss the economy (Akwetey 2001).

Ghana has often been presented as a model for neoliberal economic and political reform in Africa. By strengthening its organisation, allying it to other civil-society organisations and adopting a number of new initiatives in response to globalisation, the GTUC, too, appears to be a trendsetter in state-union relations in West Africa.

The Cameroonian Trade Union Movement and Neoliberal Reforms

Until the mid 1980s Cameroon was lauded by many observers, including World Bank staff, as one of the most prosperous and stable countries in sub-Saharan Africa. Today this rosy assessment has been replaced by gloom. The country is facing an unprecedented economic and political crisis (Konings 1996). After some initial hesitation but due to the deteriorating economic crisis, the Biya government could no longer avoid calling upon the Bretton Woods institutions. In 1988–89, it was forced to implement an SAP and, in the early 1990s, it was also required by international donors to introduce neoliberal political reforms.

There is nevertheless ample evidence to demonstrate that the Biya government has constantly attempted to undermine the economic and political reforms advocated by western donors and international financial institutions (Konings 2004). As a result, the process of economic liberalisation has been slow and inconsistent. The necessary institutional reforms in the public and parastatal sectors, for example, have been largely thwarted by government delaying tactics and half-hearted implementation. This is particularly grave as the reform of these sectors – marked by excessive costs and inefficiencies – has been a cornerstone of the SAP. In its 1994 report 'Adjustment in Africa: Reform, Results, and the Road Ahead', the World Bank asserted that in the area of privatisation, little progress had been made in Cameroon. The report constantly rated Cameroon very poorly for its economic policy and adjustment performance and it pointed out that the IMF had signed and cancelled three successive stand-by agreements because of the government's failure to achieve negotiated targets (World Bank 1994). Political liberalisation has barely gone beyond the introduction of a multi-party system and a larger measure of freedom of press and association. Since the mid 1990s, however, western donors and international financiers have intensified their pressure on the regime to conform to new standards of economic and political liberalisation.

I have argued elsewhere (Konings 1996) that the Biya government's persistent opposition to neoliberal economic and political reforms can be largely explained by the class character of the Cameroonian post-colonial state. In his seminal book on Cameroonian politics, Bayart (1979) claimed that the first President of Cameroon, Ahmadou Ahidjo (1961–1982), was instrumental in creating a highly centralised, authoritarian and neo-patrimonial state and in shaping a hegemonic alliance out of the various ethnic elite groups in society which were given access to state resources and rent-seeking activities so as to cement their loyalty to him. Such a hegemonic alliance has a vested interest in the status quo and is inclined to resist any economic and political liberalisation measures that threaten both its control over state resources and rent-seeking activities and the considerable measure of political stability characteristic of the neo-patrimonial post-colonial state. Apparently, its resistance has been successful: none of the reforms implemented so far seems to have struck at the roots of the authoritarian and neo-patrimonial state as yet.

Given the fusion between the post-colonial state and civil society, it is not altogether surprising that the Cameroonian trade union movement played hardly any role in the neoliberal reforms. Following independence and reunification in 1961, the Ahidjo regime (1961–1982) gradually succeeded in merging all the existing trade union organisations in the Anglophone and Francophone parts of the country into a single body, the National Union of Cameroon Workers (NUCW), and in subordinating it to the state for the sake of national reconstruction (Konings 1993, 1998). The close relationship between the state and trade unions continued under Ahidjo's successor, Paul Biya. At the 1985 Bamenda Congress, Biya changed the name of the single party from the Cameroon National Union to the Cameroon

People's Democratic Movement (CPDM), and commended the central labour organisation for the constructive role it had played in society. The NUCW, in turn, immediately changed its name to the Cameroon Trade Union Congress (CTUC) and its then President, J.-E. Abondo, 'thanked President Paul Biya a thousand times for all that he had done for the workers' (Fondation Friedrich-Ebert 1994). Soon afterwards, Abondo was appointed Minister of Defence, a clear reward for his services to the regime.

Although the corrupt and authoritarian Biya regime swiftly lost its legitimacy during the severe economic and political crisis, the CTUC continued to support the regime. Like the ruling CPDM party, it strongly condemned the increasing calls in civil society for political liberalisation and the introduction of a multi-party system. When the first opposition party, the Social Democratic Front (SDF), was formed in the Anglophone part of the country in 1990, the then CTUC President, D. Fouda Sima, expressed, as did other CPDM loyalists, 'his total rejection of what the Head of State has called political models imported from abroad' (Konings 2000: 179). Together with other CTUC leaders, he subsequently participated in anti-democracy marches organised by the regime.

After the Biya government, under considerable pressure from the Bretton Woods institutions and western donors, notably France, had been compelled to introduce a multi-party system and increased freedom of speech and association in December of that same year (Konings 1996), growing dissatisfaction could be felt among the rank and file with the CTUC's performance and its continuing alliance with the ruling CPDM party. This was manifest in a series of strikes, particularly in the parastatal sector, against retrenchment and other SAP measures, and in the workers' support of the opposition. Many workers participated in the protracted 1991 'Ghost Town' Campaign – essentially a civil disobedience action aimed at bringing the economy to a complete standstill and called by the radical opposition to force the Biya regime to hold a sovereign national conference (Takougang and Krieger 1998: 126–31).

Even within the CTUC regional and local leadership, severe criticism of its position and calls for union autonomy versus the state and political parties could be heard (Mehler 1997). The President of the CTUC in the Fako Division of Anglophone Cameroon, C.P.N. Vewessee, who in the meantime had joined the opposition, was to become the most vocal opponent of the corrupt national leadership of the CTUC, openly condemning it for its continued alliance with the ruling party and its complete neglect of the defence of workers' interests during the economic crisis and the SAP. Moreover, he advocated the unions' direct involvement in the struggle for the establishment of a truly democratic system in the country. In February 1991, he declared:

> The workers expect an independent and strong trade union organisation that would be autonomous in relation to all political parties and state bodies and institutions. [...] This will relieve the trade unions of the rubber-stamp element in the country's political life. If the trade union does not become more militant and resolute in its demands, then the CTUC won't be of much help to the workers. (Konings 1995: 531)

Under mounting pressure, the CTUC finally recognised the right of its members to join the political party of their choice on 2 April 1991. The new Labour Code of 1992 guaranteed trade union autonomy towards the state, and the CTUC subsequently changed its name to the Confederation of Cameroon Trade Unions (CCTU) to reflect its newly acquired autonomous status. This did not mean the end of government intervention in the unions, however. The government developed several strategies to keep the unions under its control. The 1992 CCTU elections were clearly manipulated by the government buying the support of a number of delegates to make sure that Etame Ndedi, the trade union representative in the CPDM Central Committee, instead of Vewessee, the popular and outspoken Anglophone trade union leader, would be elected President of the central labour organisation. While the government succeeded in this endeavour, it could not forestall the election of a number of autonomous trade union leaders. One of them, Louis Sombès, became Secretary-General.

Government intervention in the union became even more overt in late 1993 when Sombès was sacked by the union President, Etame Ndedi, for having called a general strike of civil servants in protest at severe cuts in their remuneration. Both the regime and the union

President tried to prevent a meeting of the union executive, the majority of whom advocated Sombès's reinstatement. Not even protests from the ILO could dissuade the government from further intervening in the matter. It openly supported the installation of Jules Mousseni, a CPDM loyalist and Second Vice-Secretary-General of the CCTU, who had been unilaterally nominated by Etame Ndedi as the new Secretary-General of the union. This led the ILO to rebuff Etame Ndedi and the government at its June 1994 annual convention in Geneva by refusing to accredit Mousseni. Given the stalemate Sombès's dismissal had caused in the union and the Geneva debacle, the First Vice-President of the CCTU convened a meeting of the union executive in July 1994, which decided to reinstate Sombès and sack Etame Ndedi instead. A few months later, in September 1994, security forces raided the union headquarters in Yaoundé and forcibly removed Sombès from office, throwing him into prison (Fondation Friedrich-Ebert 1994: 78; Eboussi Boulaga 1997: 347–48). Realising that not even the arrest of Sombès could prevent the CCTU from asserting its autonomy, the regime decided to sponsor a rival trade union centre, the Union of Free Trade Unions of Cameroon, which was to serve as an instrument for the continuing incorporation of trade unionism into the state (Konings 2000).

Unfortunately, it soon became manifest that the CCTU was not going to play a more significant role in economic and political liberalisation than its new rival. From 1997 onwards, it split into two factions, with both having claimed leadership ever since. Their struggles for power appear to have been motivated not only by differences over the federation's policies and strategies but also by sheer material interests: leadership positions in the federation offered the incumbents multiple opportunities to divert the substantial union dues to personal ends and to travel abroad regularly at the invitation of international labour organisations. The leadership struggle has led to numerous court cases, the organisation of several 'unity' conferences held under the auspices of the ILO and international labour organisations, and renewed government interference in the federation. The Minister of Labour has persistently refused to recognise the leadership of the reformist faction backed by the ILO and the ICFTU, openly supporting the other faction that appeared closer to the government and its policies, and to meet and negotiate with the federation. On 12 September 2001, the Secretary-General of the ICFTU, Bill Jordan, informed President Biya that his organisation would lodge a complaint with the ILO about renewed government interference in trade union matters (*Le Messager,* 1 October 2001).

Given the two federations' lack of defence of workers' interests, workers were increasingly inclined to resort to strike action during political liberalisation. This was particularly the case in the Francophone area where trade unionism tended to be centrally organised. In the Anglophone area where trade unionism had a stronger base at the local and regional level, union leaders usually played a more active role in the defence of workers' interests (Konings 1993). For example, in the Cameroon Development Corporation, a huge agro-industrial parastatal in Anglophone Cameroon with a current labour force of approximately 14,000, trade unionism has continued to play a significant mediating role between workers and management. When the corporation was in need of restructuring during the severe fiscal crisis starting in 1986–87, both management and labour called upon the union for assistance. To the management, the union was a vital organisation in controlling the anticipated resistance of the militant labour force to a painful adjustment programme. To the workers, it offered a defence in a situation where their bargaining power was extremely weak. To save the corporation from total collapse, in 1990 the union agreed with the management on austere adjustment measures, including a drastic cut in the salaries and fringe benefits of all the workers and managerial staff members, an increase in workers' productivity, and the introduction of a compulsory savings scheme, in return for management promises to safeguard workers' jobs. As soon as it became clear that the management was not keeping to the terms of the agreement and was laying off a considerable number of workers, the union called a strike in May 1992 that brought about several modifications favourable to the workers (Konings 1995).

The most important development during political liberalisation was the emergence of several autonomous trade unions in the civil and public services, especially in the educational sector. Their leaders strongly condemned the inactivity of the existing labour federations and pledged to contribute to the resurgence of militant trade unionism in Cameroon and to serve as a countervailing power to the ruling regime (Fondation Friedrich-Ebert 1994; Sindjoun 1999). Unsurprisingly, they soon became victims of state repression under the pretext that public servants were prohibited by law from forming trade unions.

The first autonomous trade union in the educational sector was set up by university lecturers when the *Syndicat National des Enseignants du Supérieur* (SYNES) was founded at the University of Yaoundé on 1 June 1991 after security forces and pro-government militia had terrorised student opponents (Konings 2002). The main objective of the new trade union was to defend its members' interests in the grave crisis bedevilling the university system. The crisis was clearly multi-dimensional: the existing universities had been grossly underfunded, especially during the economic malaise and structural adjustment, their autonomy and academic freedom had been severely eroded, and their teaching staff had suffered a sharp fall in income, livelihood and status. The regime did everything to weaken or eliminate SYNES. Its leadership was intimidated and even physically attacked. Its members were frequently subjected to arbitrary punitive measures, including the suspension of salaries, transfers and dismissals. The government and the university authorities resorted to police violence to quell any demonstrations and strikes by SYNES. Even the building housing the union office was set on fire. After a complaint by SYNES, the ILO insisted in 1993 that civil servants in Cameroon be given the right to unionise. The Biya government simply ignored the ILO demand, arguing that an 'illegal' organisation like SYNES could not lodge a complaint against the government.

Soon after the establishment of SYNES, a number of autonomous unions were formed in secondary and primary education (Konings forthcoming). In January and February 1994, these teachers' trade unions participated in a general strike in the civil service in protest against two drastic cuts in their salaries (amounting to 70 percent) in 1993, the non-payment of their September–October 1993 salaries, and the 50 percent devaluation of the CFA franc in January 1994. Despite the government's repressive, divisive and clientelist tactics, these unions continued to display a high degree of militancy. From 1995 onwards, they have undertaken a variety of actions that have tended to paralyse the educational system, including demonstrations, regular boycotting of examinations, and intermittent strikes. These actions aimed to pressurise the government into negotiating on necessary educational reforms and improvements in teachers' deplorable working and living conditions. In the end, the government appears to have recognised that trade union participation in the decision-making process is a more effective way of tackling the enormous problems facing the country's educational sector than evasive and repressive tactics. While still refusing to give teachers' unions a legal status, it shows a greater willingness to enter into dialogue.

Cameroon has often been presented as a bad adjuster. Cameroonian trade unions appear to have performed no better, having largely failed to play any significant role in economic and political liberalisation. The emergence of autonomous trade unions in the public sector is a sign of hope.

Conclusion

This study has highlighted the large variation in trade union responses to the challenges of neoliberal globalisation. One has therefore to be extremely careful when making pessimistic or optimistic generalisations about the future of trade unions in Africa. My case studies provide ample evidence that the widespread pessimism about the role of African unions in economic and political liberalisation seems to be more relevant to Cameroon than to Ghana, especially during the NDC era. A number of factors have been shown to be responsible for the better performance of trade unions in Ghana than in Cameroon, notably their stronger organisational capacity, their greater autonomy towards the state and political parties, and their search for innovative ways to respond to neoliberal economic and political reforms and to defend workers' interests.

Although the Ghanaian trade union movement was able to maintain a certain measure of autonomy during the PNDC era, it largely failed to achieve any meaningful say in economic decision-making or to win any substantial concessions for its members. The military PNDC was one of the few regimes in Africa that succeeded in rigorously implementing the austere SAP measures, essentially on the basis of an ascetic, populist style of leadership and through severe repression. Strongly convinced that a constitutional government would provide more space for the defence of workers' interests than a military regime, the GTUC became a strong advocate of neoliberal political reform. It thus provided a mass popular base for the country's democratic movement that had hitherto been derided by the regime as the preserve of the elite. Unlike the Zambian trade union movement, the GTUC refused to enter into any formal alliance with the opposition, fearing in part that such an alliance would harm its representation of workers' interests in a multi-party system.

During the NDC era, the Ghanaian government found it hard to execute its SAP in an environment of political liberalisation and electoral competition, leading to the resurgence of worker militancy and the development of increased trade union autonomy. The latter enabled the unions to better defend workers' interests and promote trade union rights. And, even more significantly, the economic and political reforms have since become a source of inspiration for Ghanaian union leaders in their pursuit of new and innovative ways to mobilise workers. They have attempted to strengthen the organisation by recruiting new members from outside the traditional trade union constituency, notably senior staff members, informal-sector workers and women, and have begun to establish worker-owned enterprises. They have taken a number of initiatives to improve workers' participation in the national decision-making process and in enterprises. And finally, they have created or intensified relations with other civil-society organisations. Here one observes a typical example of a movement in search of its mission under changed circumstances.

Unlike its Ghanaian counterpart, the Cameroonian trade union movement has failed to play any significant role in economic and political liberalisation, largely due to the close links between the neo-patrimonial regime and the union leadership. Even after the CCTU had finally achieved a certain measure of autonomy during political liberalisation, the government continued to intervene in trade union matters for the purpose of political control and even sponsored the foundation of a rival federation led by members of the ruling party. Moreover, the CCTU has become almost completely paralysed by internal factional divisions and struggles for power. One of the direct consequences of the two federations' blatant neglect of the defence of workers' interests has been the emergence of militant autonomous trade unions in the public service, particularly in the educational sector. This development provides grounds for optimism that the Cameroonian labour movement, too, will eventually succeed in loosening the controls of the corporatist state machine and become more meaningful to its members.

References

Adesina, J. (1994) *Labour in the Explanation of an African Crisis*, Dakar: Codesria Book Series.

Adu-Amankwah, K. (1990) 'The State, Trade Unions and Democracy in Ghana, 1982–1990', M.A. Thesis, Institute of Social Studies, The Hague.

— and Tutu, K. (1997) 'Ghana: Going Beyond Politics', in G. Kester and O.O. Sidibé (eds) *Trade Unions and Sustainable Democracy in Africa*, Aldershot: Ashgate.

Akwetey, E.O. (1994) *Trade Unions and Democratization: A Comparative Study of Zambia and Ghana*, Stockholm: University of Stockholm.

— (2001) 'Democratic Transition and Post-Colonial Labour Regimes in Zambia and Ghana', in B. Beckman and L.M. Sachikonye (eds) *Labour Regimes and Liberalization: The Restructuring of State-Society Relations in Africa*, Harare: University of Zimbabwe Publications.

Ayee, J.R.A. (1994) *Anatomy of Public Policy Implementation: The Case of Decentralization in Ghana*, London: Avebury.

Bangura, Y. and Beckman, B. (1993) 'African Workers and Structural Adjustment in Nigeria', in A.O. Olukoshi (ed.) *The Politics of Structural Adjustment in Nigeria*, London: James Currey.

Bayart, J.-F. (1979) *L'État au Cameroun*, Paris: Presses de la Fondation Nationale des Sciences Politiques.

Beckman, B. (2002) 'Trade Unions and Institutional Reform: Nigerian Experiences with South African and Ugandan Comparisons', *Transformation* 48: 83–115.

Beckman, B. and Sachikonye, L.M. (eds) *Labour Regimes and Liberalization: The Restructuring of State–Society Relations in Africa*, Harare: University of Zimbabwe Publications.

Buijtenhuijs, R. and Thiriot, C. (1995) *Democratization in Sub-Saharan Africa, 1992–1995: An Overview of the Literature*, Leiden: African Studies Centre.

Crisp, J. (1984) *The Story of an African Working Class: Ghanaian Miners' Struggles, 1870–1980*, London: Zed Books.

Damachi, U. (1974) *The Role of Trade Unions in the Development Process with a Case Study of Ghana*, New York: Praeger.

Eboussi Boulaga, F. (1997) *La Démocratie de Transit au Cameroun*, Paris: L'Harmattan.

Ferguson, J. (1999) *Expectations of Modernity: Myths and Meanings of Urban Life on the Zambian Copperbelt*, Berkeley: University of California Press.

Fondation Friedrich-Ebert (1994) *Le Syndicalisme dans le Processus de Démocratisation*, Yaoundé: Imprimerie Saint John.

Freund, B. (1988) *The African Worker*, Cambridge: Cambridge University Press.

Gabriel, J.M. (1999) 'Cameroon's Neopatrimonial Dilemma', *Journal of Contemporary African Studies* 17(2): 173–96.

Gibbon, P. (ed.) (1995) *Structural Adjustment and the Working Poor in Zimbabwe: Studies on Labour, Women Informal Sector Workers and Health*, Uppsala: Nordiska Afrikainstitutet.

Ghana Trades Union Congress (1996) 'Report of the Executive Board on the Activities of the Trades Union Congress (Ghana) covering the period 1st September 1992 to 7th June 1996 presented to the 5th Quadrennial Delegates Congress of the TUC (Ghana) held at the University of Cape Coast from 18th to 22nd August 1996', Accra: Key Publications.

Gyimah-Boadi, E. and Essuman-Johnson, A. (1993) 'The PNDC and Organised Labour: The Anatomy of Political Control', in E. Gyimah-Boadi (ed.) *Ghana Under PNDC Rule*, Dakar: Codesria.

Hansen, E. and Ninsin, K.A. (eds) (1989) *The State, Development and Politics in Ghana*, London: Codesria.

Herbst, J. (1991) 'Labor in Ghana under Structural Adjustment: The Politics of Acquiescence', in D. Rothchild (ed.) *Ghana: The Political Economy of Recovery*, Boulder, Colo: Lynne Rienner.

Hutchful, E. (2002) *Ghana's Adjustment Experience: The Paradox of Reform*, Geneva: UNRISD.

Iheduru, C.O. (2001) 'Organised Labour, Globalisation and Economic Reform: Union Investment in South Africa', *Transformation* 46: 1–31.

Isamah, I. (1994) 'Unions and Development: The Role of Labour under Structural Adjustment Programmes', in E. Osaghae (ed.) *Between State and Civil Society in Africa*, Dakar: Codesria.

Jamal, V. and Weeks, J. (1993) *Africa Misunderstood*, London: Macmillan.

Jeffries, R. (1978) *Class, Power and Ideology in Ghana: The Railwaymen of Sekondi*, Cambridge: Cambridge University Press.

Kester, G. and Sidibé, O.O. (eds) *Trade Unions and Sustainable Democracy in Africa*, Aldershot: Ashgate.

Konings, P. (1977) 'Trade Unionism and Government Development Strategy in Ghana, 1874–1976', Ph.D. dissertation, Catholic University of Brabant, Tilburg.

— (1986) *The State and the Defence Committees in the Ghanaian Revolution, 1981–1984*, Lagos: Revolutionary Monographs on Culture and Society, Series 2(2).

— (1993) *Labour Resistance in Cameroon*. London: James Currey.

— (1995) 'Plantation Labour and Economic Crisis in Cameroon', *Development and Change* 26(3): 525–49.

— (1996) 'The Post-Colonial State and Economic and Political Reforms in Cameroon', in A.E. Fernández Jilberto and A. Mommen (eds) *Liberalization in the Developing World: Institutional and Economic Changes in Latin America, Africa and Asia*, London: Routledge.

— (1998) *Unilever Estates in Crisis and the Power of Organizations in Cameroon*, Hamburg: LIT Verlag.

— (2000) 'Trade Unions and Democratisation in Africa', in P. Konings, W. van Binsbergen and G. Hesseling (eds) *Trajectoires de Libération en Afrique Contemporaine*, Paris: Karthala.

— (2002) 'University Students' Revolt, Ethnic Militia and Violence during Political Liberalization in Cameroon', *African Studies Review* 45(2): 179–204.

— (2004) 'Good Governance, Privatisation and Ethno-Regional Conflict in Cameroon', in J. Demmers, A.E. Fernández Jilberto and B. Hogenboom (eds) *Good Governance in the Era of Global Neoliberalism: Conflict and Depolitisation in Latin America, Eastern Europe, Asia and Africa*, London: Routledge.

— (forthcoming) 'Trade Union Activism among Teachers during Cameroon's Political Liberalisation', Leiden: African Studies Centre.

Kraus, J. (1991) 'The Political Economy of Stabilization and Structural Adjustment in Ghana', in D. Rothchild (ed.) *Ghana: The Political Economy of Recovery*, Boulder, Colo: Lynne Rienner.

LET Company (2000) 'Company Profile of Labour Enterprises Trust Company', Accra: GTUC.

Lipton, M. (1977) *Why Poor People Stay Poor: Urban Bias in World Development*, London: Temple Smith.

Mehler, A. (1997) 'Cameroun: une transition qui n'a pas eu lieu', in J.-F. Daloz and P. Quantin (eds) *Transitions Démocratiques Africaines: Dynamiques et Contraintes (1990–1994)*, Paris: Karthala.

Mihyo, P. and Schiphorst, F. (1995) 'A Context of Sharp Decline', in H. Thomas (ed.) *Globalization and Third World Trade Unions*, London: Zed Books.

Ninsin, K. (1989) 'State, Capital and Labour Relations, 1961–1987', in E. Hansen and K. Ninsin (eds) *The State, Development and Politics in Ghana*, London: Codesria.

Nugent, P. (1995) *Big Men, Small Boys and Politics in Ghana*, London: Pinter.

Nyamnjoh, F.B. (1996) *Mass Media and Democratisation in Cameroon*, Yaoundé: Foundation Friedrich Ebert.

Panford, K. (2001) *IMF-World Bank and Labor's Burdens in Africa: Ghana's Experience*, Westport: Praeger.

Rakner, L. (2001) 'The Pluralist Paradox: The Decline of Economic Interest Groups in Zambia in the 1990s', *Development and Change,* 32(3): 521–43.

Rothchild, D. (ed.) (1991) *Ghana: The Political Economy of Recovery*, Boulder: Lynne Rienner, 1991.

Sandbrook, R. (1982) *The Politics of Basic Needs: Urban Aspects of Assaulting Poverty in Africa*, London: Heinemann.

— and Oelbaum, J. (1997) 'Reforming Dysfunctional Institutions Through Democratisation?: Reflections on Ghana', *The Journal of Modern African Studies* 35(4): 603–46.

Simutanyi, N.R. (1996) 'Organised Labour, Economic Crisis and Structural Adjustment in Africa: The Case of Zambia', in O. Sichone and B.C. Chikulo (eds) *Democracy in Zambia: Challenges for the Third Republic*, Harare: SAPES Books.

Takougang, J. and Krieger, M. (1998) *African State and Society in the 1990s: Cameroon's Political Crossroads*, Boulder: Westview Press.

Van de Walle, N. (1993) 'The Politics of Nonreform in Cameroon', in T.M. Callaghy and J. Ravenhill (eds) *Hemmed In: Responses to Africa's Economic Decline,* New York: Columbia University Press.

Waterman, P. (1975) 'The "Labour Aristocracy" in Africa: Introduction to a Debate', *Development and Change* 6(3): 50–64.

Webster, E. and Adler, G. (2001) 'Exodus Without a Map?: The Labour Movement in a Liberalizing South Africa', in B. Beckman and L.M. Sachikonye (eds) *Labour Regimes and Liberalization: The Restructuring of State-Society Relations in Africa,* Harare: University of Zimbabwe Publications.

World Bank (1992) *Governance and Development,* Washington, D.C.: World Bank.

— (1994) *Adjustment in Africa: Reforms, Results and the Road Ahead,* New York: Oxford University Press.

— (1995) *World Development Report 1995: Workers in an Integrated World,* Washington, D.C.: World Bank.

Yanney, I.K. (2000) 'The Changing Roles of Trade Unions: The Case of Trades Union Congress of Ghana', M.A. thesis, Institute of Social Studies, The Hague.

Yeebo, Z. (1991) *Ghana: The Struggle for Popular Power; Rawlings: Saviour or Demagogue,* London: New Beacon.

Notes on Contributors

MARK ANNER is an assistant professor of Industrial Relations and Political Science at the Pennsylvania State University. He holds a Ph.D. in government from Cornell University and a Master's degree in Latin American Studies from Stanford University. Before beginning his academic career, Mark worked as a union organiser in the US and as an advisor to the labour movement in El Salvador, where he lived for eight years.

ANITA CHAN is a sociologist specialising on China at the Australian National University. She is the author of five books including *China's Workers under Assault*; *Children of Mao*; and *Chen Village under Mao and Deng*. Her current research focuses on Chinese management styles, worker-management relations in Chinese firms, the Chinese trade union, global production chains and corporate social responsibility.

DAN CLAWSON teaches sociology at the University of Massachusetts Amherst, where he is also president of the faculty union. He is a former national chair of Scholars, Artists, and Writers for Social Justice (SAWSJ), and was chair of the Labor and Labor Movements section of the American Sociological Association. His sole, co-authored, or edited books include *The Next Upsurge: Labor and the New Social Movements*; *Dollars and Votes: How Business Campaign Contributions Subvert Democracy*; *Money Talks: Corporate PACs and Political Influence*; *Bureaucracy and the Labor Process The Transformation of U.S. Industry 1860–1920*; and *Work and Families: Expanding the Bounds*. His articles have appeared in numerous labour and sociology journals. His current project, with Naomi Gerstel, examines overtime and extended hours, and the ways workers do or do not contest those hours.

BILL DUNN teaches in the discipline of Political Economy at the University of Sydney. He previously taught International Political Economy at Leeds and Bristol Universities and Sociology at the University of the West of England. His principal research interests are in contemporary socio-economic change, particularly with reference to work and to workers. These were most recently elaborated in his book *Global Restructuring and the Power of Labour*, published by Palgrave in 2004.

DAN GALLIN is Chair of the Global Labour Institute (GLI), a foundation established in 1997 with a secretariat in Geneva. The GLI (www.global-labour.org) investigates the consequences of the global-isation of the world economy for workers and trade unions, develops and proposes counterstrategies and promotes international thinking and action in the labour movement. Gallin worked from August 1960 until April 1997 for the International Union of Food, Agricultural, Hotel, Restaurant and Catering, Tobacco and Allied Workers' Associations (IUF), since 1968 as General Secretary. He has served as President of the International Federation of Workers' Education Associations (IFWEA) from 1992 to 2003 and has been Director of the Organization and Representation Program of WIEGO (Women in Informal Employment Globalizing and Organizing) from June 2000 to July 2002. He continues to serve on the IFWEA Executive and on the WIEGO Steering Committee.

ANDRÉIA GALVÃO is Professor of Political Science at the State University of Campinas (Brazil) and a researcher at the Marxist Centre of Studies at the same university. She writes about trade unions and labour relations in Brazil.

STEVE JEFFERYS is Professor of European Employment Studies and Director of the Working Lives Research Institute at London Metropolitan University. He is the author of *Liberté, Egalité and Fraternité at Work: Changing French Employment Relations and Management* (2003), and joint author of *Management, Work and Welfare in Western Europe* (2000). Previously he worked at Keele University and at Manchester Polytechnic after spending fifteen years first as a car worker and then as a journalist, and writing a book in 1986 on the history of trade unionism in Chrysler US between 1930 and 1980.

PIET KONINGS is a senior researcher at the African Studies Centre, University of Leiden (The Netherlands). He has published widely on political economy and labour in Africa, especially in Ghana and Cameroon. His major current research interests are the politics of Anglophone identity in Cameroon and the role of civil society in Africa. His most recent publications include *Unilever Estates and the Power of Organization in Cameroon* (Hamburg: LIT Verlag, 1998), *Trajectoires de Libération en Afrique Contemporaine* (Paris: Karthala, 2000), and *Negotiating an Anglophone Identity: A Study of the Politics of Recognition and Representation in Cameroon* (Leiden: Brill, 2003).

ROB LAMBERT is Associate Professor and Chair of the University of Western Australia's International and Global Studies programme. He is also the Chair of the Human Resources and Industrial Relations Programme. He has been appointed Director of the Australian Global Studies Research Centre and is the Coordinator of the Southern Initiative on Globalization and Trade Union Rights (SIGTUR), which he founded with other Australian union leaders in 1990.

SUE LEDWITH teaches women's studies and labour studies at Ruskin College, Oxford, UK, where she also runs international scholarship programmes for overseas trade unionists, and a regular round table for women trade unionists and women academics working in the field. Her main research and writing is around women in trade unions, and in the 1980s she edited the women's pages of the journal of the print industry union SOGAT '82. With Fiona Colgan, she has co-edited *Women in Organisations: Challenging Gender Politics* (1996) and *Gender, Diversity and Trade Unions: International Perspectives* (2002).

RONALDO MUNCK is at Dublin City University where he leads the internationalisation and social development strategic theme, and he is also visiting Professor of Sociology at the University of Liverpool. He has written widely on labour struggles in Latin America, South Africa and Ireland. He has also intervened in the ongoing 'globalisation and its discontents' literature with *Globalisation and Labour: The New 'Great Transformation'* (2002) and *Globalisation and Social Exclusion: Towards a Transformationalist Perspective* (2004).

DAVID OST is Professor of political science at Hobart and William Smith Colleges in Geneva, New York, and occasional visiting professor at Central European University. He has written extensively on political economy, democratization, and labour in eastern Europe. He is co-author (with Stephen Crowley) of *Workers After Workers' States* (Rowman and Littlefield, 2001), and his most recent work is *The Defeat of Solidarity: Anger and Politics in Postcommunist Europe* (Cornell University Press, 2005).

CRAIG PHELAN is senior lecturer at the University of Wales Swansea. He is editor of the journal *Labor History* and the author of numerous books and articles on that subject.

PETER WATERMAN (London 1936) retired from the Institute of Social Studies, The Hague in 1998, and has since devoted himself to the old and new labour internationalisms, the World Social Forum and related matters. In 2004 he co-edited *World Social Forum: Challenging Empires* (New Delhi: Viveka). His current obsession is with auto/biographical historical work intended to make internationalism more accessible and attractive to those who do not or will not read academic work on the subject.

Index